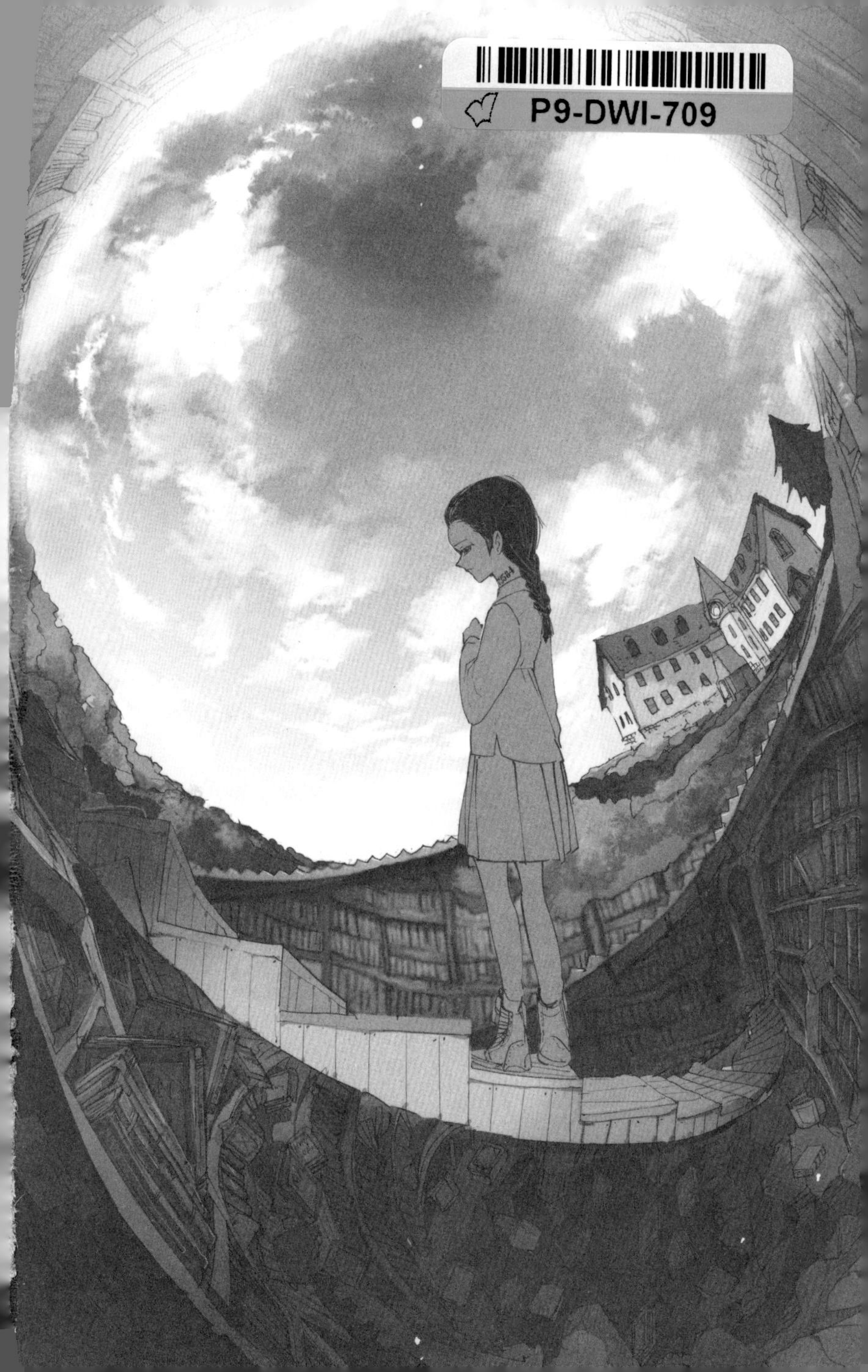

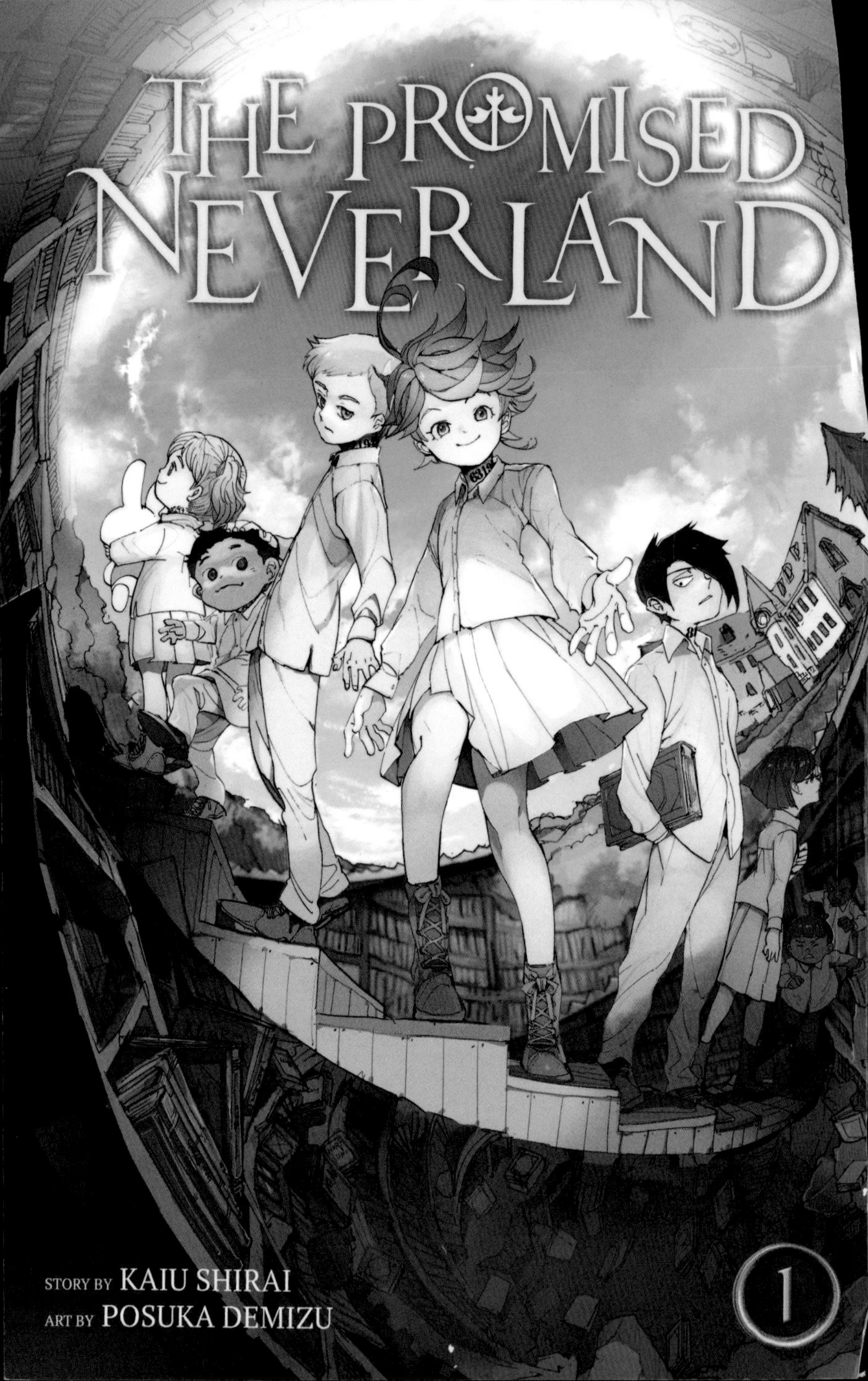
THE PROMISED NEVERLAND
STORY BY KAIU SHIRAI
ART BY POSUKA DEMIZU
1

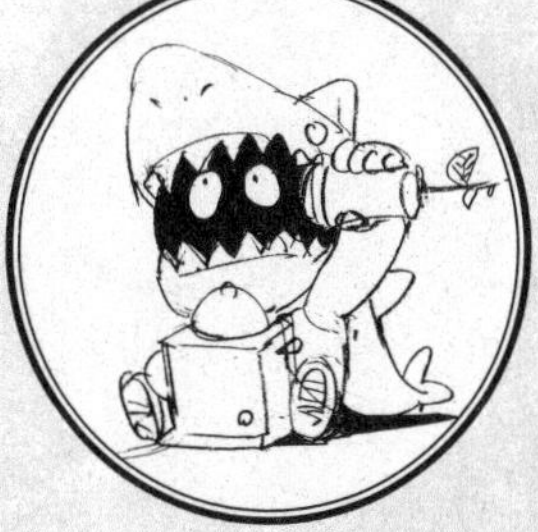

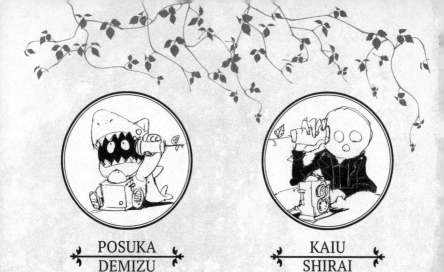

POSUKA DEMIZU

This is my first weekly series! I'm so excited, flustered and energized every day! I'm gonna draw and draw!

Thank you for reading! I'll work hard on volume 2 as well.

All my thanks to Shirai Sensei.

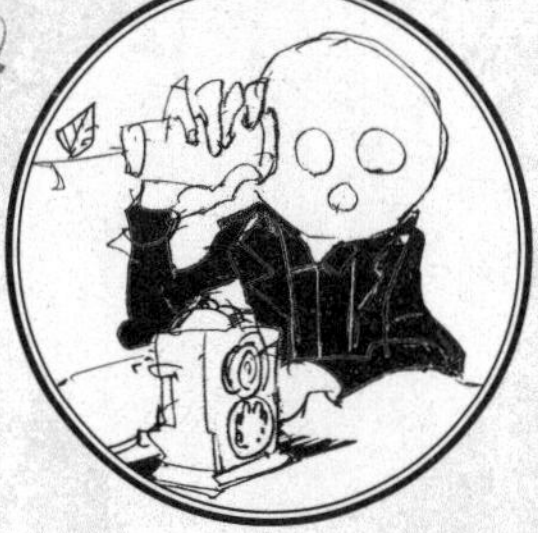

KAIU SHIRAI

Writer Shirai's personal highlights for *The Promised Neverland* fanatics:

1. The foreshadowing in the art (but I'm not telling where)

2. The liveliness of the characters in the background (check out Conny's eyes on page 20, panel 2)

3. The amazing quality of the little kids' drawings on the wall! (chapter 3)

Okay, everyone! Please enjoy this series!

Posuka Demizu debuted as a manga artist with the 2013 *CoroCoro* series *Oreca Monster Bouken Retsuden*. A collection of illustrations, *The Art of Posuka Demizu*, was released in 2016 by PIE International.

Kaiu Shirai debuted in 2015 with *Ashley Gate no Yukue* on the *Shonen Jump+* website. Shirai first worked with Posuka Demizu on the two-shot *Poppy no Negai*, which was released in February 2016.

THE PROMISED NEVERLAND

VOLUME 1
SHONEN JUMP Manga Edition

STORY BY KAIU SHIRAI
ART BY POSUKA DEMIZU

Translation/Satsuki Yamashita
Touch-Up Art & Lettering/Mark McMurray
Design/Julian [JR] Robinson
Editor/Alexis Kirsch

YAKUSOKU NO NEVERLAND © 2016 by Kaiu Shirai, Posuka Demizu
All rights reserved.
First published in Japan in 2016 by SHUEISHA Inc., Tokyo.
English translation rights arranged by SHUEISHA Inc.

The stories, characters and incidents mentioned in this publication are
entirely fictional.

Printed in the U.S.A.

Published by VIZ Media, LLC
P.O. Box 77010
San Francisco, CA 94107

10 9 8
First printing, December 2017
Eighth printing, June 2021

PARENTAL ADVISORY
THE PROMISED NEVERLAND is rated T+
and is recommended for ages 16 and up.
This volume contains fantasy violence and
adult themes.

THE PROMISED NEVERLAND

1

Grace Field House

STORY	KAIU SHIRAI
ART	POSUKA DEMIZU

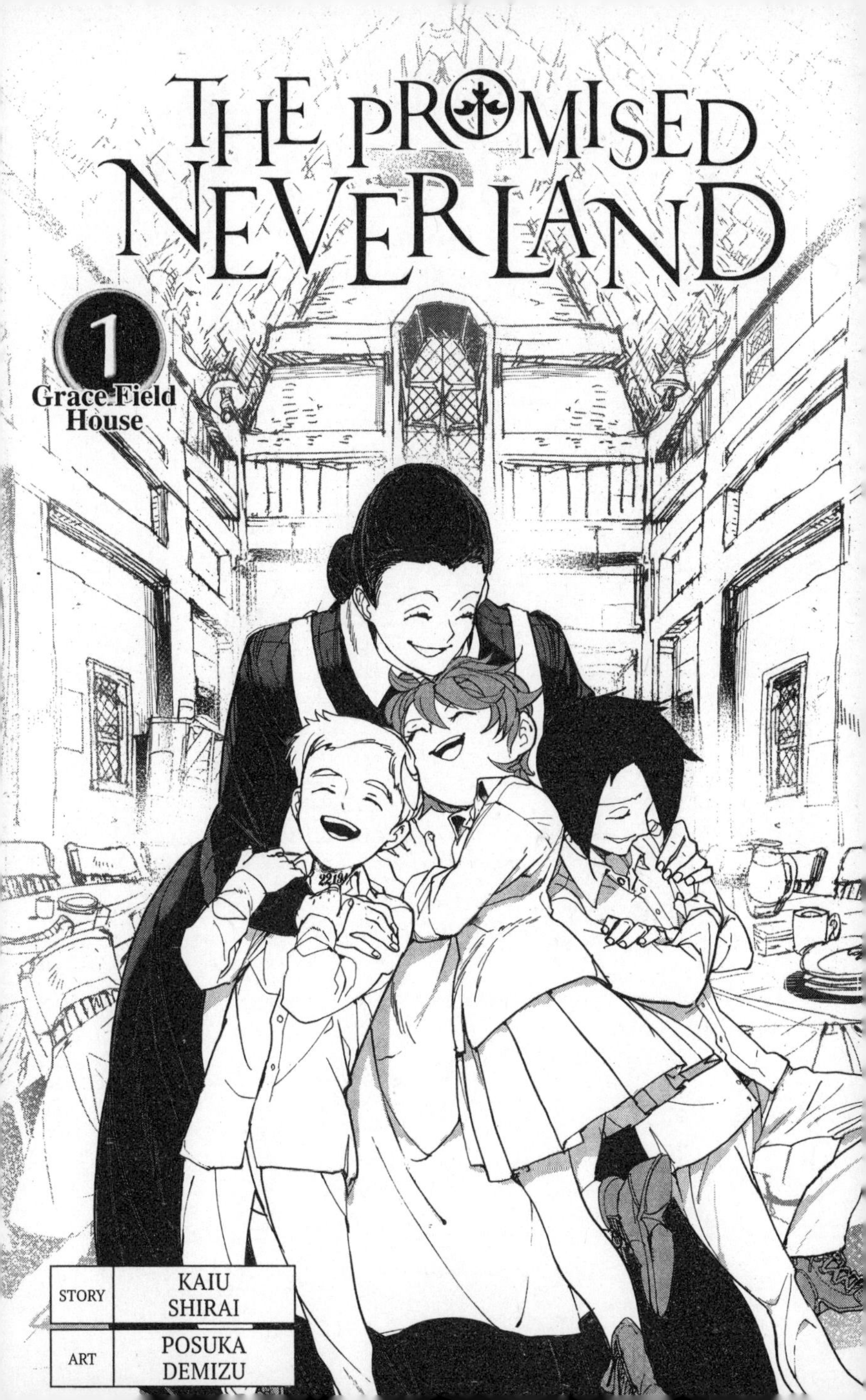

THE PROMISED NEVERLAND 1

Grace Field House

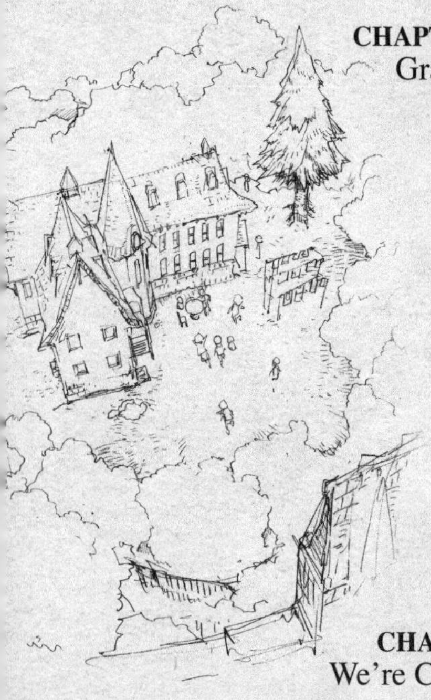

CHAPTER 1: GRACE FIELD HOUSE

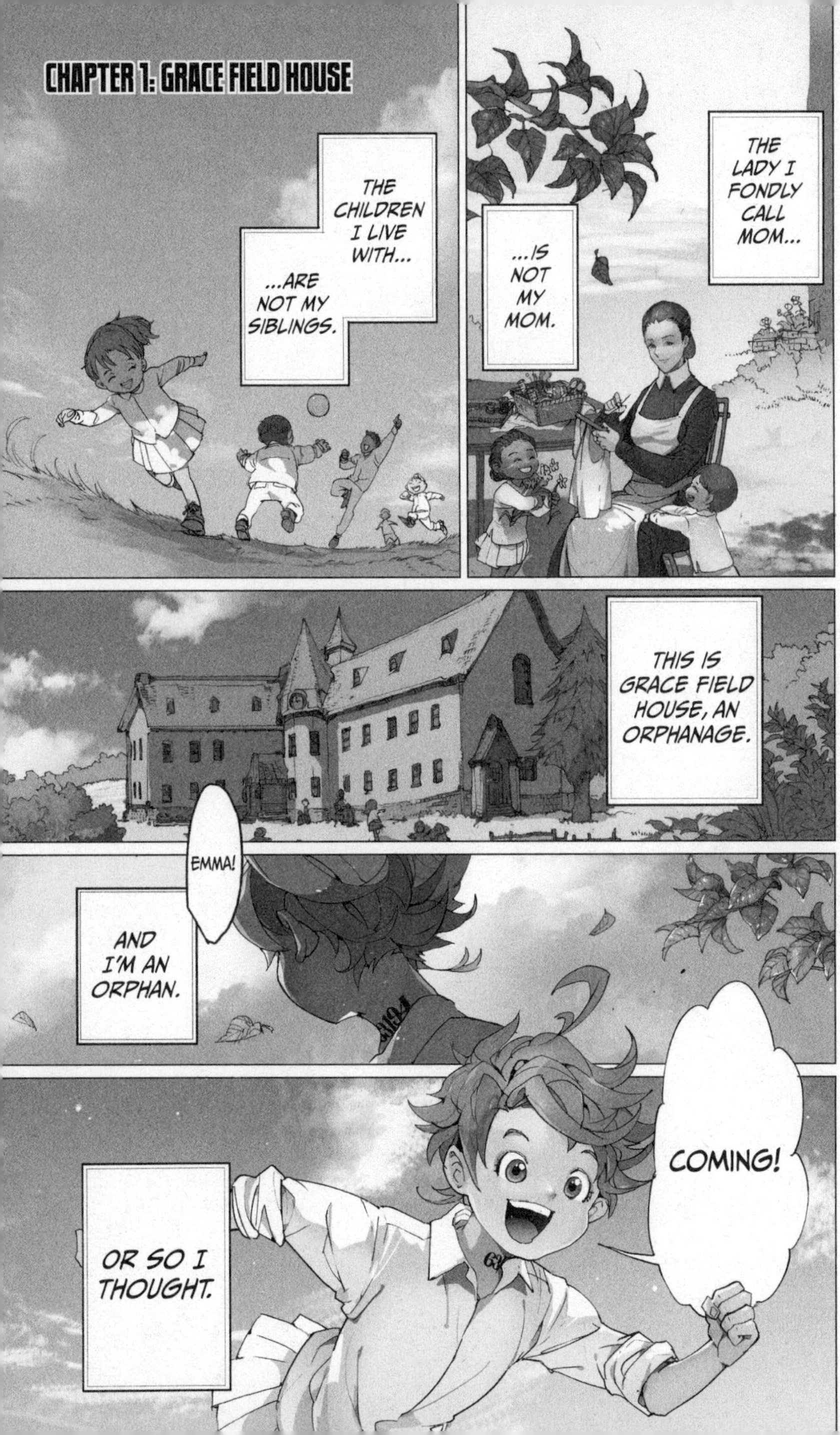

THE LADY I FONDLY CALL MOM...
...IS NOT MY MOM.
THE CHILDREN I LIVE WITH...
...ARE NOT MY SIBLINGS.
THIS IS GRACE FIELD HOUSE, AN ORPHANAGE.
EMMA!
AND I'M AN ORPHAN.
COMING!
OR SO I THOUGHT.

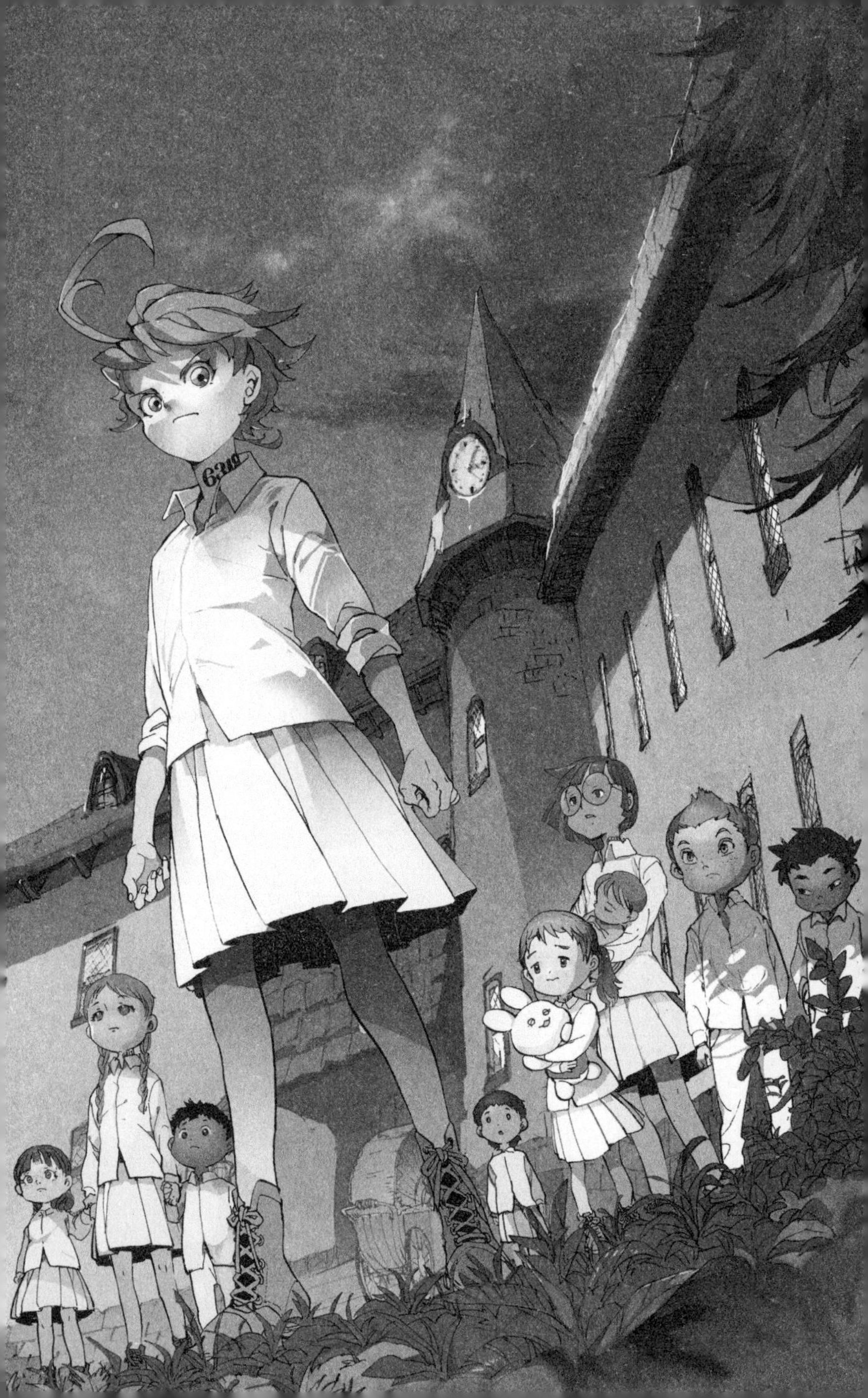
63194

CHAPTER 1: GRACE FIELD HOUSE

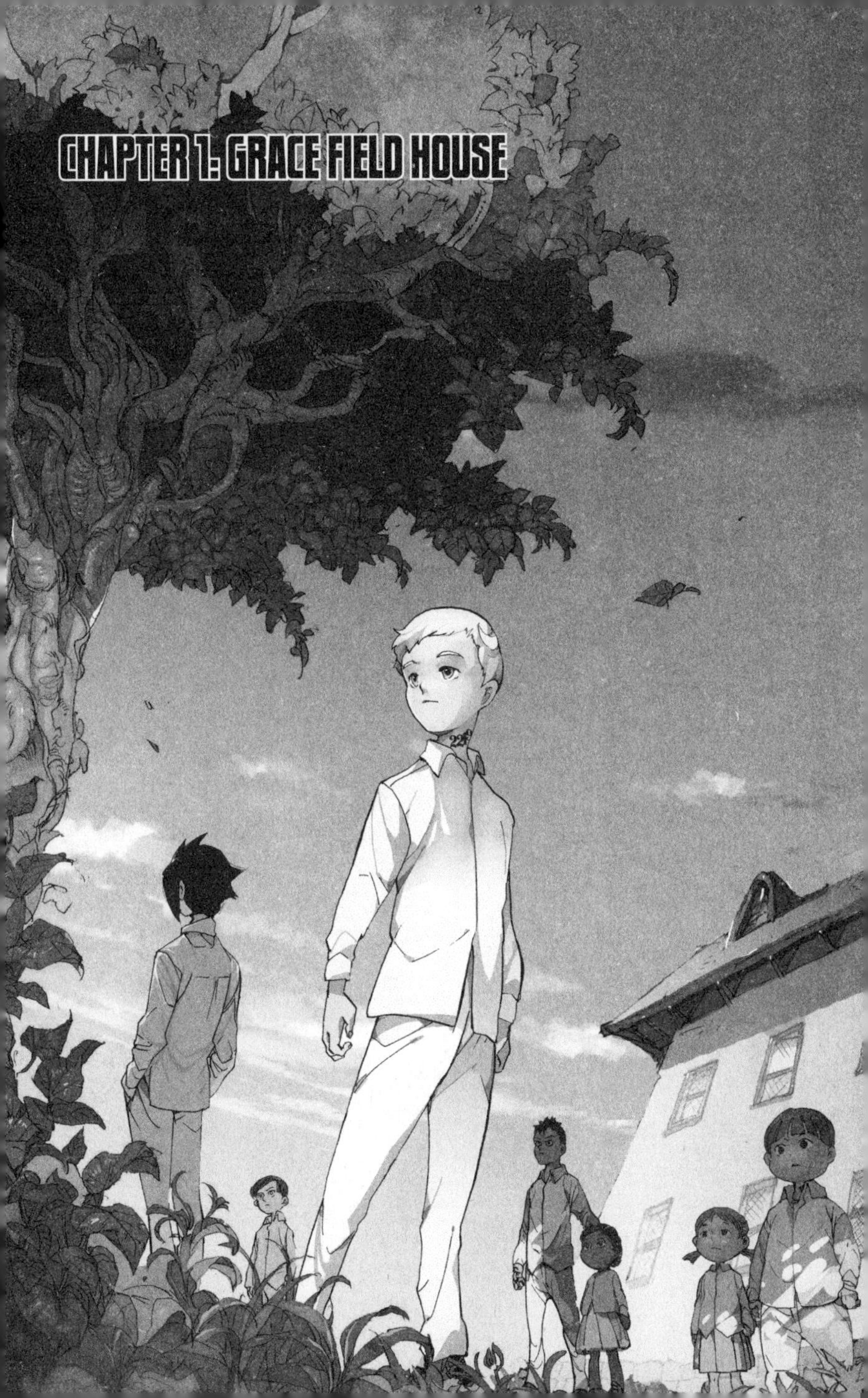

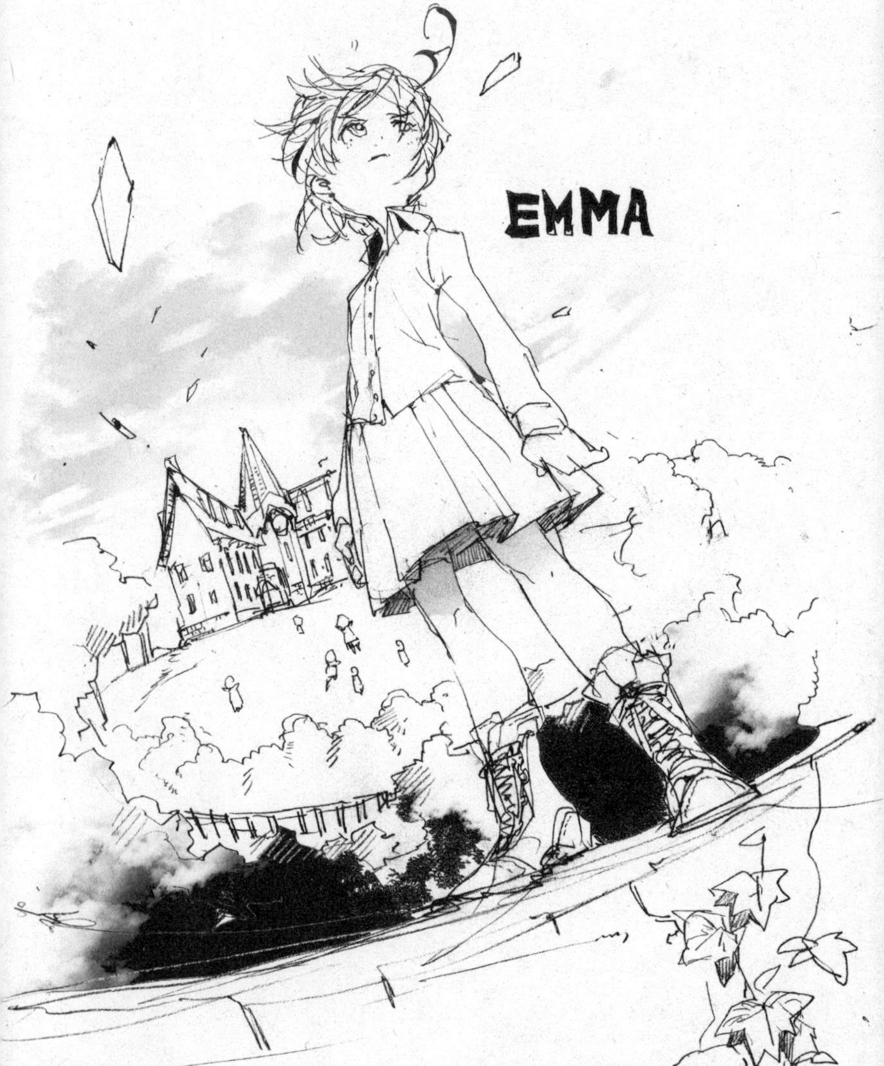
EMMA

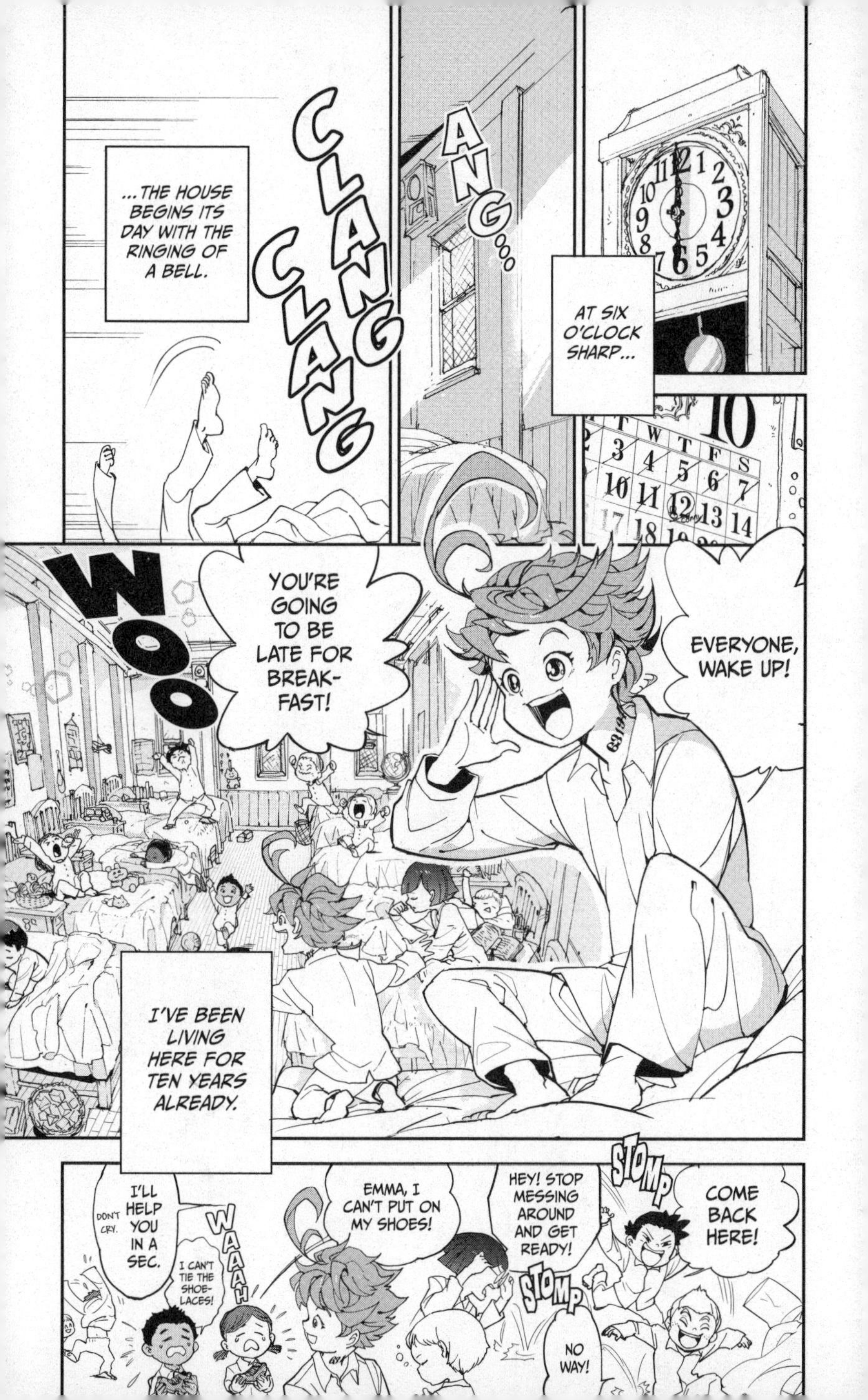
AT SIX O'CLOCK SHARP...
ANG
CLANG CLANG
...THE HOUSE BEGINS ITS DAY WITH THE RINGING OF A BELL.
EVERYONE, WAKE UP!
YOU'RE GOING TO BE LATE FOR BREAK-FAST!
WOOO
I'VE BEEN LIVING HERE FOR TEN YEARS ALREADY.
COME BACK HERE!
STOMP
HEY! STOP MESSING AROUND AND GET READY!
STOMP
NO WAY!
EMMA, I CAN'T PUT ON MY SHOES!
WAAAH
I CAN'T TIE THE SHOE-LACES!
I'LL HELP YOU IN A SEC.
DON'T CRY.

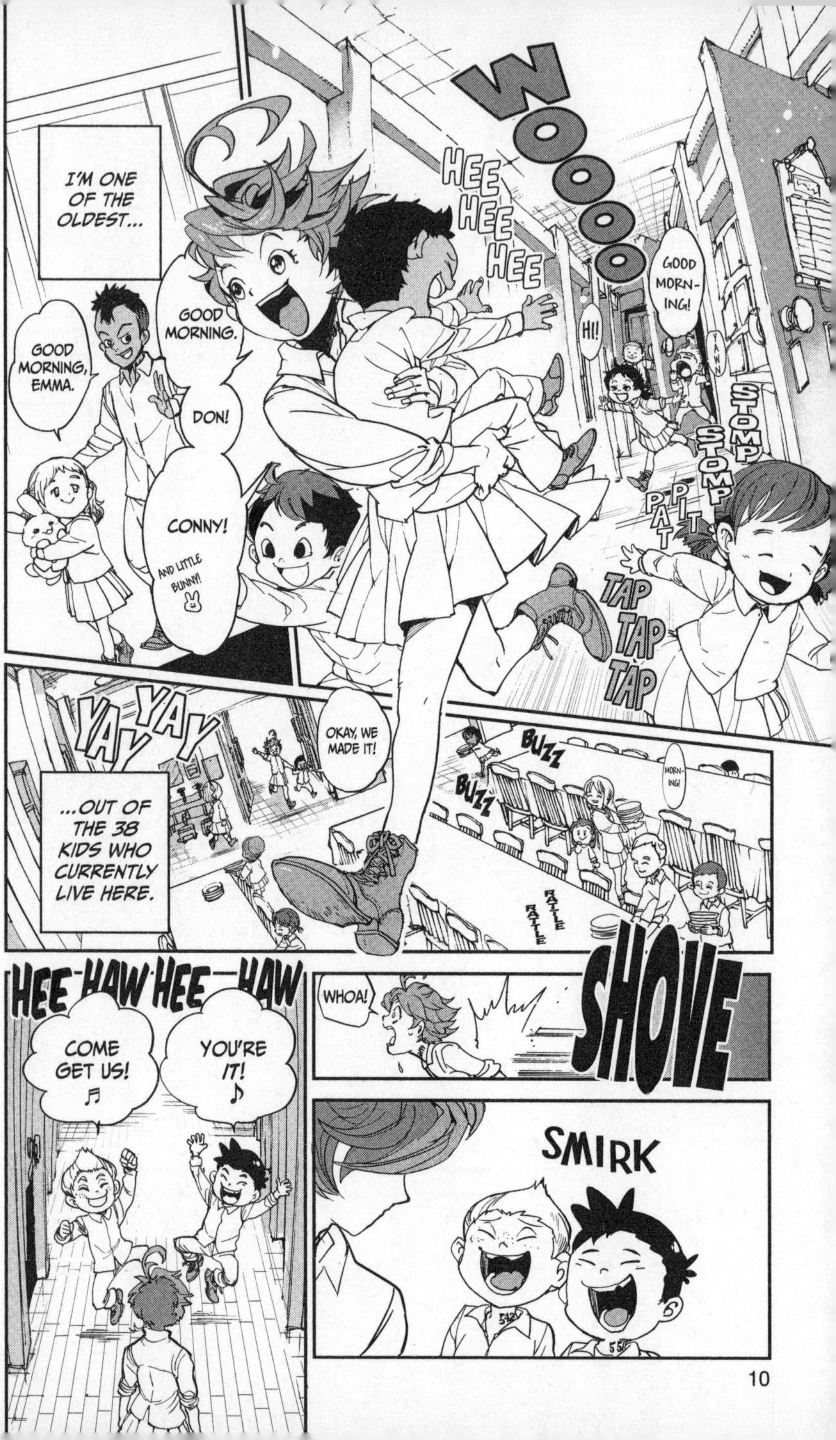
WOOOOO
HEE HEE HEE
GOOD MORN-ING!
HI!
YAWN
STOMP STOMP
PIT PAT
TAP TAP TAP
GOOD MORNING.
DON!
CONNY!
AND LITTLE BUNNY!
I'M ONE OF THE OLDEST...
GOOD MORNING, EMMA.
BUZZ BUZZ
MORN-ING!
RATTLE RATTLE
YAY YAY YAY
OKAY, WE MADE IT!
...OUT OF THE 38 KIDS WHO CURRENTLY LIVE HERE.
SHOVE
WHOA!
SMIRK
HEE-HAW HEE-HAW
YOU'RE IT! ♪
COME GET US! ♬

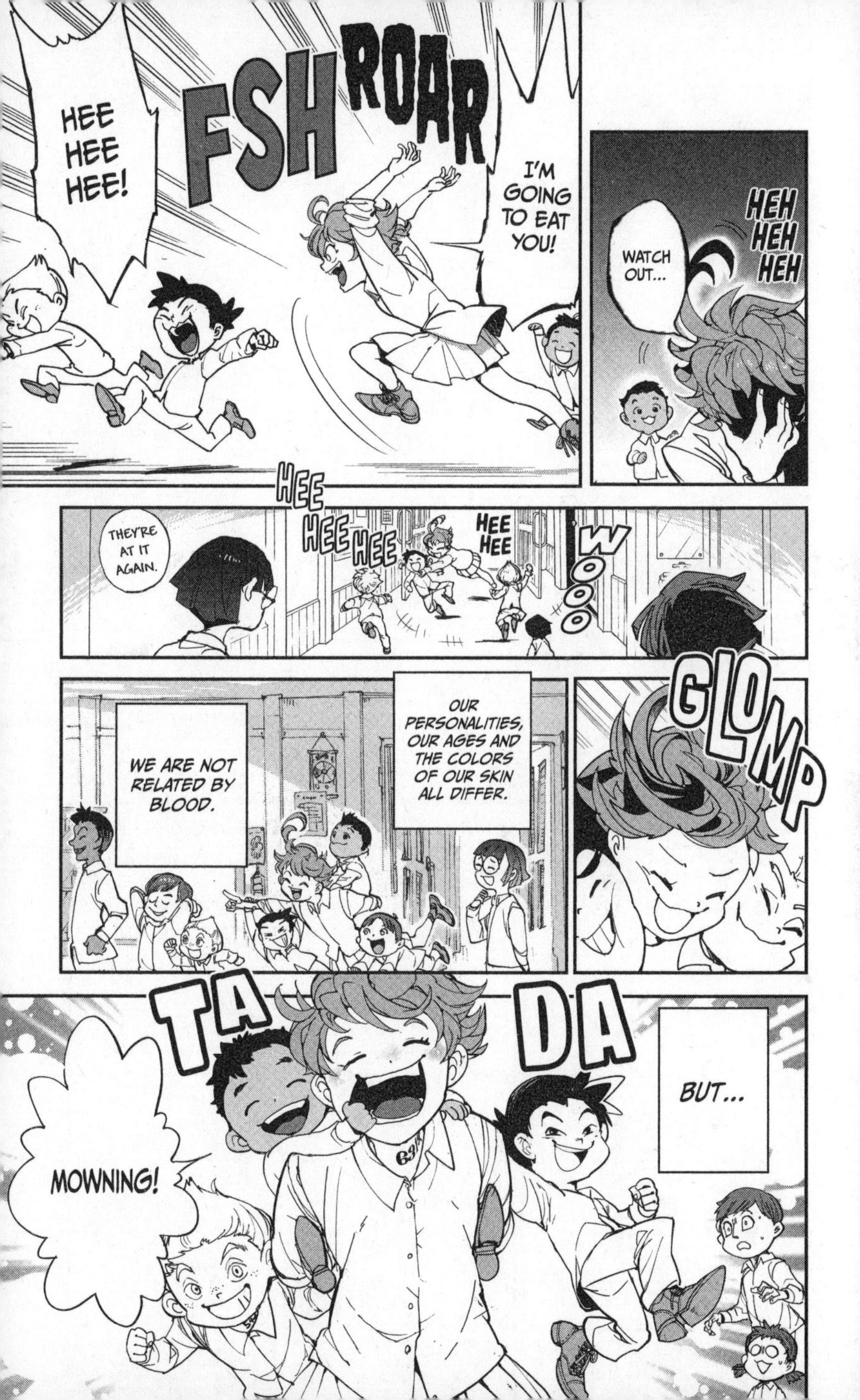
HEH HEH HEH
WATCH OUT...
ROAR
I'M GOING TO EAT YOU!
FSH
HEE HEE HEE!
HEE HEE HEE
WOOOO
HEE HEE
THEY'RE AT IT AGAIN.
GLOMP
OUR PERSONALITIES, OUR AGES AND THE COLORS OF OUR SKIN ALL DIFFER.
WE ARE NOT RELATED BY BLOOD.
BUT...
DA
TA
MOWNING!

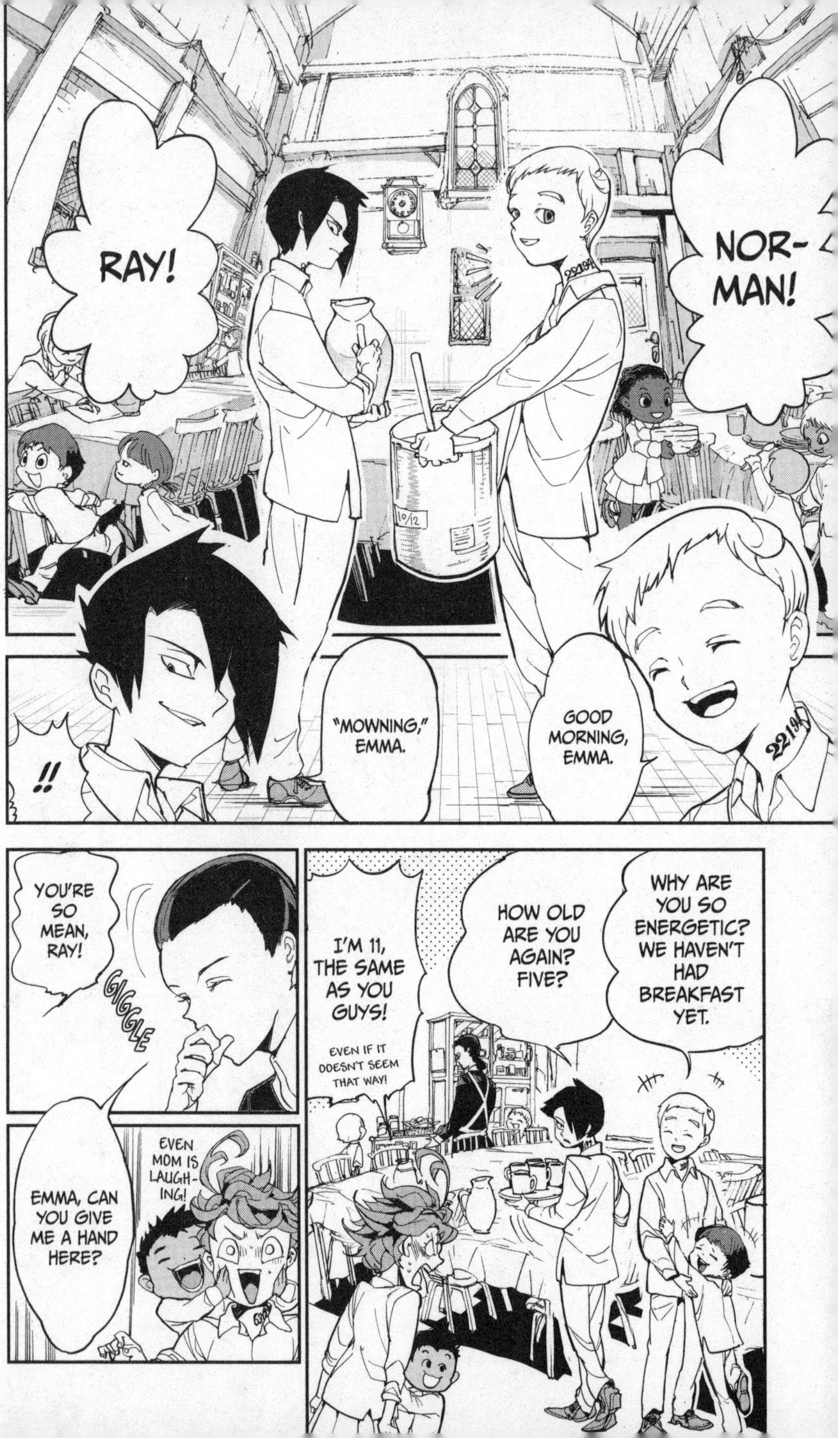
NOR-MAN!
RAY!
GOOD MORNING, EMMA.
"MOWNING," EMMA.
!!
WHY ARE YOU SO ENERGETIC? WE HAVEN'T HAD BREAKFAST YET.
HOW OLD ARE YOU AGAIN? FIVE?
I'M 11, THE SAME AS YOU GUYS!
EVEN IF IT DOESN'T SEEM THAT WAY!
YOU'RE SO MEAN, RAY!
GIGGLE
EVEN MOM IS LAUGHING!
EMMA, CAN YOU GIVE ME A HAND HERE?

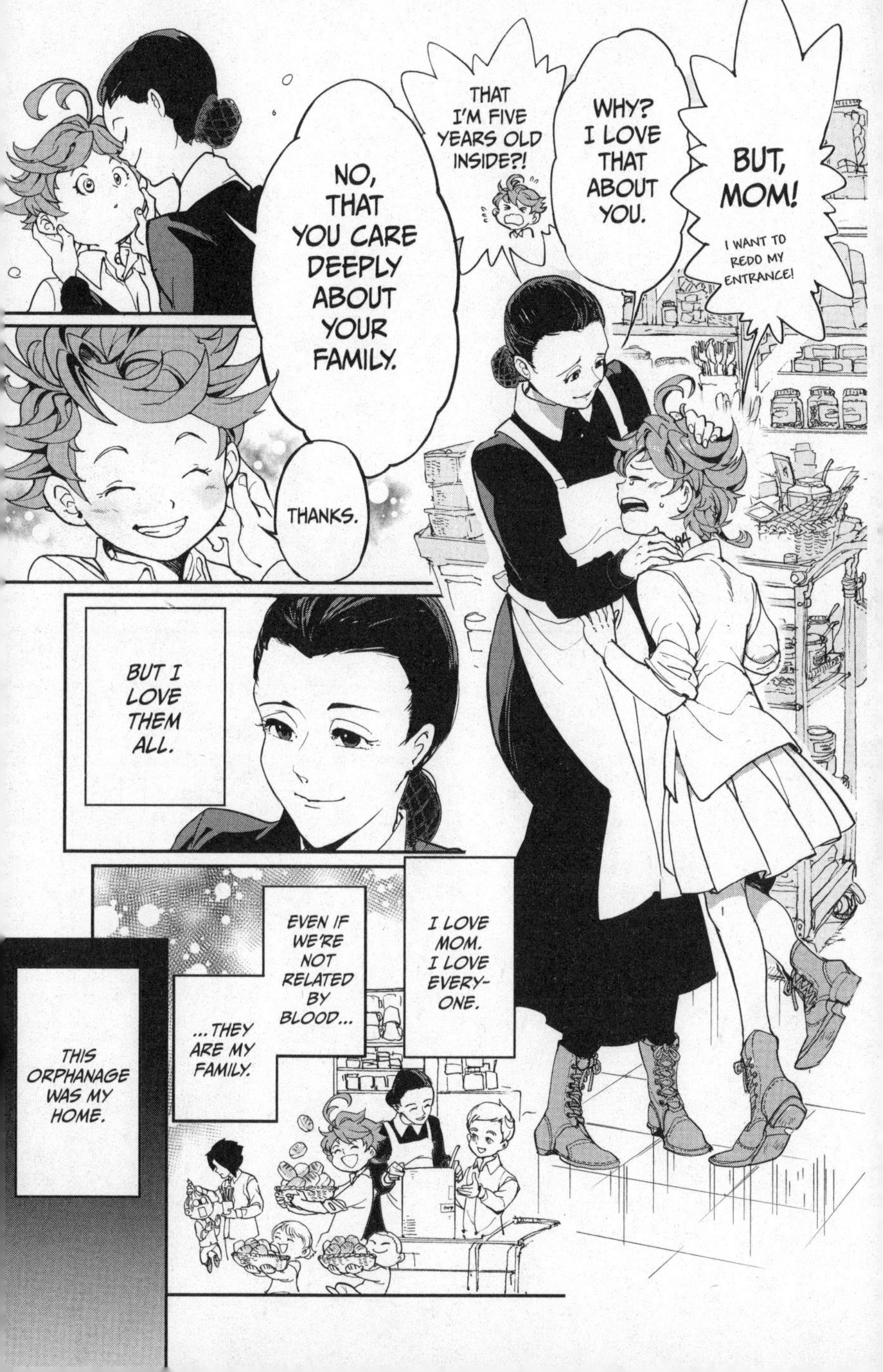

BUT, MOM!
I WANT TO REDO MY ENTRANCE!
WHY? I LOVE THAT ABOUT YOU.
THAT I'M FIVE YEARS OLD INSIDE?!
NO, THAT YOU CARE DEEPLY ABOUT YOUR FAMILY.
THANKS.
BUT I LOVE THEM ALL.
I LOVE MOM. I LOVE EVERY-ONE.
EVEN IF WE'RE NOT RELATED BY BLOOD...
...THEY ARE MY FAMILY.
THIS ORPHANAGE WAS MY HOME.

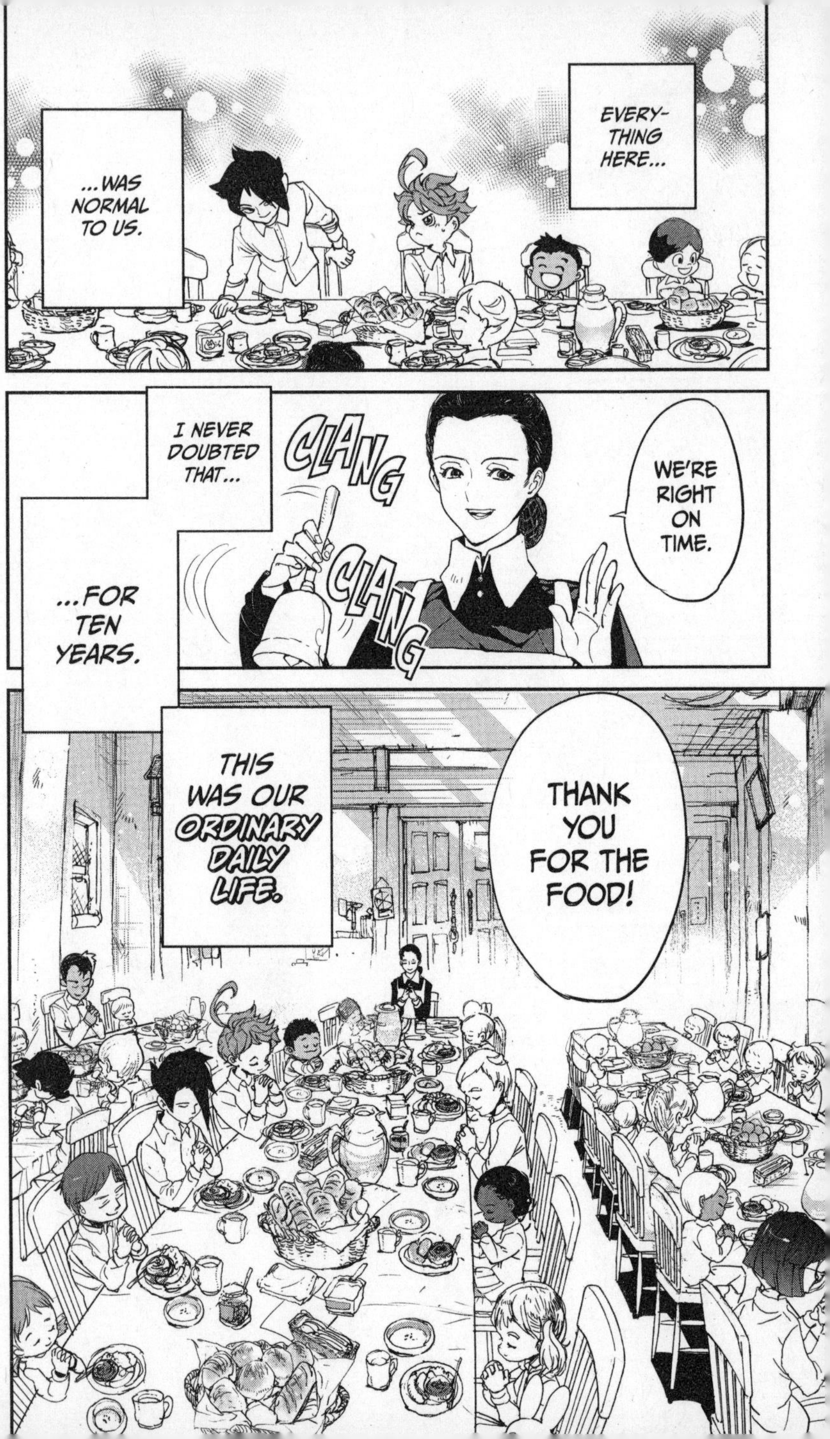
EVERY-THING HERE...
...WAS NORMAL TO US.
WE'RE RIGHT ON TIME.
CLANG
CLANG
I NEVER DOUBTED THAT...
...FOR TEN YEARS.
THANK YOU FOR THE FOOD!
THIS WAS OUR ORDINARY DAILY LIFE.

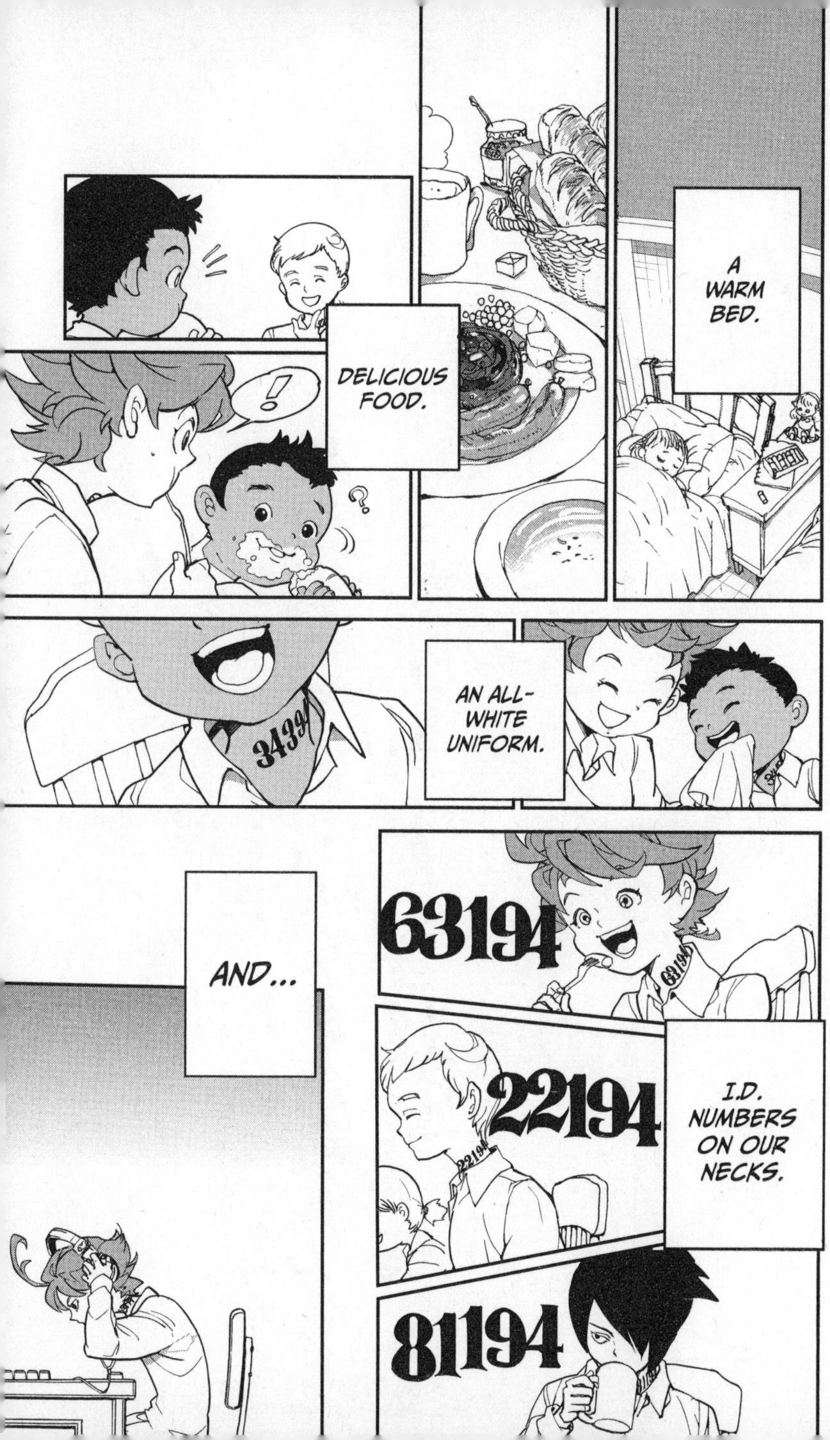

A WARM BED.
DELICIOUS FOOD.
!
?
AN ALL-WHITE UNIFORM.
AND...
63194
22194
I.D. NUMBERS ON OUR NECKS.
81194

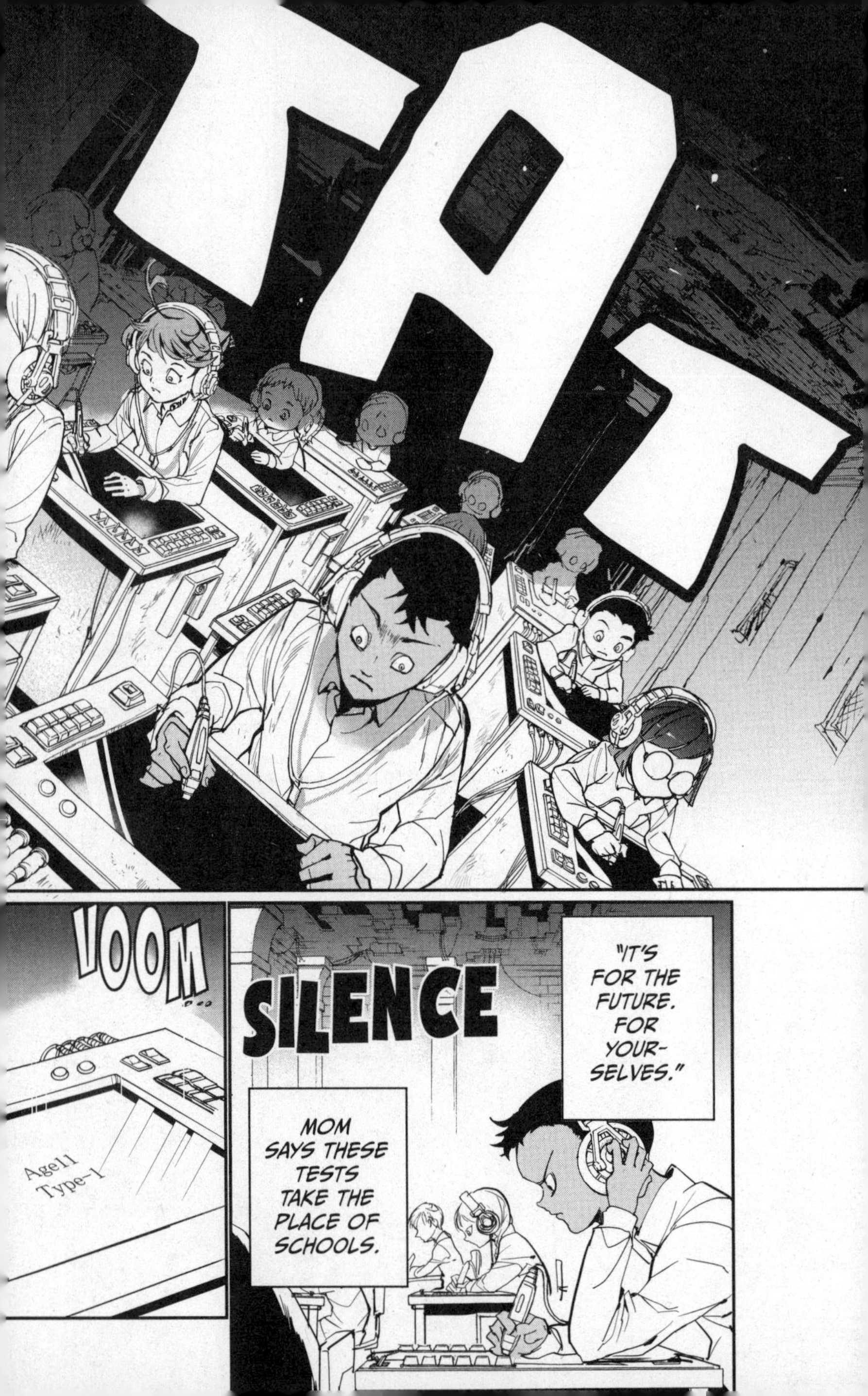
"IT'S FOR THE FUTURE. FOR YOURSELVES."
SILENCE
MOM SAYS THESE TESTS TAKE THE PLACE OF SCHOOLS.
VOOM
Age11
Type-1

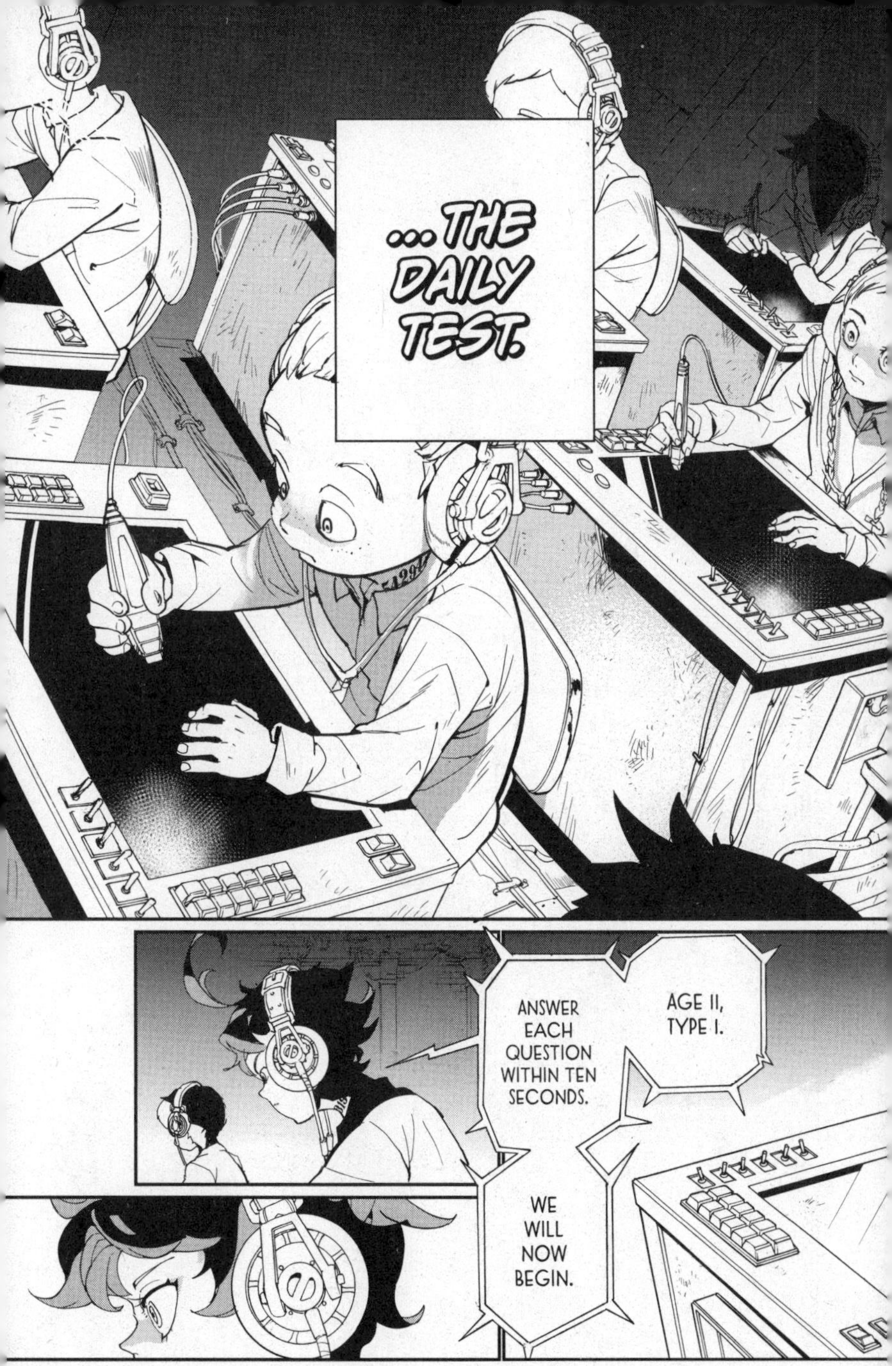
...THE DAILY TEST.
AGE 11, TYPE 1.
ANSWER EACH QUESTION WITHIN TEN SECONDS.
WE WILL NOW BEGIN.

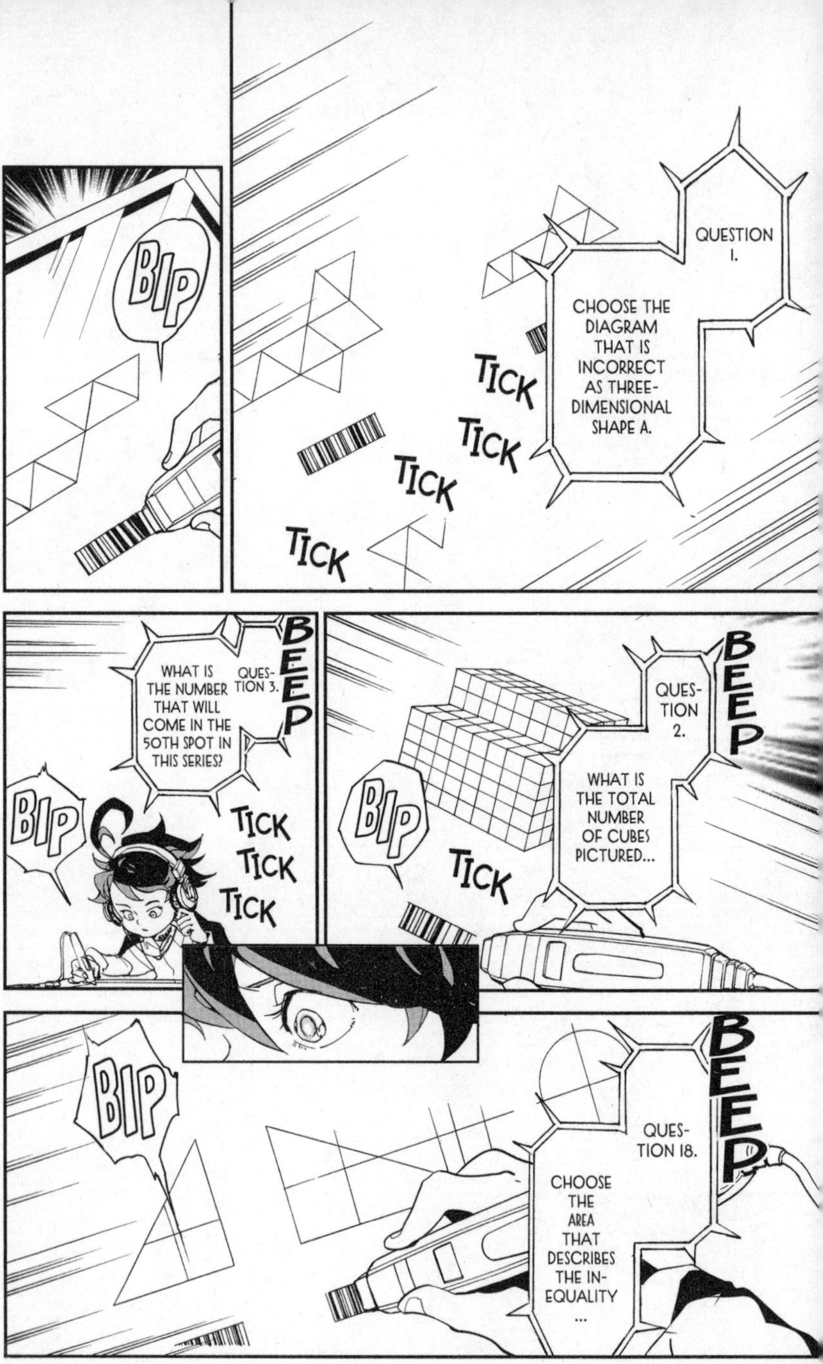
QUESTION 1.
CHOOSE THE DIAGRAM THAT IS INCORRECT AS THREE-DIMENSIONAL SHAPE A.
TICK
TICK
TICK
TICK
BIP
BEEP
QUES-TION 2.
WHAT IS THE TOTAL NUMBER OF CUBES PICTURED...
BIP
TICK
BEEP
QUES-TION 3.
WHAT IS THE NUMBER THAT WILL COME IN THE 50TH SPOT IN THIS SERIES?
TICK
TICK
TICK
BIP
BEEP
QUES-TION 18.
CHOOSE THE AREA THAT DESCRIBES THE IN-EQUALITY ...
BIP

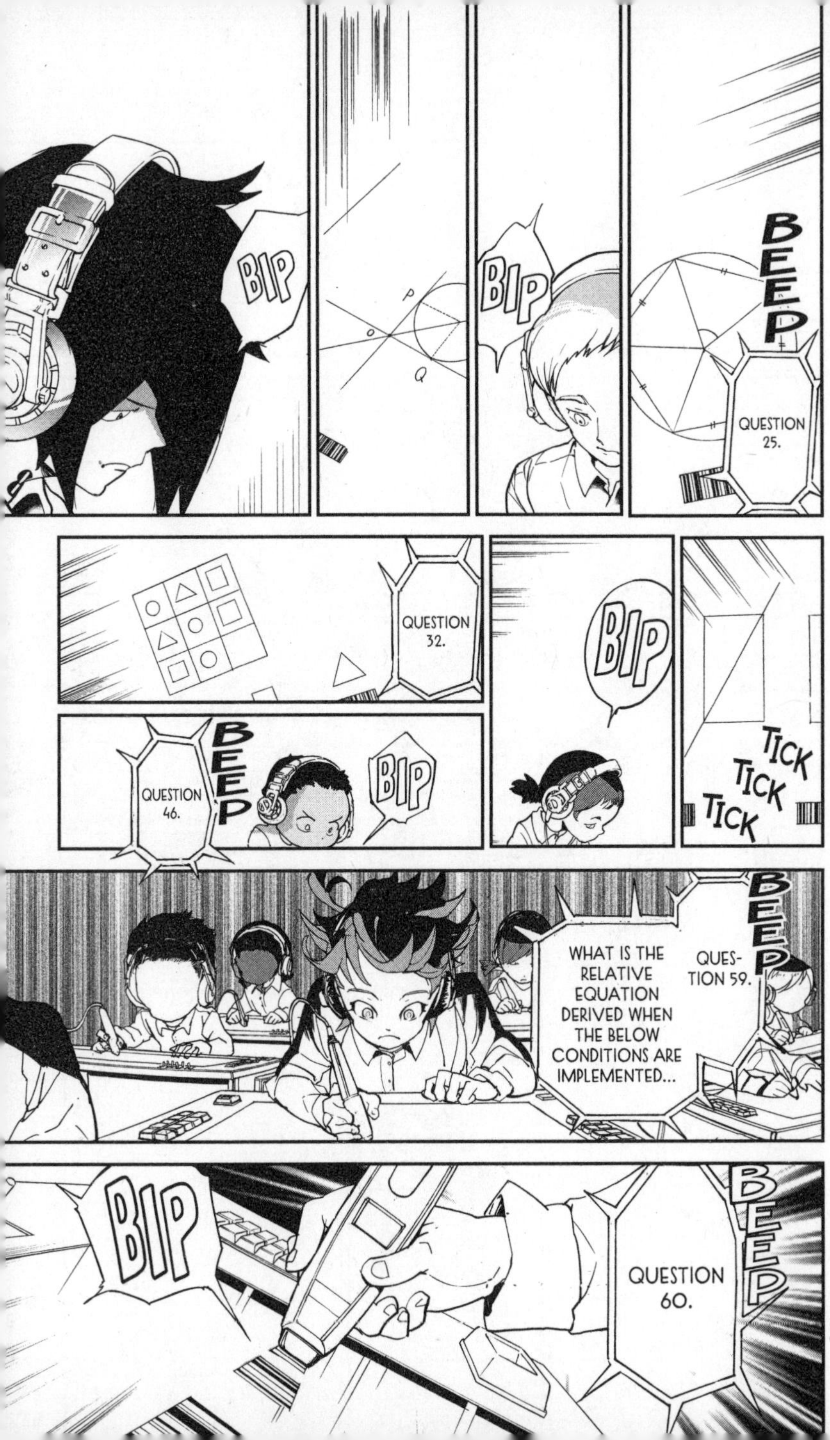
BEEP
QUESTION 25.
BIP
P
O
Q
BIP
TICK TICK TICK
BIP
QUESTION 32.
BEEP
QUESTION 46.
BIP
BEEP
QUES-TION 59.
WHAT IS THE RELATIVE EQUATION DERIVED WHEN THE BELOW CONDITIONS ARE IMPLEMENTED...
BEEP
QUESTION 60.
BIP

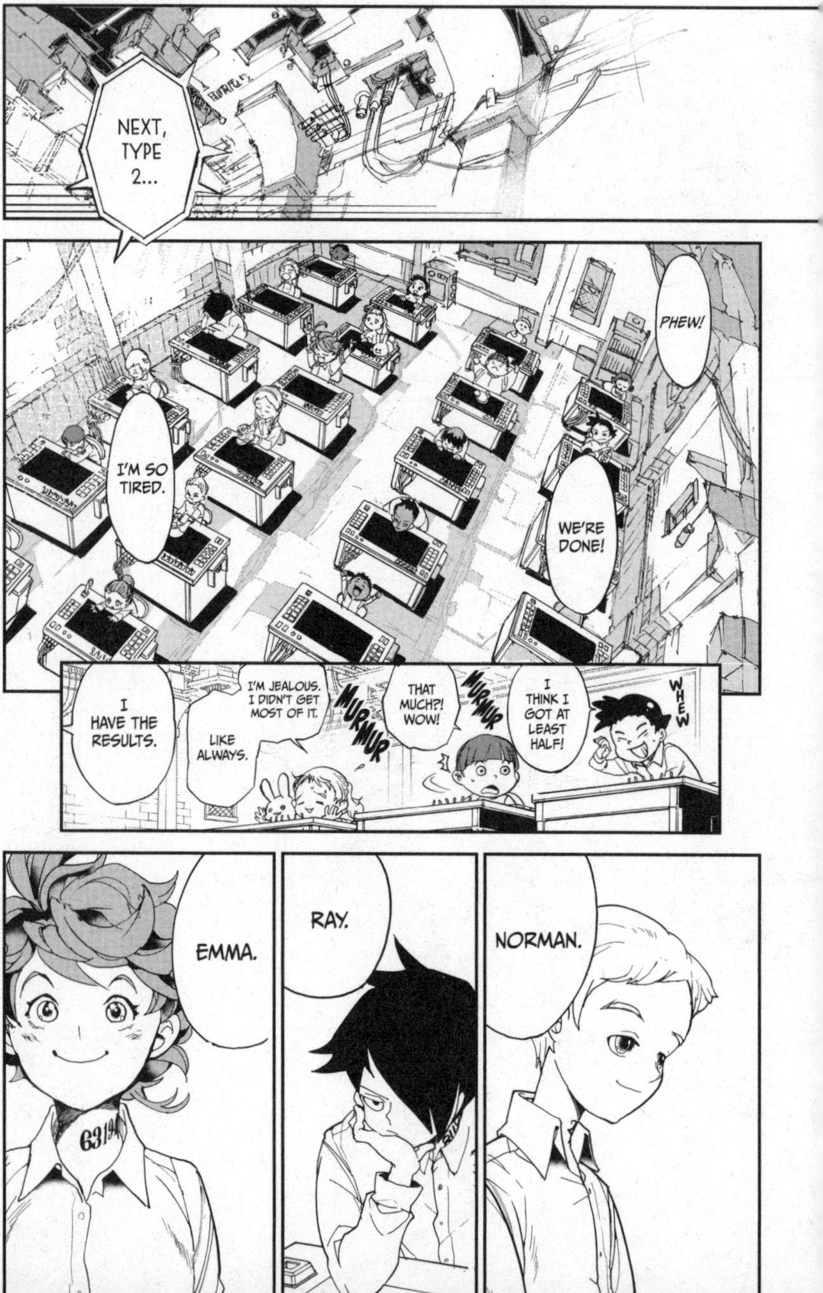
NEXT, TYPE 2...
PHEW!
WE'RE DONE!
I'M SO TIRED.
WHEW
I THINK I GOT AT LEAST HALF!
MURMUR
THAT MUCH?! WOW!
MURMUR
I'M JEALOUS. I DIDN'T GET MOST OF IT.
LIKE ALWAYS.
I HAVE THE RESULTS.
NORMAN.
RAY.
EMMA.

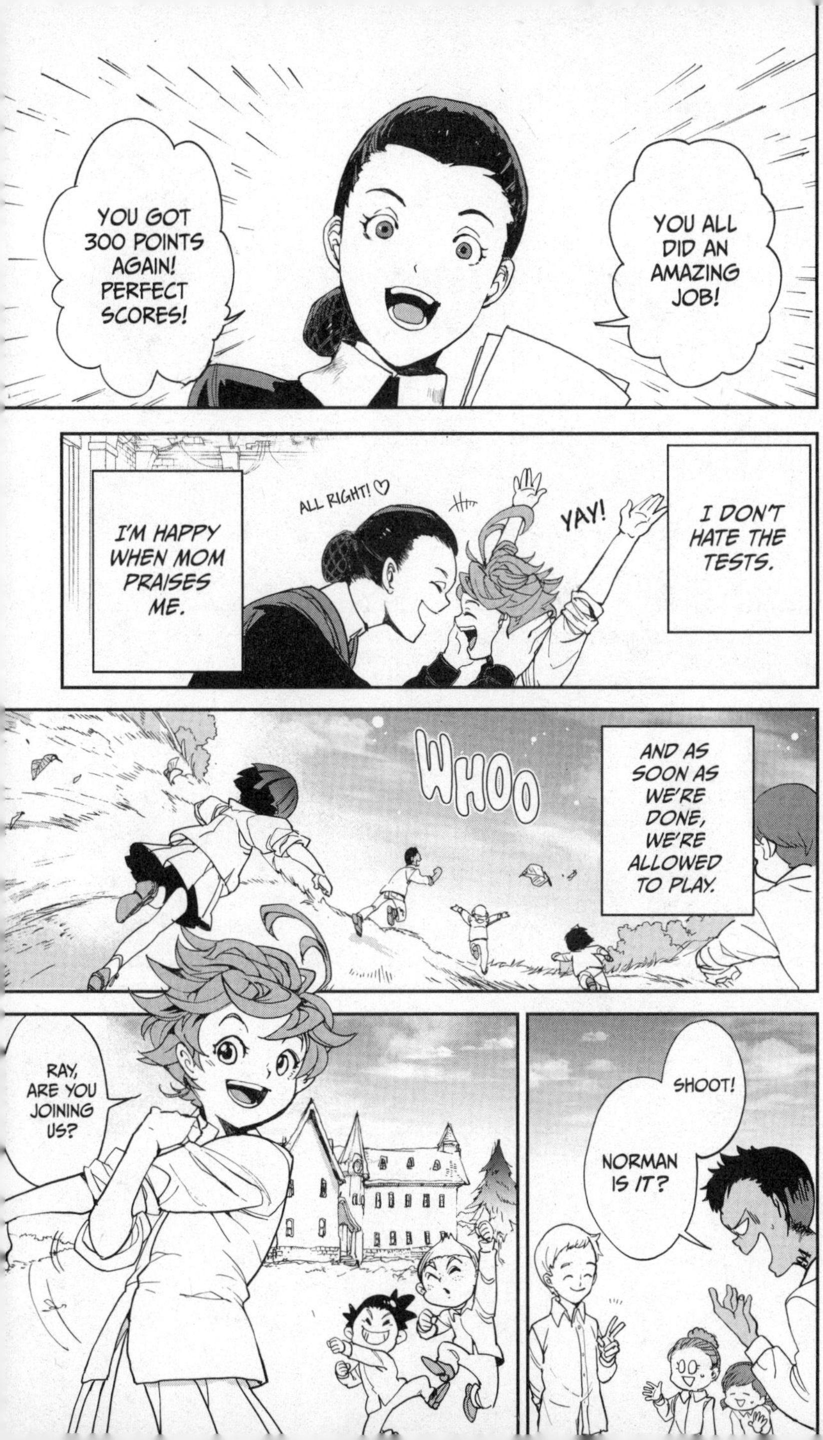
YOU ALL DID AN AMAZING JOB!
YOU GOT 300 POINTS AGAIN! PERFECT SCORES!
I DON'T HATE THE TESTS.
YAY!
ALL RIGHT! ♡
I'M HAPPY WHEN MOM PRAISES ME.
AND AS SOON AS WE'RE DONE, WE'RE ALLOWED TO PLAY.
WHOO
SHOOT!
NORMAN IS IT?
RAY, ARE YOU JOINING US?

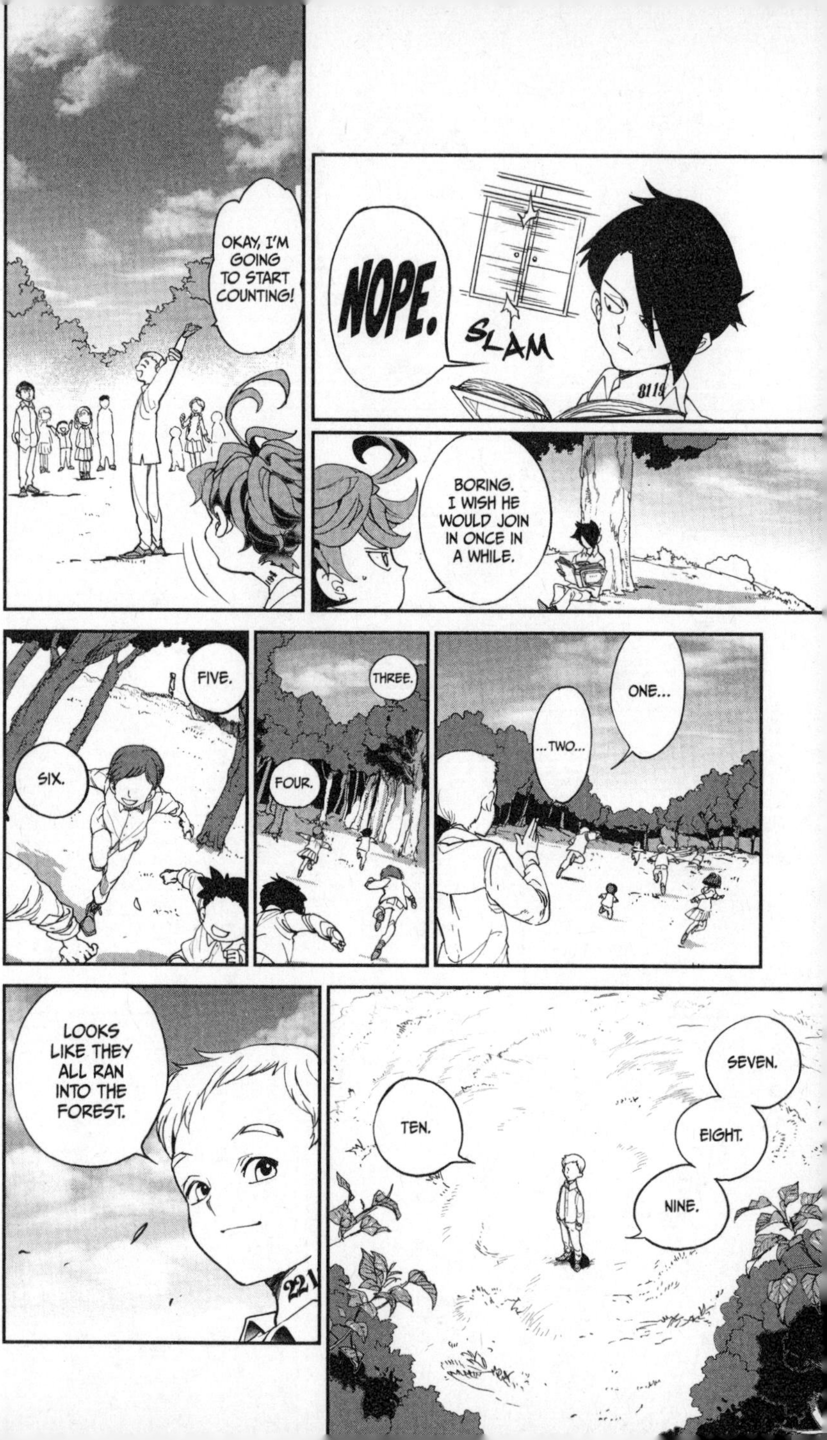
OKAY, I'M GOING TO START COUNTING!
NOPE.
SLAM
BORING. I WISH HE WOULD JOIN IN ONCE IN A WHILE.
ONE...
...TWO...
THREE.
FOUR.
FIVE.
SIX.
SEVEN.
EIGHT.
NINE.
TEN.
LOOKS LIKE THEY ALL RAN INTO THE FOREST.

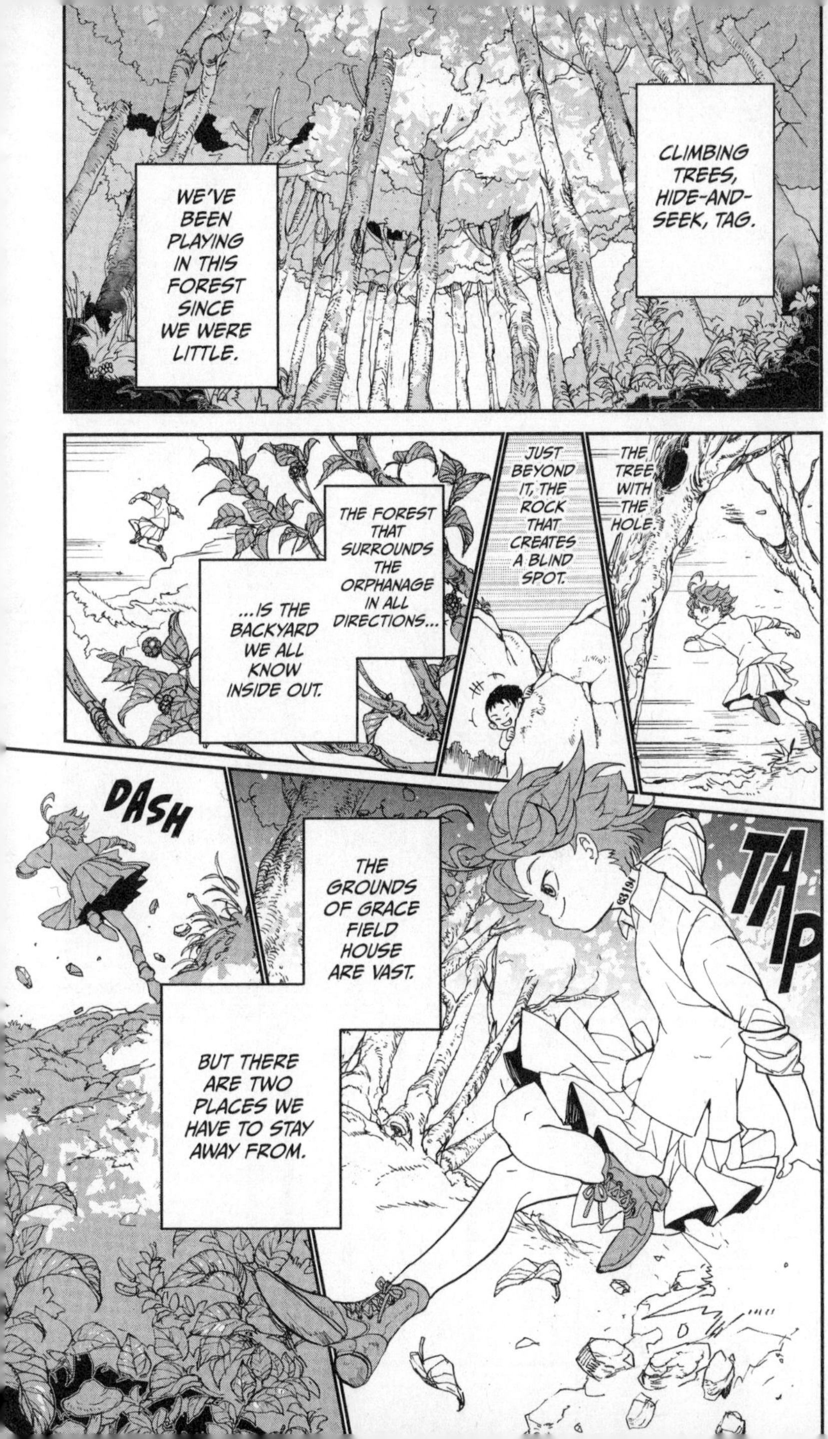
CLIMBING TREES, HIDE-AND-SEEK, TAG.
WE'VE BEEN PLAYING IN THIS FOREST SINCE WE WERE LITTLE.
THE TREE WITH THE HOLE.
JUST BEYOND IT, THE ROCK THAT CREATES A BLIND SPOT.
THE FOREST THAT SURROUNDS THE ORPHANAGE IN ALL DIRECTIONS...
...IS THE BACKYARD WE ALL KNOW INSIDE OUT.
TAP
THE GROUNDS OF GRACE FIELD HOUSE ARE VAST.
BUT THERE ARE TWO PLACES WE HAVE TO STAY AWAY FROM.
DASH

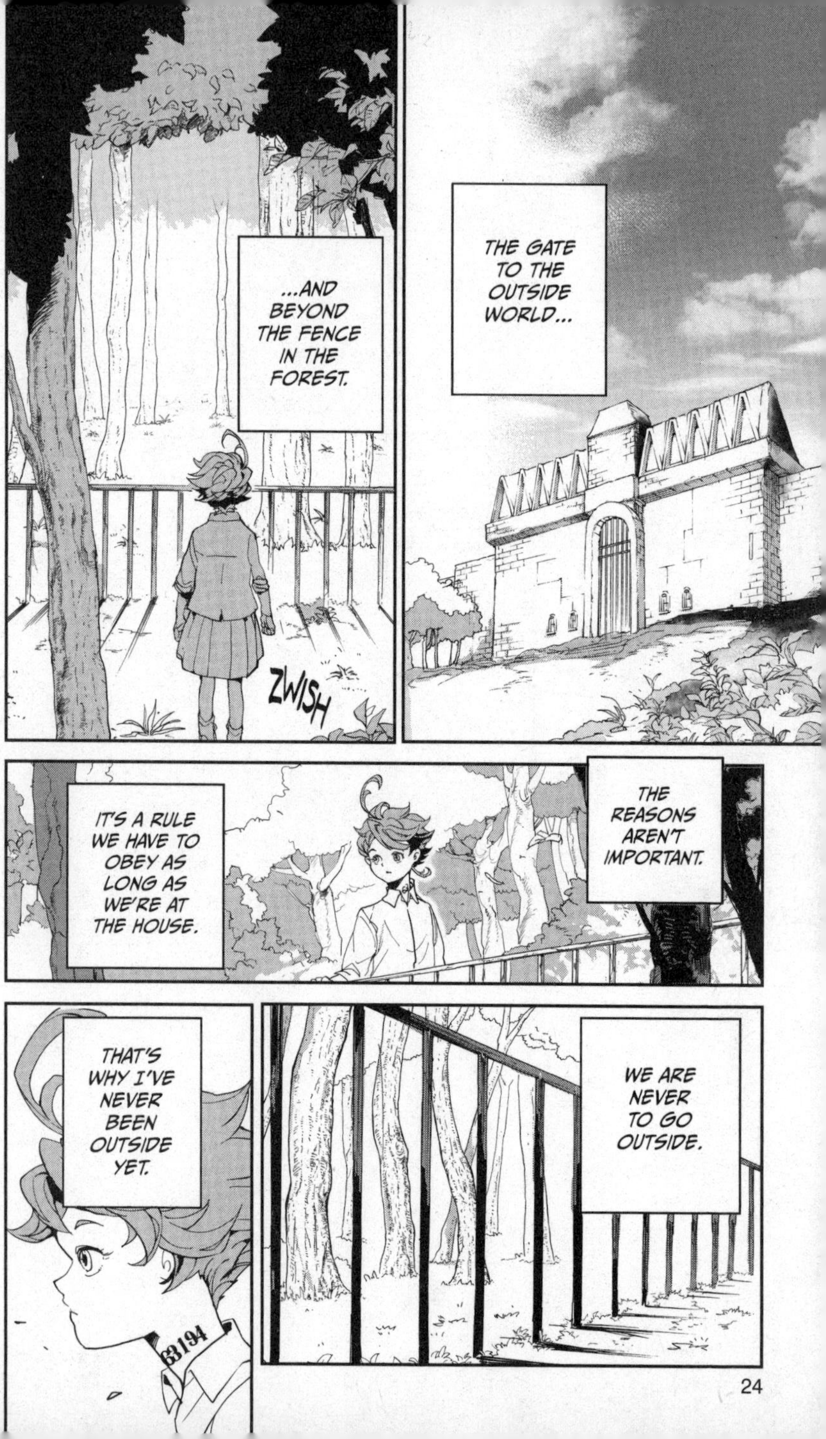
THE GATE TO THE OUTSIDE WORLD...
...AND BEYOND THE FENCE IN THE FOREST.
ZWISH
THE REASONS AREN'T IMPORTANT.
IT'S A RULE WE HAVE TO OBEY AS LONG AS WE'RE AT THE HOUSE.
WE ARE NEVER TO GO OUTSIDE.
THAT'S WHY I'VE NEVER BEEN OUTSIDE YET.
63194

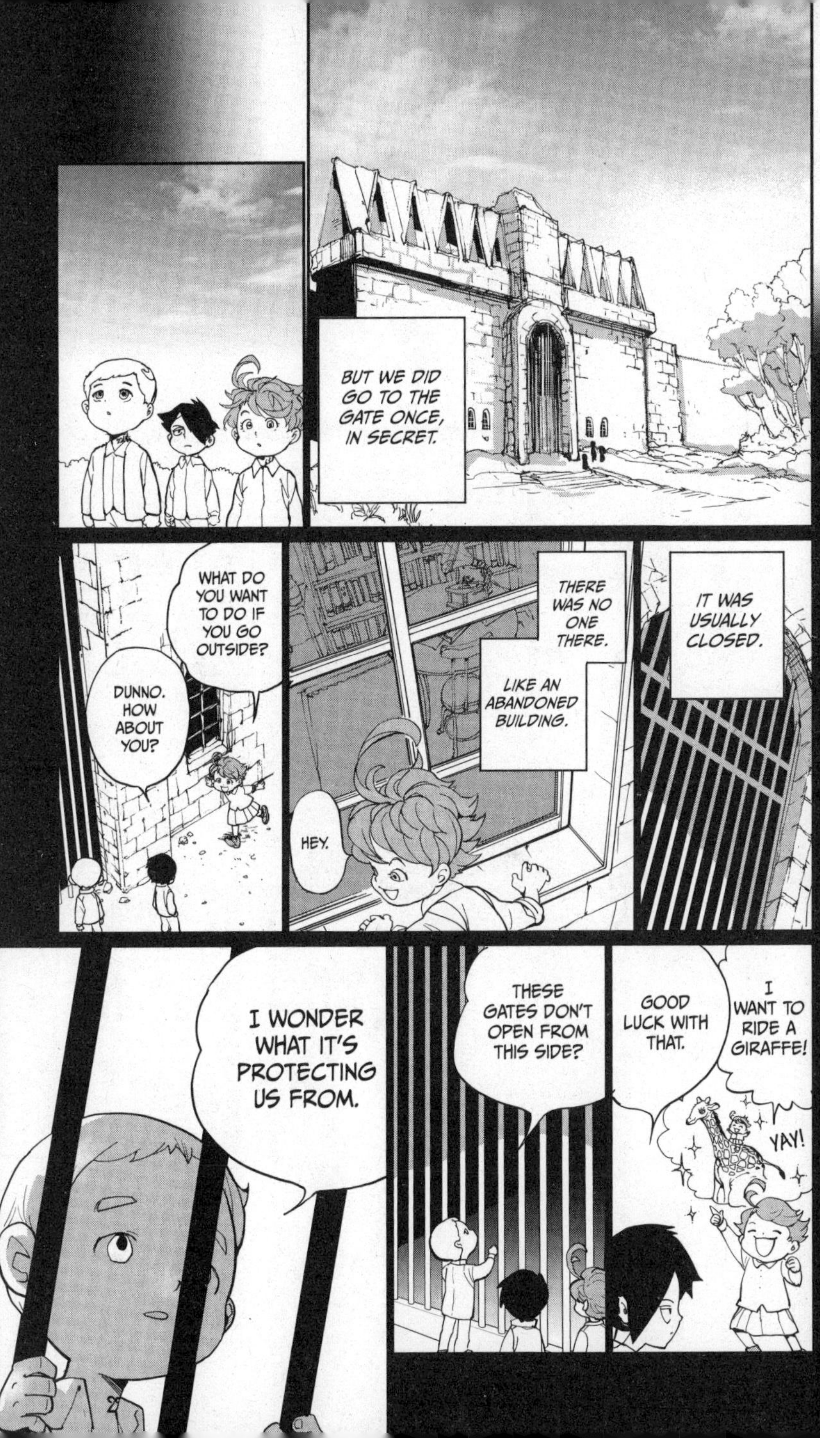
BUT WE DID GO TO THE GATE ONCE, IN SECRET.
IT WAS USUALLY CLOSED.
THERE WAS NO ONE THERE.
LIKE AN ABANDONED BUILDING.
HEY.
WHAT DO YOU WANT TO DO IF YOU GO OUTSIDE?
DUNNO. HOW ABOUT YOU?
I WANT TO RIDE A GIRAFFE!
YAY!
GOOD LUCK WITH THAT.
THESE GATES DON'T OPEN FROM THIS SIDE?
I WONDER WHAT IT'S PROTECTING US FROM.

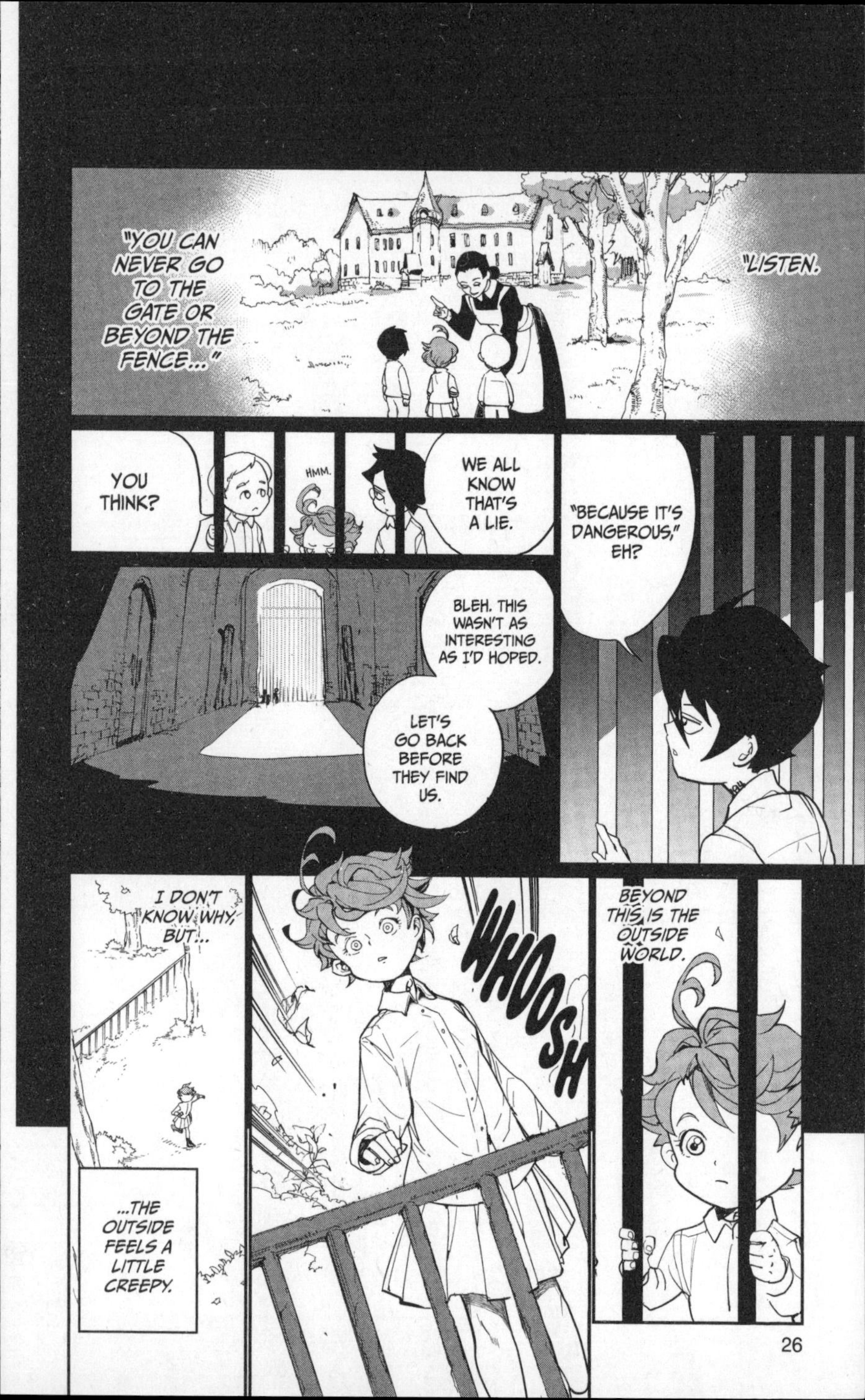
"LISTEN.
"YOU CAN NEVER GO TO THE GATE OR BEYOND THE FENCE..."
"BECAUSE IT'S DANGEROUS," EH?
WE ALL KNOW THAT'S A LIE.
HMM.
YOU THINK?
BLEH. THIS WASN'T AS INTERESTING AS I'D HOPED.
LET'S GO BACK BEFORE THEY FIND US.
BEYOND THIS IS THE OUTSIDE WORLD.
WHOOSH
I DON'T KNOW WHY, BUT...
...THE OUTSIDE FEELS A LITTLE CREEPY.

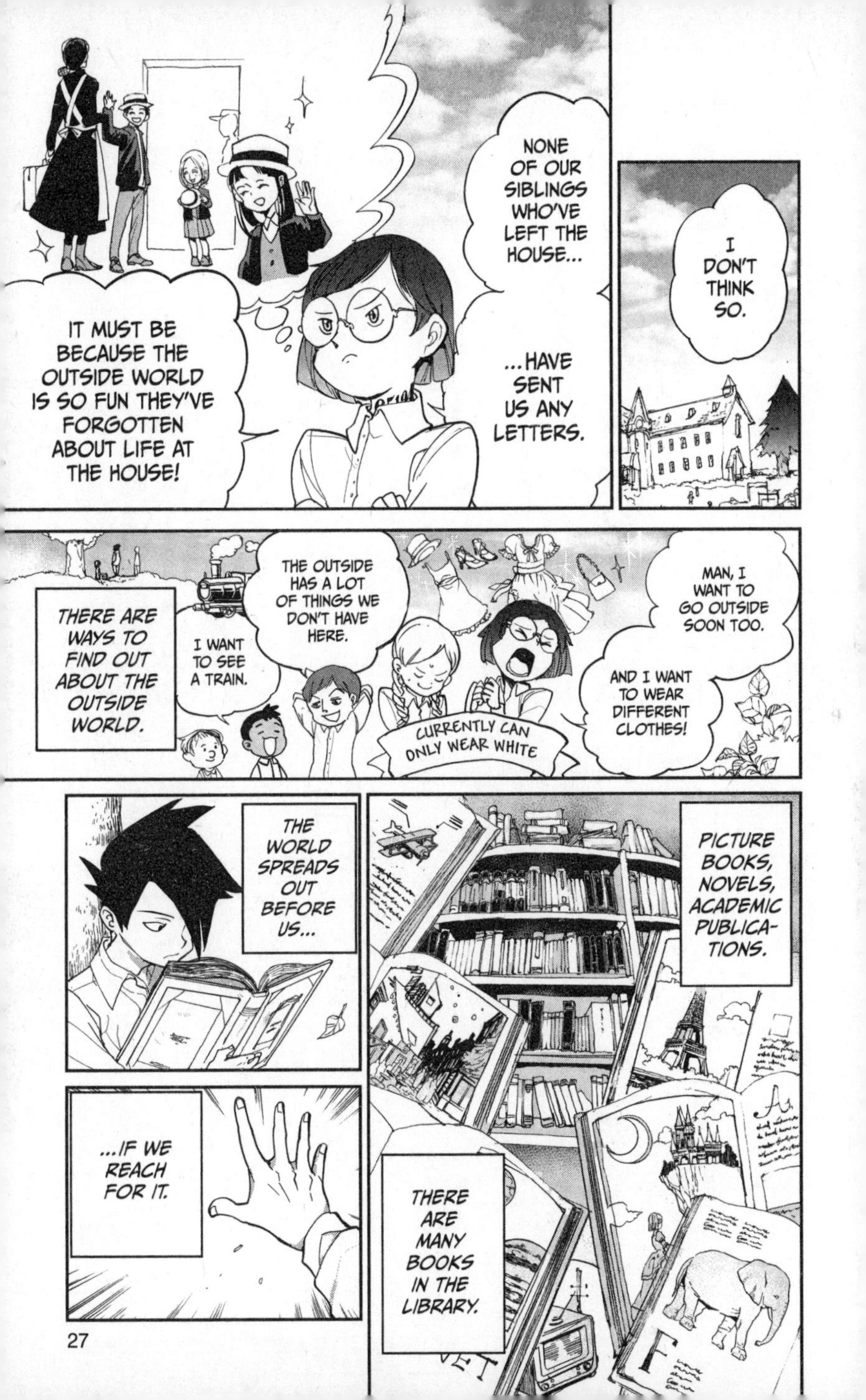
I DON'T THINK SO.
NONE OF OUR SIBLINGS WHO'VE LEFT THE HOUSE...
...HAVE SENT US ANY LETTERS.
IT MUST BE BECAUSE THE OUTSIDE WORLD IS SO FUN THEY'VE FORGOTTEN ABOUT LIFE AT THE HOUSE!
MAN, I WANT TO GO OUTSIDE SOON TOO.
AND I WANT TO WEAR DIFFERENT CLOTHES!
CURRENTLY CAN ONLY WEAR WHITE
THE OUTSIDE HAS A LOT OF THINGS WE DON'T HAVE HERE.
I WANT TO SEE A TRAIN.
THERE ARE WAYS TO FIND OUT ABOUT THE OUTSIDE WORLD.
PICTURE BOOKS, NOVELS, ACADEMIC PUBLICATIONS.
THERE ARE MANY BOOKS IN THE LIBRARY.
THE WORLD SPREADS OUT BEFORE US...
...IF WE REACH FOR IT.

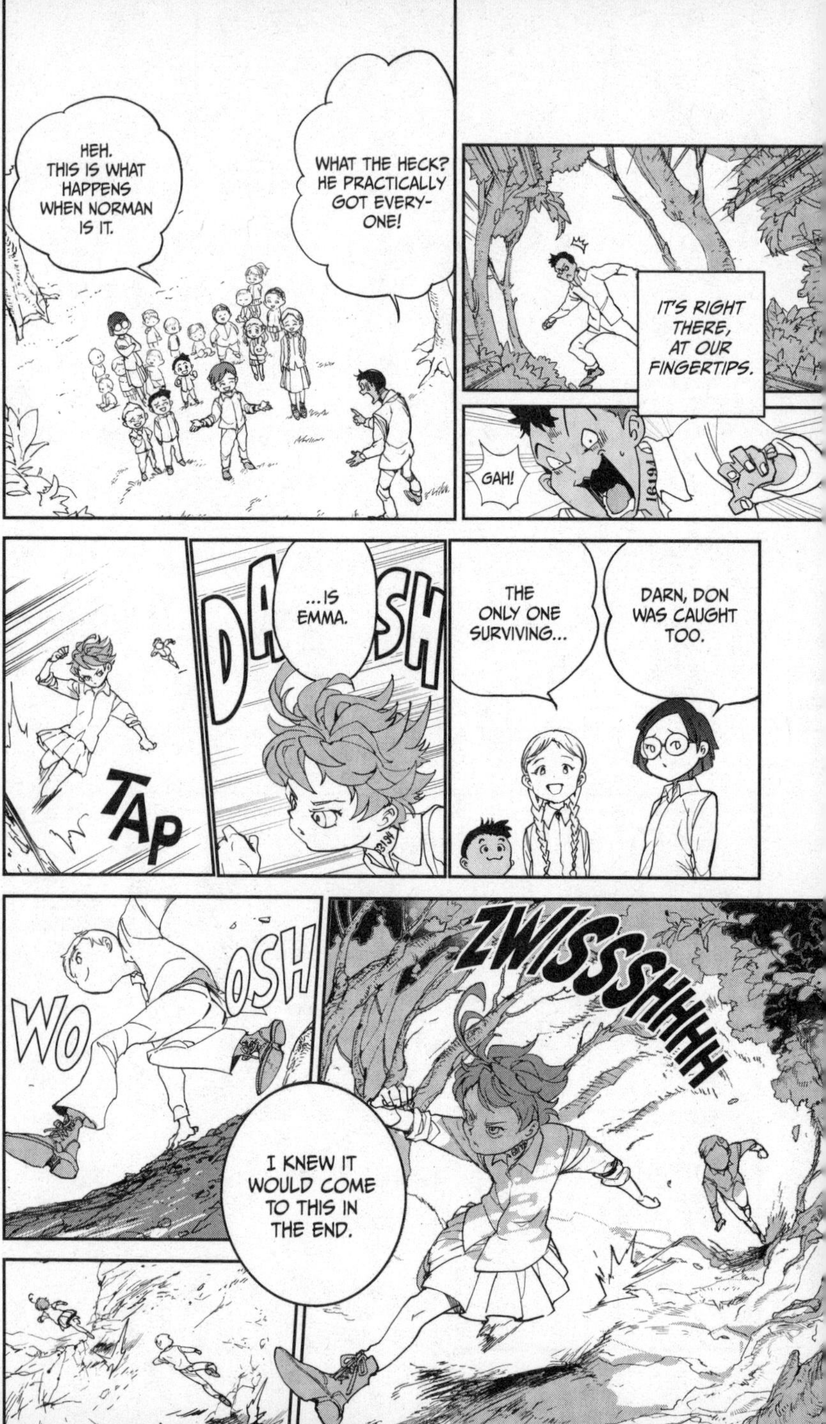
IT'S RIGHT THERE, AT OUR FINGERTIPS.
GAH!
WHAT THE HECK? HE PRACTICALLY GOT EVERY-ONE!
HEH. THIS IS WHAT HAPPENS WHEN NORMAN IS IT.
DARN, DON WAS CAUGHT TOO.
THE ONLY ONE SURVIVING...
DASH
...IS EMMA.
TAP
ZWISSSHHHH
I KNEW IT WOULD COME TO THIS IN THE END.
WOOSH

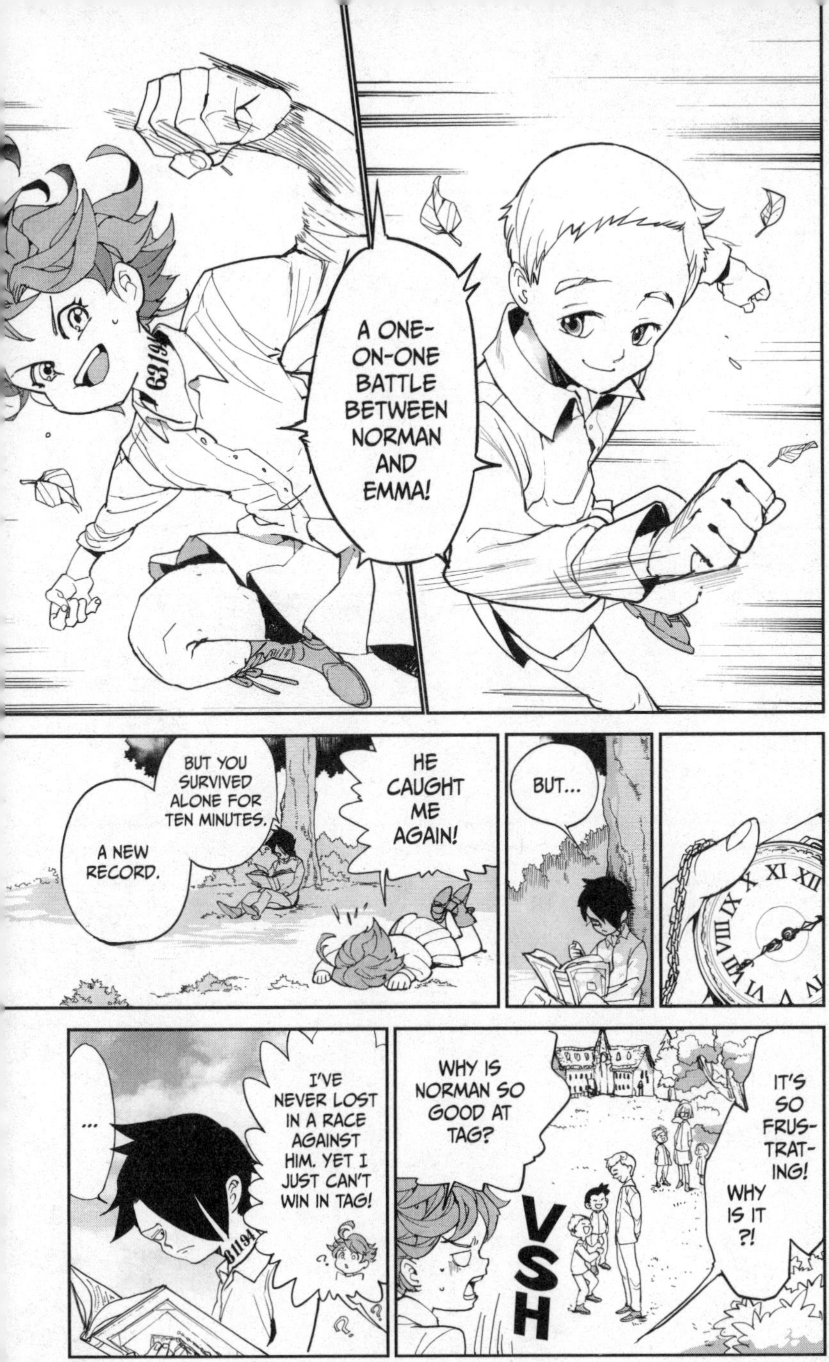
A ONE-ON-ONE BATTLE BETWEEN NORMAN AND EMMA!
BUT...
HE CAUGHT ME AGAIN!
BUT YOU SURVIVED ALONE FOR TEN MINUTES.
A NEW RECORD.
IT'S SO FRUS-TRATING!
WHY IS IT ?!
WHY IS NORMAN SO GOOD AT TAG?
VSH
I'VE NEVER LOST IN A RACE AGAINST HIM. YET I JUST CAN'T WIN IN TAG!
...

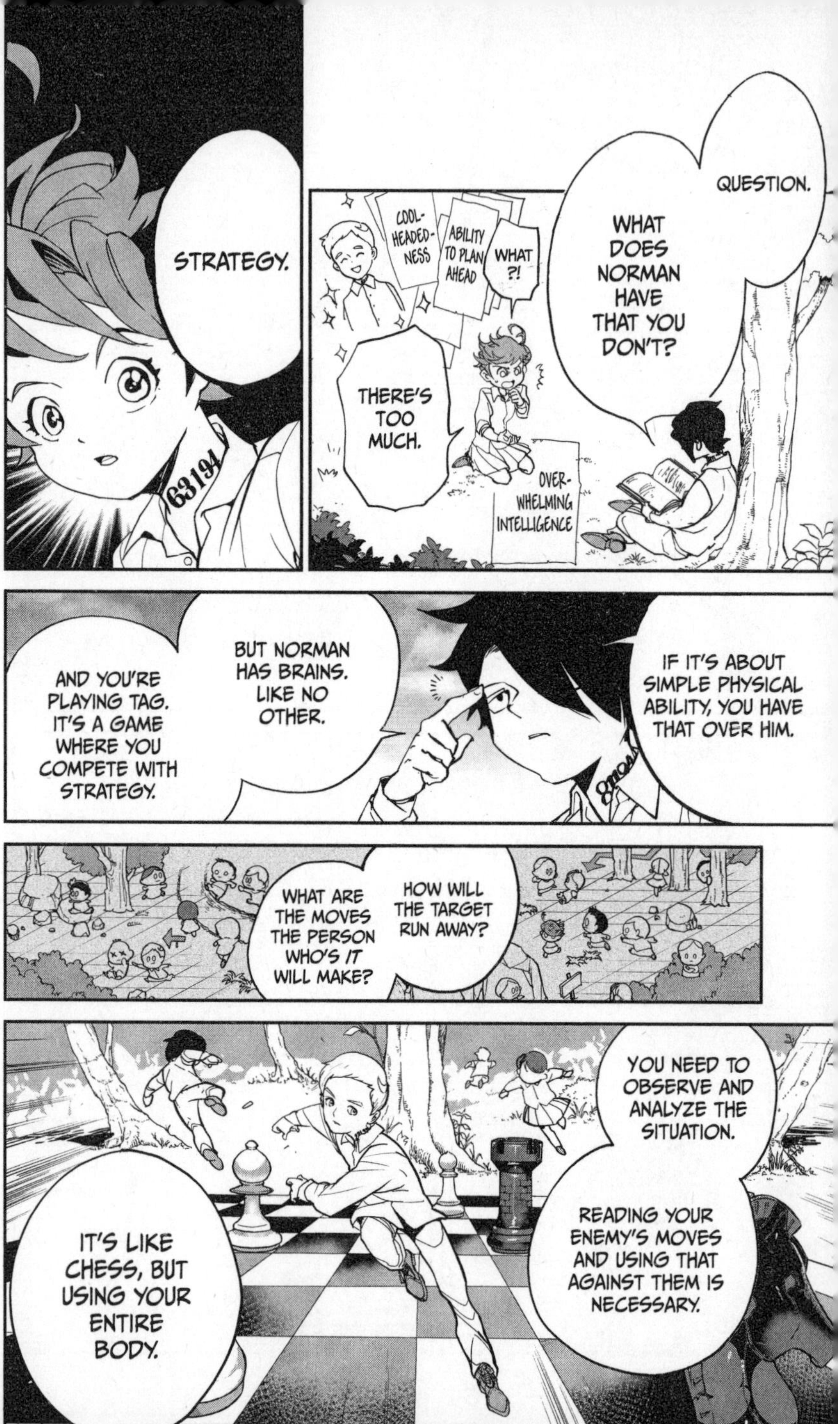
QUESTION.
WHAT DOES NORMAN HAVE THAT YOU DON'T?
COOL-HEADED-NESS
ABILITY TO PLAN AHEAD
WHAT ?!
THERE'S TOO MUCH.
OVER-WHELMING INTELLIGENCE
STRATEGY.
63194
IF IT'S ABOUT SIMPLE PHYSICAL ABILITY, YOU HAVE THAT OVER HIM.
BUT NORMAN HAS BRAINS. LIKE NO OTHER.
AND YOU'RE PLAYING TAG. IT'S A GAME WHERE YOU COMPETE WITH STRATEGY.
HOW WILL THE TARGET RUN AWAY?
WHAT ARE THE MOVES THE PERSON WHO'S IT WILL MAKE?
YOU NEED TO OBSERVE AND ANALYZE THE SITUATION.
READING YOUR ENEMY'S MOVES AND USING THAT AGAINST THEM IS NECESSARY.
IT'S LIKE CHESS, BUT USING YOUR ENTIRE BODY.

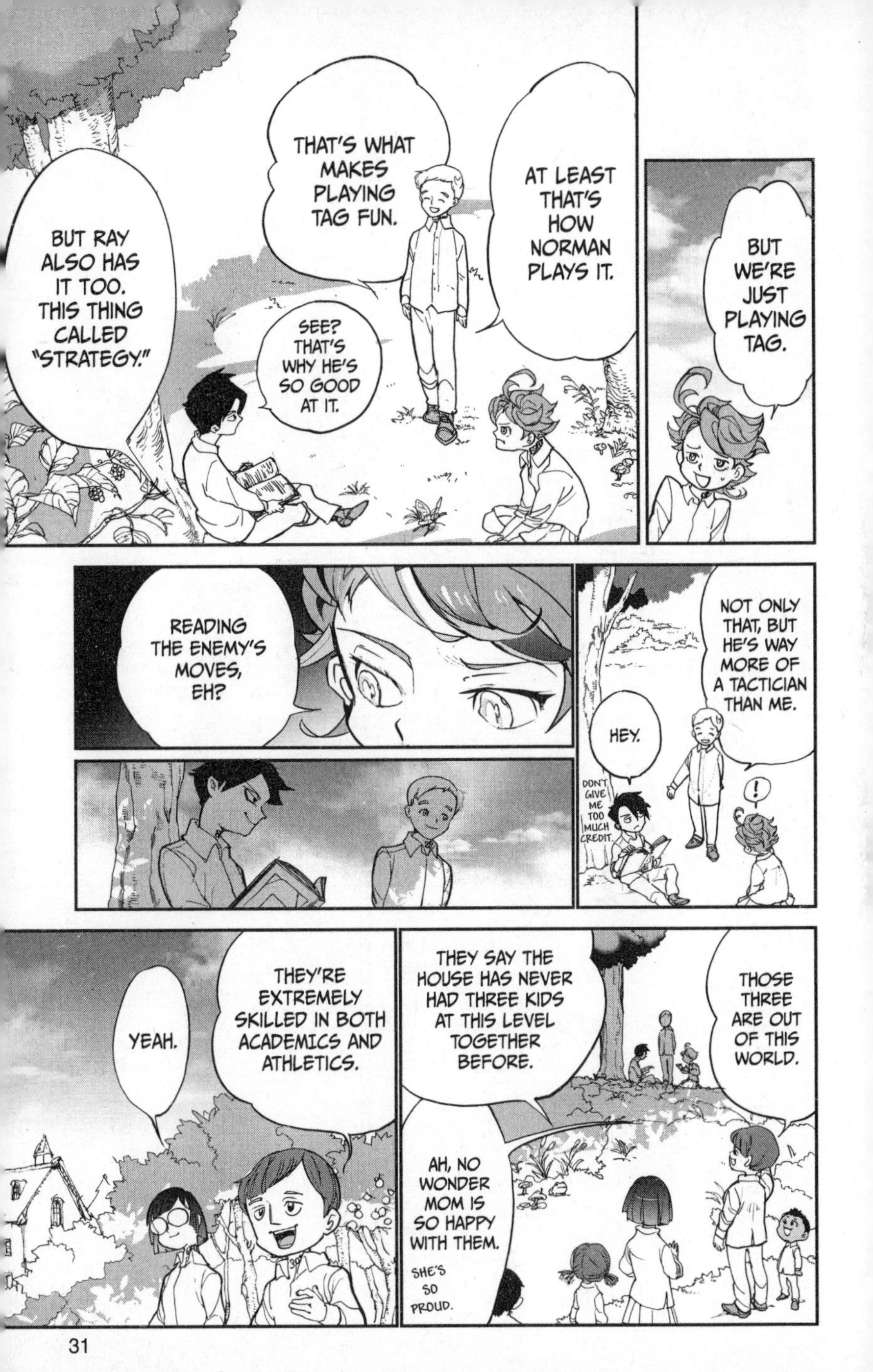
BUT WE'RE JUST PLAYING TAG.
THAT'S WHAT MAKES PLAYING TAG FUN.
AT LEAST THAT'S HOW NORMAN PLAYS IT.
SEE? THAT'S WHY HE'S SO GOOD AT IT.
BUT RAY ALSO HAS IT TOO. THIS THING CALLED "STRATEGY."
NOT ONLY THAT, BUT HE'S WAY MORE OF A TACTICIAN THAN ME.
!
HEY.
DON'T GIVE ME TOO MUCH CREDIT.
READING THE ENEMY'S MOVES, EH?
THOSE THREE ARE OUT OF THIS WORLD.
THEY SAY THE HOUSE HAS NEVER HAD THREE KIDS AT THIS LEVEL TOGETHER BEFORE.
AH, NO WONDER MOM IS SO HAPPY WITH THEM.
SHE'S SO PROUD.
THEY'RE EXTREMELY SKILLED IN BOTH ACADEMICS AND ATHLETICS.
YEAH.

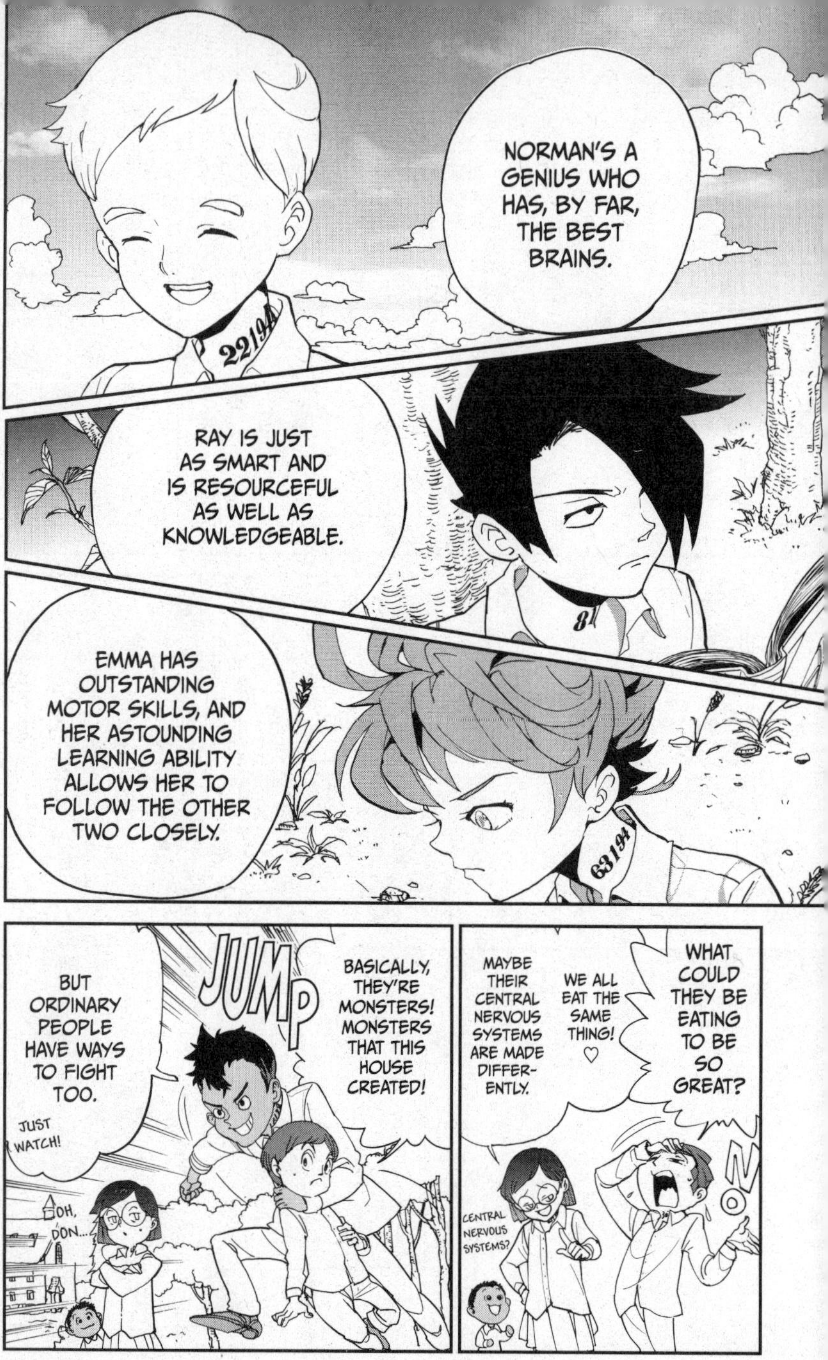
NORMAN'S A GENIUS WHO HAS, BY FAR, THE BEST BRAINS.
22194
RAY IS JUST AS SMART AND IS RESOURCEFUL AS WELL AS KNOWLEDGEABLE.
EMMA HAS OUTSTANDING MOTOR SKILLS, AND HER ASTOUNDING LEARNING ABILITY ALLOWS HER TO FOLLOW THE OTHER TWO CLOSELY.
63194
WHAT COULD THEY BE EATING TO BE SO GREAT?
WE ALL EAT THE SAME THING! ♡
MAYBE THEIR CENTRAL NERVOUS SYSTEMS ARE MADE DIFFER-ENTLY.
NO
CENTRAL NERVOUS SYSTEMS?
BASICALLY, THEY'RE MONSTERS! MONSTERS THAT THIS HOUSE CREATED!
JUMP
BUT ORDINARY PEOPLE HAVE WAYS TO FIGHT TOO.
JUST WATCH!
OH, DON...

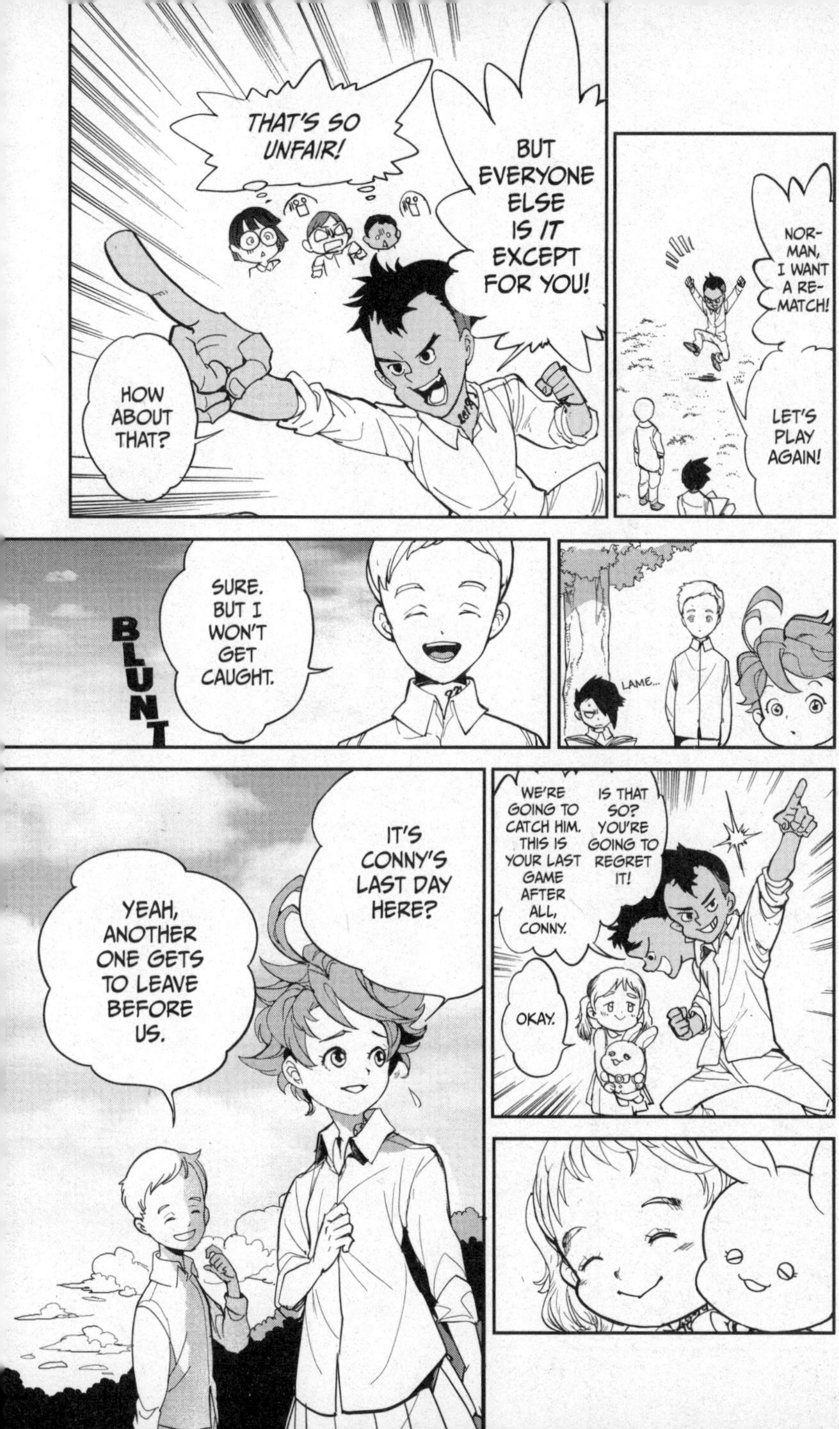
NOR-MAN, I WANT A RE-MATCH!
LET'S PLAY AGAIN!
BUT EVERYONE ELSE IS IT EXCEPT FOR YOU!
THAT'S SO UNFAIR!
HOW ABOUT THAT?
LAME...
SURE. BUT I WON'T GET CAUGHT.
BLUNT
IS THAT SO? YOU'RE GOING TO REGRET IT!
WE'RE GOING TO CATCH HIM. THIS IS YOUR LAST GAME AFTER ALL, CONNY.
OKAY.
IT'S CONNY'S LAST DAY HERE?
YEAH, ANOTHER ONE GETS TO LEAVE BEFORE US.

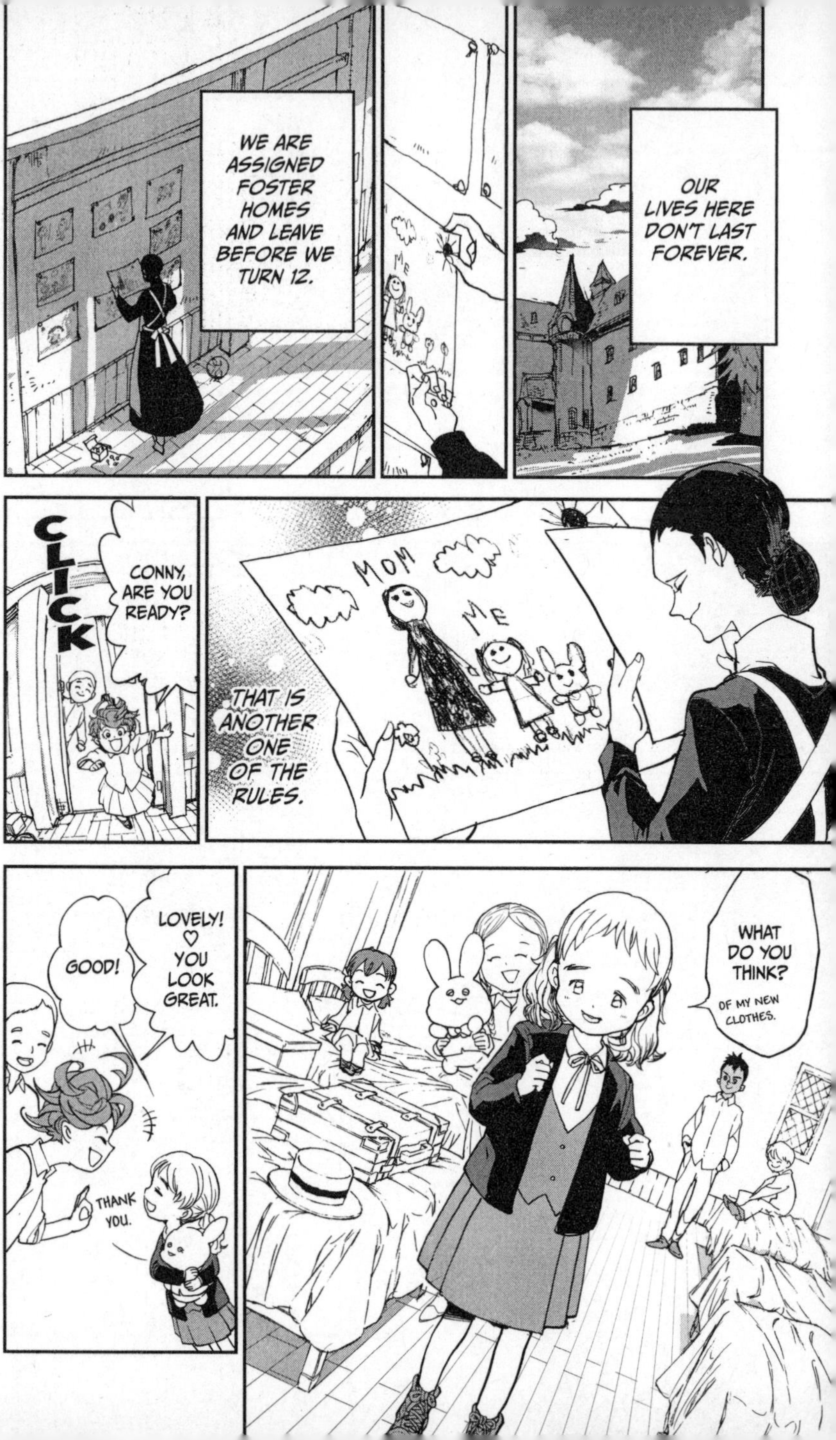
OUR LIVES HERE DON'T LAST FOREVER.
ME
WE ARE ASSIGNED FOSTER HOMES AND LEAVE BEFORE WE TURN 12.
MOM
ME
THAT IS ANOTHER ONE OF THE RULES.
CLICK
CONNY, ARE YOU READY?
WHAT DO YOU THINK?
OF MY NEW CLOTHES.
LOVELY! ♡ YOU LOOK GREAT.
GOOD!
THANK YOU.

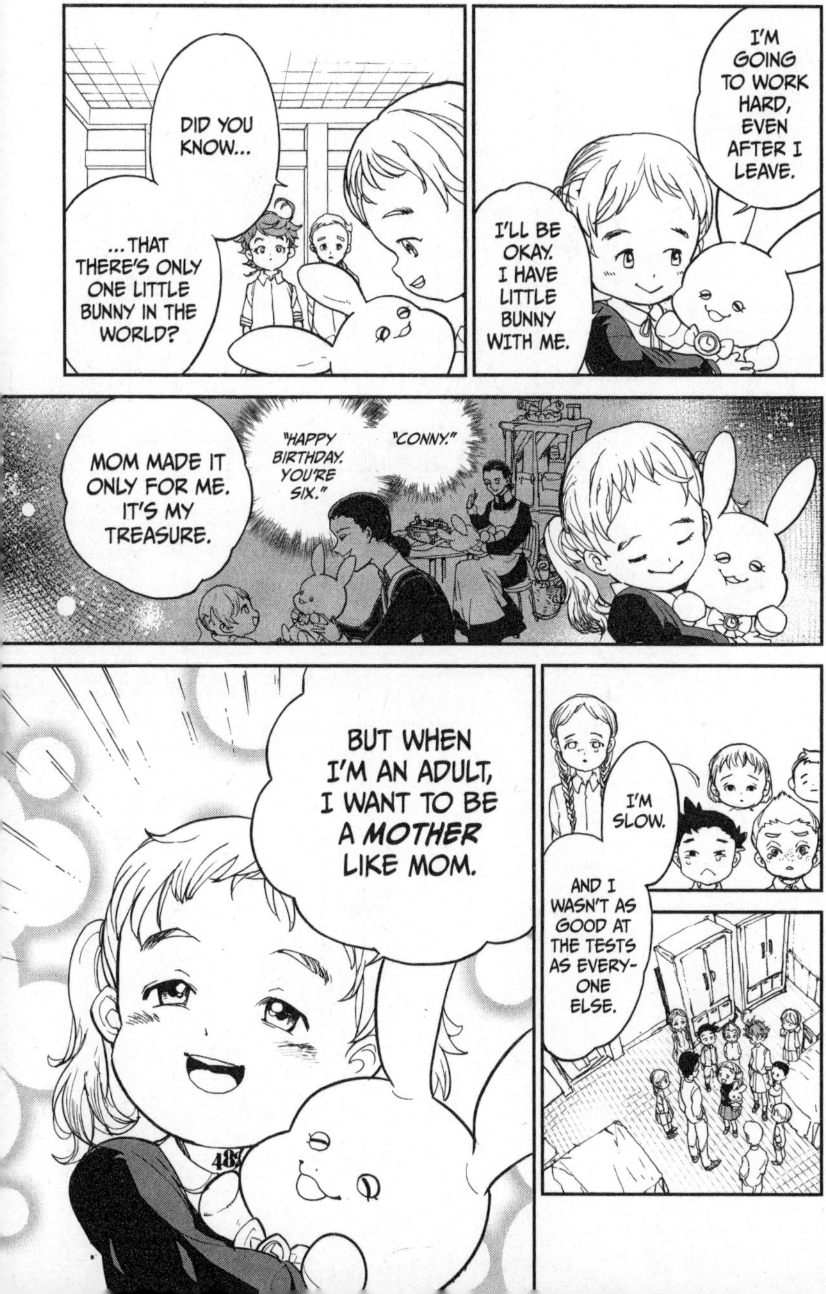
I'M GOING TO WORK HARD, EVEN AFTER I LEAVE.
I'LL BE OKAY. I HAVE LITTLE BUNNY WITH ME.
DID YOU KNOW...
...THAT THERE'S ONLY ONE LITTLE BUNNY IN THE WORLD?
"CONNY."
"HAPPY BIRTHDAY. YOU'RE SIX."
MOM MADE IT ONLY FOR ME. IT'S MY TREASURE.
I'M SLOW.
AND I WASN'T AS GOOD AT THE TESTS AS EVERY-ONE ELSE.
BUT WHEN I'M AN ADULT, I WANT TO BE A *MOTHER* LIKE MOM.

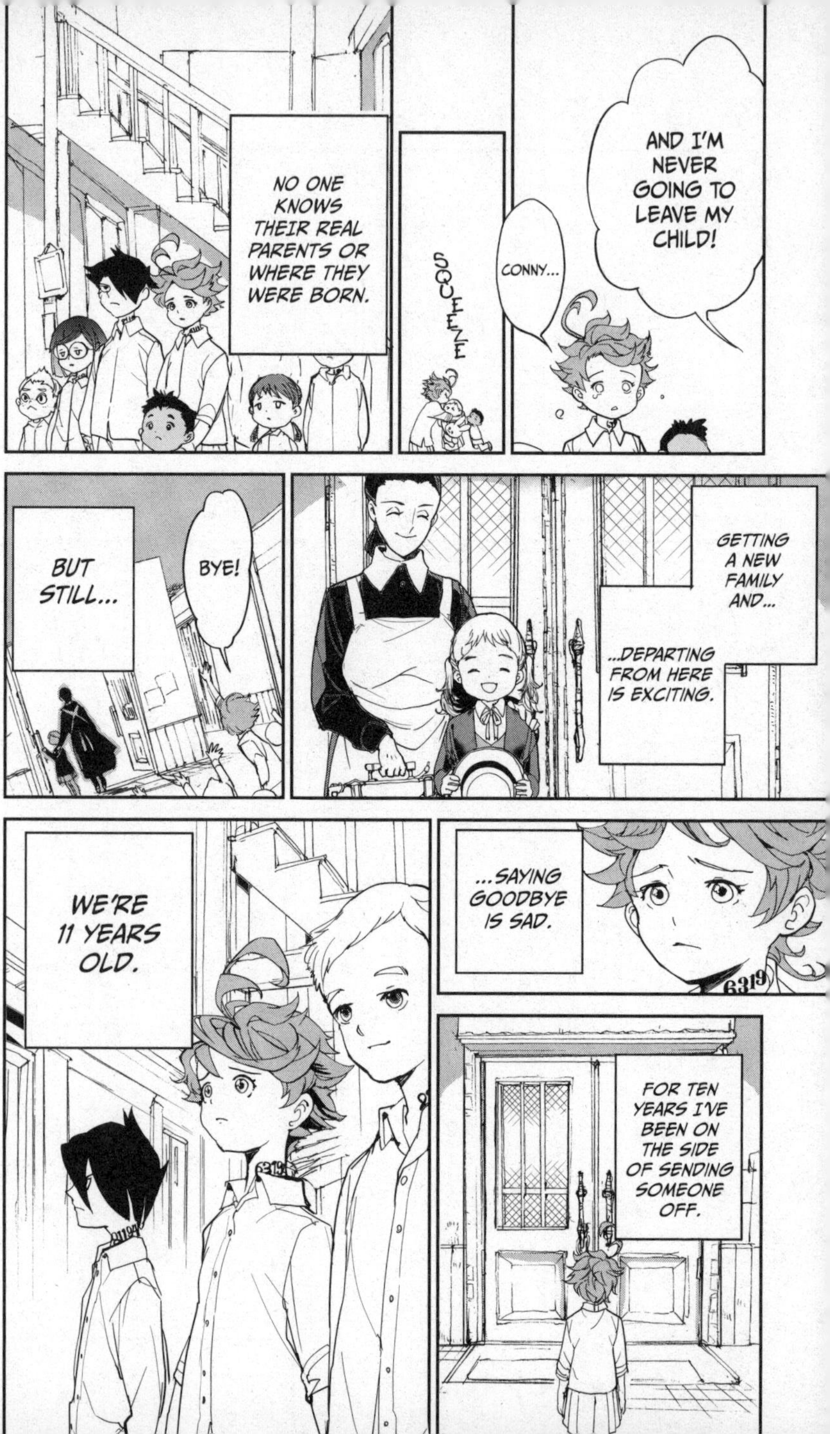
AND I'M NEVER GOING TO LEAVE MY CHILD!
CONNY...
SQUEEZE
NO ONE KNOWS THEIR REAL PARENTS OR WHERE THEY WERE BORN.
GETTING A NEW FAMILY AND...
...DEPARTING FROM HERE IS EXCITING.
BYE!
BUT STILL...
...SAYING GOODBYE IS SAD.
63194
FOR TEN YEARS I'VE BEEN ON THE SIDE OF SENDING SOMEONE OFF.
WE'RE 11 YEARS OLD.

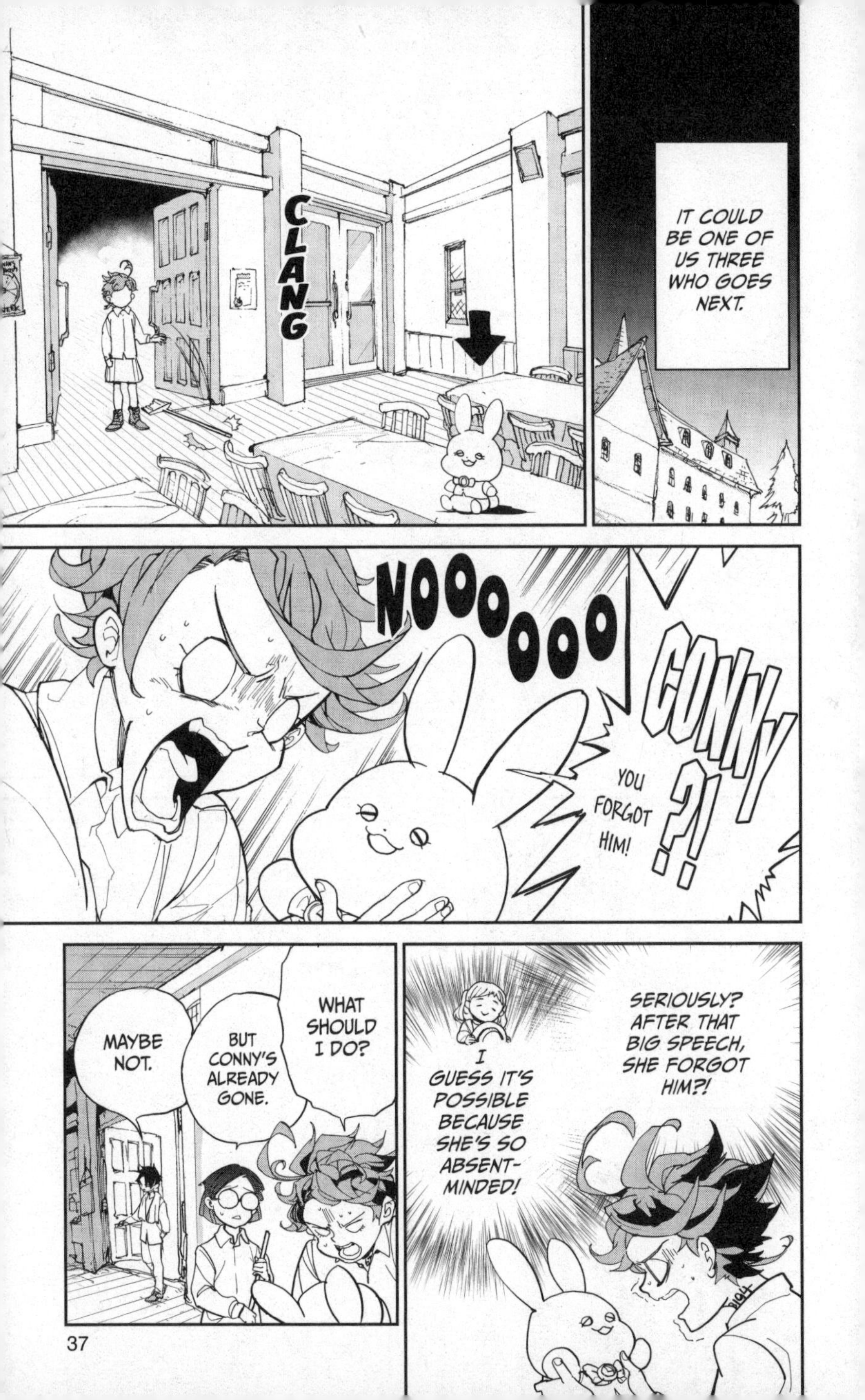
IT COULD BE ONE OF US THREE WHO GOES NEXT.
CLANG
NOOOOOO
CONNY?!
YOU FORGOT HIM!
SERIOUSLY? AFTER THAT BIG SPEECH, SHE FORGOT HIM?!
I GUESS IT'S POSSIBLE BECAUSE SHE'S SO ABSENT-MINDED!
WHAT SHOULD I DO?
BUT CONNY'S ALREADY GONE.
MAYBE NOT.

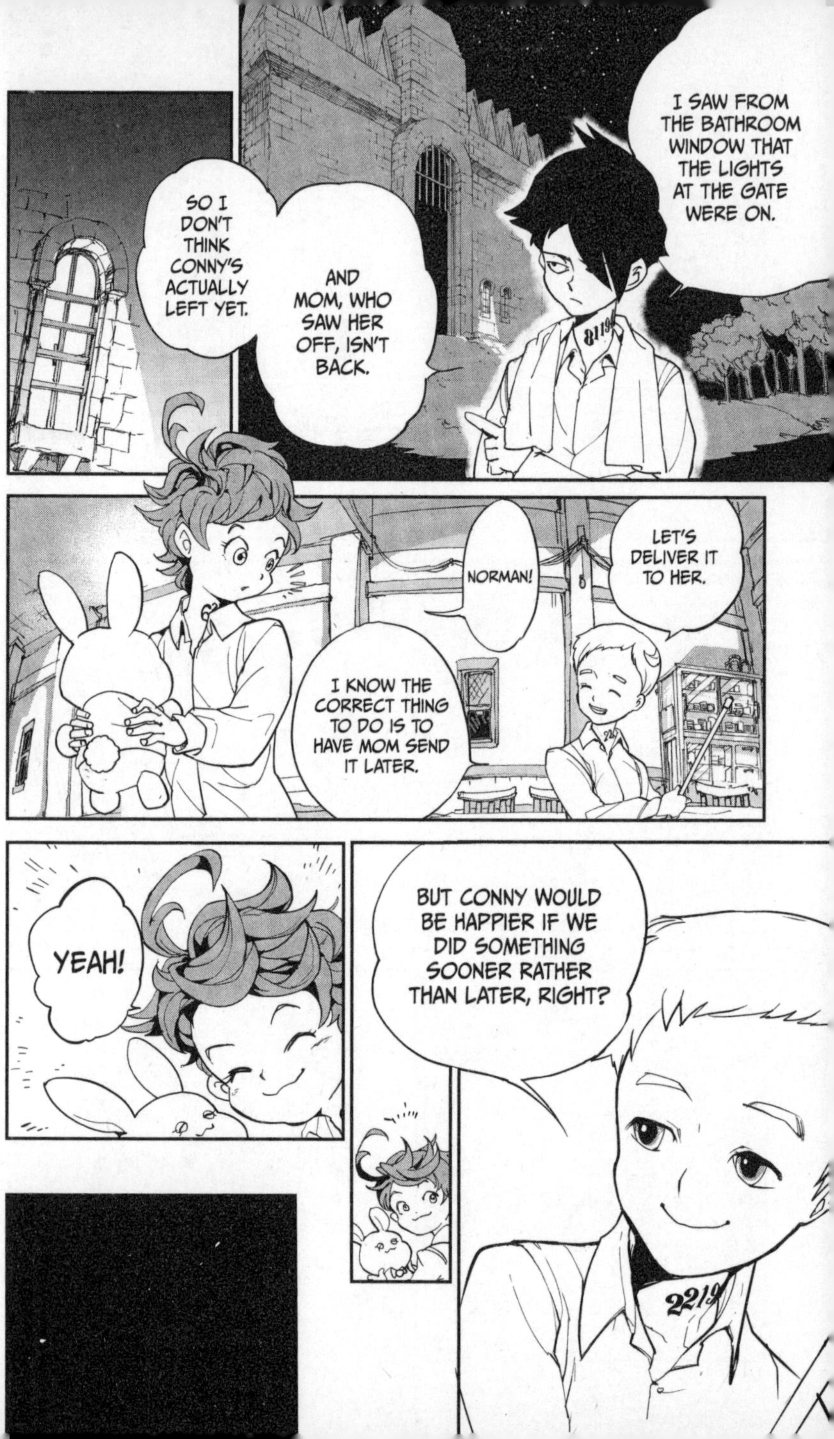
I SAW FROM THE BATHROOM WINDOW THAT THE LIGHTS AT THE GATE WERE ON.
AND MOM, WHO SAW HER OFF, ISN'T BACK.
SO I DON'T THINK CONNY'S ACTUALLY LEFT YET.
LET'S DELIVER IT TO HER.
NORMAN!
I KNOW THE CORRECT THING TO DO IS TO HAVE MOM SEND IT LATER.
BUT CONNY WOULD BE HAPPIER IF WE DID SOMETHING SOONER RATHER THAN LATER, RIGHT?
YEAH!

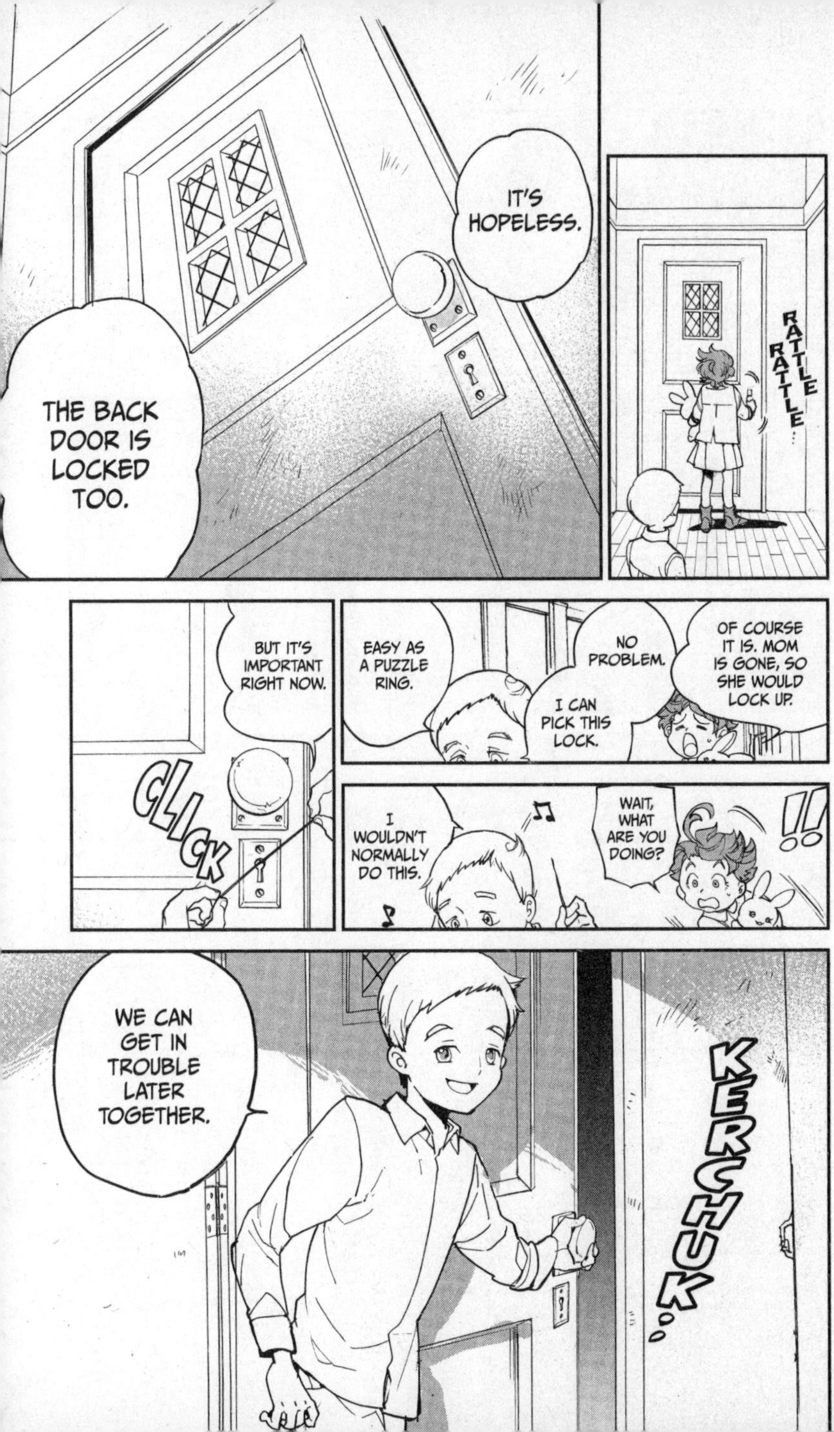
RATTLE RATTLE...
IT'S HOPELESS.
THE BACK DOOR IS LOCKED TOO.
OF COURSE IT IS. MOM IS GONE, SO SHE WOULD LOCK UP.
NO PROBLEM.
I CAN PICK THIS LOCK.
EASY AS A PUZZLE RING.
!!
WAIT, WHAT ARE YOU DOING?
I WOULDN'T NORMALLY DO THIS.
BUT IT'S IMPORTANT RIGHT NOW.
CLICK
KERCHUK...
WE CAN GET IN TROUBLE LATER TOGETHER.

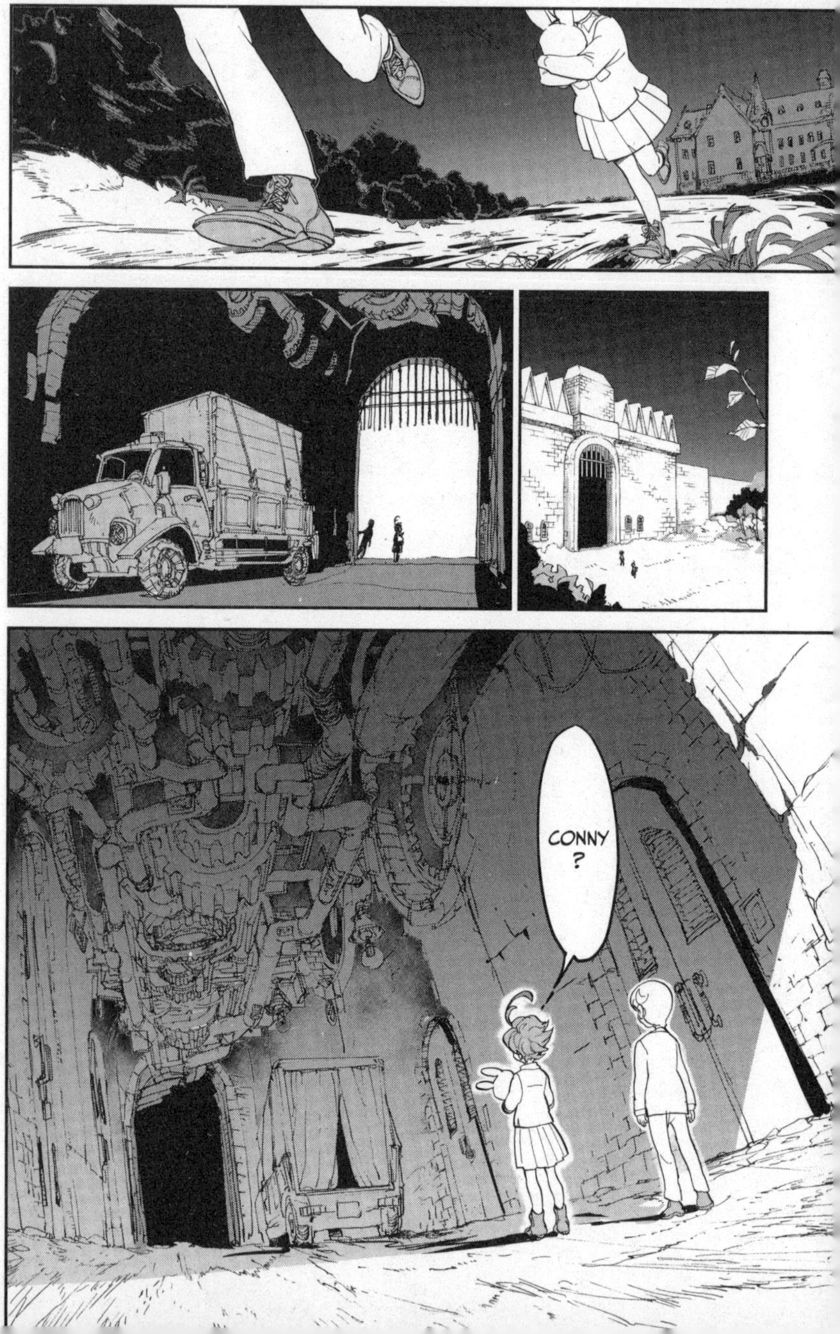
CONNY
?

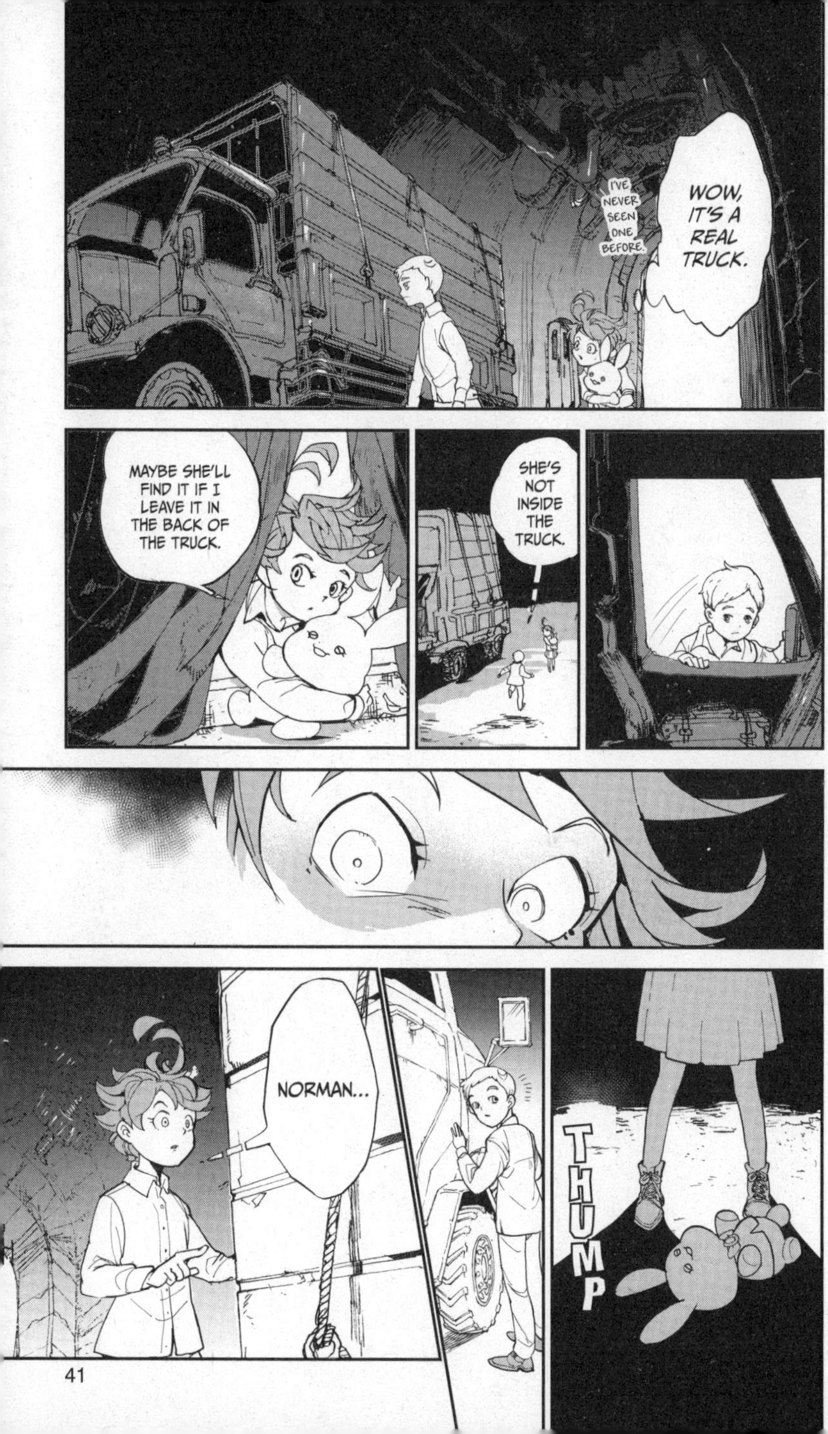
WOW, IT'S A REAL TRUCK.
I'VE NEVER SEEN ONE BEFORE.
SHE'S NOT INSIDE THE TRUCK.
MAYBE SHE'LL FIND IT IF I LEAVE IT IN THE BACK OF THE TRUCK.
THUMP
NORMAN...

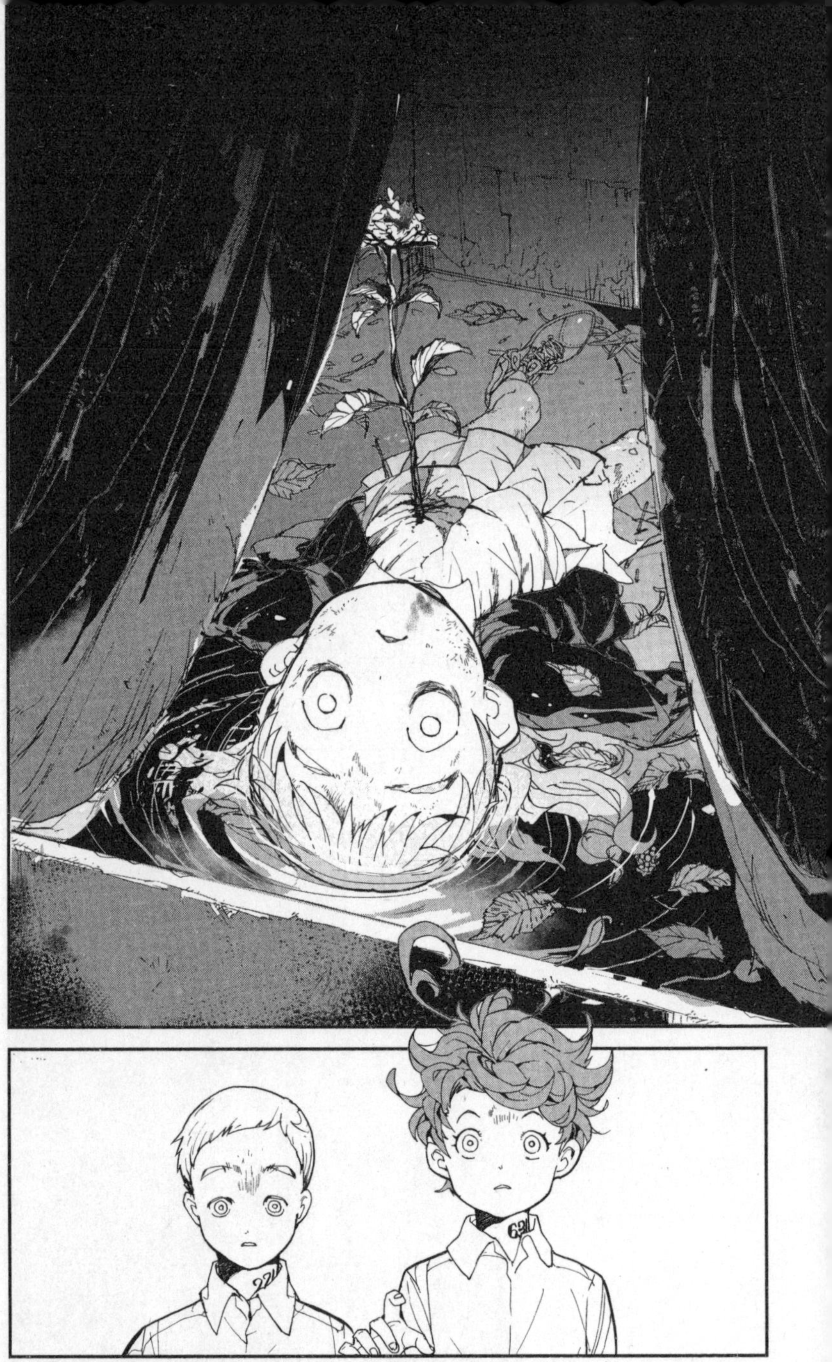

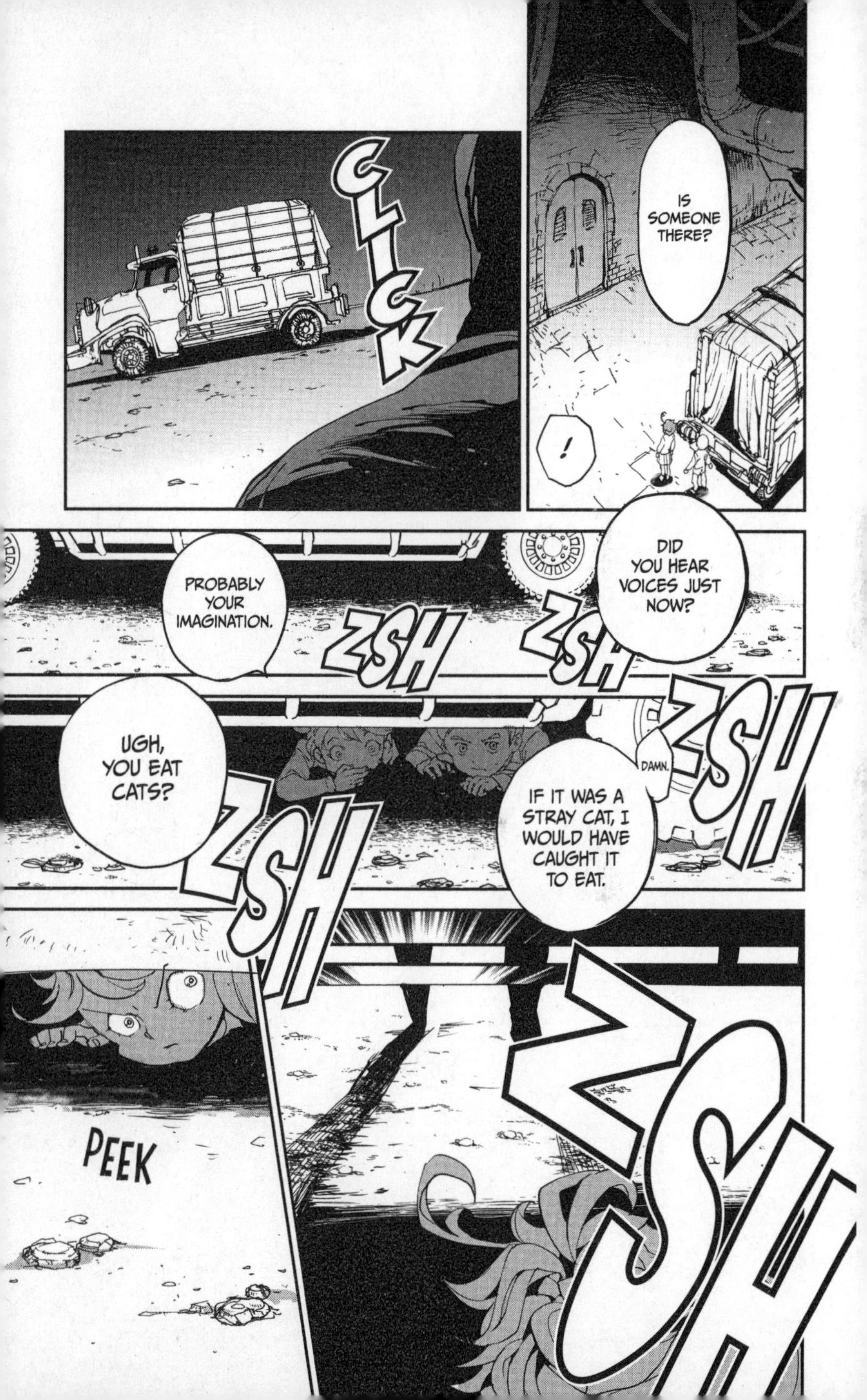
IS SOMEONE THERE?
!
CLICK
DID YOU HEAR VOICES JUST NOW?
ZSH
ZSH
PROBABLY YOUR IMAGINATION.
ZSH
DAMN.
IF IT WAS A STRAY CAT, I WOULD HAVE CAUGHT IT TO EAT.
UGH, YOU EAT CATS?
ZSH
ZSH
PEEK

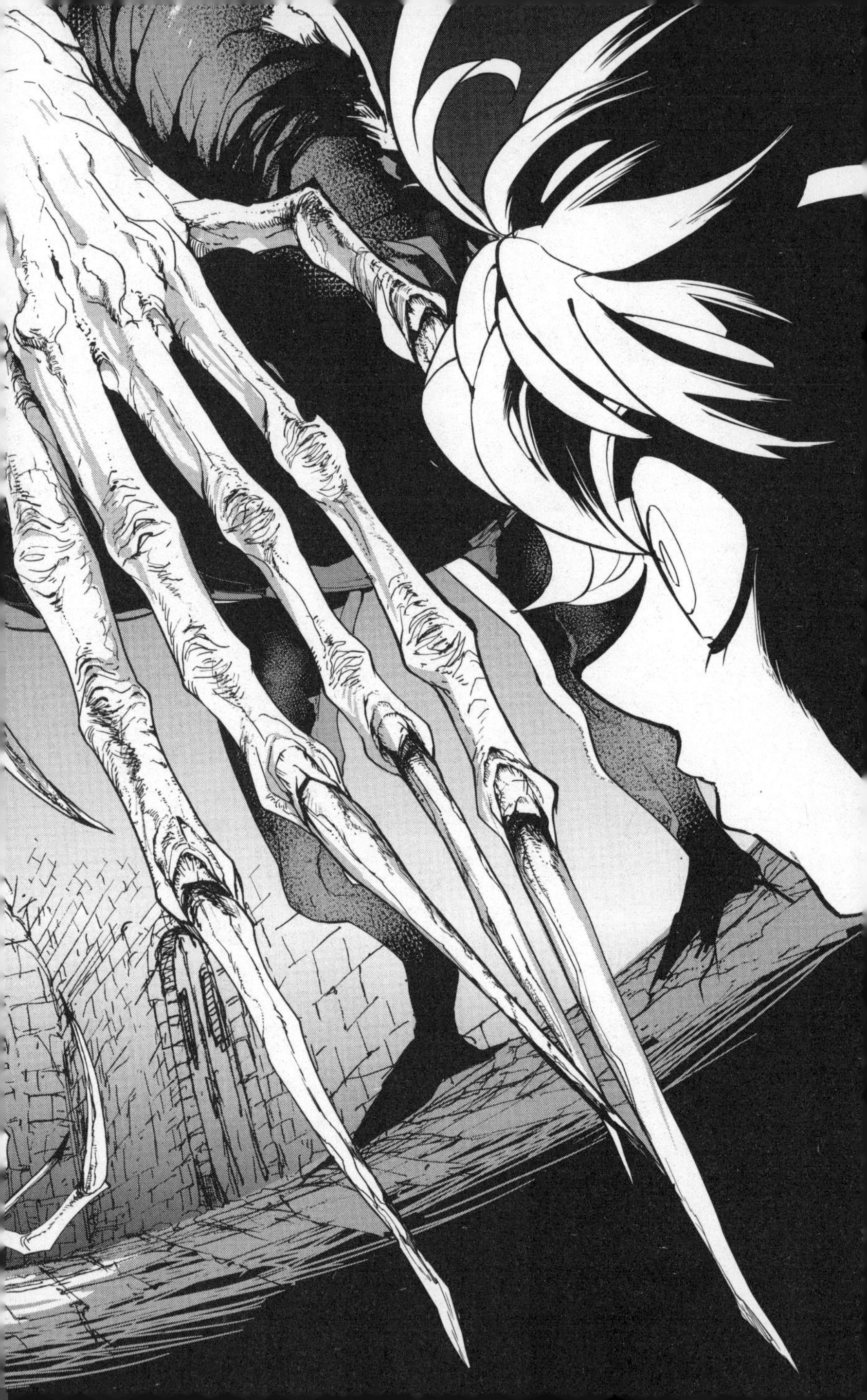

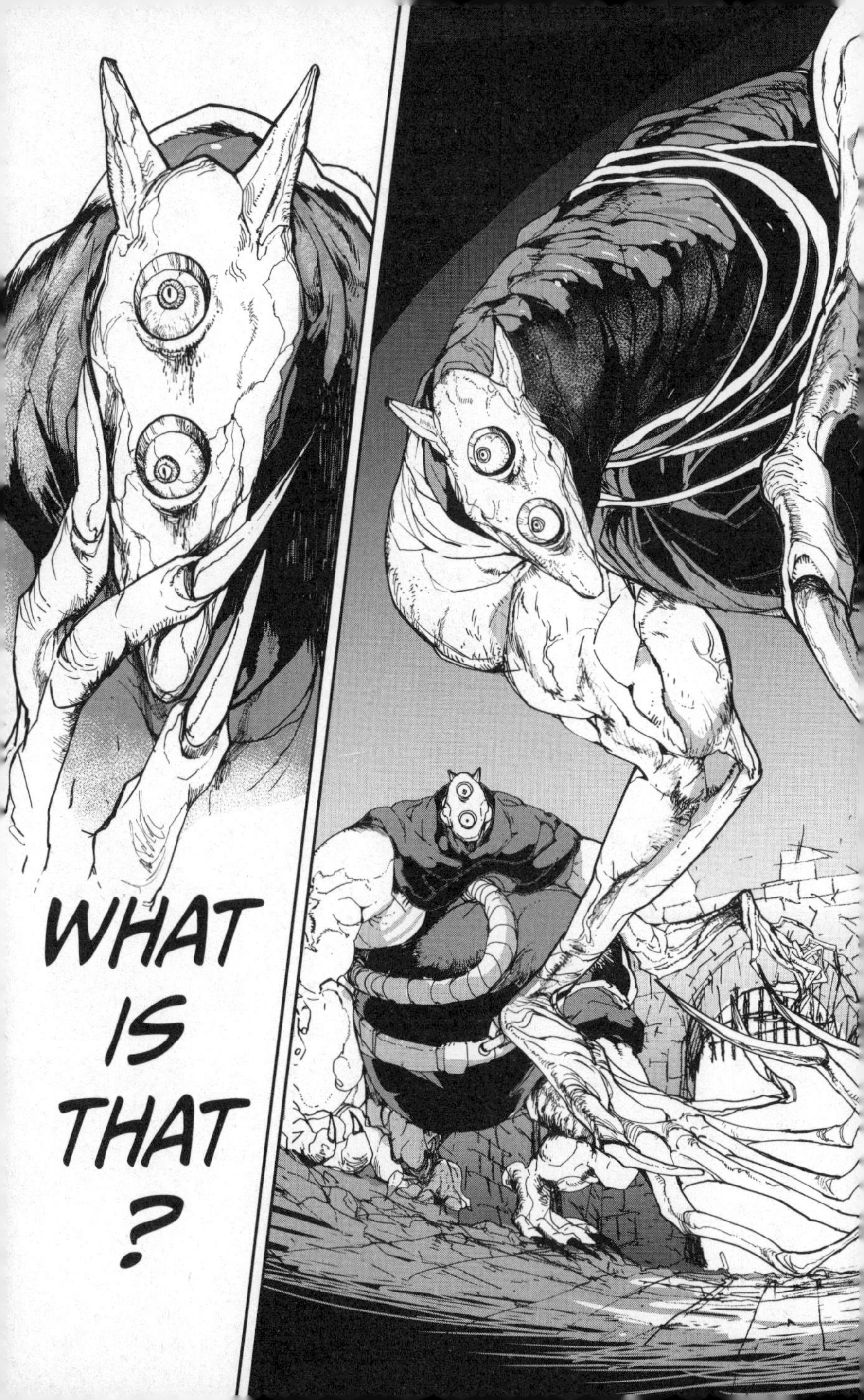
WHAT IS THAT ?

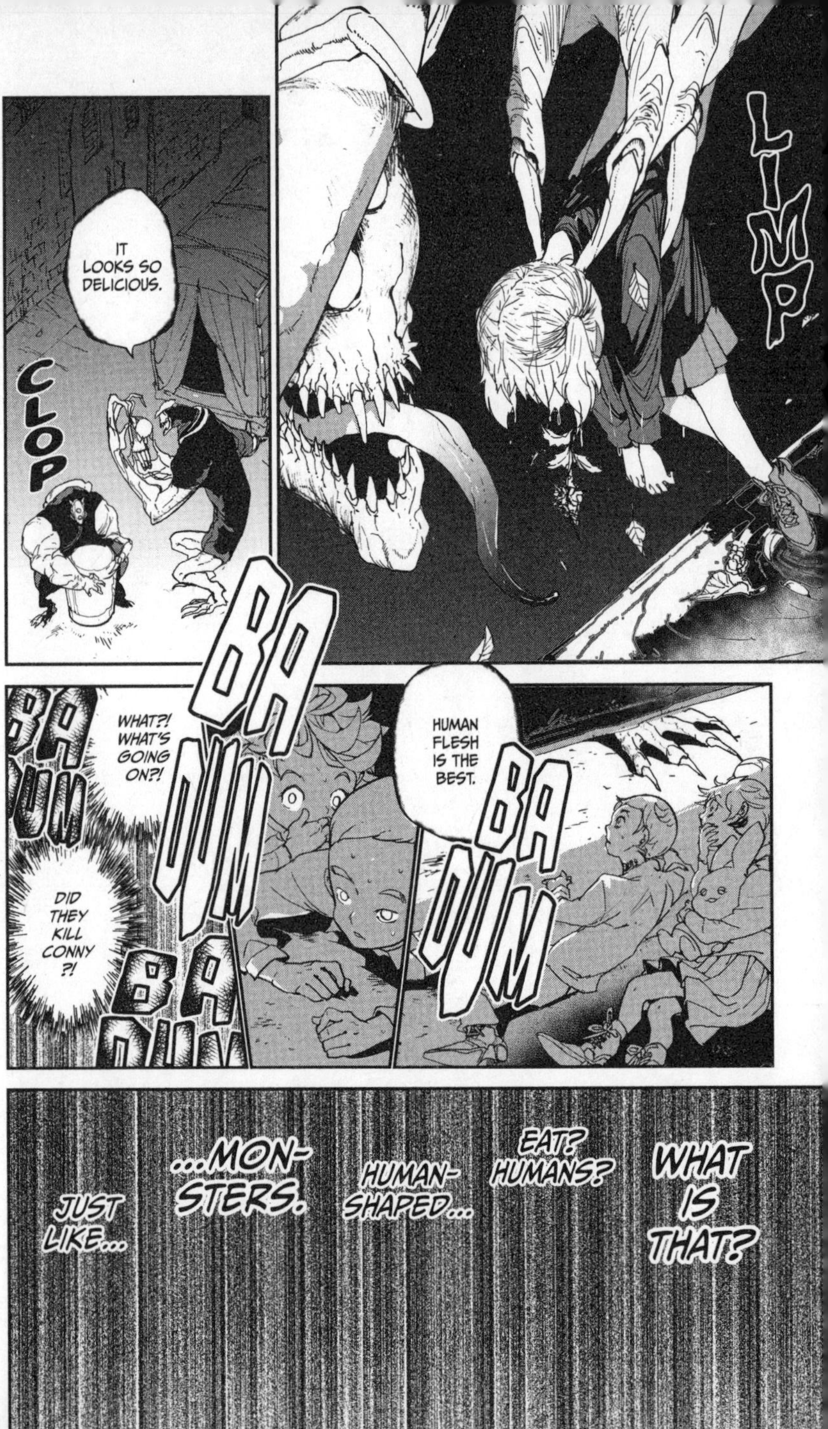
LIMP
IT LOOKS SO DELICIOUS.
CLOP
BA DUM
HUMAN FLESH IS THE BEST.
BA DUM
WHAT?! WHAT'S GOING ON?!
BA DUM
DID THEY KILL CONNY?!
BA
WHAT IS THAT?
EAT? HUMANS?
HUMAN-SHAPED...
...MON-STERS.
JUST LIKE...

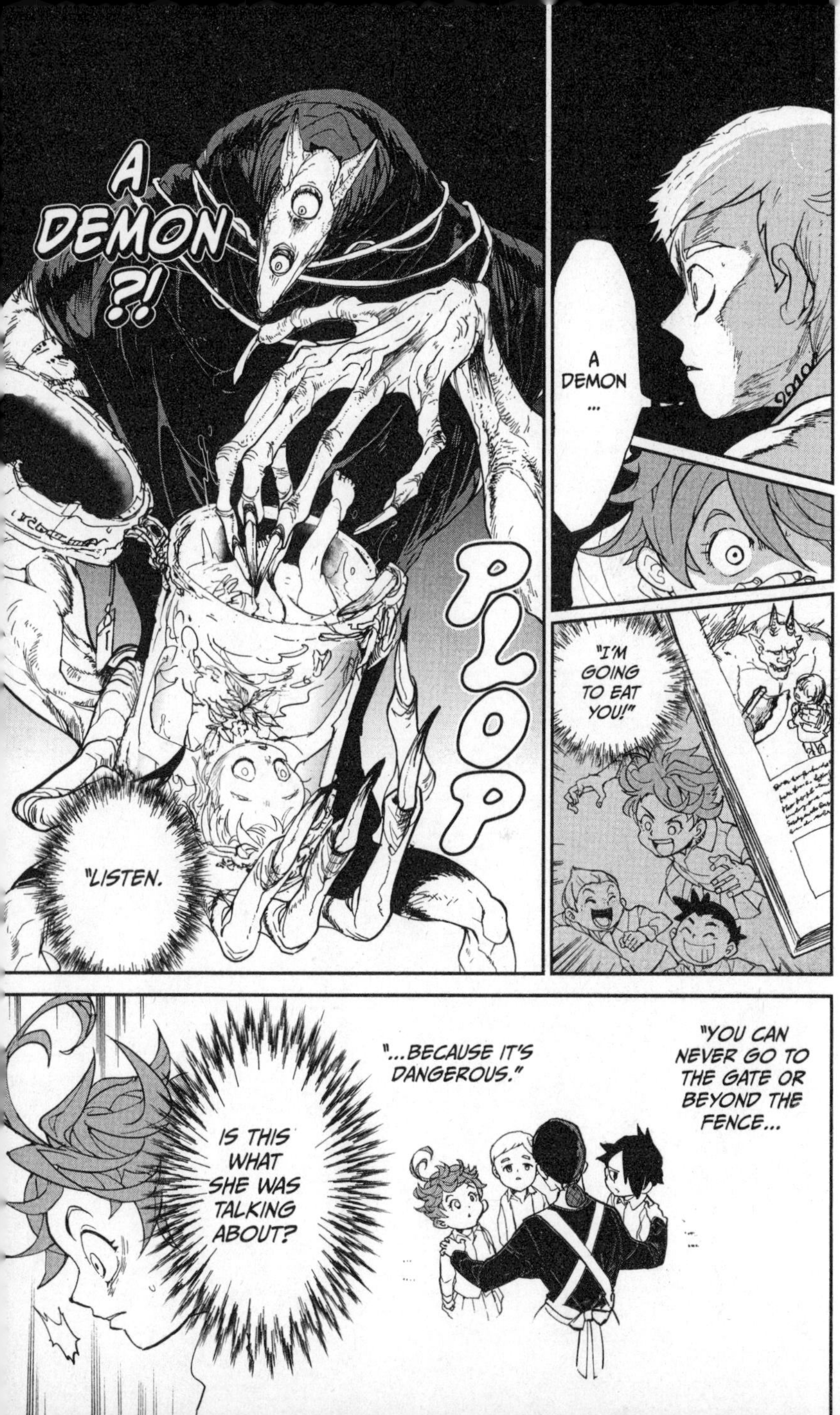
A DEMON...
"I'M GOING TO EAT YOU!"
A DEMON ?!
PLOP
"LISTEN.
"YOU CAN NEVER GO TO THE GATE OR BEYOND THE FENCE...
"...BECAUSE IT'S DANGEROUS."
IS THIS WHAT SHE WAS TALKING ABOUT?

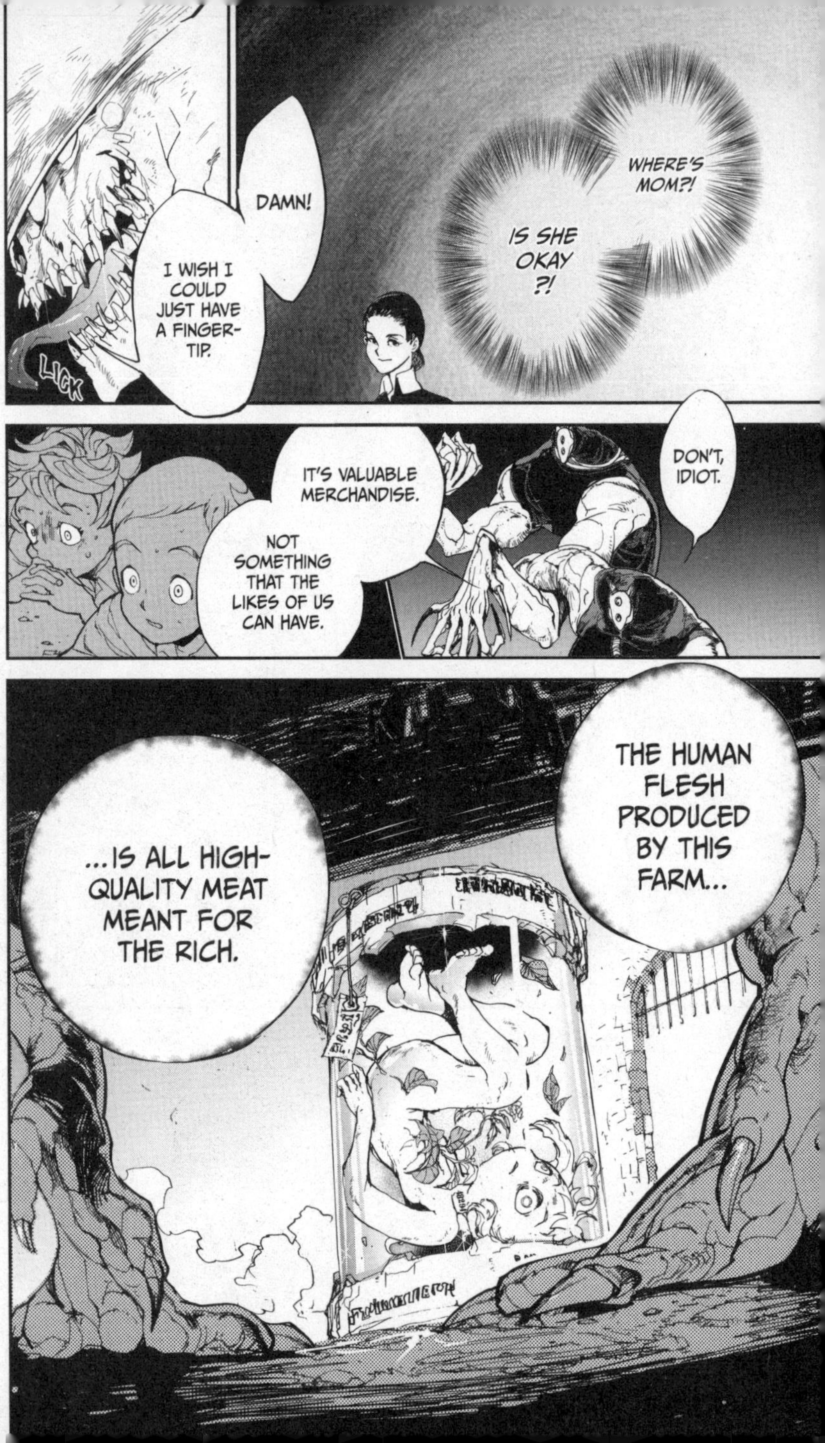
WHERE'S MOM?!
IS SHE OKAY ?!
DAMN!
I WISH I COULD JUST HAVE A FINGER-TIP.
LICK
DON'T, IDIOT.
IT'S VALUABLE MERCHANDISE.
NOT SOMETHING THAT THE LIKES OF US CAN HAVE.
THE HUMAN FLESH PRODUCED BY THIS FARM...
...IS ALL HIGH-QUALITY MEAT MEANT FOR THE RICH.

A FARM
?

HUMAN
FLESH
?

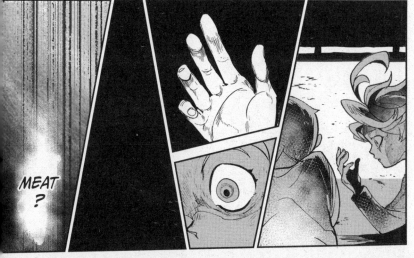

MEAT
?

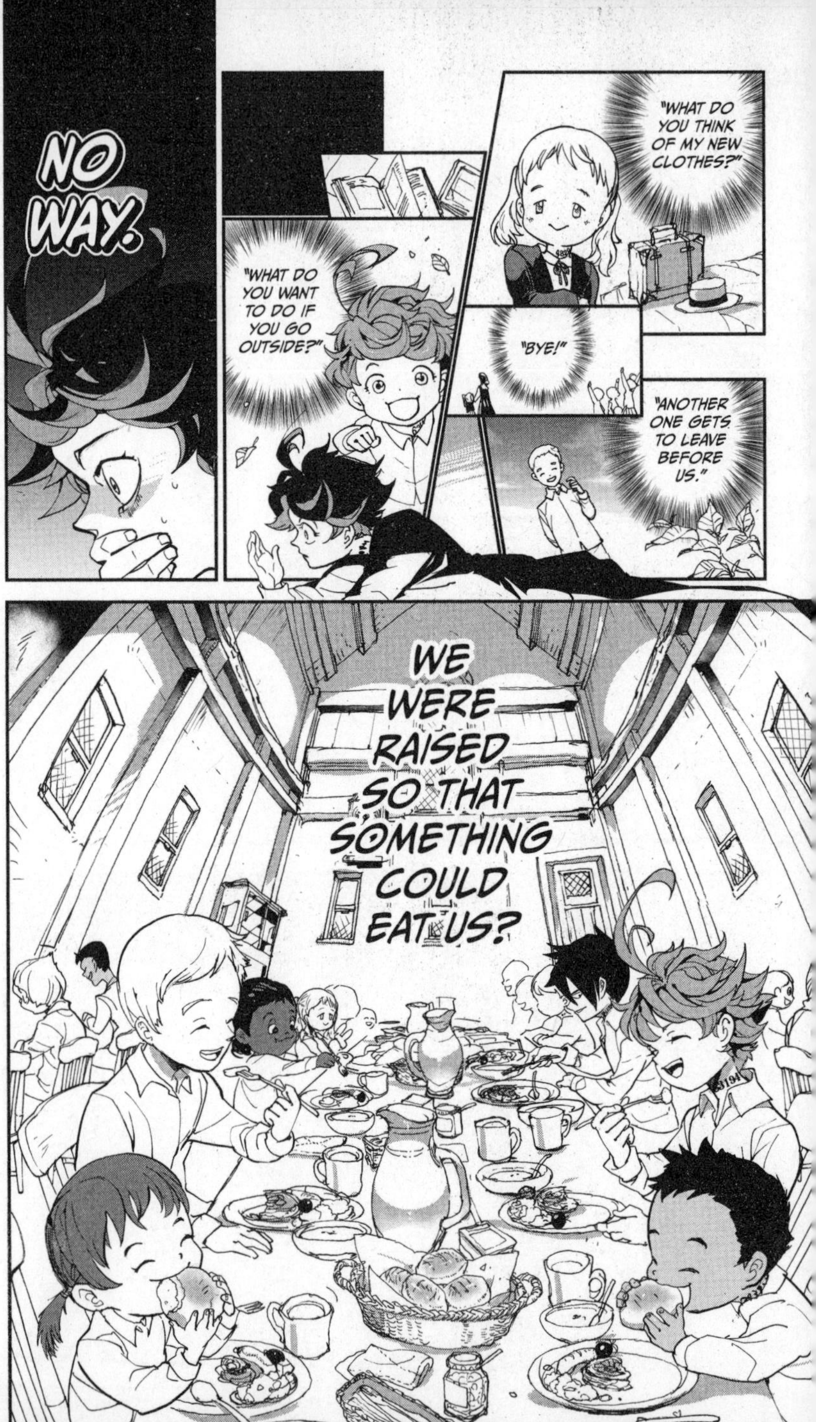
"WHAT DO YOU THINK OF MY NEW CLOTHES?"
"BYE!"
"ANOTHER ONE GETS TO LEAVE BEFORE US."
"WHAT DO YOU WANT TO DO IF YOU GO OUTSIDE?"
NO WAY.
WE WERE RAISED SO THAT SOMETHING COULD EAT US?

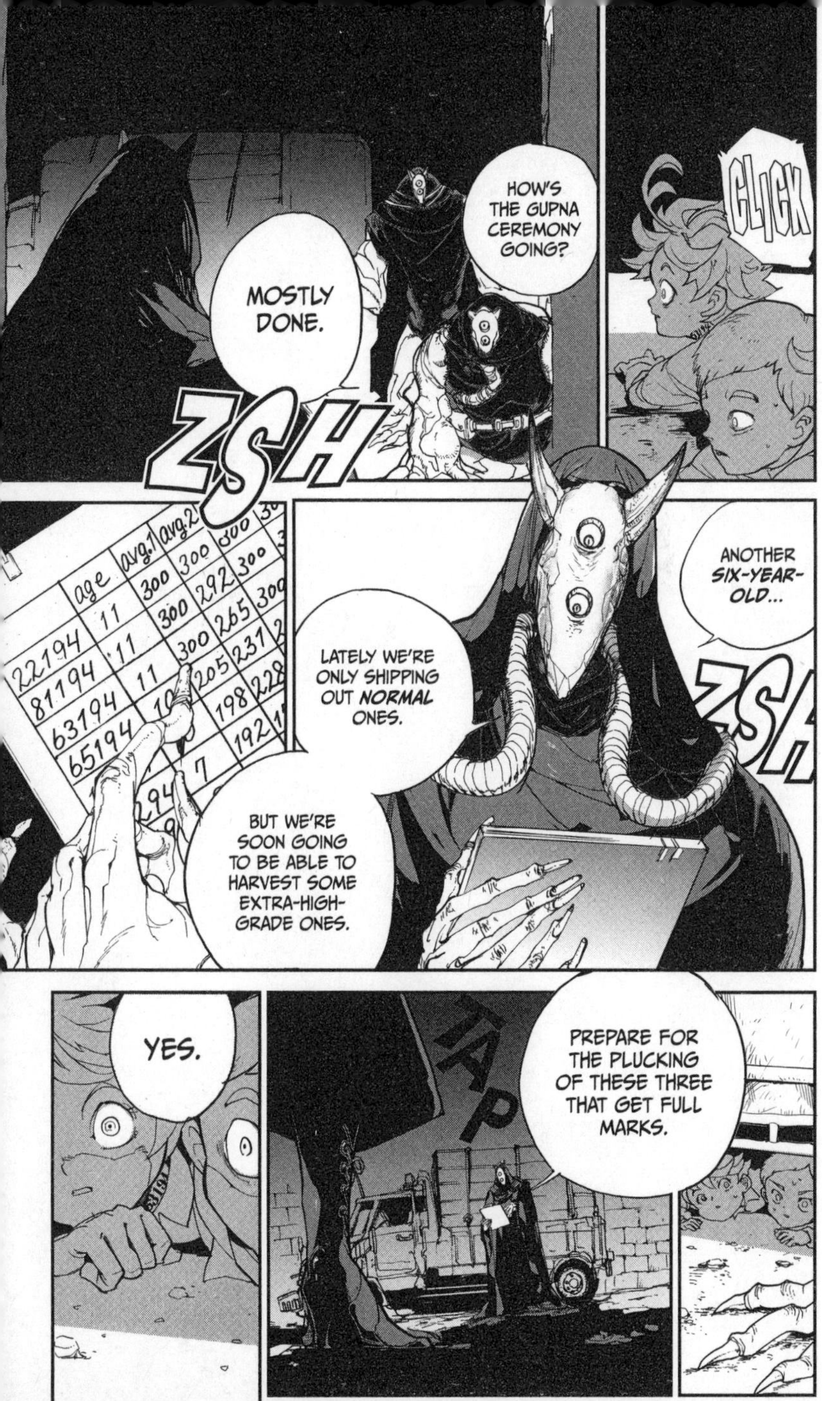
CLICK
HOW'S THE GUPNA CEREMONY GOING?
MOSTLY DONE.
ZSH
ANOTHER *SIX-YEAR-OLD*...
ZSH
LATELY WE'RE ONLY SHIPPING OUT *NORMAL* ONES.
BUT WE'RE SOON GOING TO BE ABLE TO HARVEST SOME EXTRA-HIGH-GRADE ONES.
PREPARE FOR THE PLUCKING OF THESE THREE THAT GET FULL MARKS.
TAP
YES.

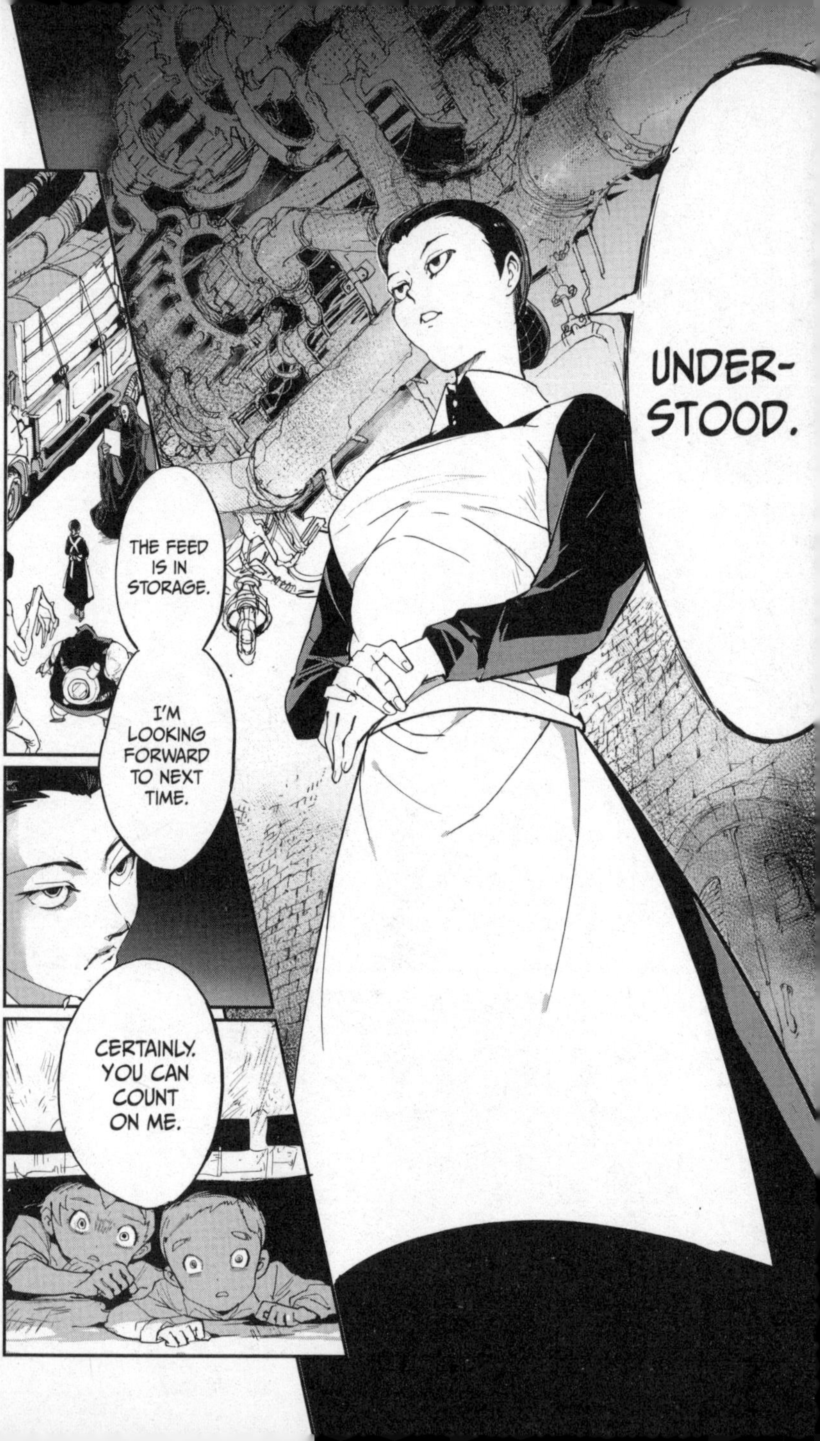
UNDER-STOOD.
THE FEED IS IN STORAGE.
I'M LOOKING FORWARD TO NEXT TIME.
CERTAINLY. YOU CAN COUNT ON ME.

HEAD OUT.

TWITCH

!

HOLD ON.

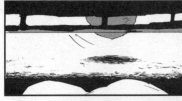

I SMELL SOME-THING.

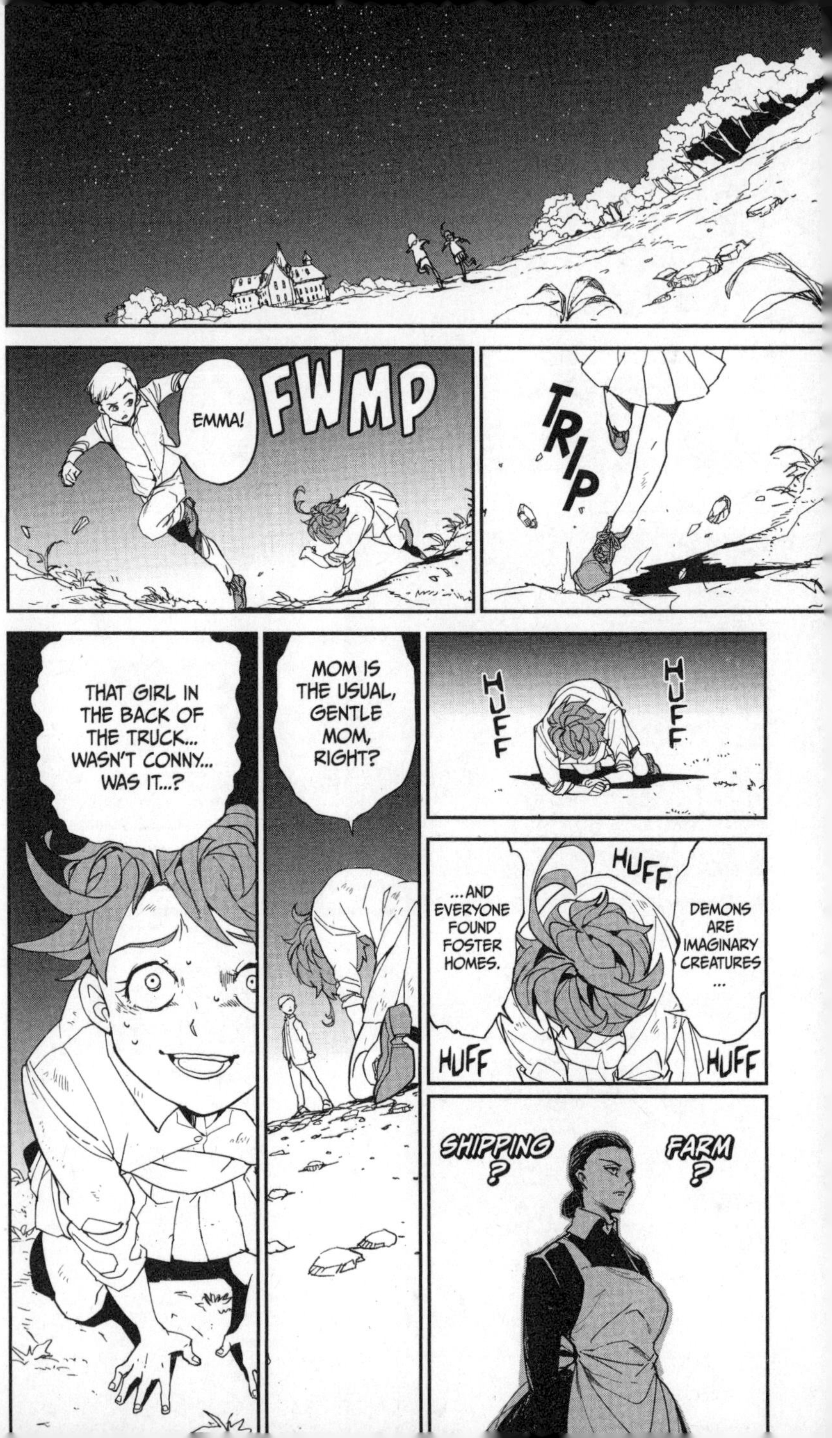
TRIP
FWMP
EMMA!
HUFF
HUFF
HUFF
DEMONS ARE IMAGINARY CREATURES...
...AND EVERYONE FOUND FOSTER HOMES.
HUFF
HUFF
FARM?
SHIPPING?
MOM IS THE USUAL, GENTLE MOM, RIGHT?
THAT GIRL IN THE BACK OF THE TRUCK... WASN'T CONNY... WAS IT...?

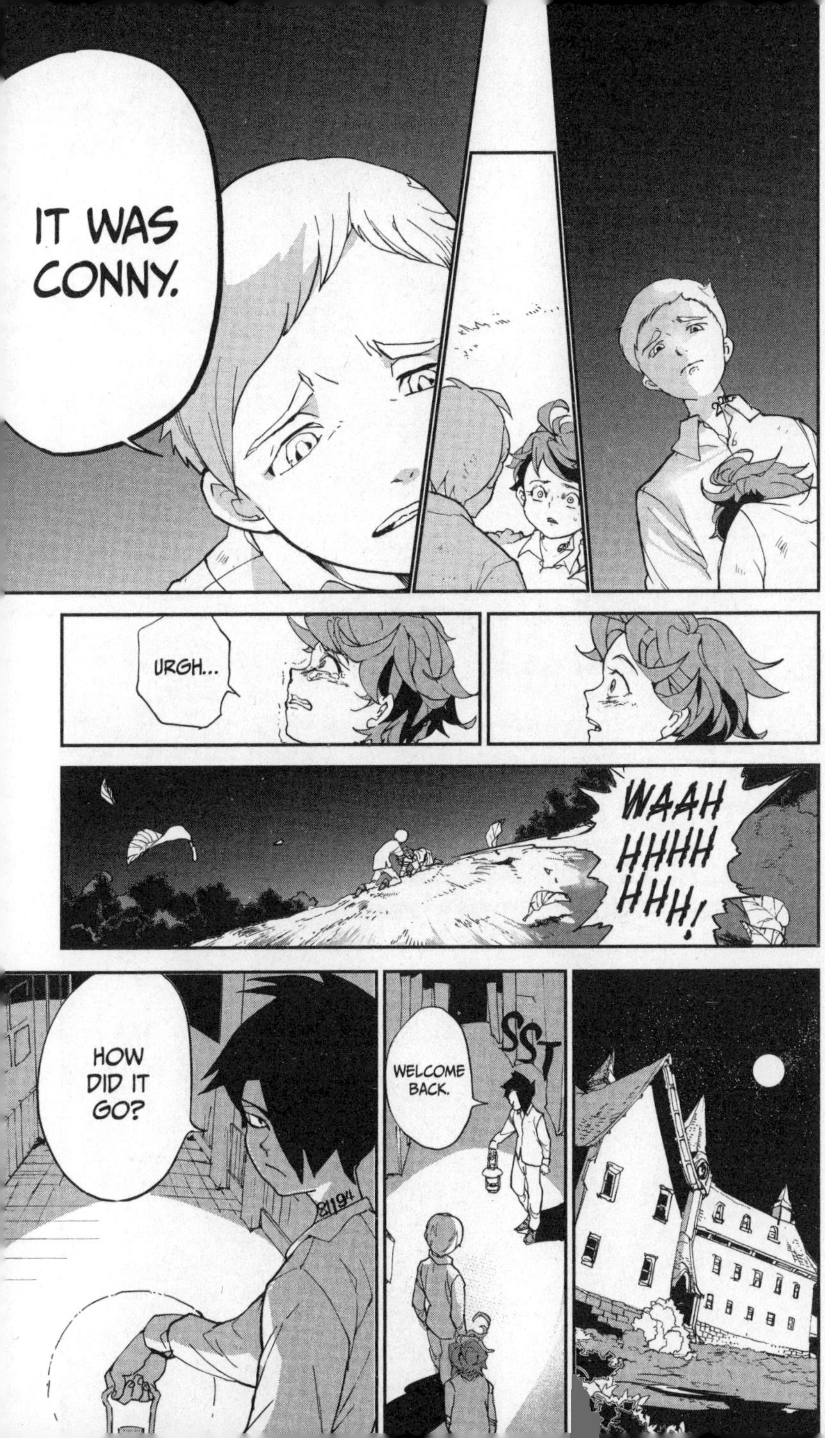
IT WAS CONNY.
URGH...
WAAHHHHHHHH!
SST
WELCOME BACK.
HOW DID IT GO?

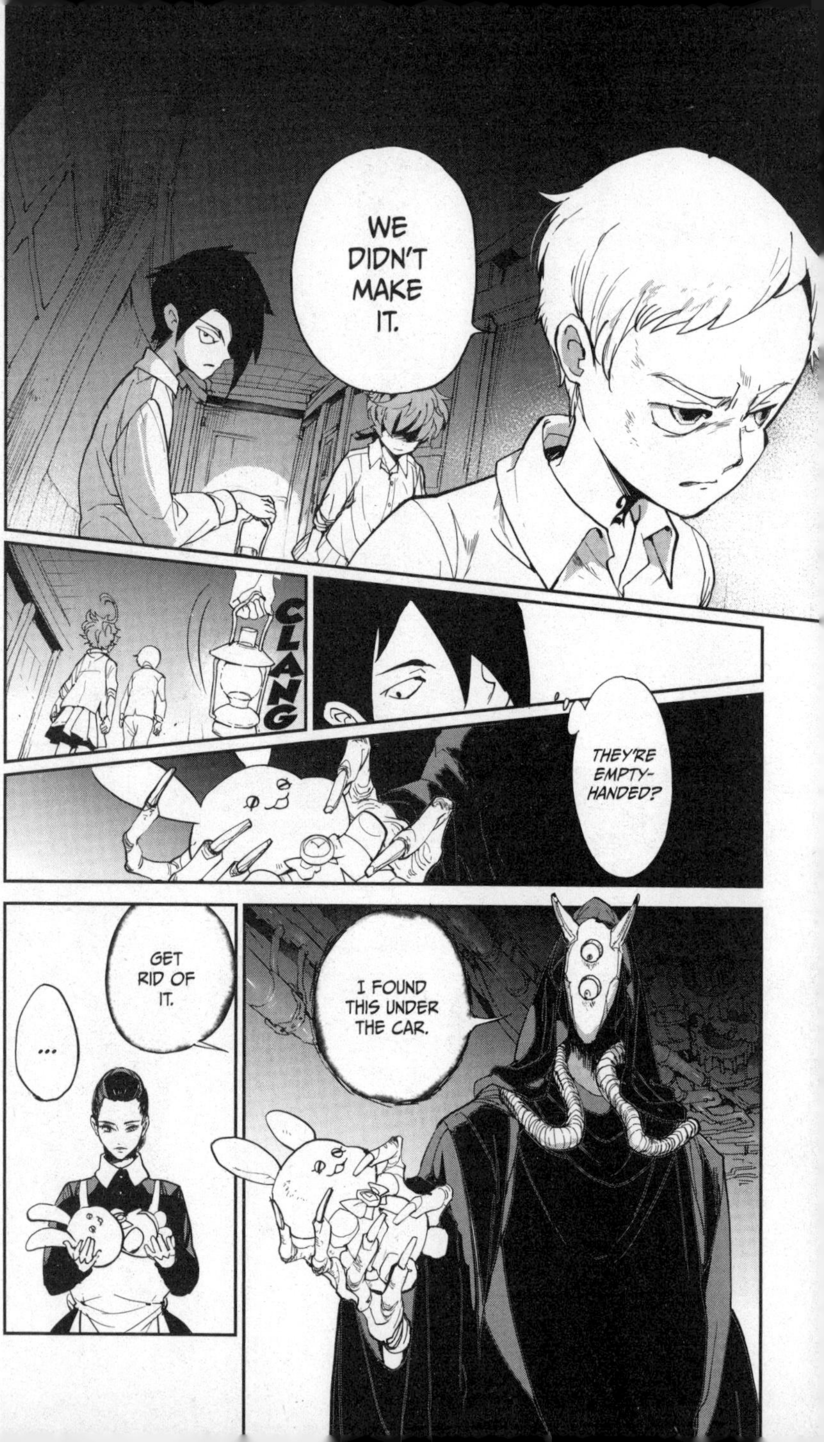
WE DIDN'T MAKE IT.
CLANG
THEY'RE EMPTY-HANDED?
I FOUND THIS UNDER THE CAR.
GET RID OF IT.
...

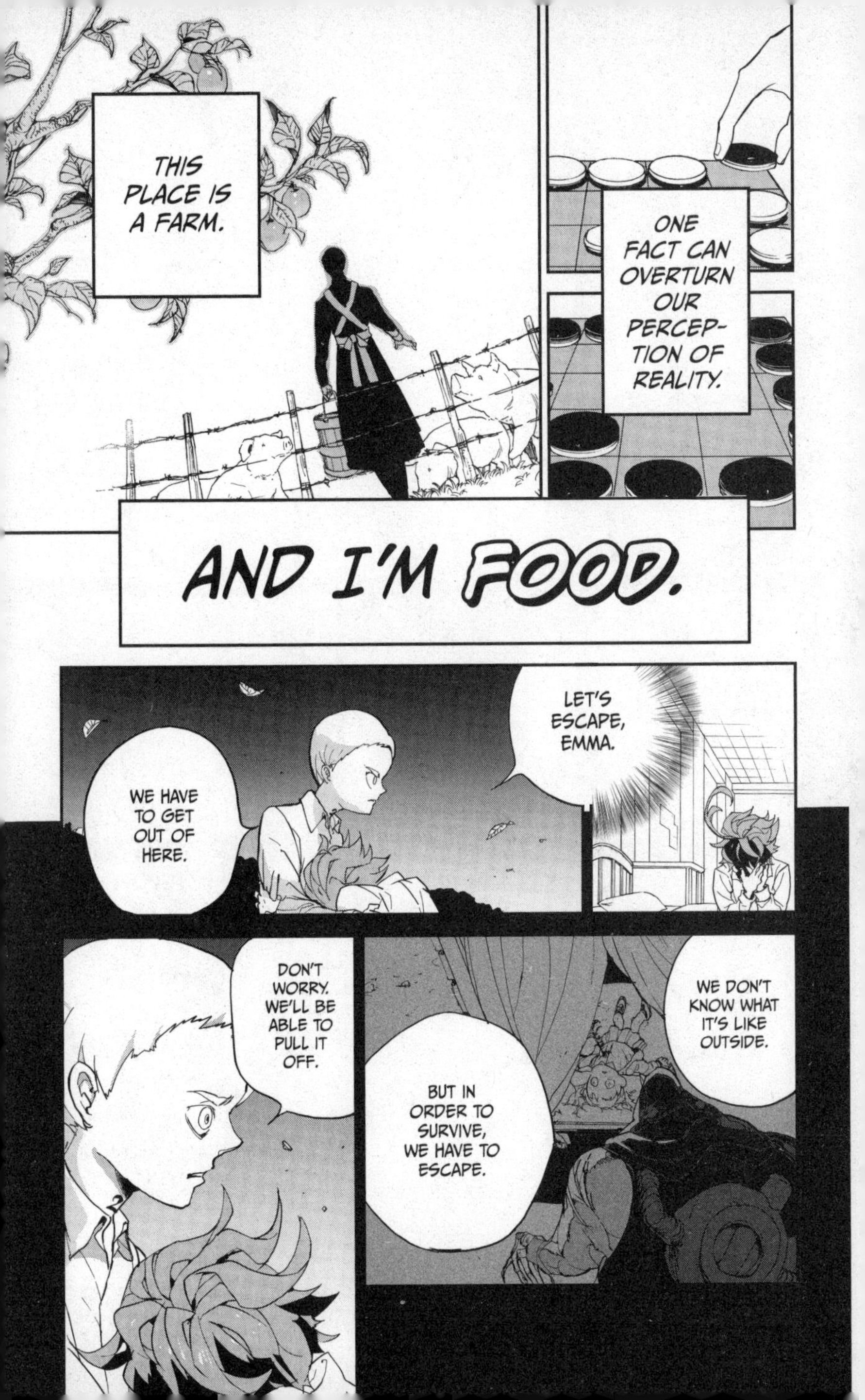
ONE FACT CAN OVERTURN OUR PERCEPTION OF REALITY.
THIS PLACE IS A FARM.
AND I'M FOOD.
LET'S ESCAPE, EMMA.
WE HAVE TO GET OUT OF HERE.
WE DON'T KNOW WHAT IT'S LIKE OUTSIDE.
BUT IN ORDER TO SURVIVE, WE HAVE TO ESCAPE.
DON'T WORRY. WE'LL BE ABLE TO PULL IT OFF.

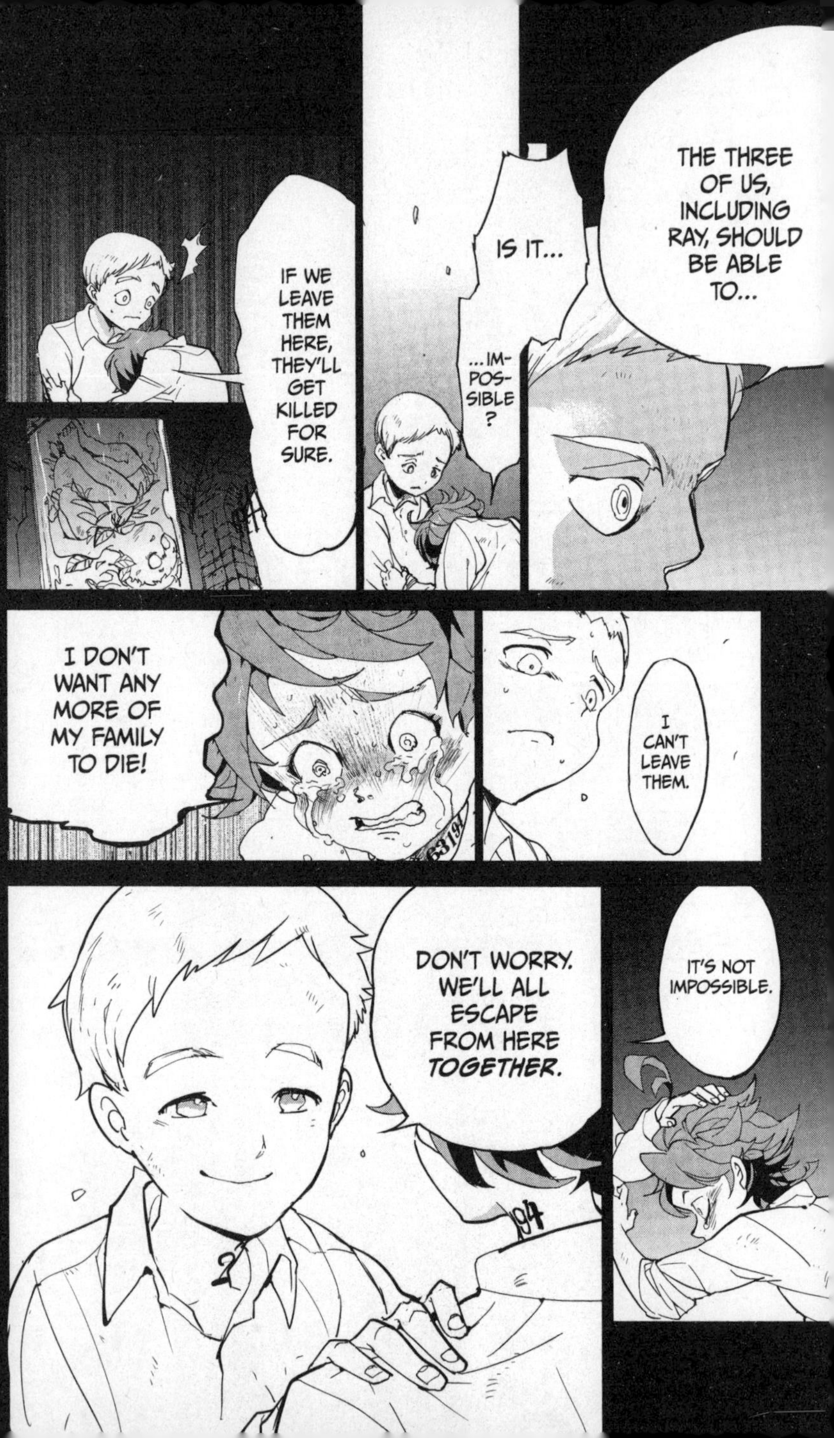
THE THREE OF US, INCLUDING RAY, SHOULD BE ABLE TO...
IS IT...
...IMPOSSIBLE?
IF WE LEAVE THEM HERE, THEY'LL GET KILLED FOR SURE.
I CAN'T LEAVE THEM.
I DON'T WANT ANY MORE OF MY FAMILY TO DIE!
IT'S NOT IMPOSSIBLE.
DON'T WORRY. WE'LL ALL ESCAPE FROM HERE *TOGETHER*.

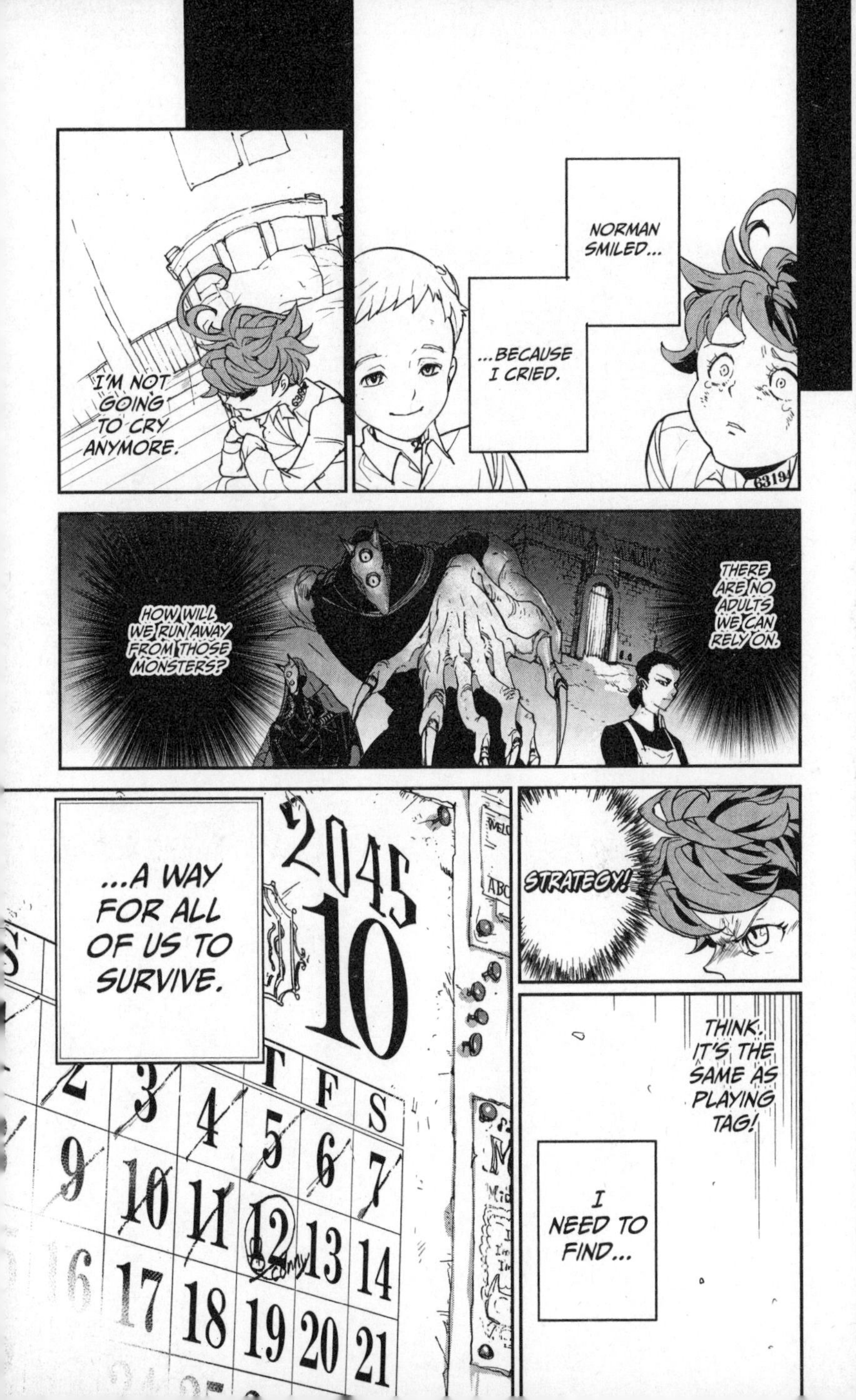
NORMAN SMILED...
...BECAUSE I CRIED.
I'M NOT GOING TO CRY ANYMORE.
THERE ARE NO ADULTS WE CAN RELY ON.
HOW WILL WE RUN AWAY FROM THOSE MONSTERS?
STRATEGY!
THINK. IT'S THE SAME AS PLAYING TAG!
I NEED TO FIND...
...A WAY FOR ALL OF US TO SURVIVE.
2045
10

THE PROMISED NEVERLAND SIDE SCENE 001

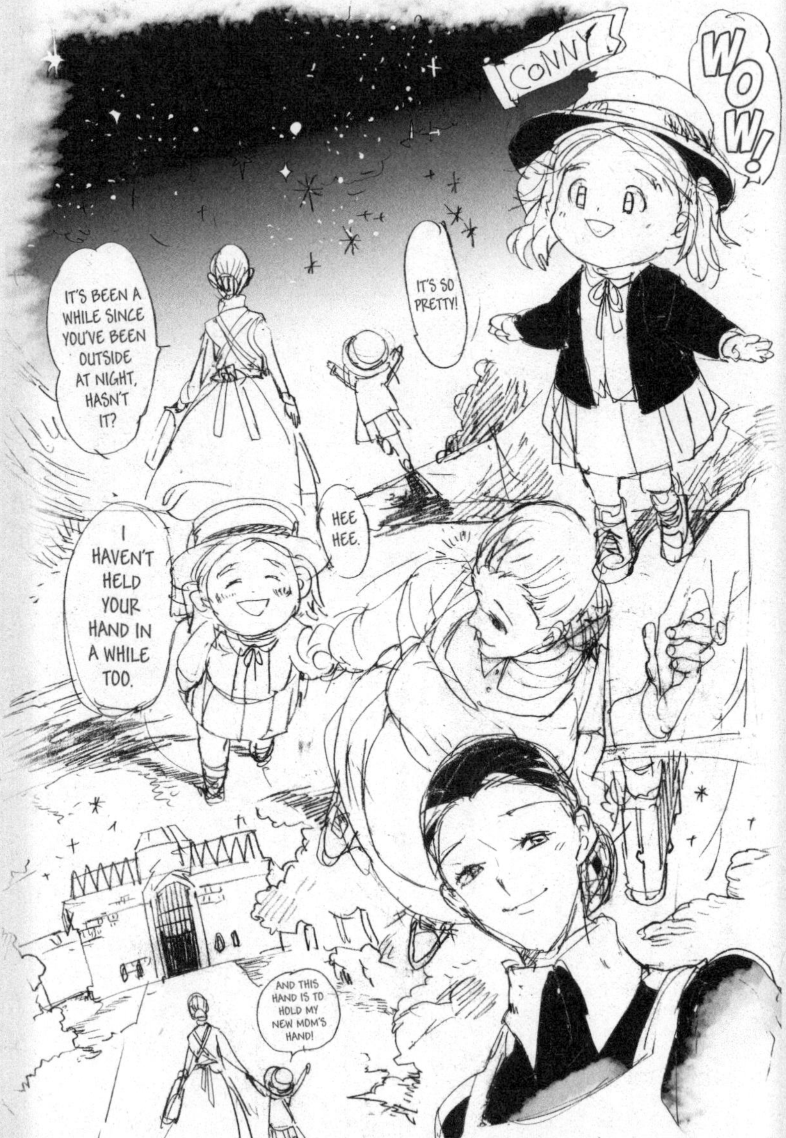

CONNY
WOW!
IT'S SO PRETTY!
IT'S BEEN A WHILE SINCE YOU'VE BEEN OUTSIDE AT NIGHT, HASN'T IT?
HEE HEE.
I HAVEN'T HELD YOUR HAND IN A WHILE TOO.
AND THIS HAND IS TO HOLD MY NEW MOM'S HAND!

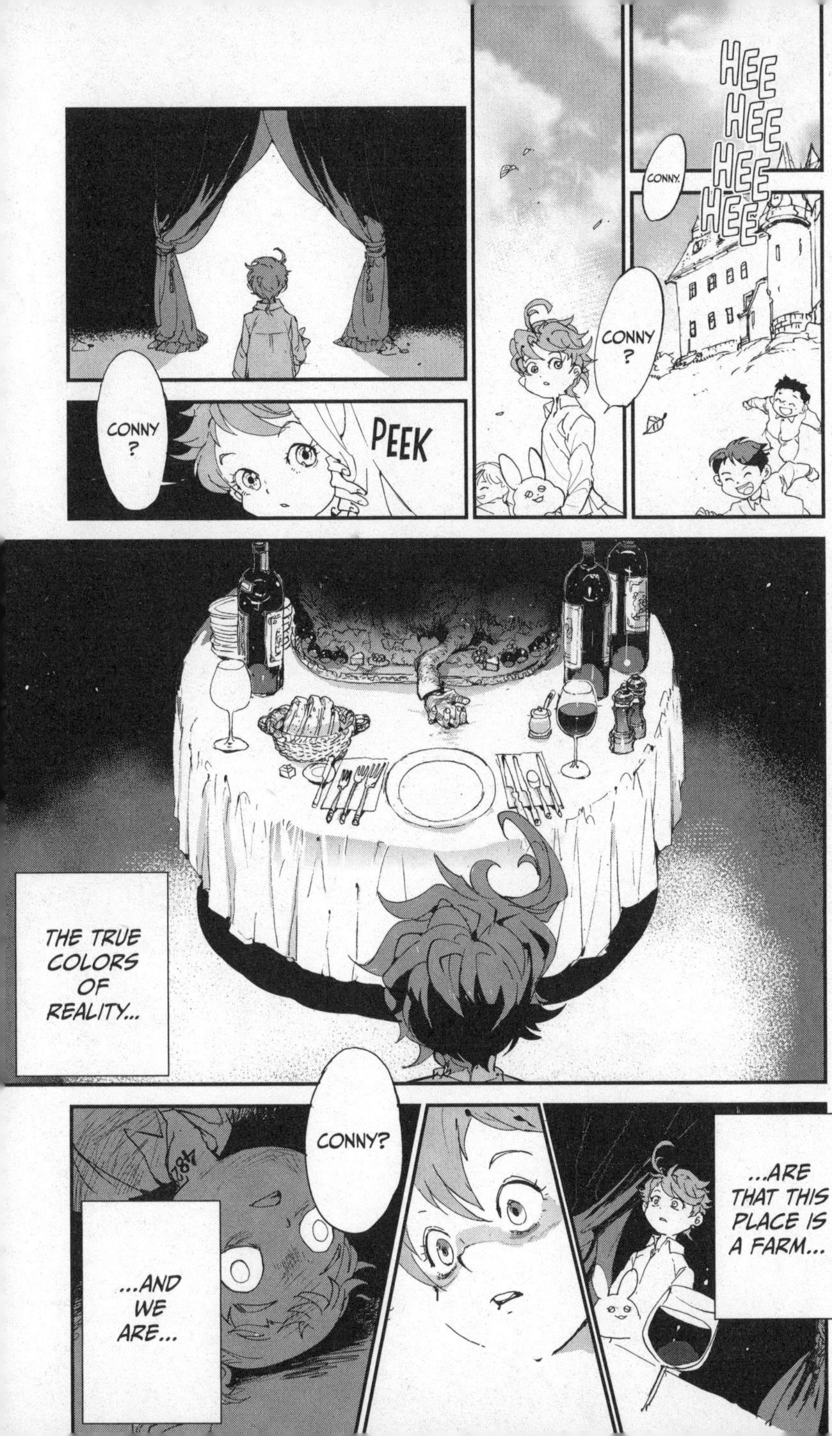
CONNY.
HEE HEE HEE HEE
CONNY ?
CONNY ?
PEEK
THE TRUE COLORS OF REALITY...
CONNY?
...ARE THAT THIS PLACE IS A FARM...
...AND WE ARE...

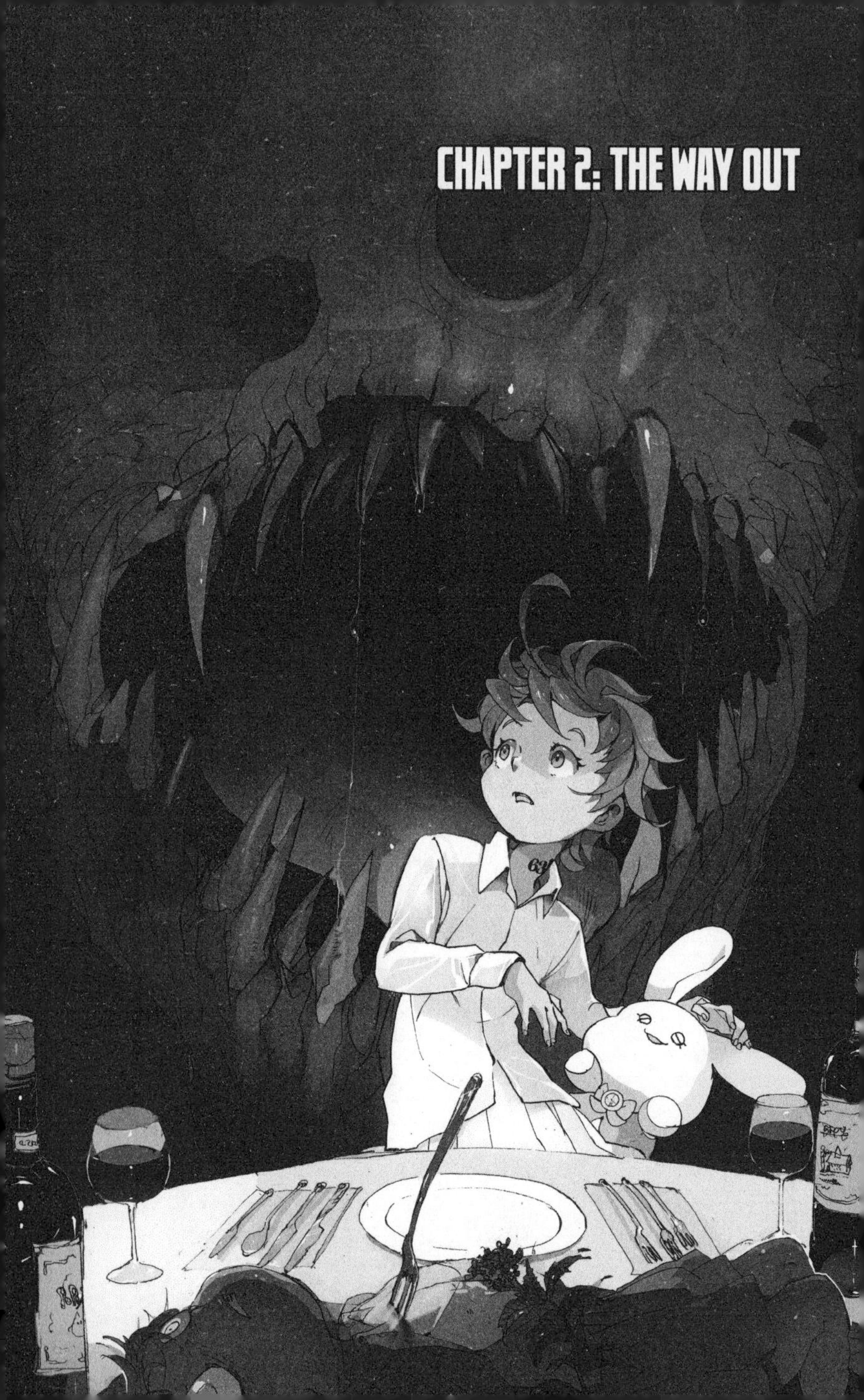
CHAPTER 2: THE WAY OUT

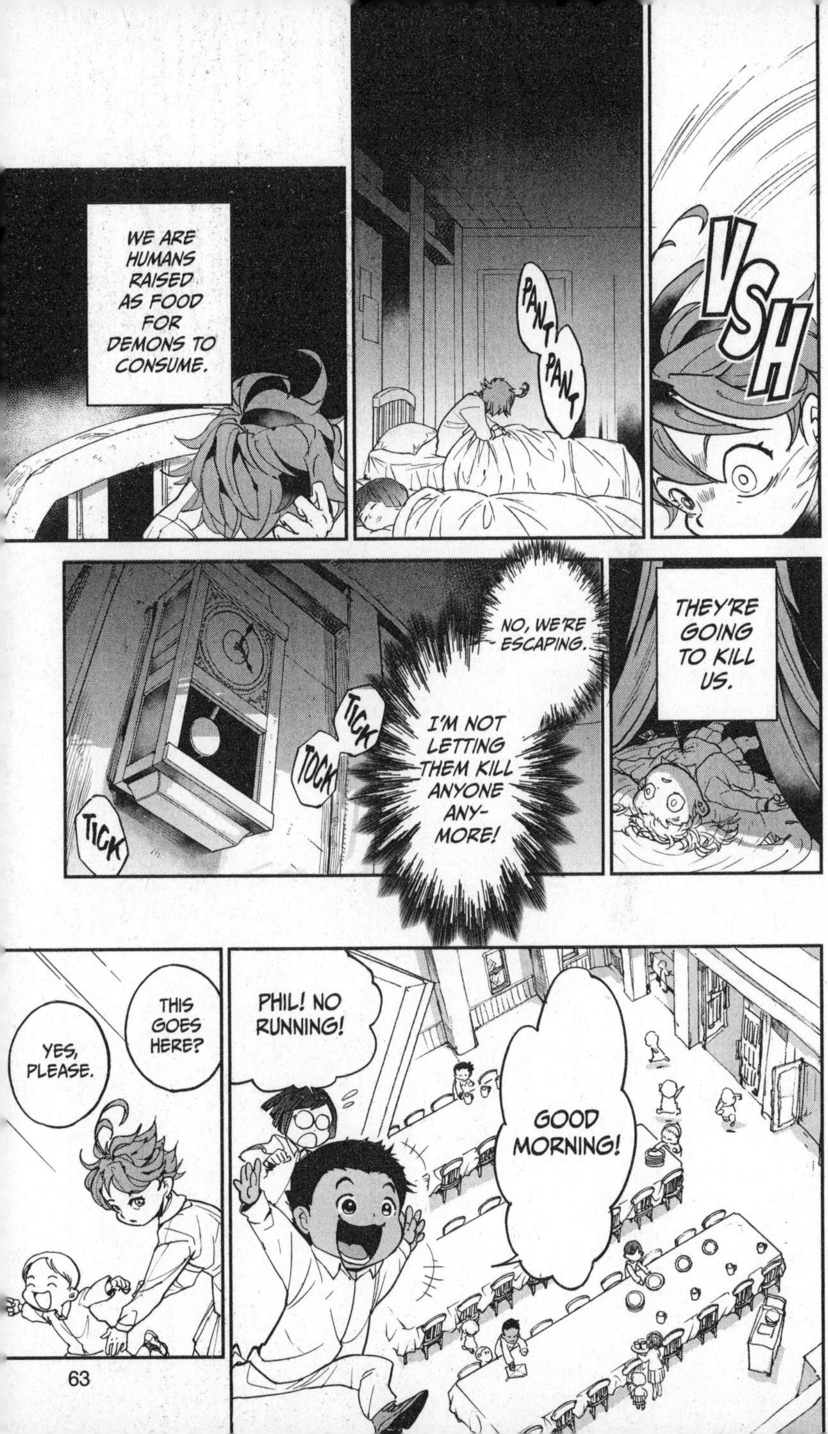
VSH
PANT PANT
WE ARE HUMANS RAISED AS FOOD FOR DEMONS TO CONSUME.
THEY'RE GOING TO KILL US.
NO, WE'RE ESCAPING.
I'M NOT LETTING THEM KILL ANYONE ANY- MORE!
TICK
TOCK
TICK
GOOD MORNING!
PHIL! NO RUNNING!
THIS GOES HERE?
YES, PLEASE.

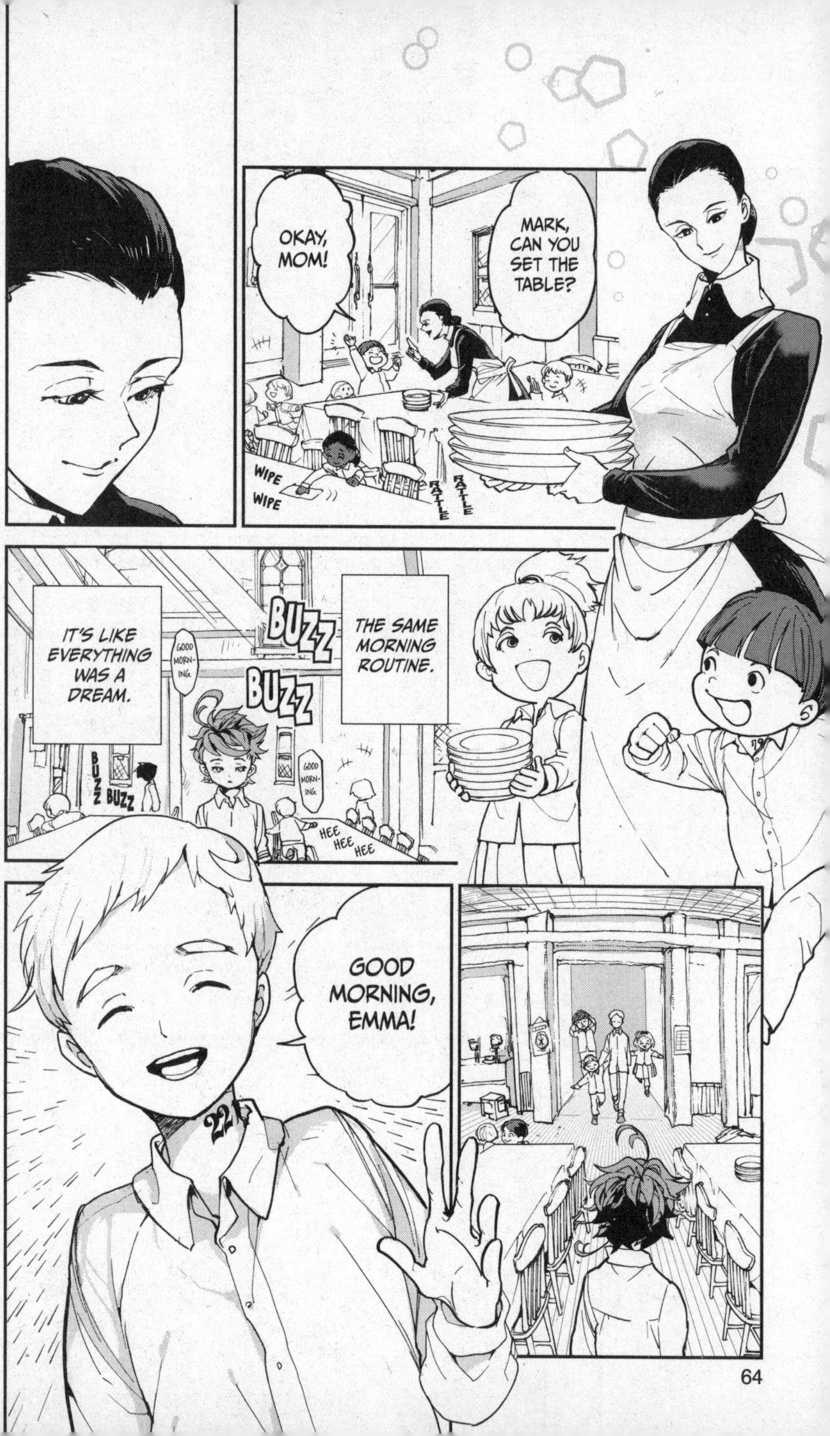
MARK, CAN YOU SET THE TABLE?
OKAY, MOM!
WIPE WIPE
RATTLE RATTLE
THE SAME MORNING ROUTINE.
BUZZ
BUZZ
GOOD MORN-ING
IT'S LIKE EVERYTHING WAS A DREAM.
GOOD MORN-ING
BUZZ BUZZ
HEE HEE HEE
GOOD MORNING, EMMA!

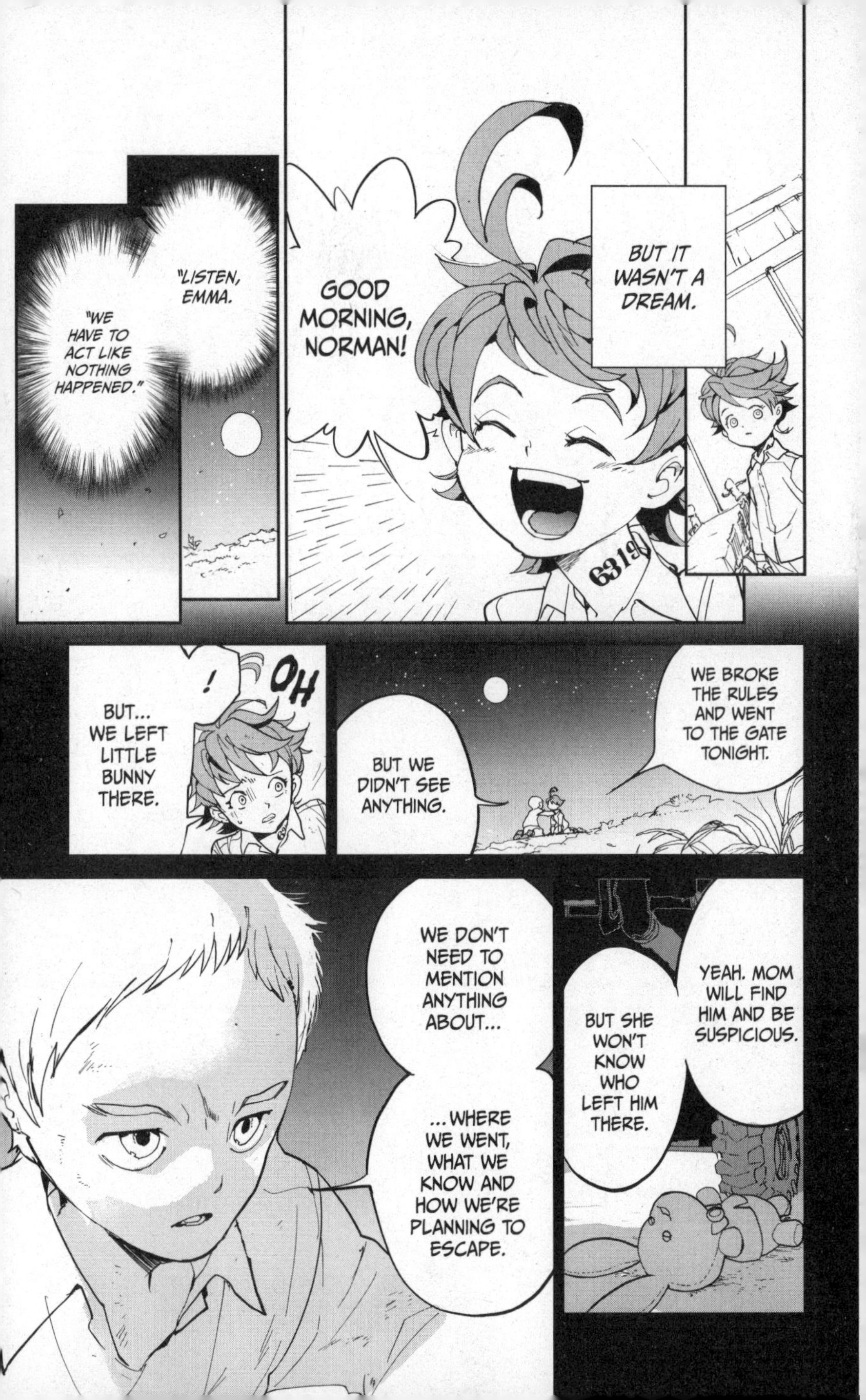
BUT IT WASN'T A DREAM.
GOOD MORNING, NORMAN!
"LISTEN, EMMA.
"WE HAVE TO ACT LIKE NOTHING HAPPENED."
WE BROKE THE RULES AND WENT TO THE GATE TONIGHT.
BUT WE DIDN'T SEE ANYTHING.
!
OH
BUT... WE LEFT LITTLE BUNNY THERE.
YEAH. MOM WILL FIND HIM AND BE SUSPICIOUS.
BUT SHE WON'T KNOW WHO LEFT HIM THERE.
WE DON'T NEED TO MENTION ANYTHING ABOUT...
...WHERE WE WENT, WHAT WE KNOW AND HOW WE'RE PLANNING TO ESCAPE.

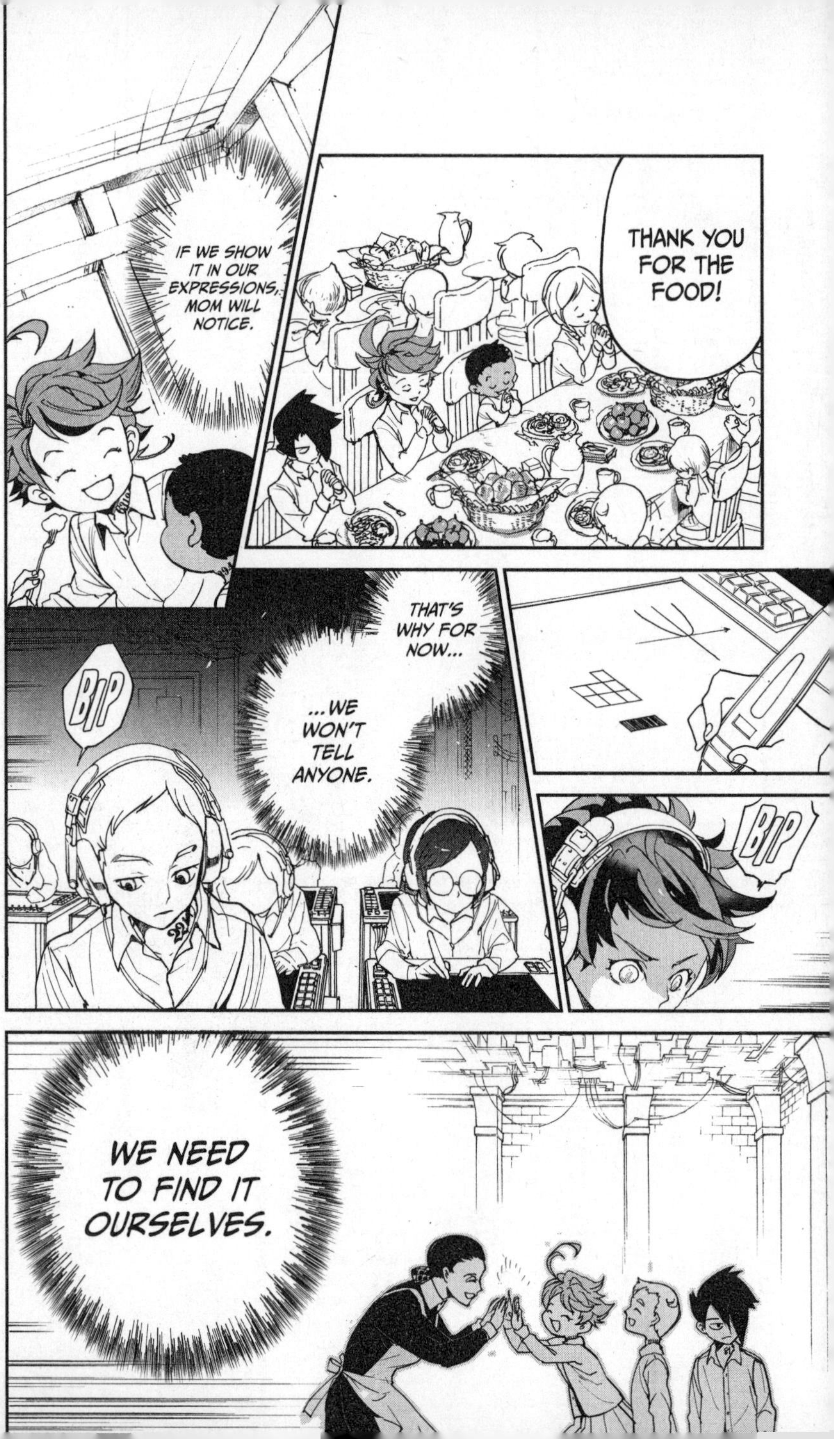
THANK YOU FOR THE FOOD!
IF WE SHOW IT IN OUR EXPRESSIONS, MOM WILL NOTICE.
BIP
THAT'S WHY FOR NOW...
...WE WON'T TELL ANYONE.
BIP
WE NEED TO FIND IT OURSELVES.

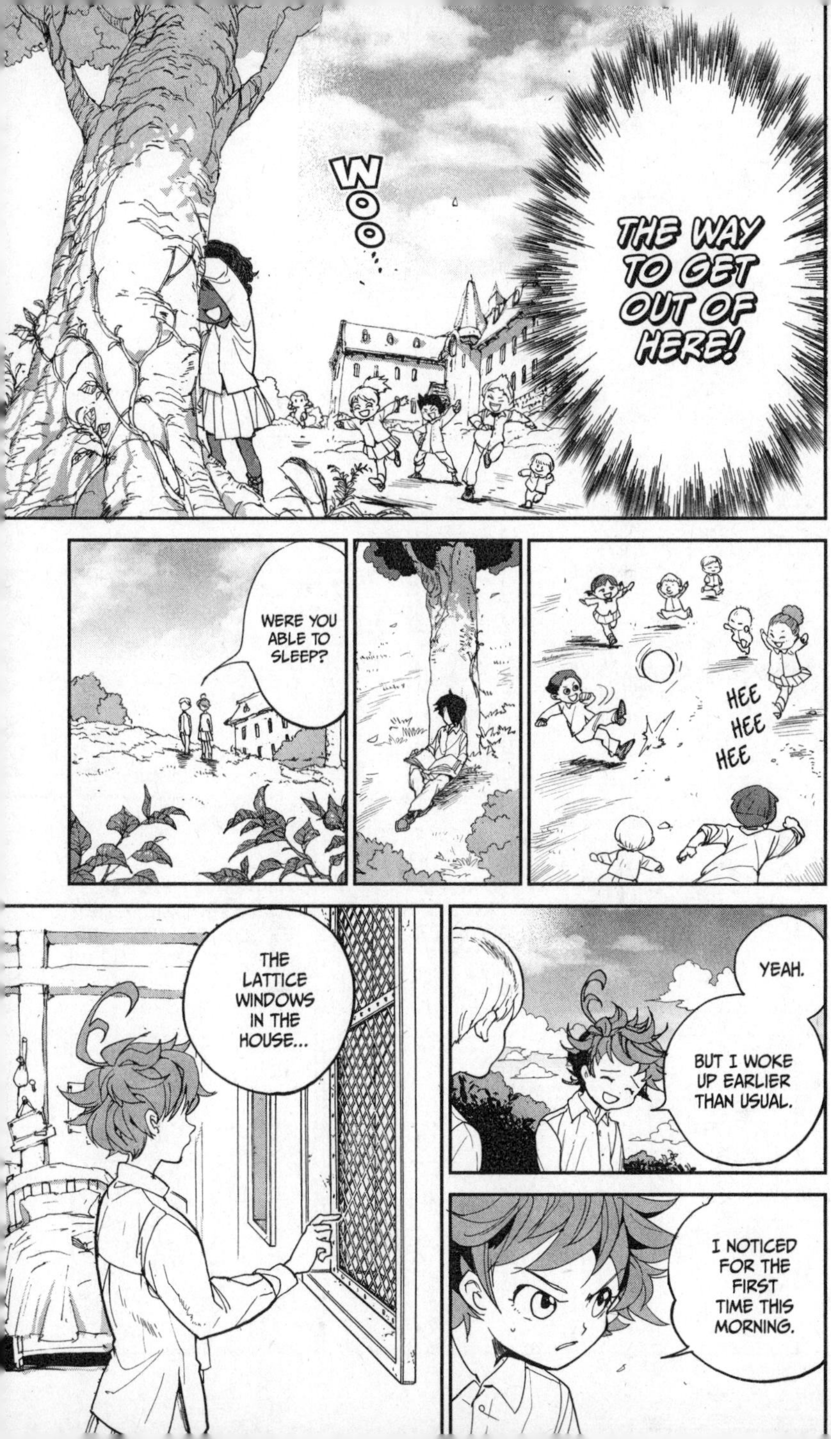
THE WAY TO GET OUT OF HERE!
WOO...
HEE HEE HEE
WERE YOU ABLE TO SLEEP?
YEAH.
BUT I WOKE UP EARLIER THAN USUAL.
I NOTICED FOR THE FIRST TIME THIS MORNING.
THE LATTICE WINDOWS IN THE HOUSE...

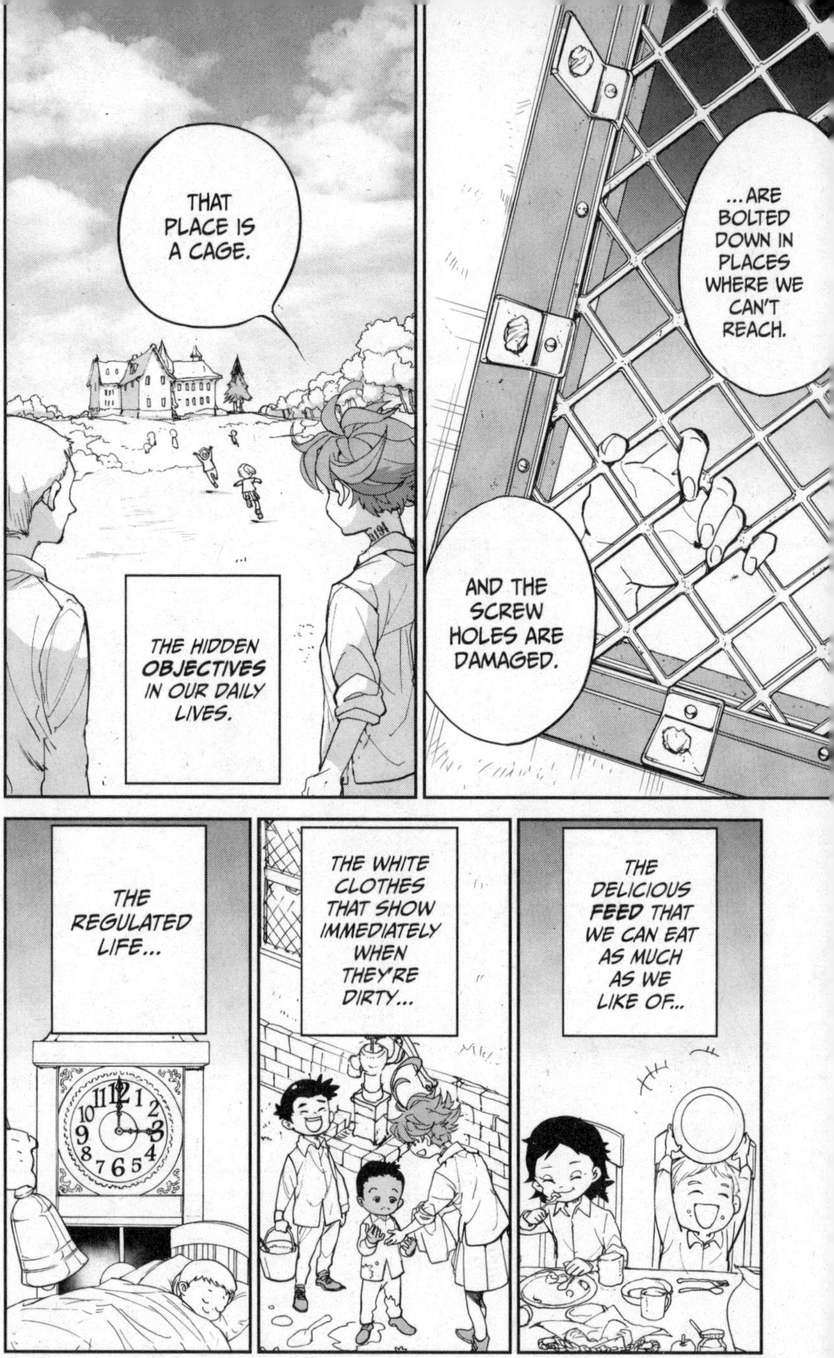
...ARE BOLTED DOWN IN PLACES WHERE WE CAN'T REACH.
AND THE SCREW HOLES ARE DAMAGED.
THAT PLACE IS A CAGE.
...
THE HIDDEN OBJECTIVES IN OUR DAILY LIVES.
THE DELICIOUS FEED THAT WE CAN EAT AS MUCH AS WE LIKE OF...
THE WHITE CLOTHES THAT SHOW IMMEDIATELY WHEN THEY'RE DIRTY...
THE REGULATED LIFE...

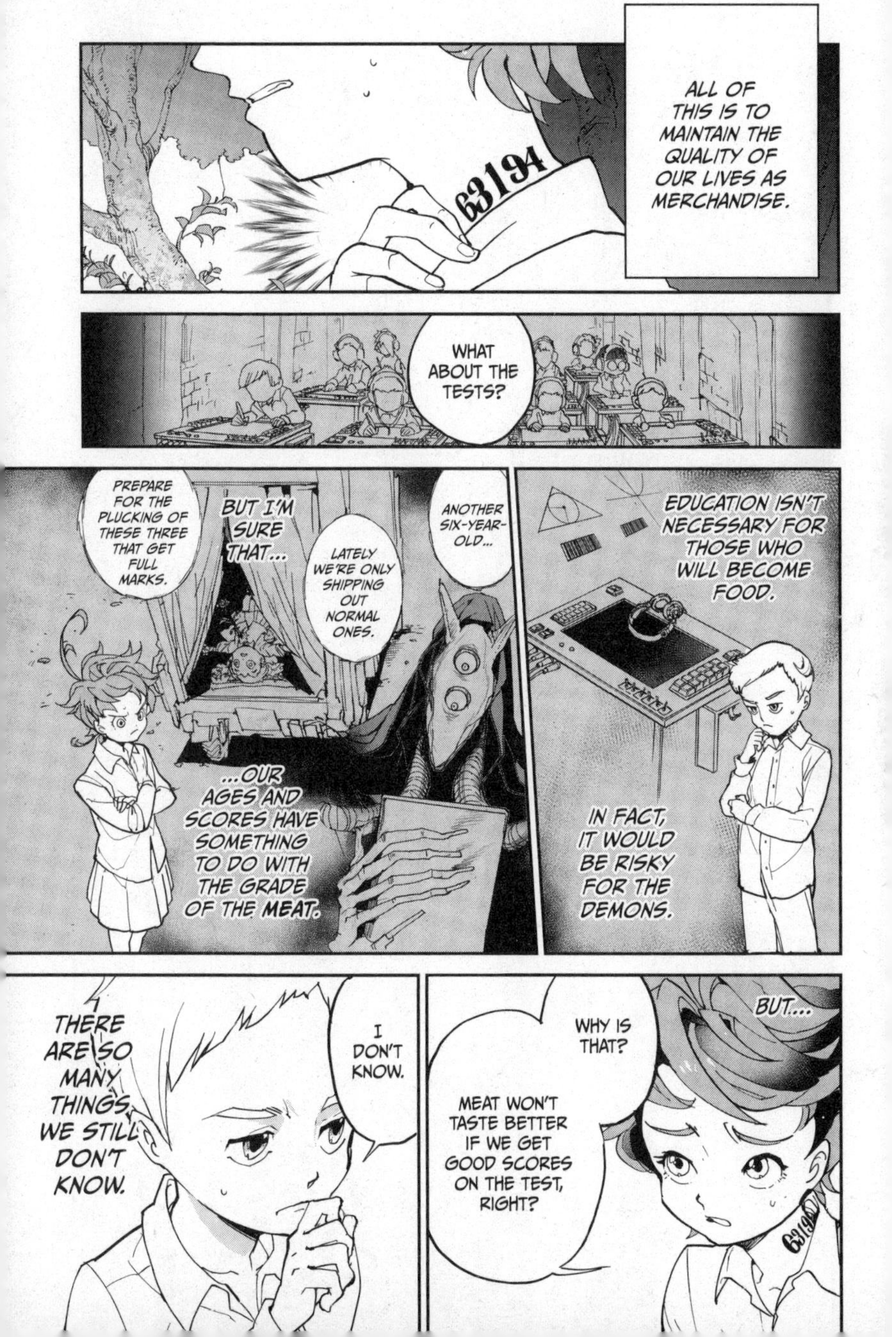
ALL OF THIS IS TO MAINTAIN THE QUALITY OF OUR LIVES AS MERCHANDISE.
63194
WHAT ABOUT THE TESTS?
EDUCATION ISN'T NECESSARY FOR THOSE WHO WILL BECOME FOOD.
IN FACT, IT WOULD BE RISKY FOR THE DEMONS.
ANOTHER SIX-YEAR-OLD...
LATELY WE'RE ONLY SHIPPING OUT NORMAL ONES.
BUT I'M SURE THAT...
PREPARE FOR THE PLUCKING OF THESE THREE THAT GET FULL MARKS.
...OUR AGES AND SCORES HAVE SOMETHING TO DO WITH THE GRADE OF THE MEAT.
BUT....
WHY IS THAT?
MEAT WON'T TASTE BETTER IF WE GET GOOD SCORES ON THE TEST, RIGHT?
I DON'T KNOW.
THERE ARE SO MANY THINGS WE STILL DON'T KNOW.

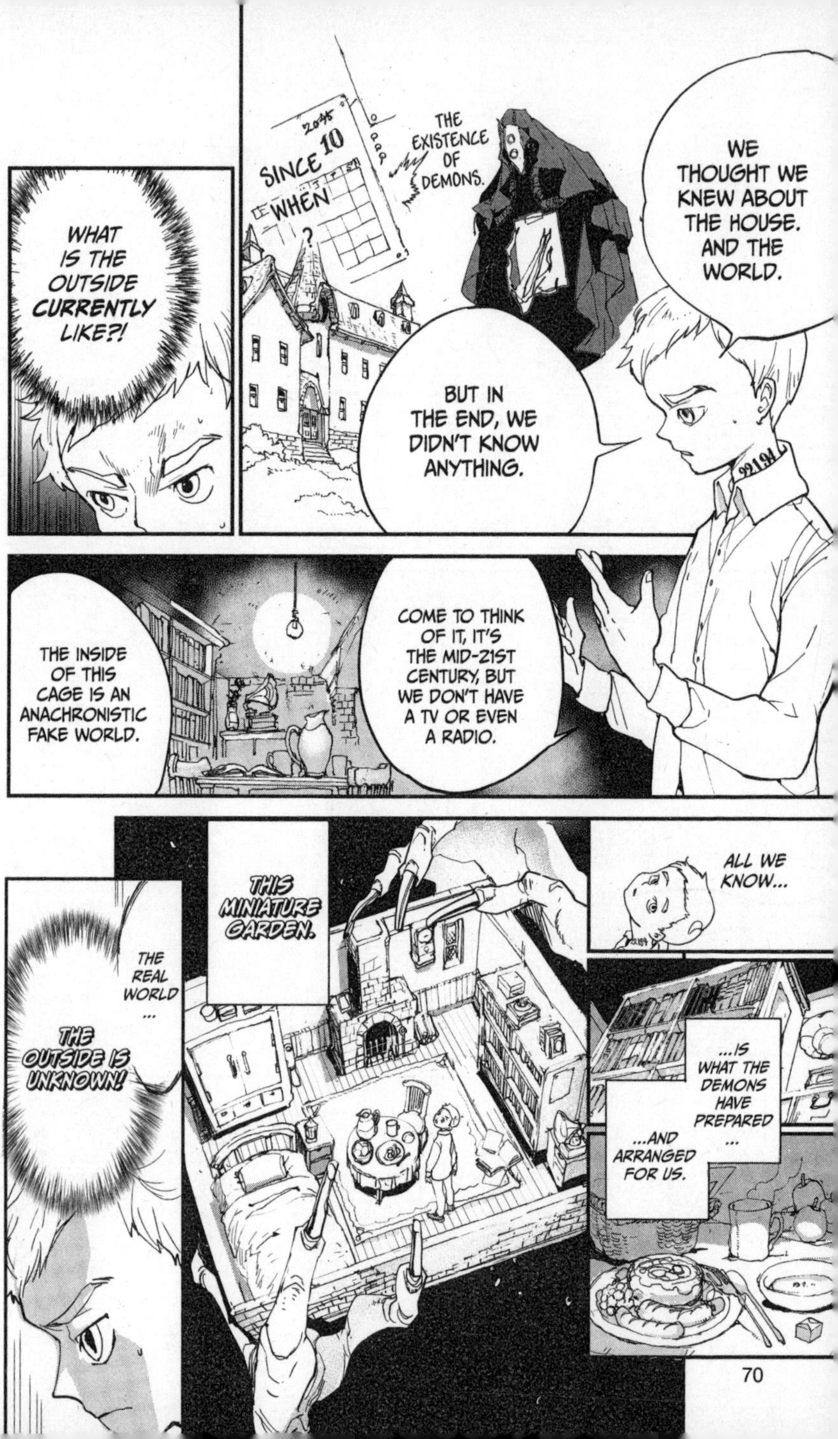
WE THOUGHT WE KNEW ABOUT THE HOUSE. AND THE WORLD.
BUT IN THE END, WE DIDN'T KNOW ANYTHING.
THE EXISTENCE OF DEMONS.
SINCE WHEN ?
WHAT IS THE OUTSIDE CURRENTLY LIKE?!
COME TO THINK OF IT, IT'S THE MID-21ST CENTURY, BUT WE DON'T HAVE A TV OR EVEN A RADIO.
THE INSIDE OF THIS CAGE IS AN ANACHRONISTIC FAKE WORLD.
ALL WE KNOW...
...IS WHAT THE DEMONS HAVE PREPARED...
...AND ARRANGED FOR US.
THIS MINIATURE GARDEN.
THE REAL WORLD...
THE OUTSIDE IS UNKNOWN!

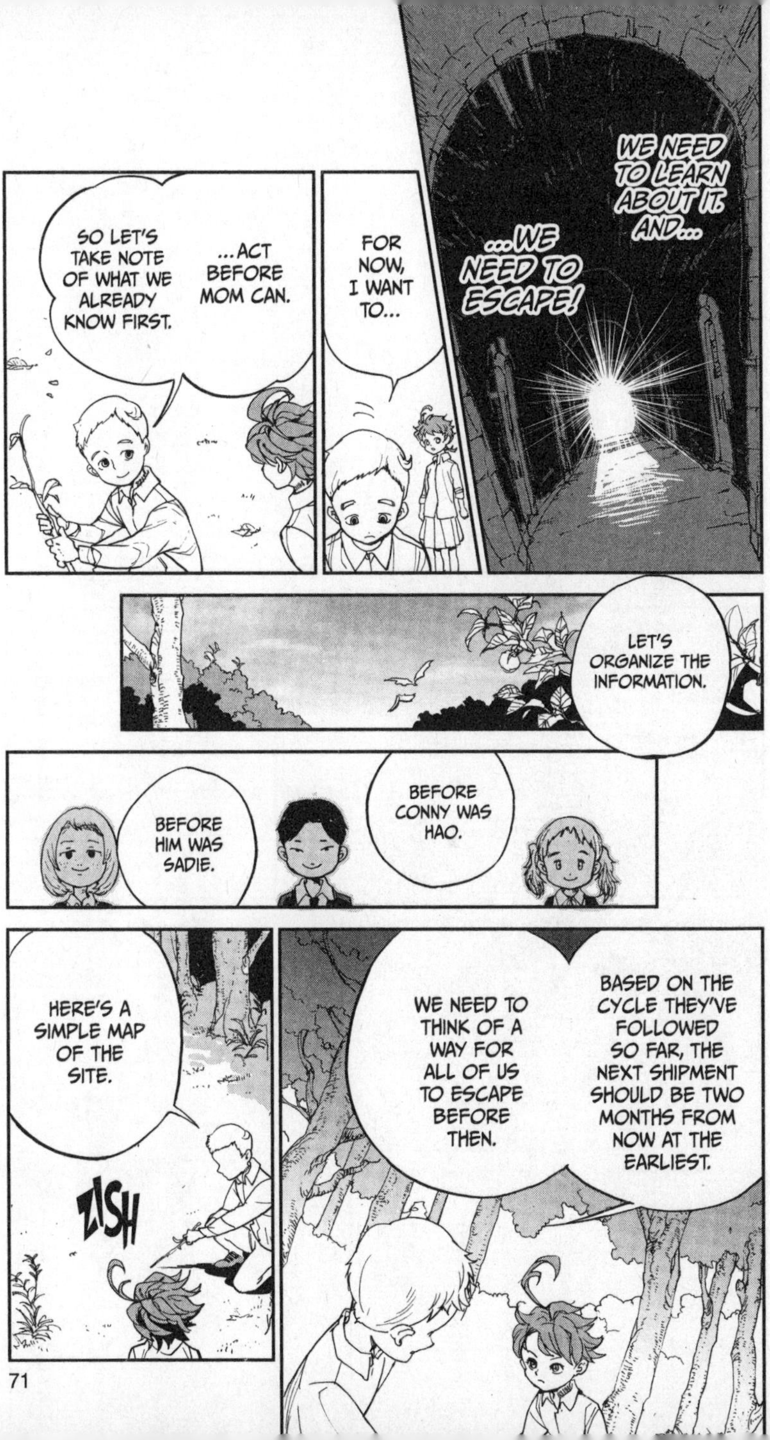

WE NEED TO LEARN ABOUT IT. AND...
...WE NEED TO ESCAPE!
FOR NOW, I WANT TO...
...ACT BEFORE MOM CAN.
SO LET'S TAKE NOTE OF WHAT WE ALREADY KNOW FIRST.
LET'S ORGANIZE THE INFORMATION.
BEFORE CONNY WAS HAO.
BEFORE HIM WAS SADIE.
BASED ON THE CYCLE THEY'VE FOLLOWED SO FAR, THE NEXT SHIPMENT SHOULD BE TWO MONTHS FROM NOW AT THE EARLIEST.
WE NEED TO THINK OF A WAY FOR ALL OF US TO ESCAPE BEFORE THEN.
HERE'S A SIMPLE MAP OF THE SITE.
ZISH

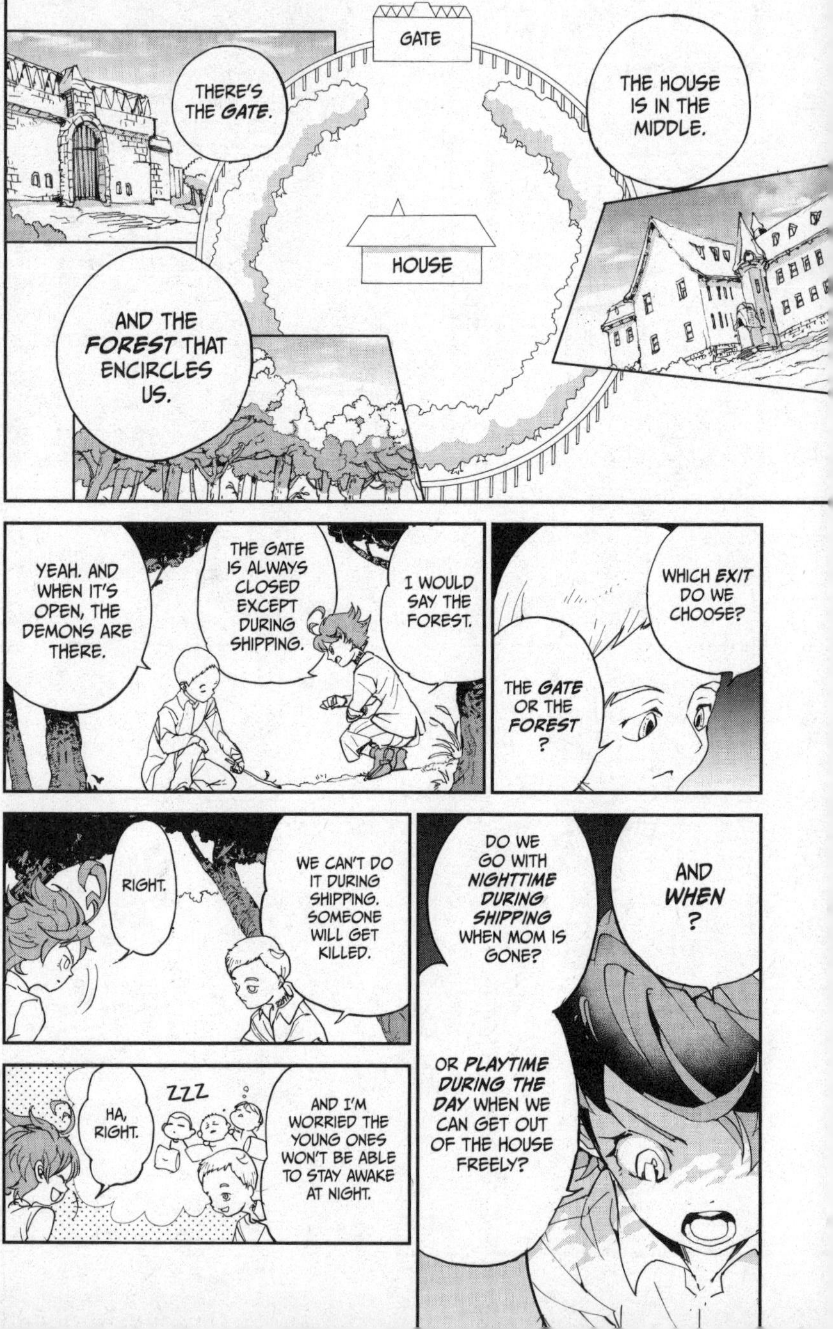
GATE
THE HOUSE IS IN THE MIDDLE.
THERE'S THE GATE.
HOUSE
AND THE FOREST THAT ENCIRCLES US.
WHICH EXIT DO WE CHOOSE?
THE GATE OR THE FOREST?
I WOULD SAY THE FOREST.
THE GATE IS ALWAYS CLOSED EXCEPT DURING SHIPPING.
YEAH. AND WHEN IT'S OPEN, THE DEMONS ARE THERE.
AND WHEN?
DO WE GO WITH NIGHTTIME DURING SHIPPING WHEN MOM IS GONE?
OR PLAYTIME DURING THE DAY WHEN WE CAN GET OUT OF THE HOUSE FREELY?
WE CAN'T DO IT DURING SHIPPING. SOMEONE WILL GET KILLED.
RIGHT.
AND I'M WORRIED THE YOUNG ONES WON'T BE ABLE TO STAY AWAKE AT NIGHT.
ZZZ
HA, RIGHT.

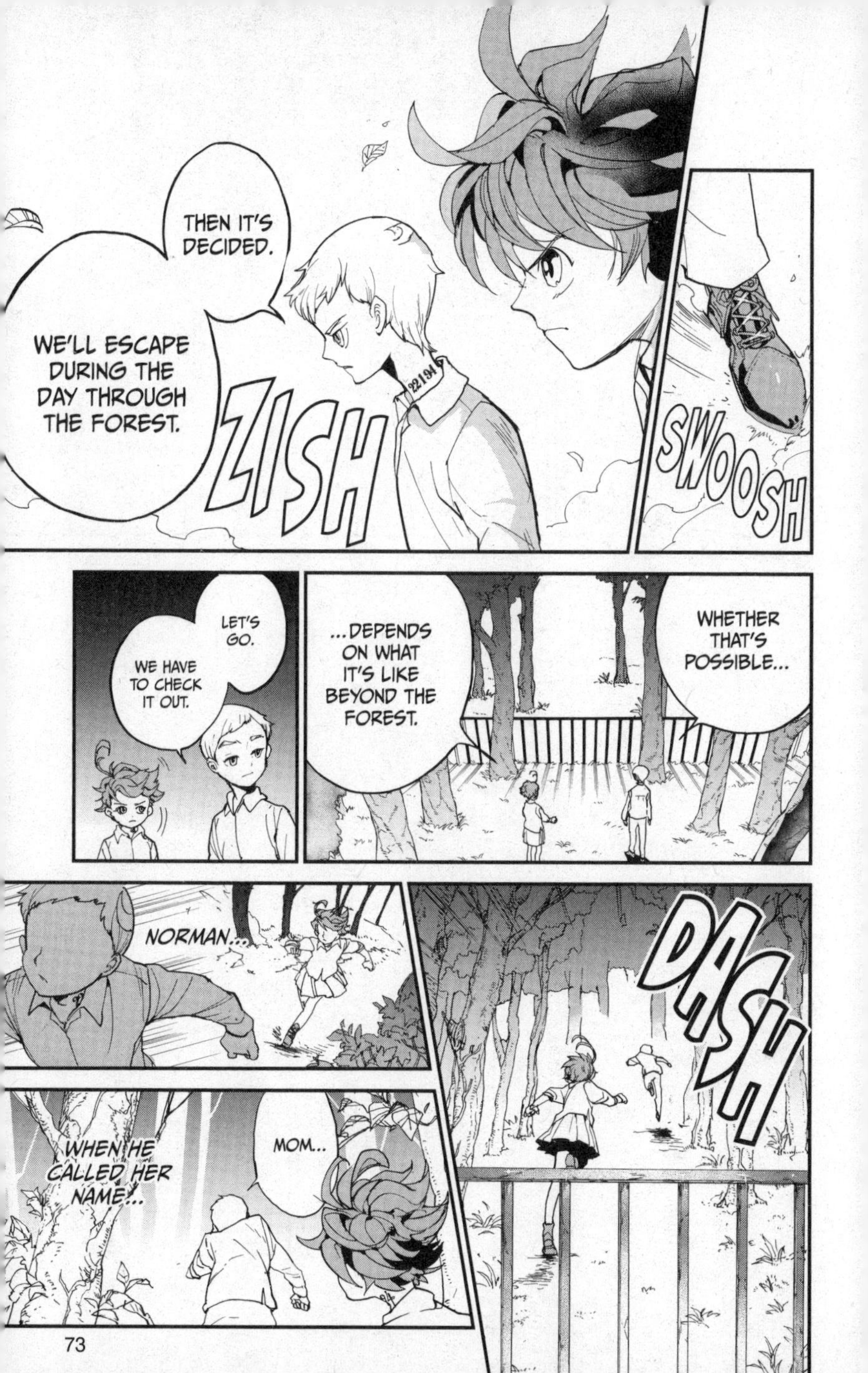
SWOOSH
THEN IT'S DECIDED.
WE'LL ESCAPE DURING THE DAY THROUGH THE FOREST.
ZISH
WHETHER THAT'S POSSIBLE...
...DEPENDS ON WHAT IT'S LIKE BEYOND THE FOREST.
LET'S GO.
WE HAVE TO CHECK IT OUT.
DASH
NORMAN...
MOM...
WHEN HE CALLED HER NAME...

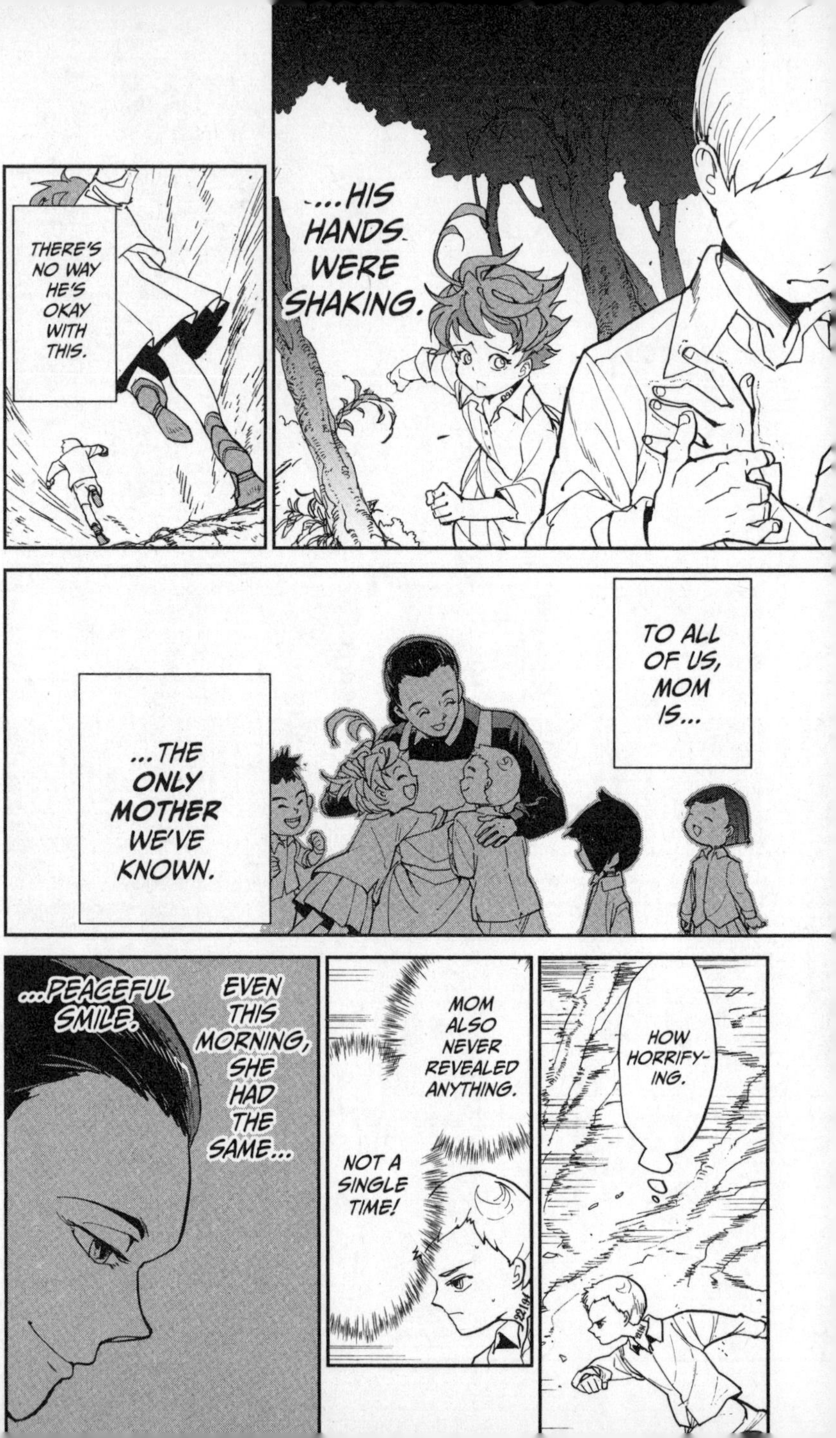
...HIS HANDS WERE SHAKING.
THERE'S NO WAY HE'S OKAY WITH THIS.
TO ALL OF US, MOM IS...
...THE ONLY MOTHER WE'VE KNOWN.
HOW HORRIFY-ING.
MOM ALSO NEVER REVEALED ANYTHING.
NOT A SINGLE TIME!
EVEN THIS MORNING, SHE HAD THE SAME...
...PEACEFUL SMILE.

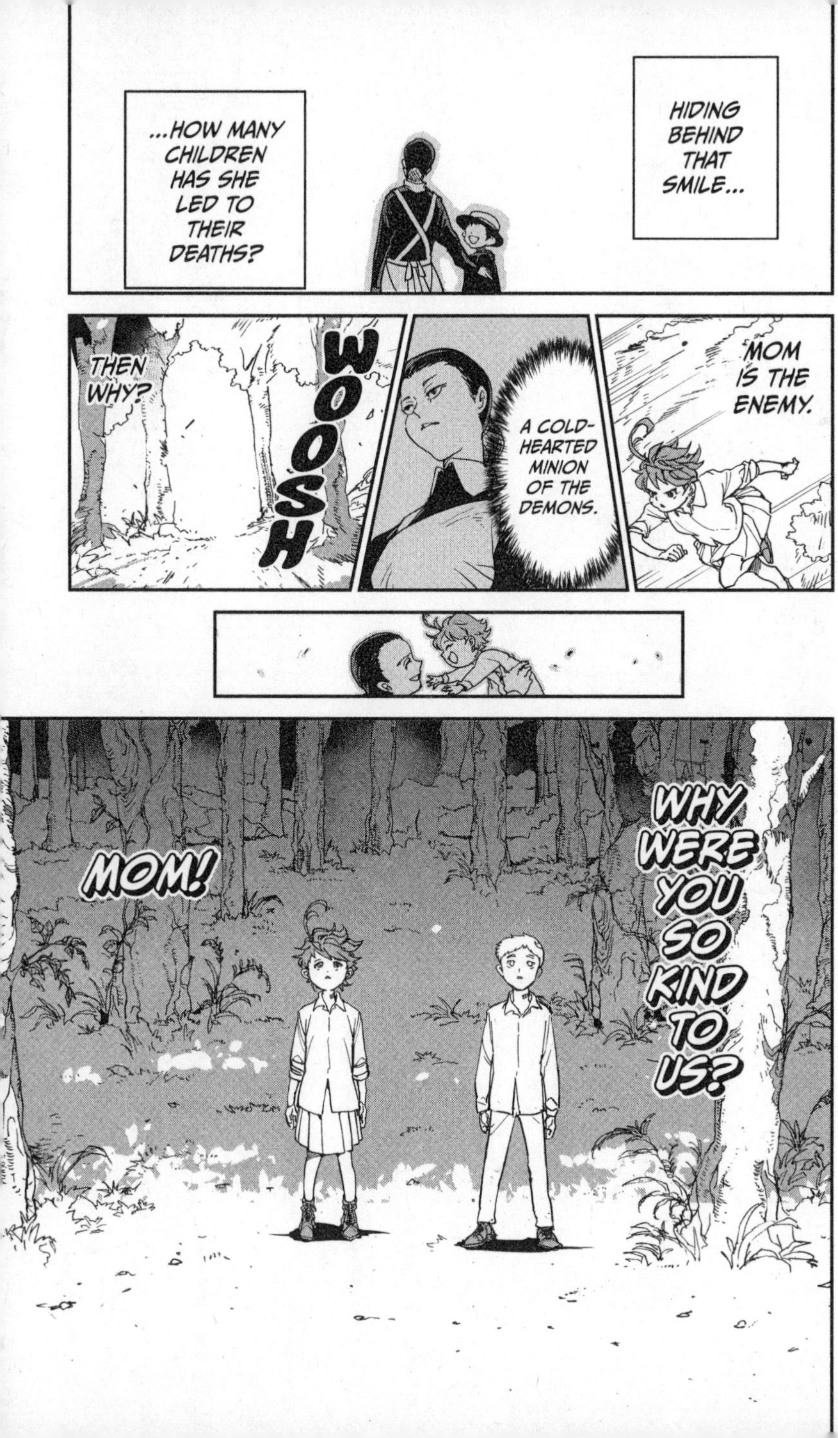
HIDING BEHIND THAT SMILE...
...HOW MANY CHILDREN HAS SHE LED TO THEIR DEATHS?
MOM IS THE ENEMY.
A COLD-HEARTED MINION OF THE DEMONS.
WOOSH
THEN WHY?
WHY WERE YOU SO KIND TO US?
MOM!

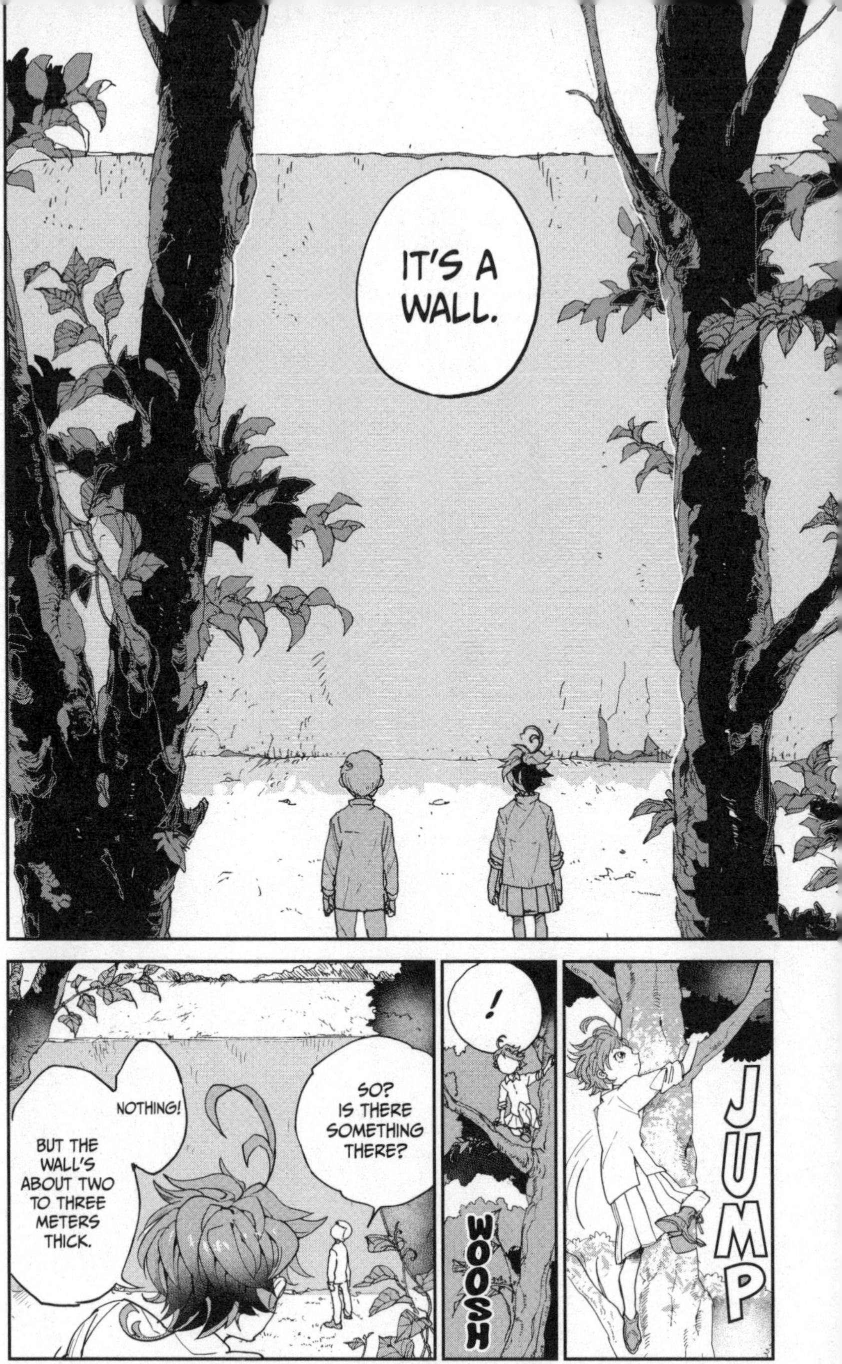
IT'S A WALL.
JUMP
!
WOOSH
SO? IS THERE SOMETHING THERE?
NOTHING!
BUT THE WALL'S ABOUT TWO TO THREE METERS THICK.

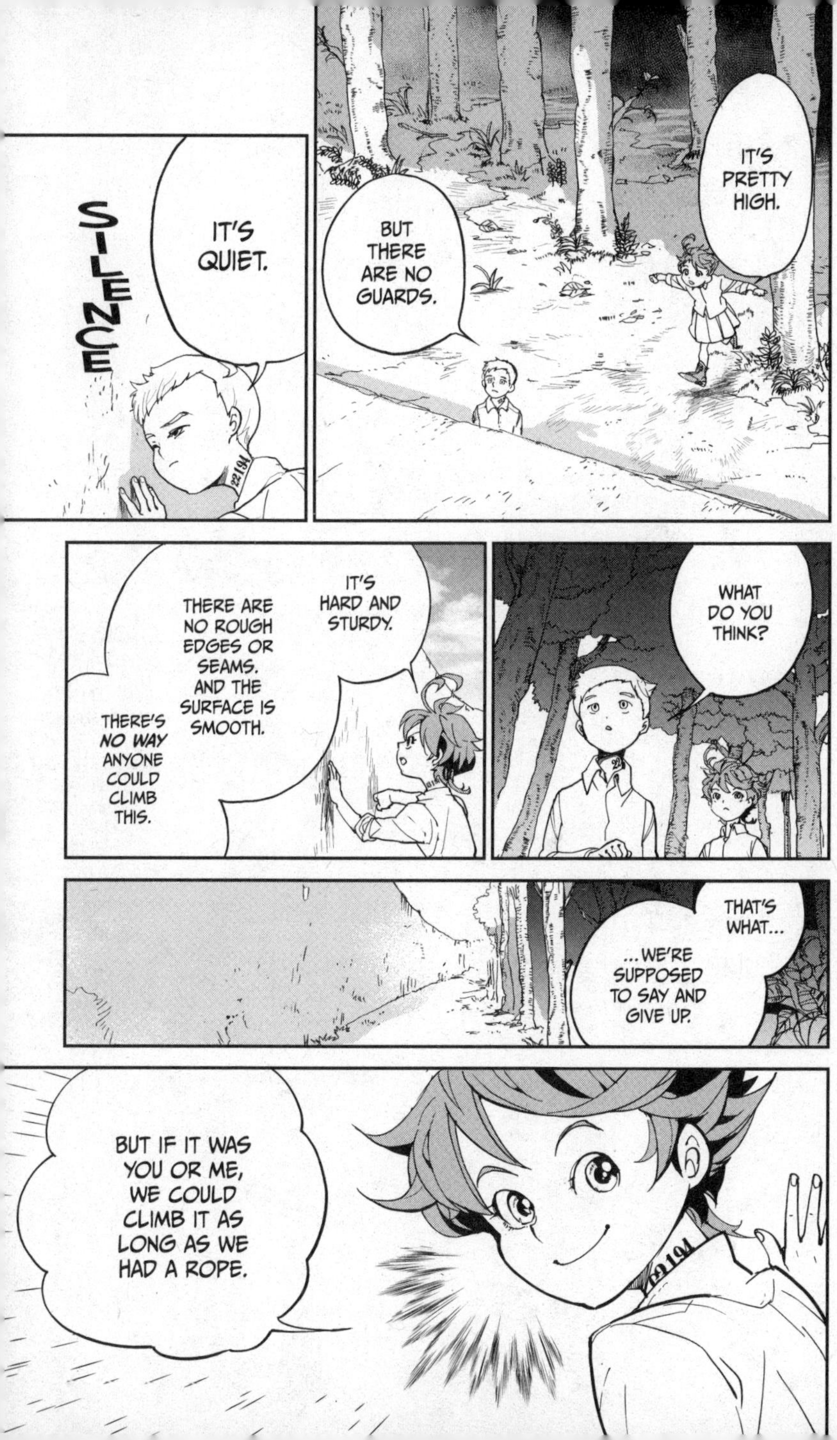
IT'S PRETTY HIGH.
BUT THERE ARE NO GUARDS.
SILENCE
IT'S QUIET.
WHAT DO YOU THINK?
IT'S HARD AND STURDY.
THERE ARE NO ROUGH EDGES OR SEAMS. AND THE SURFACE IS SMOOTH.
THERE'S *NO WAY* ANYONE COULD CLIMB THIS.
THAT'S WHAT...
...WE'RE SUPPOSED TO SAY AND GIVE UP.
BUT IF IT WAS YOU OR ME, WE COULD CLIMB IT AS LONG AS WE HAD A ROPE.

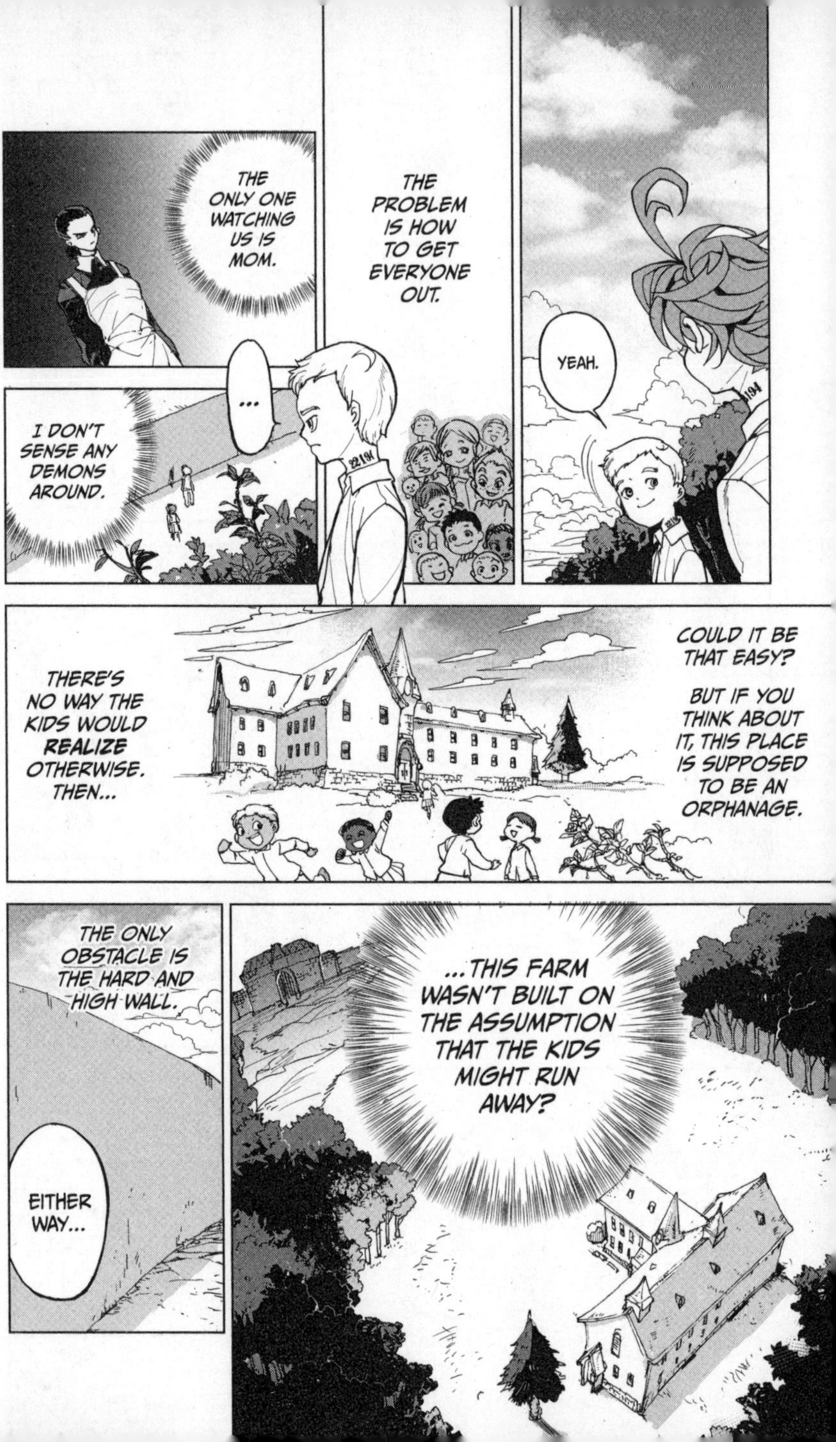
YEAH.
THE PROBLEM IS HOW TO GET EVERYONE OUT.
...
THE ONLY ONE WATCHING US IS MOM.
I DON'T SENSE ANY DEMONS AROUND.
COULD IT BE THAT EASY?
BUT IF YOU THINK ABOUT IT, THIS PLACE IS SUPPOSED TO BE AN ORPHANAGE.
THERE'S NO WAY THE KIDS WOULD REALIZE OTHERWISE. THEN...
...THIS FARM WASN'T BUILT ON THE ASSUMPTION THAT THE KIDS MIGHT RUN AWAY?
THE ONLY OBSTACLE IS THE HARD AND HIGH WALL.
EITHER WAY...

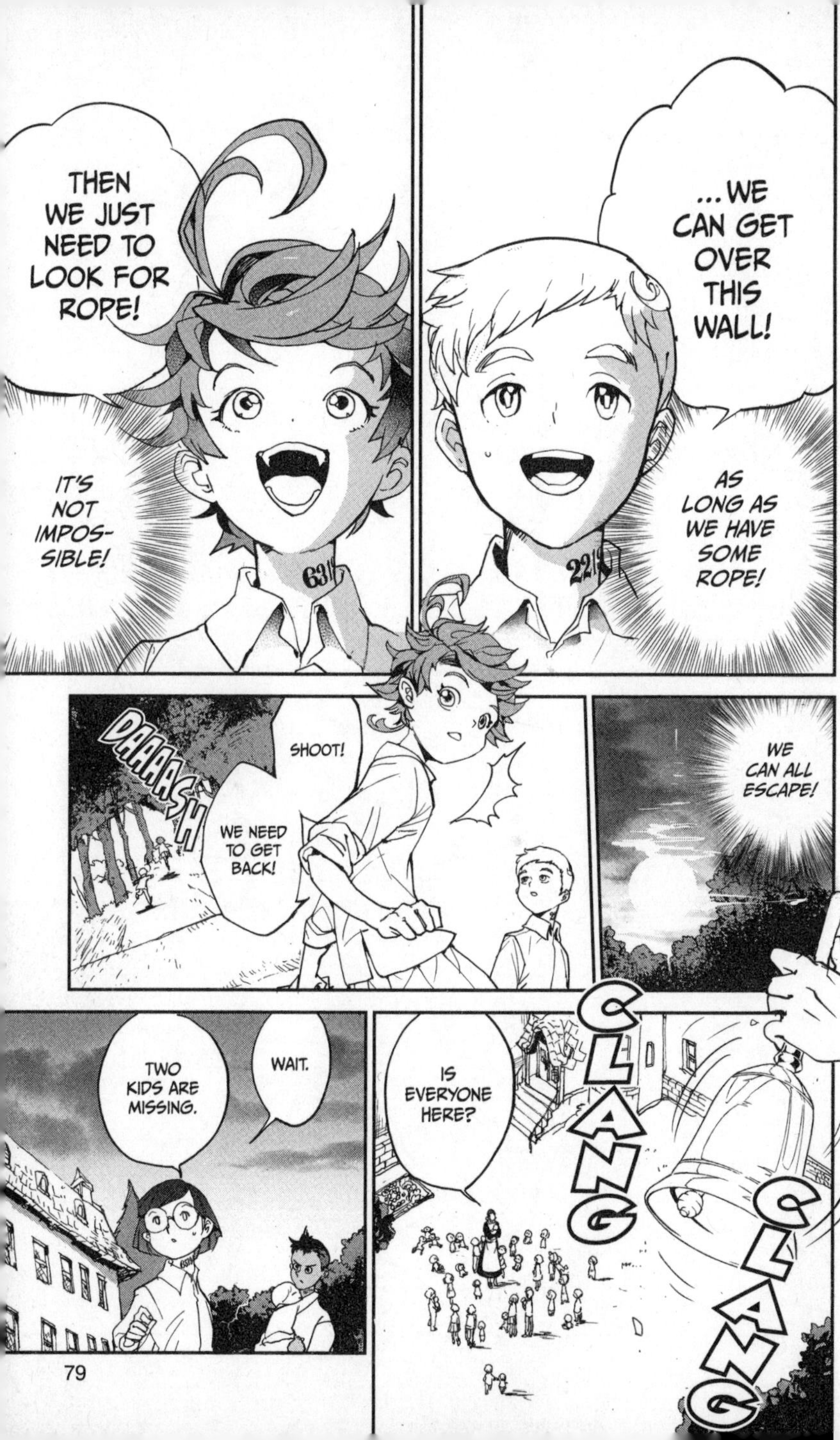
...WE CAN GET OVER THIS WALL!
AS LONG AS WE HAVE SOME ROPE!
THEN WE JUST NEED TO LOOK FOR ROPE!
IT'S NOT IMPOS-SIBLE!
WE CAN ALL ESCAPE!
SHOOT!
WE NEED TO GET BACK!
DAAAASH
IS EVERYONE HERE?
CLANG
CLANG
WAIT.
TWO KIDS ARE MISSING.

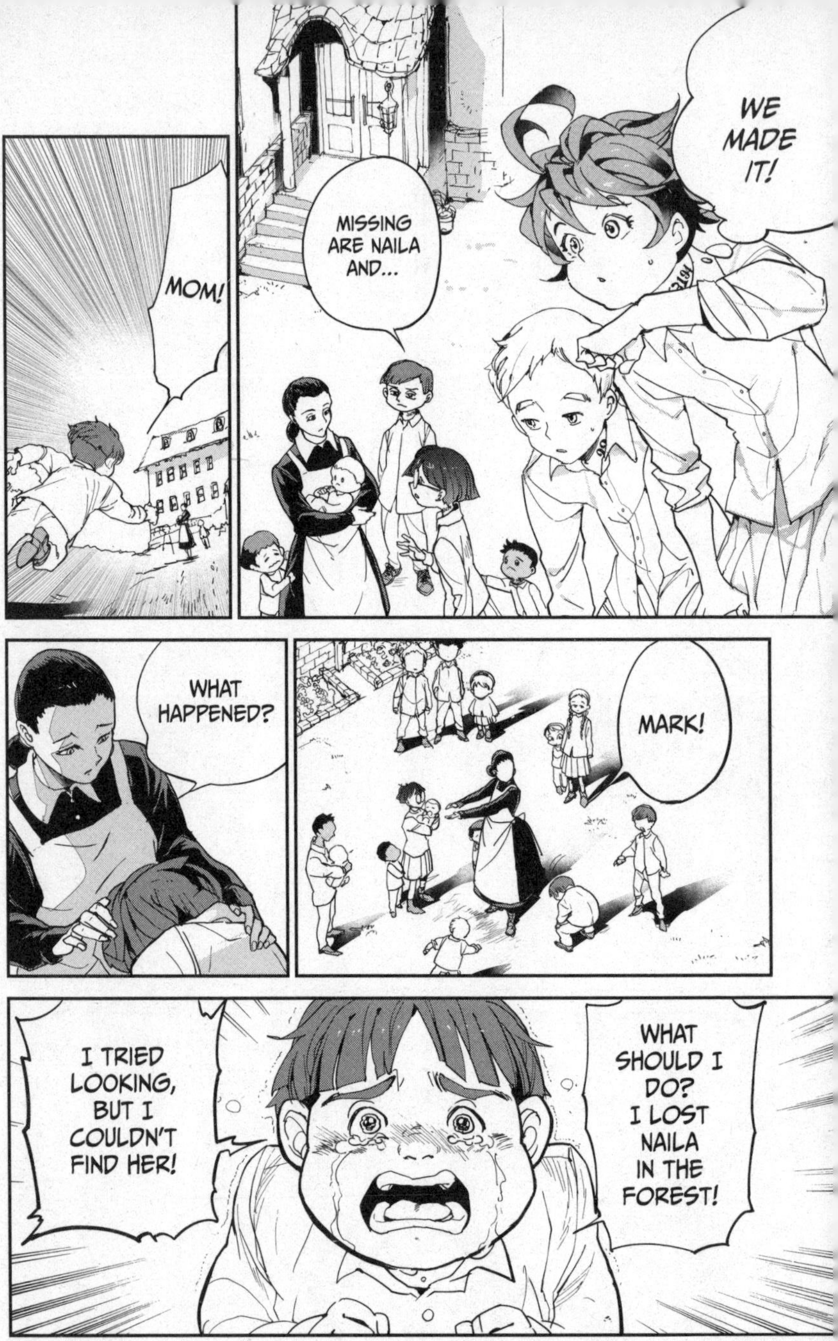
WE MADE IT!
MISSING ARE NAILA AND...
MOM!
MARK!
WHAT HAPPENED?
WHAT SHOULD I DO? I LOST NAILA IN THE FOREST!
I TRIED LOOKING, BUT I COULDN'T FIND HER!

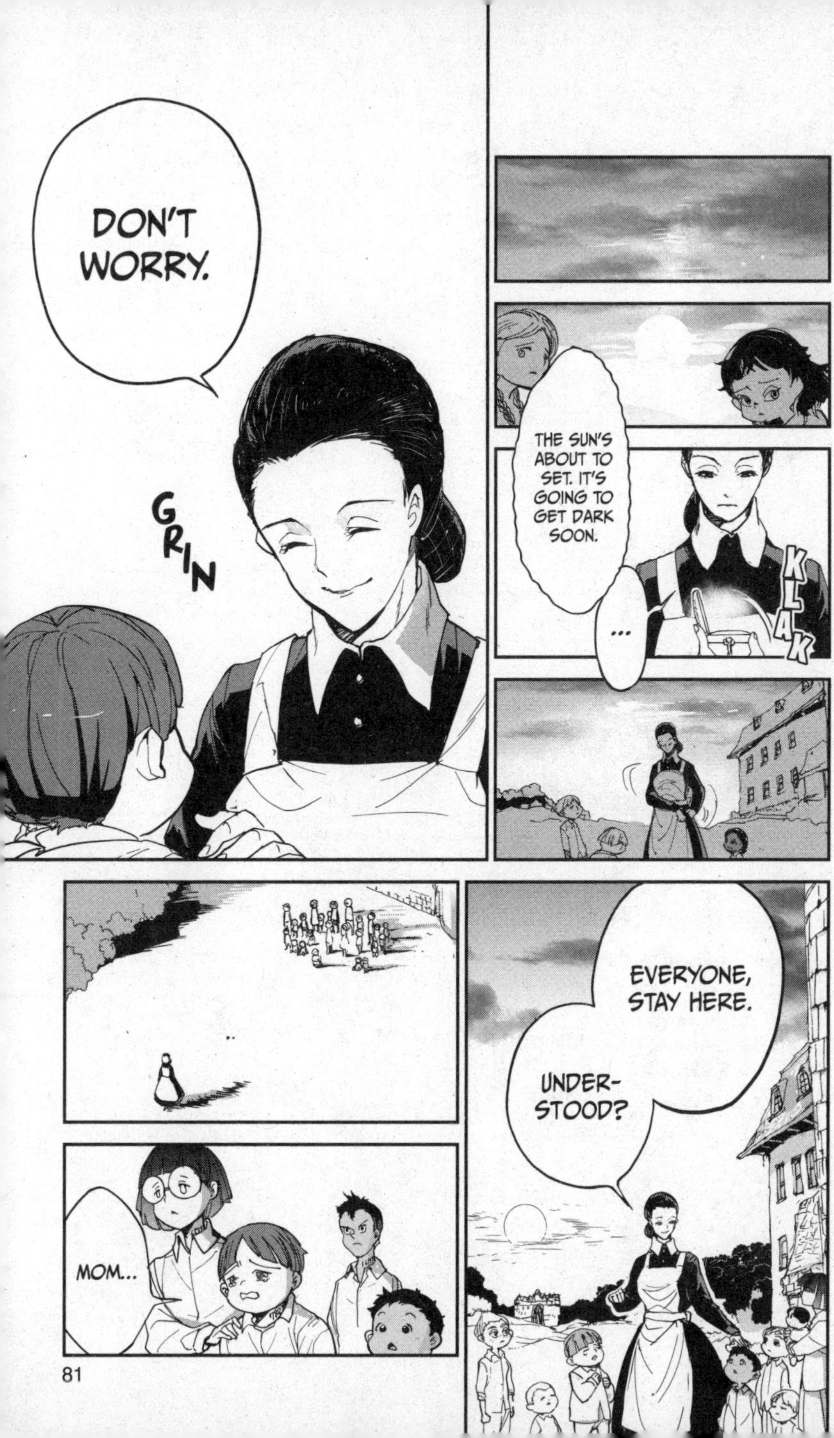
THE SUN'S ABOUT TO SET. IT'S GOING TO GET DARK SOON.
...
KLAK
DON'T WORRY.
GRIN
EVERYONE, STAY HERE.
UNDER-STOOD?
..
MOM...

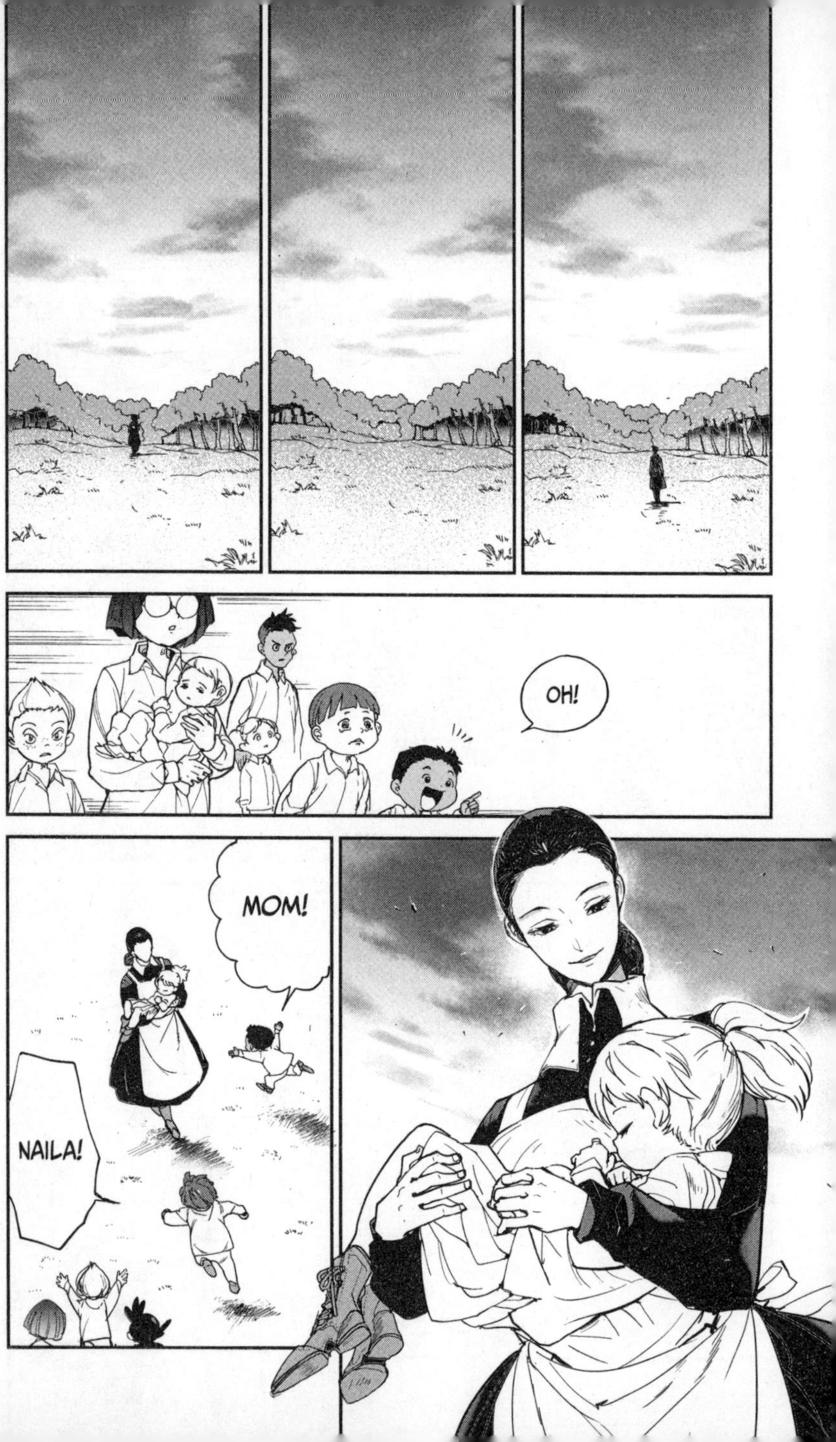
OH!
MOM!
NAILA!

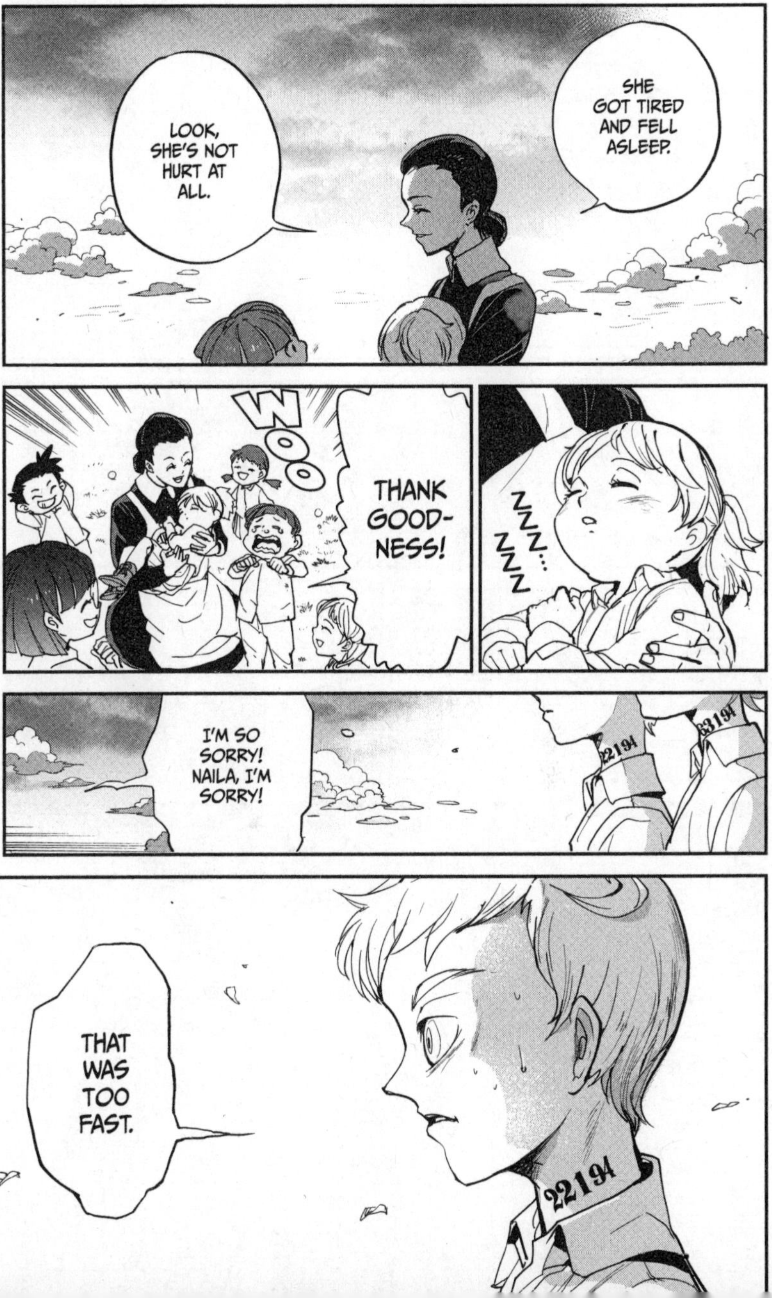
SHE GOT TIRED AND FELL ASLEEP.
LOOK, SHE'S NOT HURT AT ALL.
ZZZ... ZZZ
THANK GOODNESS!
WOO
22194
I'M SO SORRY! NAILA, I'M SORRY!
22194
THAT WAS TOO FAST.

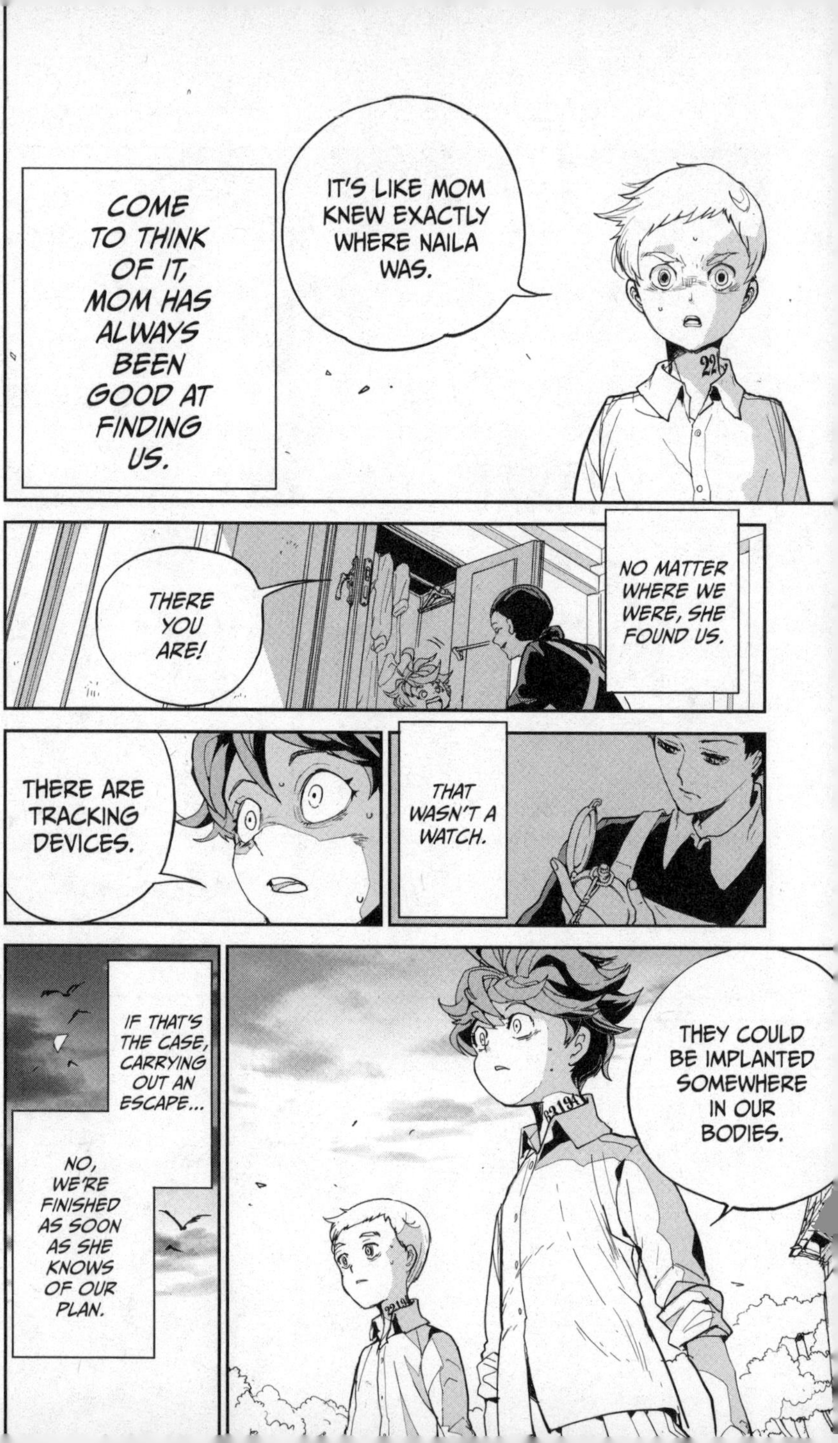
IT'S LIKE MOM KNEW EXACTLY WHERE NAILA WAS.
COME TO THINK OF IT, MOM HAS ALWAYS BEEN GOOD AT FINDING US.
NO MATTER WHERE WE WERE, SHE FOUND US.
THERE YOU ARE!
THAT WASN'T A WATCH.
THERE ARE TRACKING DEVICES.
THEY COULD BE IMPLANTED SOMEWHERE IN OUR BODIES.
IF THAT'S THE CASE, CARRYING OUT AN ESCAPE...
NO, WE'RE FINISHED AS SOON AS SHE KNOWS OF OUR PLAN.

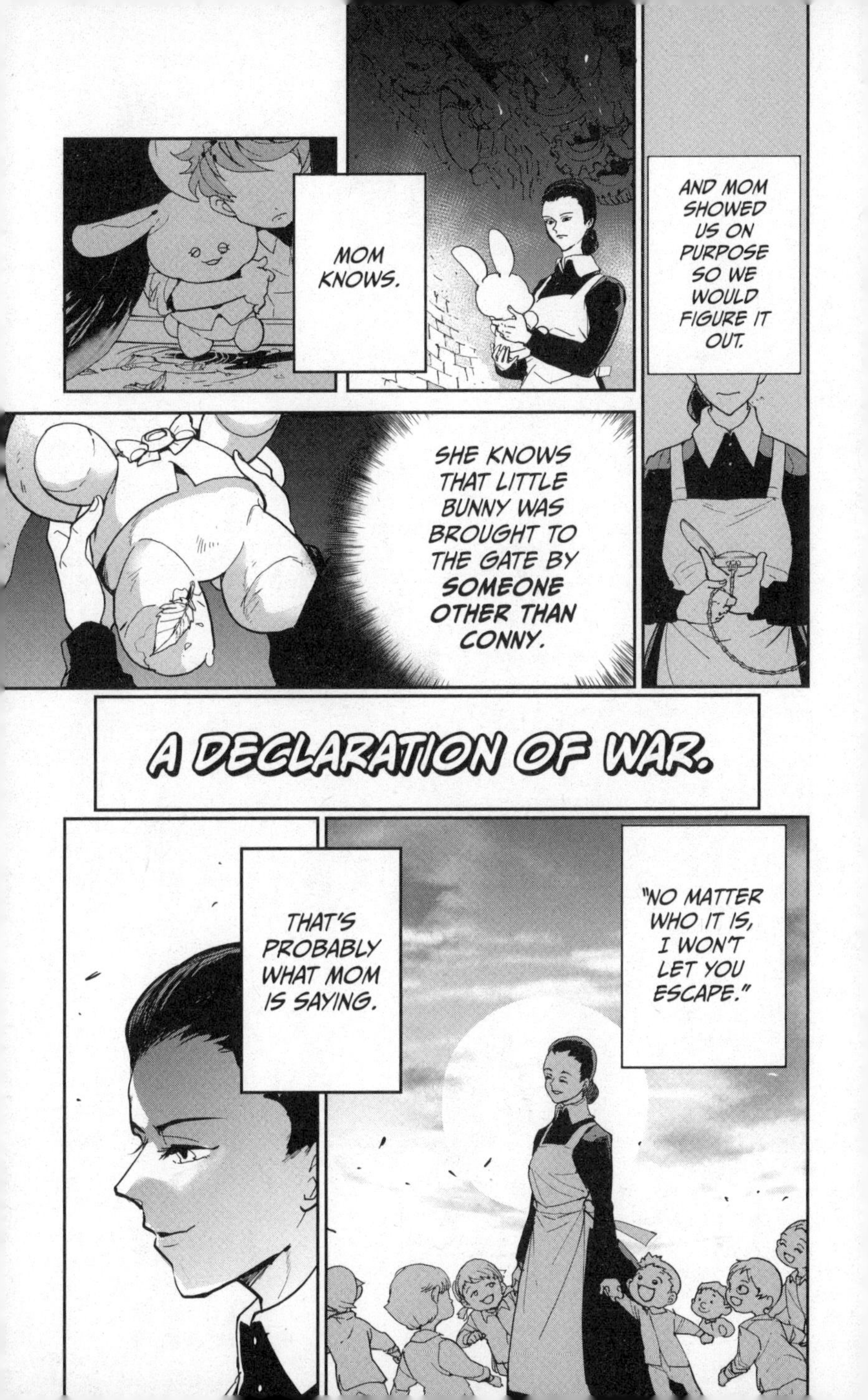
AND MOM SHOWED US ON PURPOSE SO WE WOULD FIGURE IT OUT.
MOM KNOWS.
SHE KNOWS THAT LITTLE BUNNY WAS BROUGHT TO THE GATE BY SOMEONE OTHER THAN CONNY.
A DECLARATION OF WAR.
"NO MATTER WHO IT IS, I WON'T LET YOU ESCAPE."
THAT'S PROBABLY WHAT MOM IS SAYING.

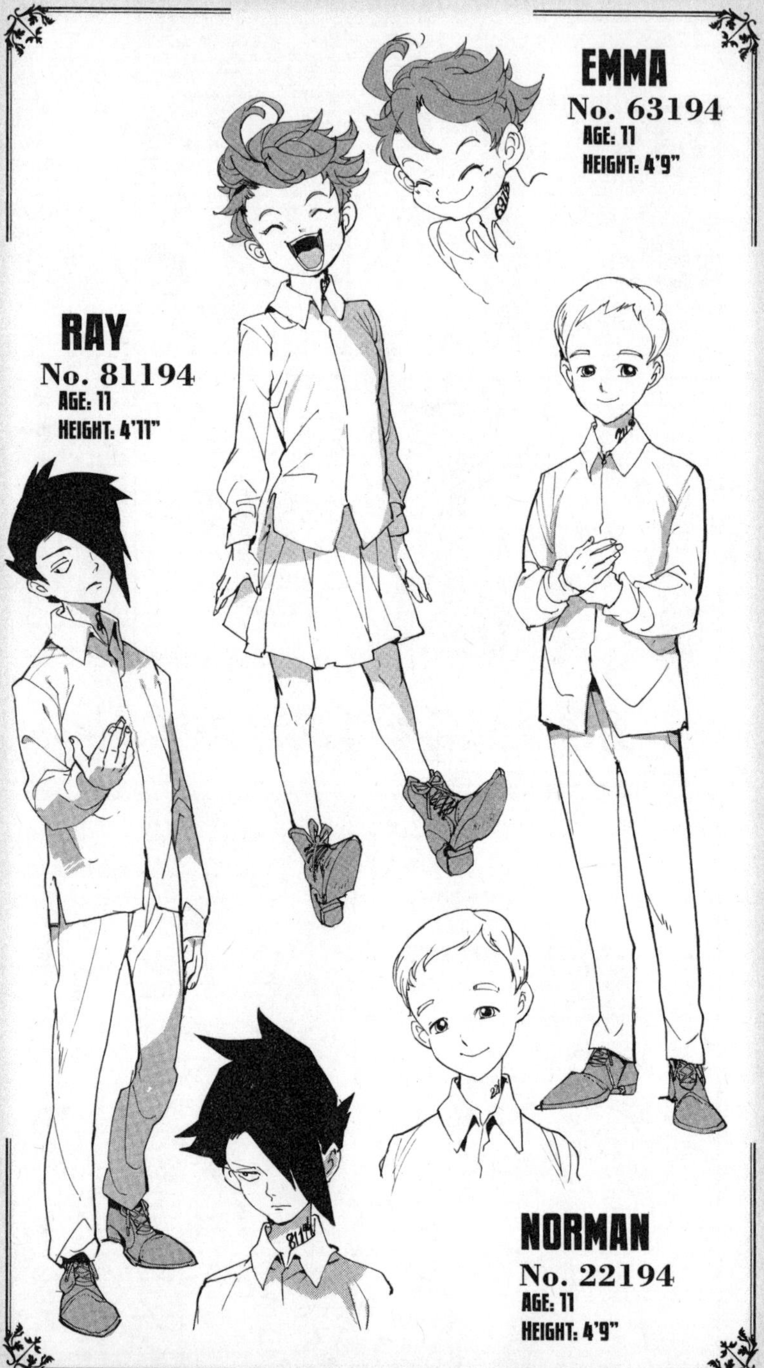
EMMA
No. 63194
AGE: 11
HEIGHT: 4'9"
RAY
No. 81194
AGE: 11
HEIGHT: 4'11"
NORMAN
No. 22194
AGE: 11
HEIGHT: 4'9"

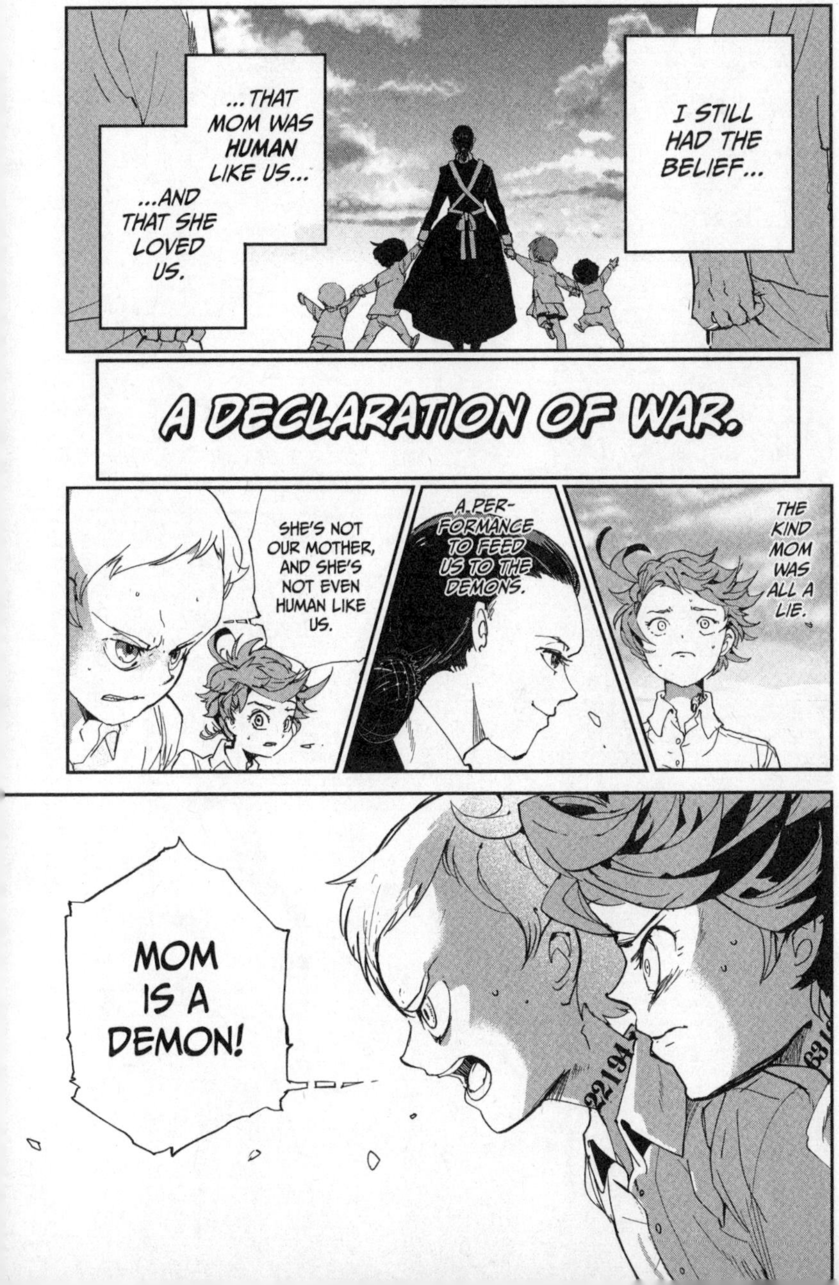
I STILL HAD THE BELIEF...
...THAT MOM WAS HUMAN LIKE US...
...AND THAT SHE LOVED US.
A DECLARATION OF WAR.
THE KIND MOM WAS ALL A LIE.
A PERFORMANCE TO FEED US TO THE DEMONS.
SHE'S NOT OUR MOTHER, AND SHE'S NOT EVEN HUMAN LIKE US.
MOM IS A DEMON!
22194

CHAPTER 3: THE IRON WOMAN

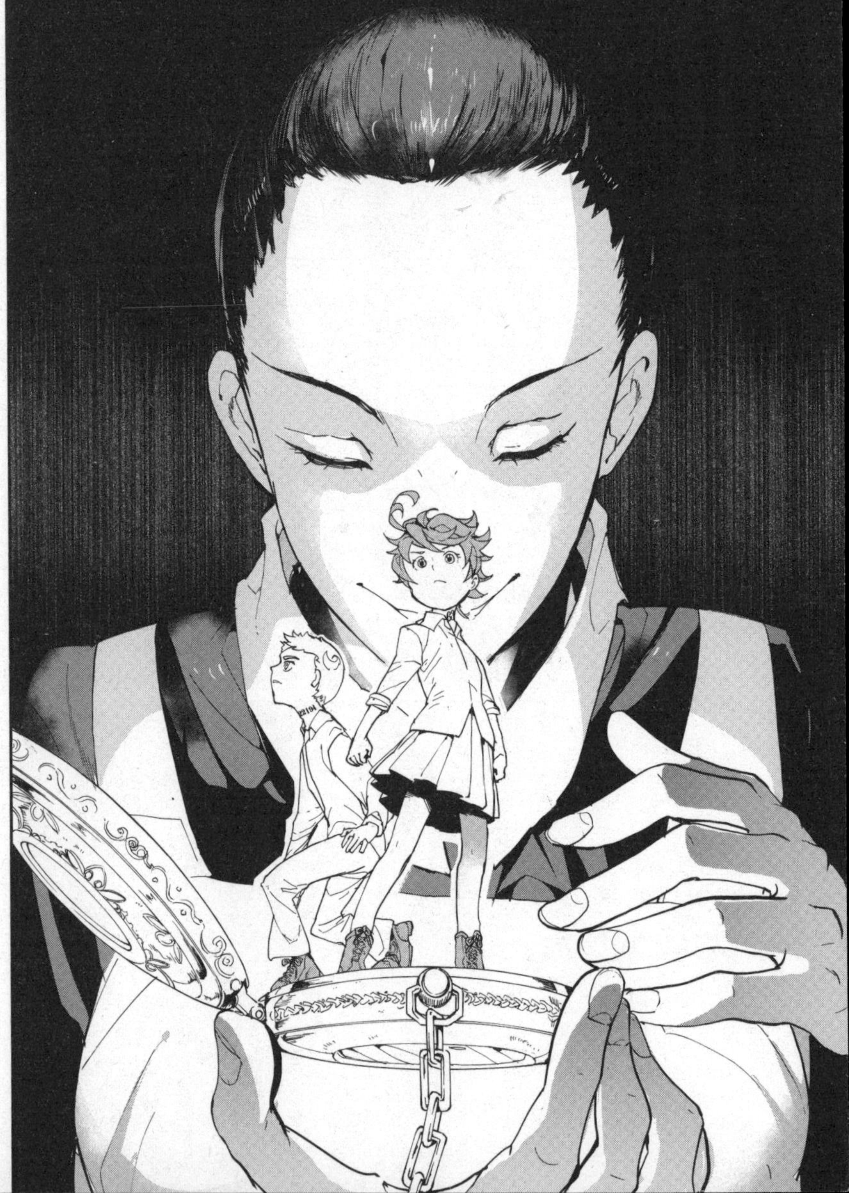

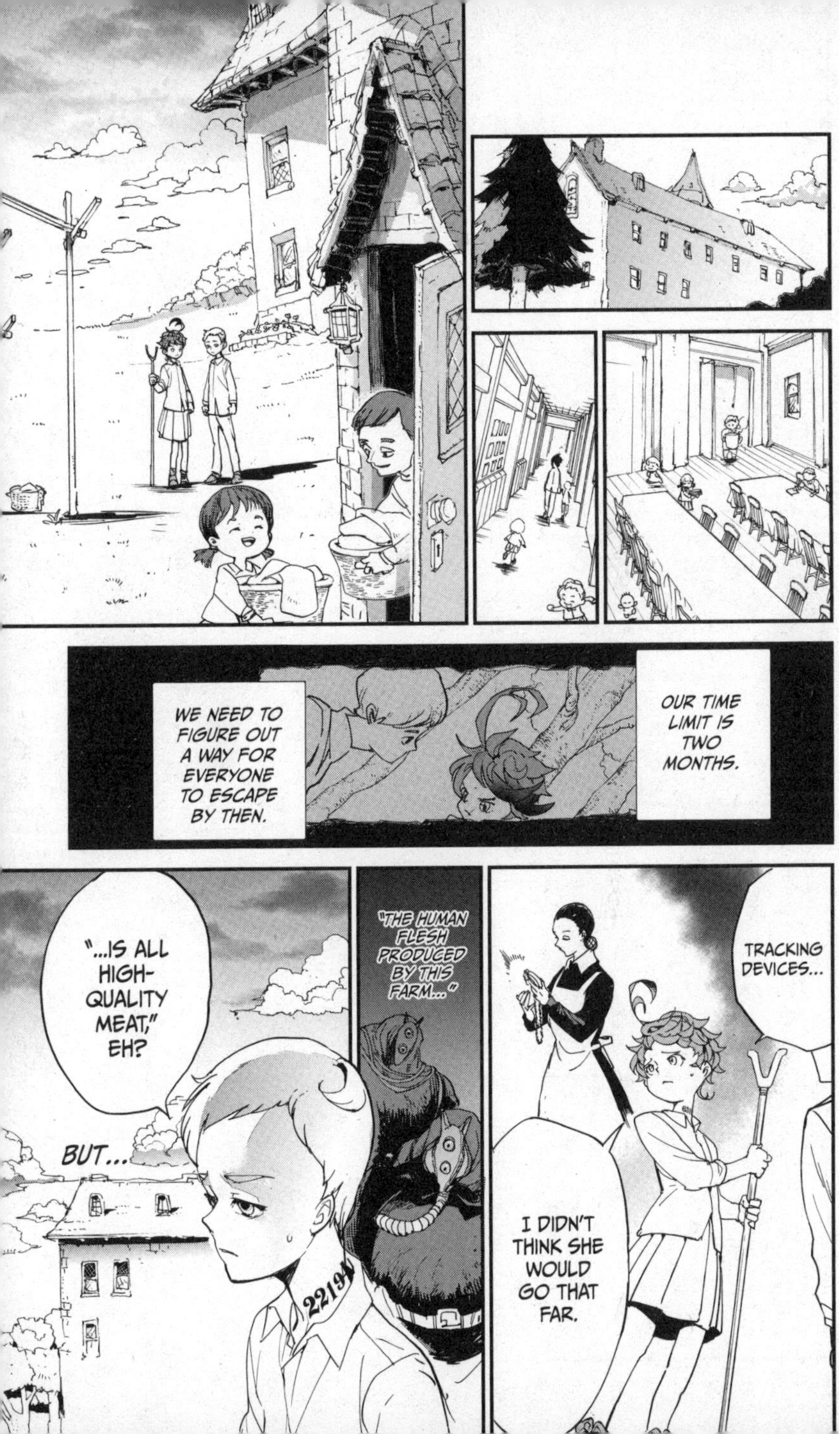
OUR TIME LIMIT IS TWO MONTHS.
WE NEED TO FIGURE OUT A WAY FOR EVERYONE TO ESCAPE BY THEN.
TRACKING DEVICES...
I DIDN'T THINK SHE WOULD GO THAT FAR.
"THE HUMAN FLESH PRODUCED BY THIS FARM..."
"...IS ALL HIGH-QUALITY MEAT," EH?
BUT...

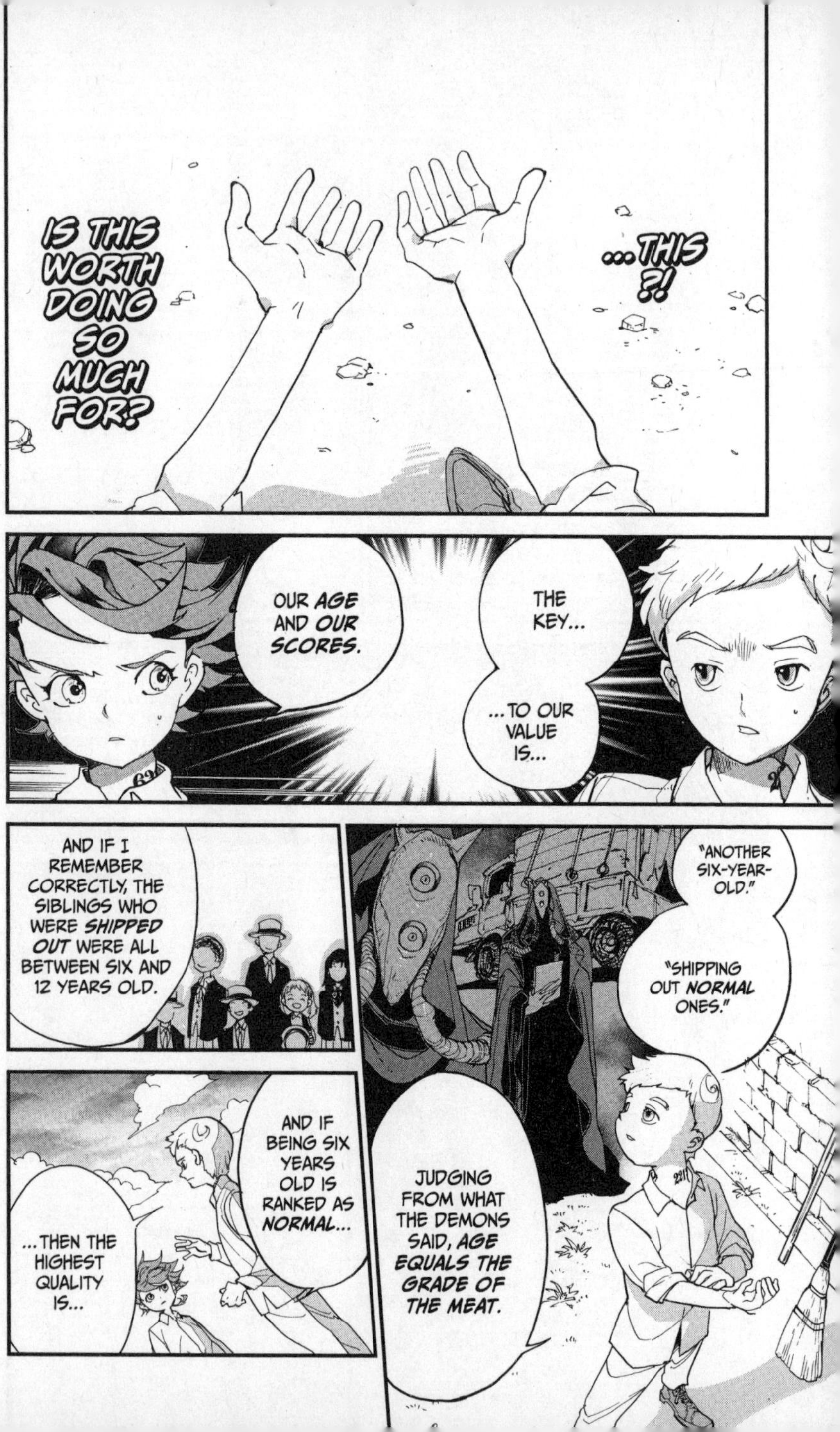
...THIS ?!
IS THIS WORTH DOING SO MUCH FOR?
THE KEY...
...TO OUR VALUE IS...
OUR AGE AND OUR SCORES.
"ANOTHER SIX-YEAR-OLD."
"SHIPPING OUT NORMAL ONES."
JUDGING FROM WHAT THE DEMONS SAID, AGE EQUALS THE GRADE OF THE MEAT.
AND IF I REMEMBER CORRECTLY, THE SIBLINGS WHO WERE SHIPPED OUT WERE ALL BETWEEN SIX AND 12 YEARS OLD.
AND IF BEING SIX YEARS OLD IS RANKED AS NORMAL...
...THEN THE HIGHEST QUALITY IS...

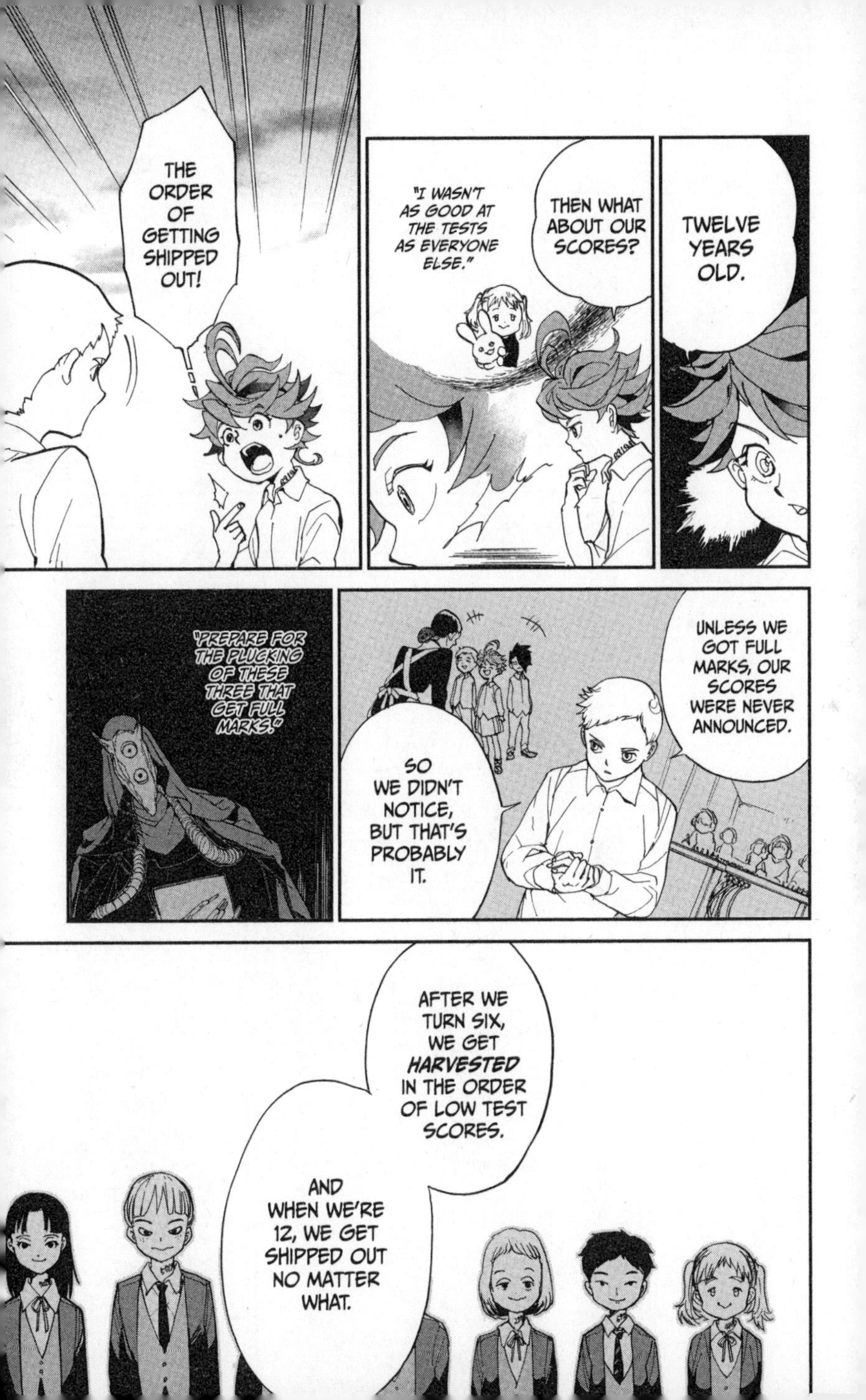
TWELVE YEARS OLD.
THEN WHAT ABOUT OUR SCORES?
"I WASN'T AS GOOD AT THE TESTS AS EVERYONE ELSE."
THE ORDER OF GETTING SHIPPED OUT!
UNLESS WE GOT FULL MARKS, OUR SCORES WERE NEVER ANNOUNCED.
SO WE DIDN'T NOTICE, BUT THAT'S PROBABLY IT.
"PREPARE FOR THE PLUCKING OF THESE THREE THAT GET FULL MARKS."
AFTER WE TURN SIX, WE GET *HARVESTED* IN THE ORDER OF LOW TEST SCORES.
AND WHEN WE'RE 12, WE GET SHIPPED OUT NO MATTER WHAT.

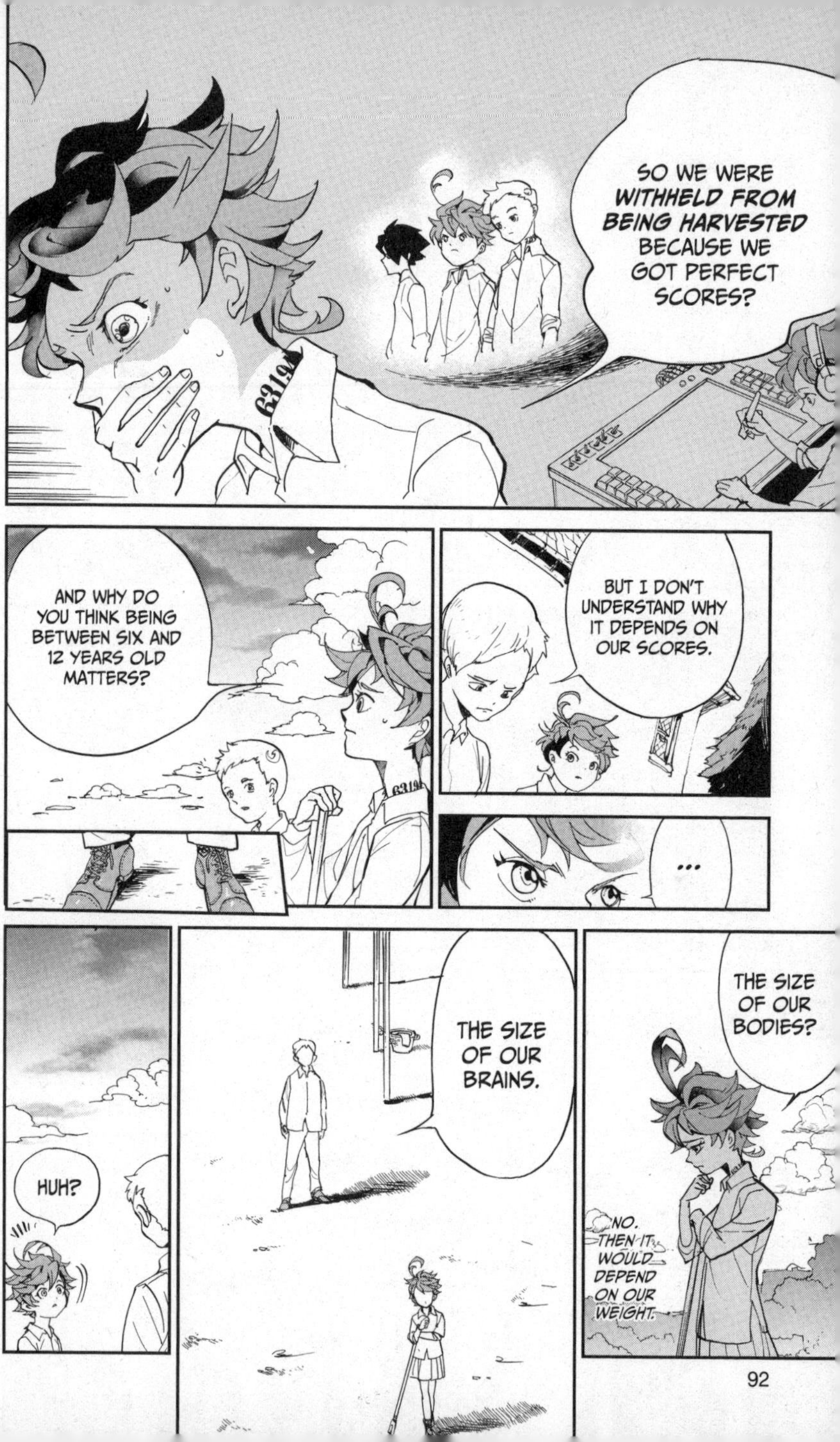
SO WE WERE WITHHELD FROM BEING HARVESTED BECAUSE WE GOT PERFECT SCORES?
BUT I DON'T UNDERSTAND WHY IT DEPENDS ON OUR SCORES.
...
AND WHY DO YOU THINK BEING BETWEEN SIX AND 12 YEARS OLD MATTERS?
THE SIZE OF OUR BODIES?
NO. THEN IT WOULD DEPEND ON OUR WEIGHT.
THE SIZE OF OUR BRAINS.
HUH?

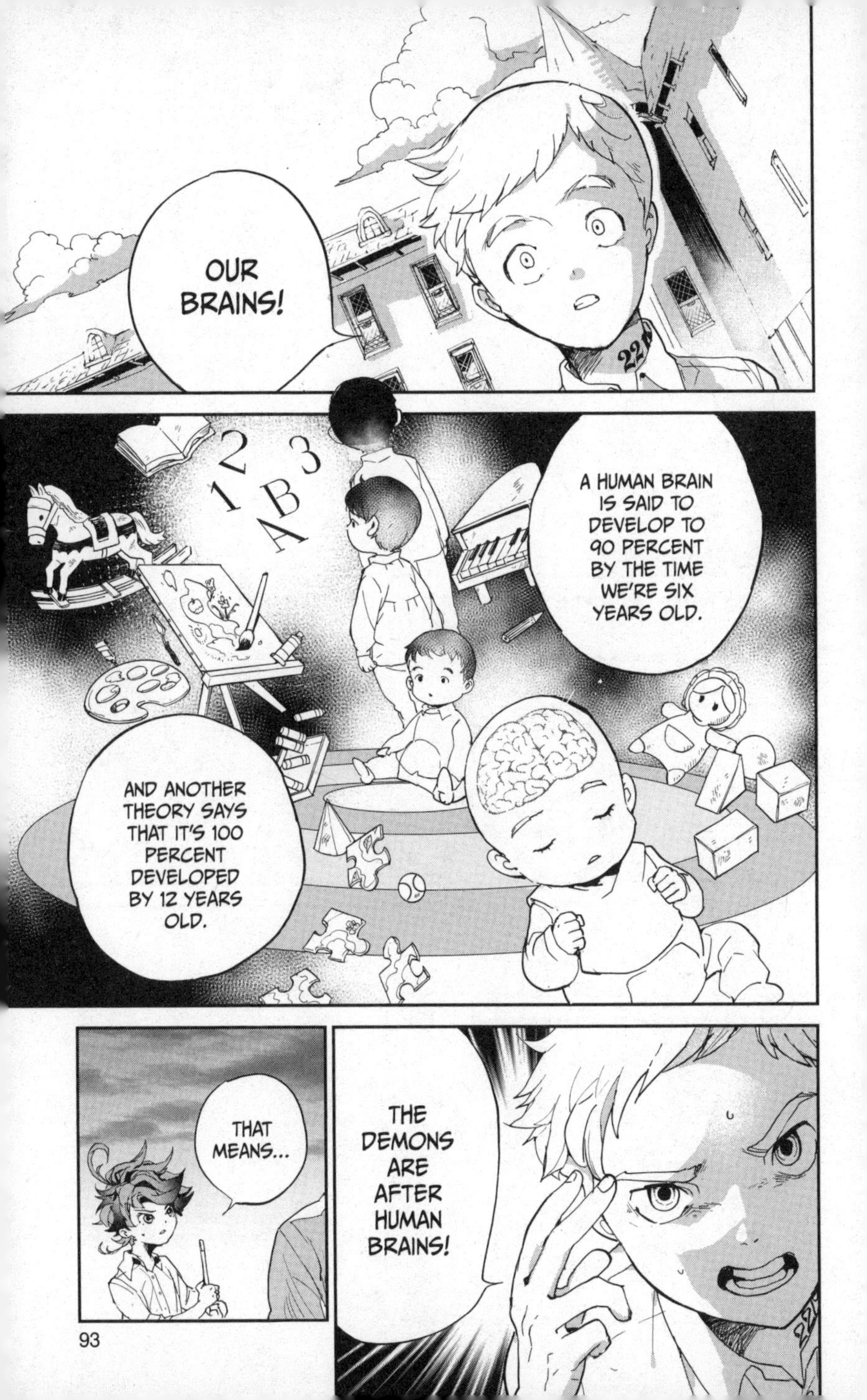
OUR BRAINS!
A HUMAN BRAIN IS SAID TO DEVELOP TO 90 PERCENT BY THE TIME WE'RE SIX YEARS OLD.
AND ANOTHER THEORY SAYS THAT IT'S 100 PERCENT DEVELOPED BY 12 YEARS OLD.
THE DEMONS ARE AFTER HUMAN BRAINS!
THAT MEANS...

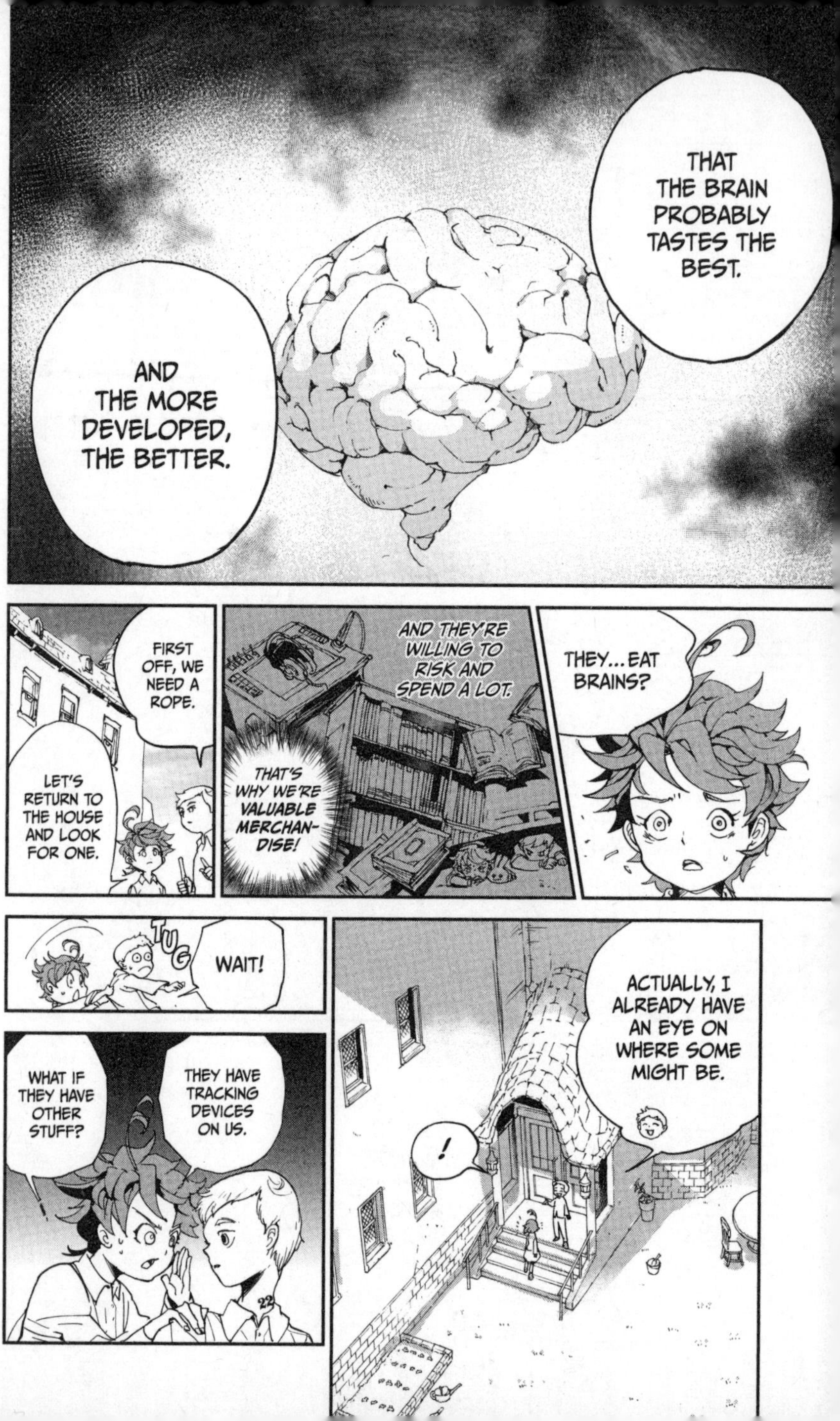
THAT THE BRAIN PROBABLY TASTES THE BEST.
AND THE MORE DEVELOPED, THE BETTER.
THEY... EAT BRAINS?
AND THEY'RE WILLING TO RISK AND SPEND A LOT.
THAT'S WHY WE'RE VALUABLE MERCHANDISE!
FIRST OFF, WE NEED A ROPE.
LET'S RETURN TO THE HOUSE AND LOOK FOR ONE.
ACTUALLY, I ALREADY HAVE AN EYE ON WHERE SOME MIGHT BE.
!
TUG
WAIT!
THEY HAVE TRACKING DEVICES ON US.
WHAT IF THEY HAVE OTHER STUFF?

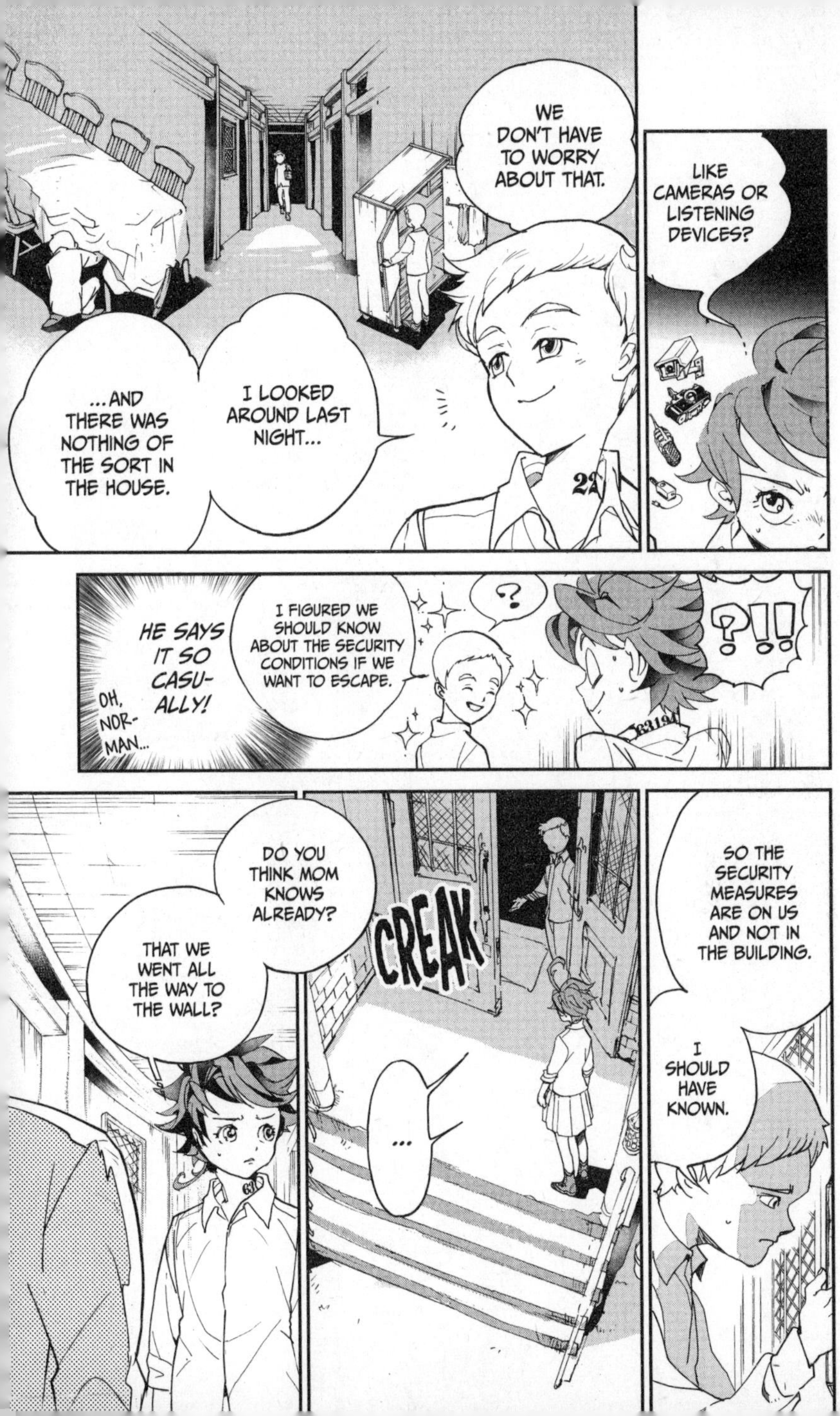
LIKE CAMERAS OR LISTENING DEVICES?
WE DON'T HAVE TO WORRY ABOUT THAT.
I LOOKED AROUND LAST NIGHT...
...AND THERE WAS NOTHING OF THE SORT IN THE HOUSE.
?!!
?
I FIGURED WE SHOULD KNOW ABOUT THE SECURITY CONDITIONS IF WE WANT TO ESCAPE.
HE SAYS IT SO CASU-ALLY!
OH, NOR-MAN...
SO THE SECURITY MEASURES ARE ON US AND NOT IN THE BUILDING.
I SHOULD HAVE KNOWN.
CREAK
...
DO YOU THINK MOM KNOWS ALREADY?
THAT WE WENT ALL THE WAY TO THE WALL?

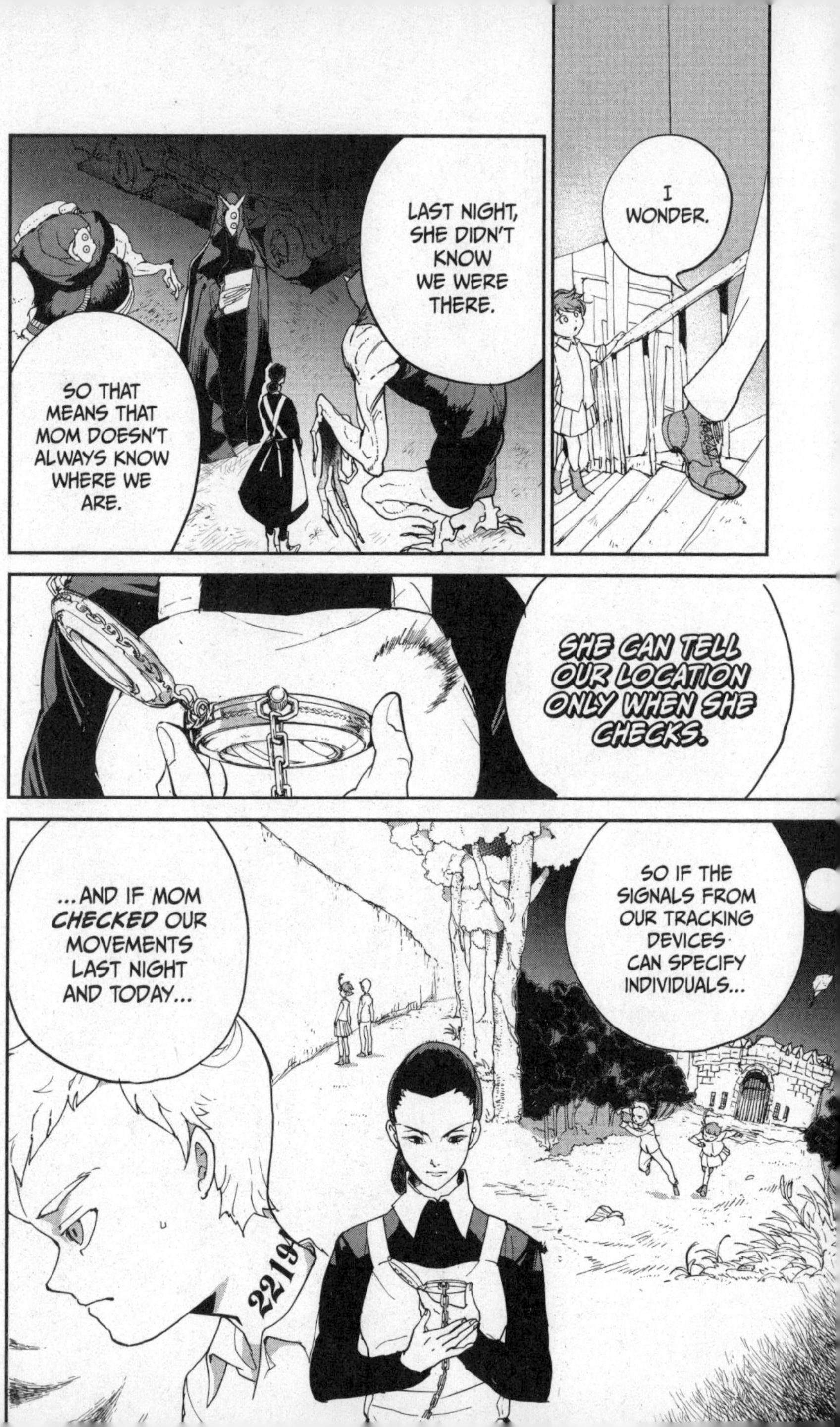
I WONDER.
LAST NIGHT, SHE DIDN'T KNOW WE WERE THERE.
SO THAT MEANS THAT MOM DOESN'T ALWAYS KNOW WHERE WE ARE.
SHE CAN TELL OUR LOCATION ONLY WHEN SHE CHECKS.
SO IF THE SIGNALS FROM OUR TRACKING DEVICES CAN SPECIFY INDIVIDUALS...
...AND IF MOM *CHECKED* OUR MOVEMENTS LAST NIGHT AND TODAY...

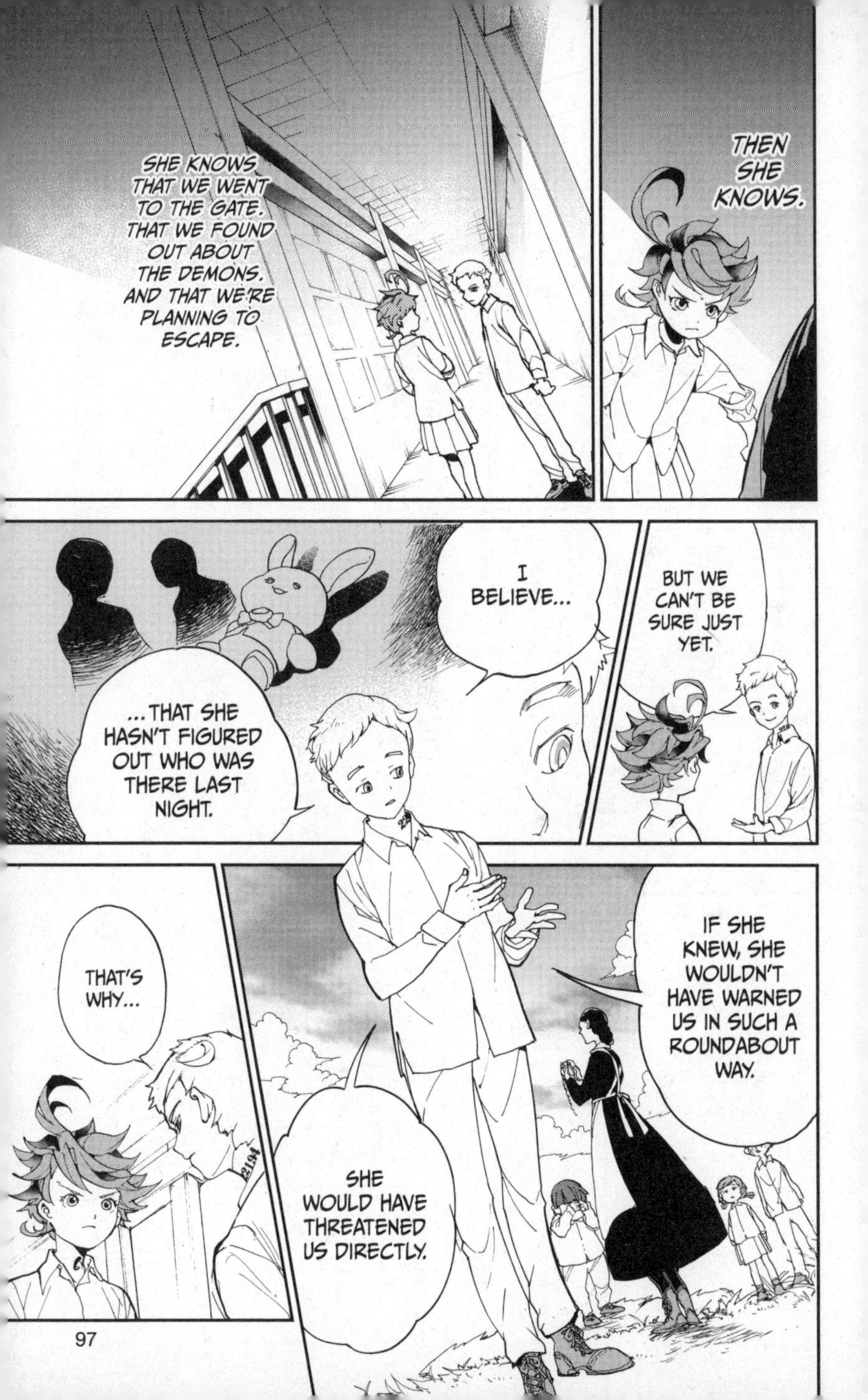
THEN SHE KNOWS.
SHE KNOWS THAT WE WENT TO THE GATE. THAT WE FOUND OUT ABOUT THE DEMONS. AND THAT WE'RE PLANNING TO ESCAPE.
BUT WE CAN'T BE SURE JUST YET.
I BELIEVE...
...THAT SHE HASN'T FIGURED OUT WHO WAS THERE LAST NIGHT.
IF SHE KNEW, SHE WOULDN'T HAVE WARNED US IN SUCH A ROUNDABOUT WAY.
SHE WOULD HAVE THREATENED US DIRECTLY.
THAT'S WHY...

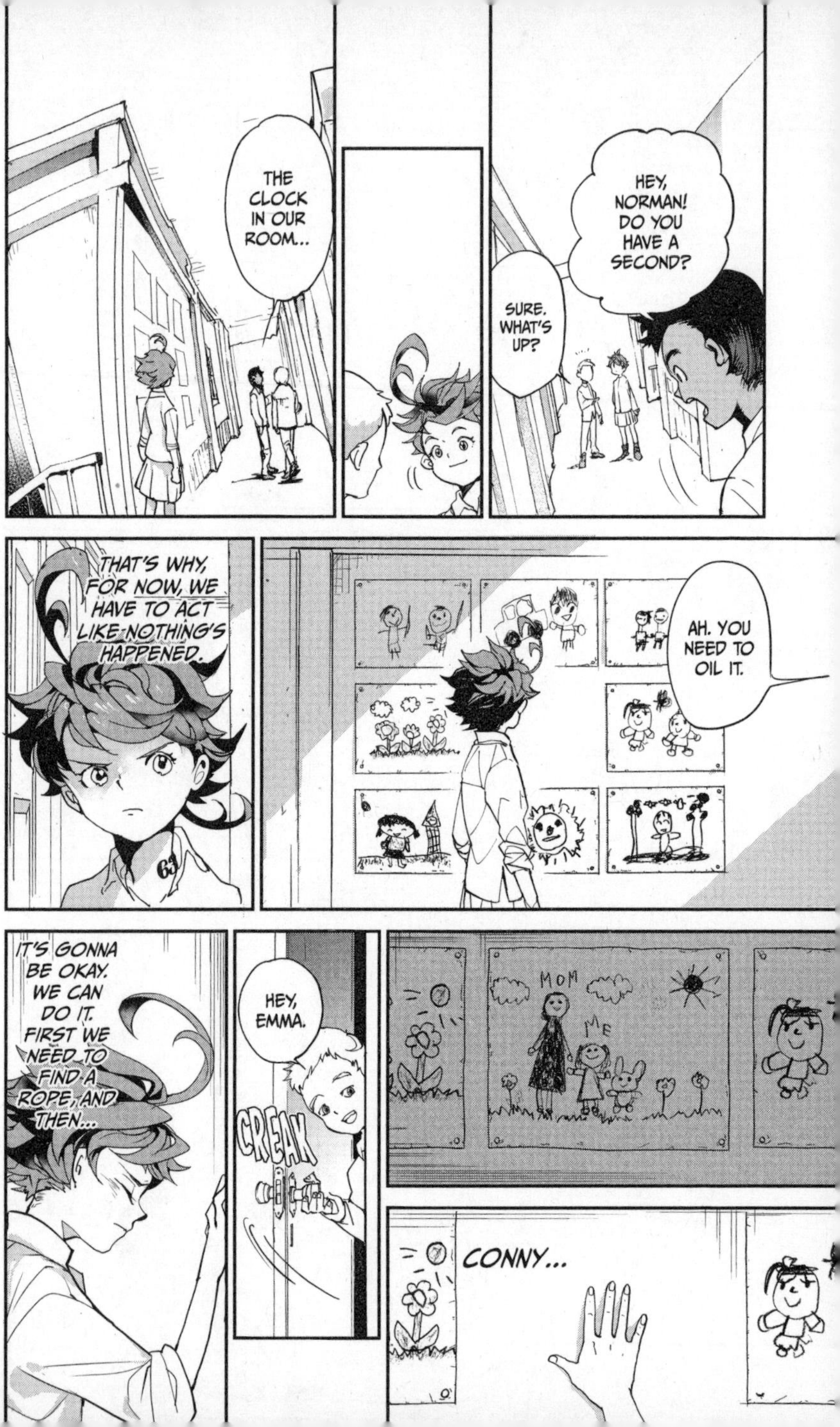
HEY, NORMAN! DO YOU HAVE A SECOND?
SURE. WHAT'S UP?
THE CLOCK IN OUR ROOM...
AH. YOU NEED TO OIL IT.
THAT'S WHY, FOR NOW, WE HAVE TO ACT LIKE NOTHING'S HAPPENED.
63
MOM
ME
CONNY...
HEY, EMMA.
CREAK
IT'S GONNA BE OKAY. WE CAN DO IT. FIRST WE NEED TO FIND A ROPE, AND THEN...

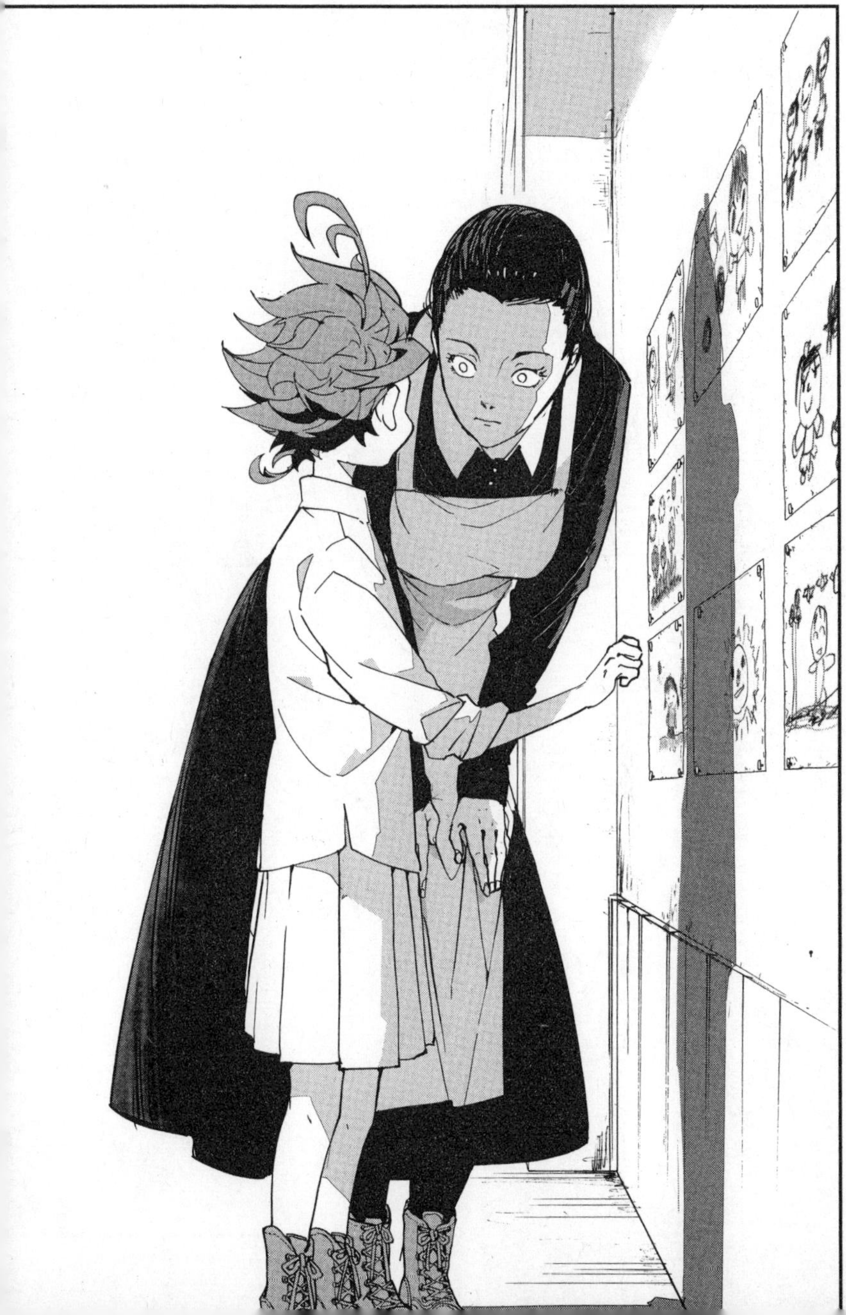

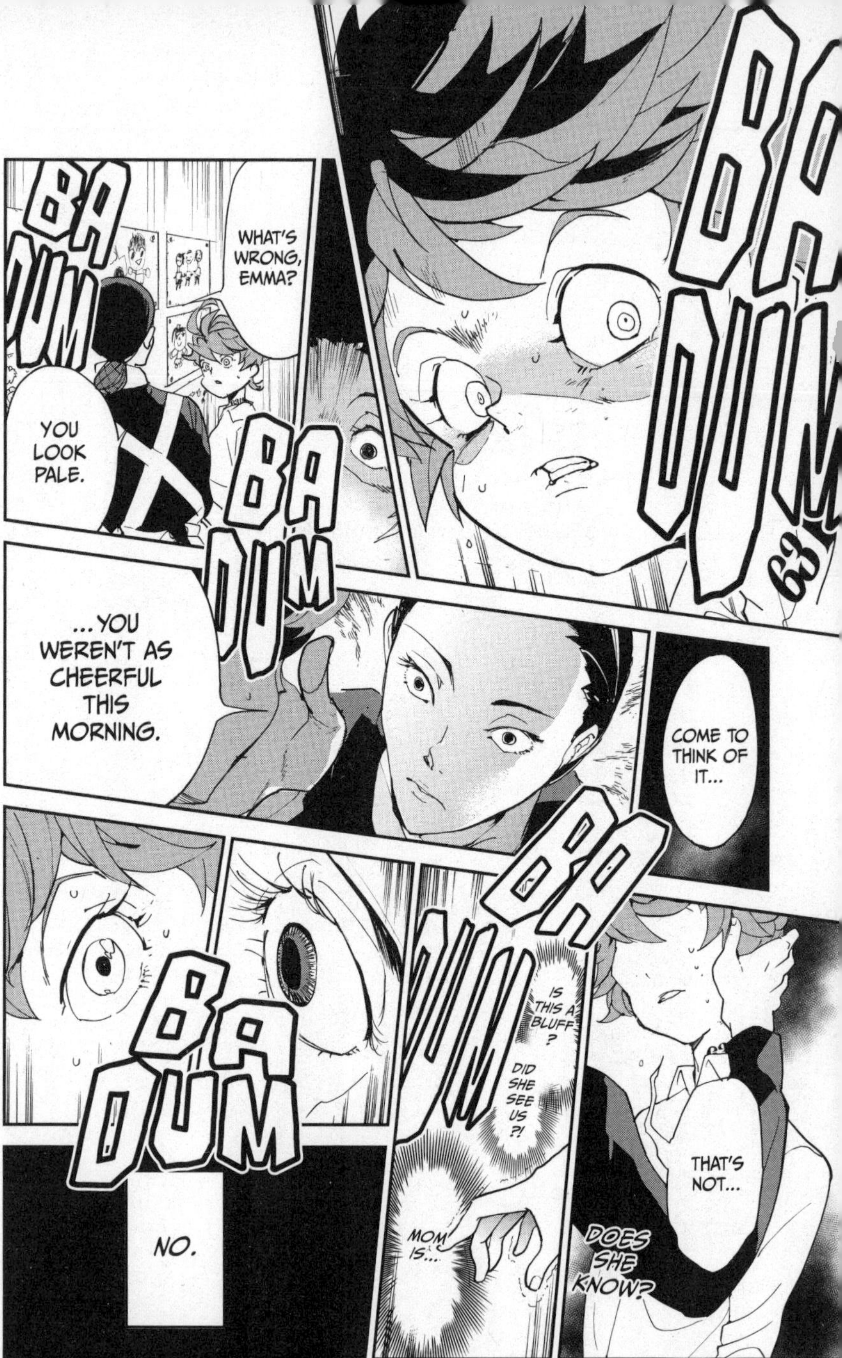
BA DUM
WHAT'S WRONG, EMMA?
YOU LOOK PALE.
BA DUM
BA DUM
COME TO THINK OF IT...
...YOU WEREN'T AS CHEERFUL THIS MORNING.
BA DUM
THAT'S NOT...
DOES SHE KNOW?
BA DUM
IS THIS A BLUFF?
DID SHE SEE US?!
MOM IS...
BA DUM
NO.

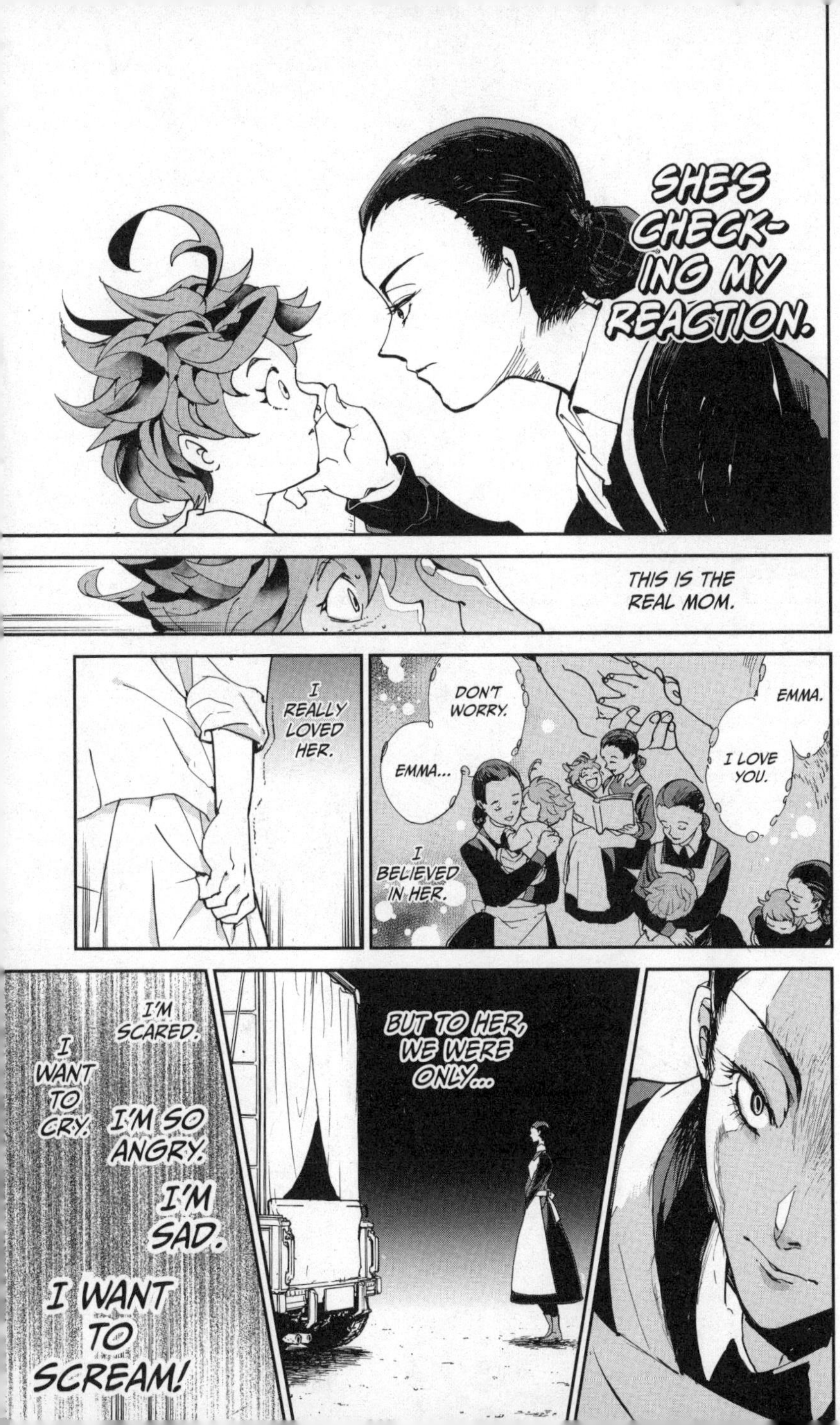
SHE'S CHECK-ING MY REACTION.
THIS IS THE REAL MOM.
EMMA.
DON'T WORRY.
I LOVE YOU.
EMMA...
I BELIEVED IN HER.
I REALLY LOVED HER.
BUT TO HER, WE WERE ONLY...
I'M SCARED.
I WANT TO CRY.
I'M SO ANGRY.
I'M SAD.
I WANT TO SCREAM!

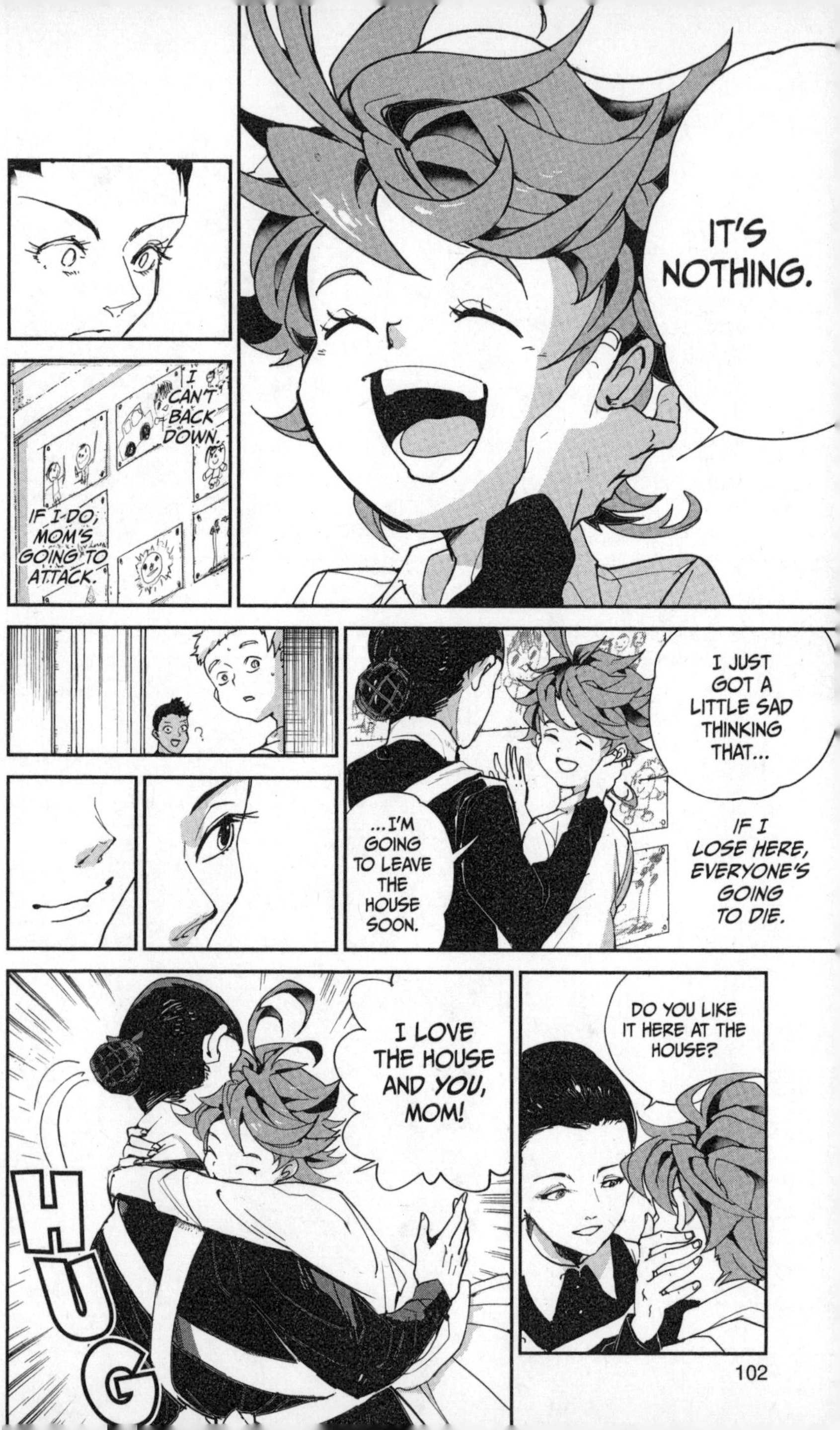
IT'S NOTHING.
I CAN'T BACK DOWN.
IF I DO, MOM'S GOING TO ATTACK.
I JUST GOT A LITTLE SAD THINKING THAT...
...I'M GOING TO LEAVE THE HOUSE SOON.
IF I LOSE HERE, EVERYONE'S GOING TO DIE.
?
DO YOU LIKE IT HERE AT THE HOUSE?
I LOVE THE HOUSE AND YOU, MOM!
HUG

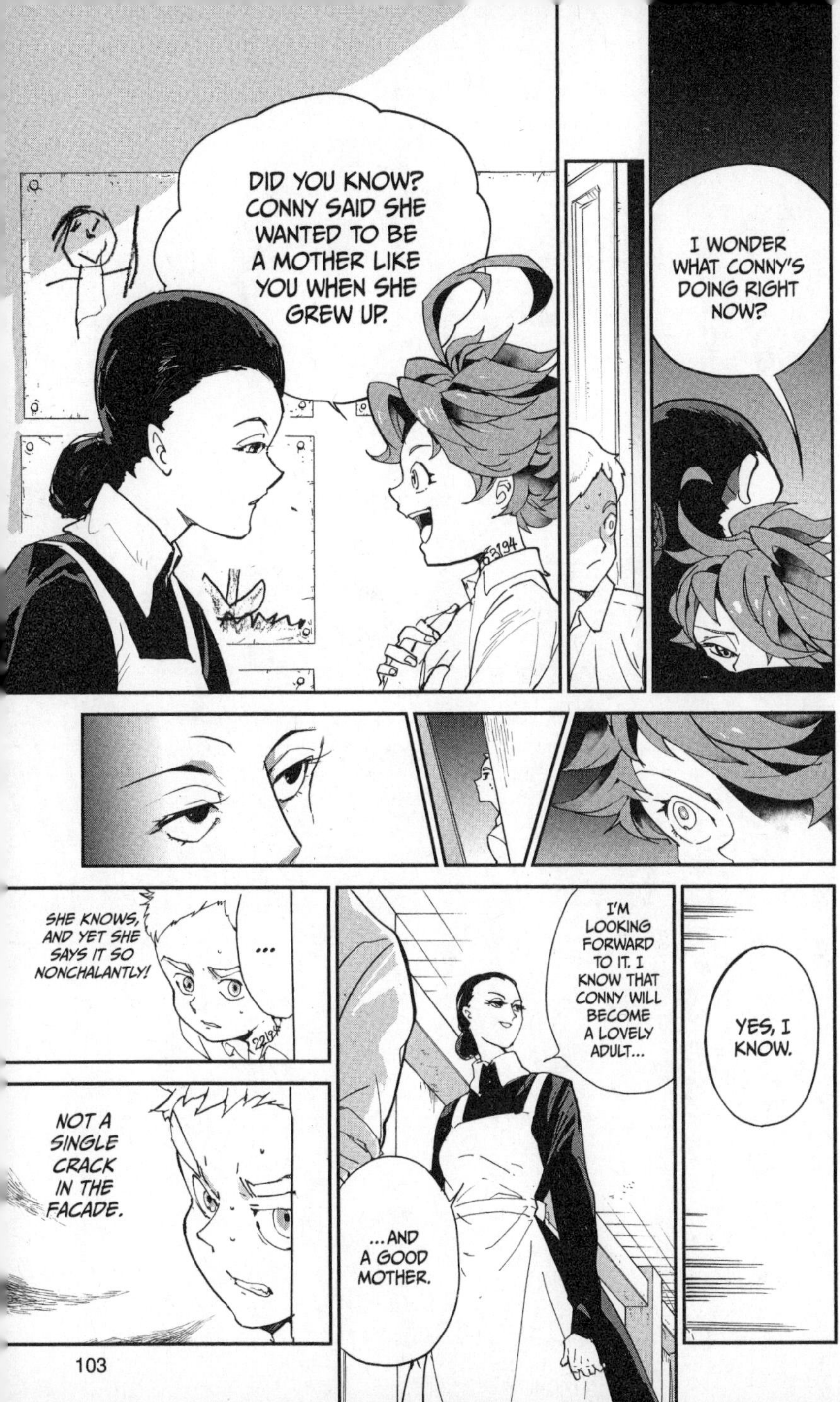
I WONDER WHAT CONNY'S DOING RIGHT NOW?
DID YOU KNOW? CONNY SAID SHE WANTED TO BE A MOTHER LIKE YOU WHEN SHE GREW UP.
YES, I KNOW.
I'M LOOKING FORWARD TO IT. I KNOW THAT CONNY WILL BECOME A LOVELY ADULT...
...AND A GOOD MOTHER.
...
SHE KNOWS, AND YET SHE SAYS IT SO NONCHALANTLY!
NOT A SINGLE CRACK IN THE FACADE.

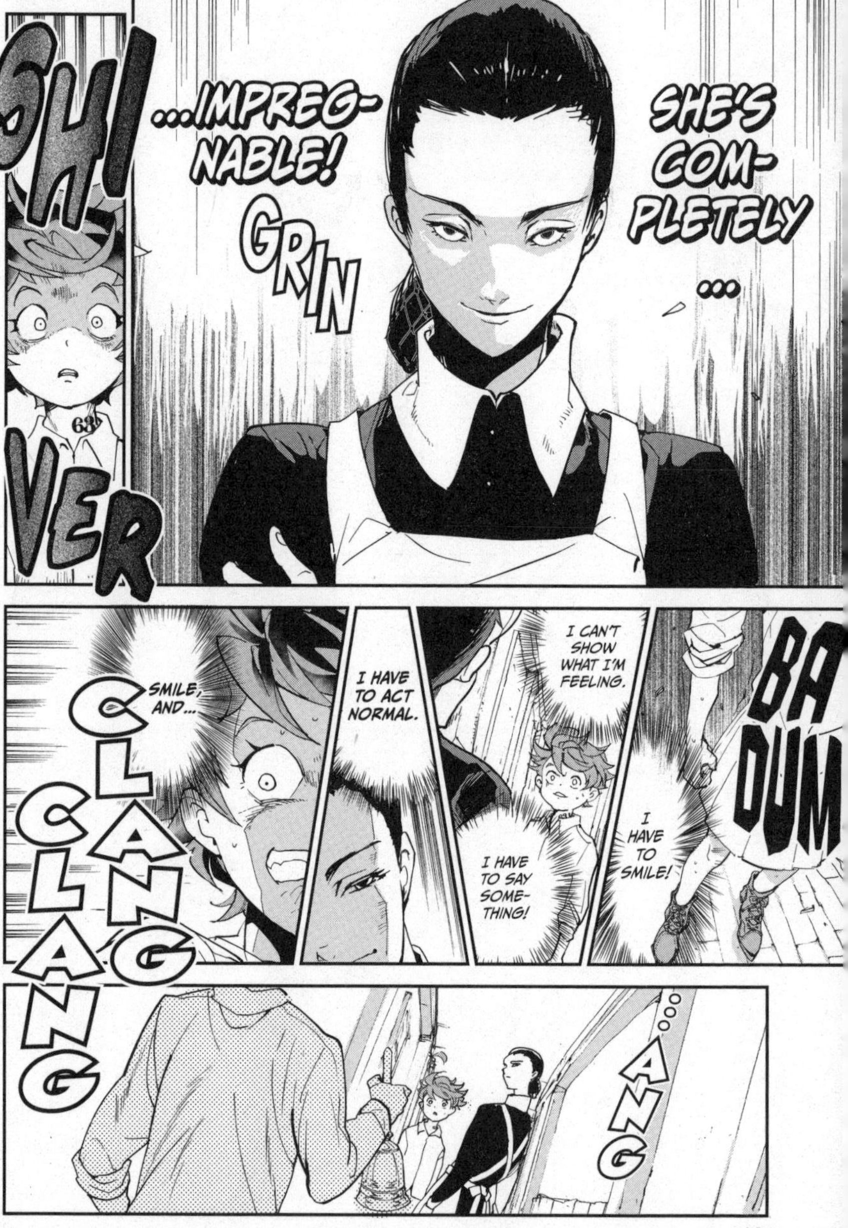
SHE'S COM-PLETELY...
...IMPREG-NABLE!
GRIN
SHIVER
BA DUM
I HAVE TO SMILE!
I CAN'T SHOW WHAT I'M FEELING.
I HAVE TO SAY SOME-THING!
I HAVE TO ACT NORMAL.
SMILE, AND...
CLANG CLANG
CLANG CLANG
...ANG

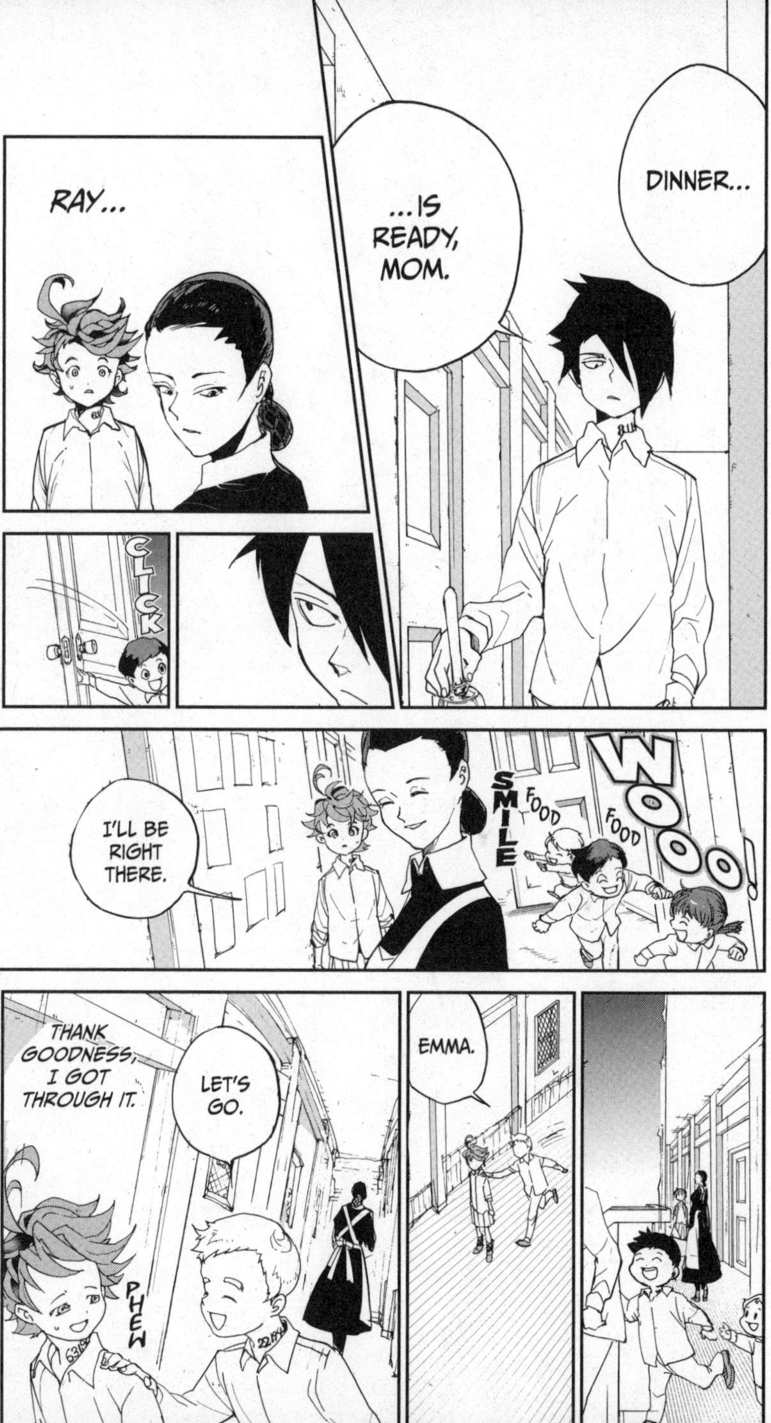
DINNER...
...IS READY, MOM.
RAY...
CLICK
WOOOO!
FOOD
FOOD
SMILE
I'LL BE RIGHT THERE.
EMMA.
LET'S GO.
THANK GOODNESS, I GOT THROUGH IT.
PHEW

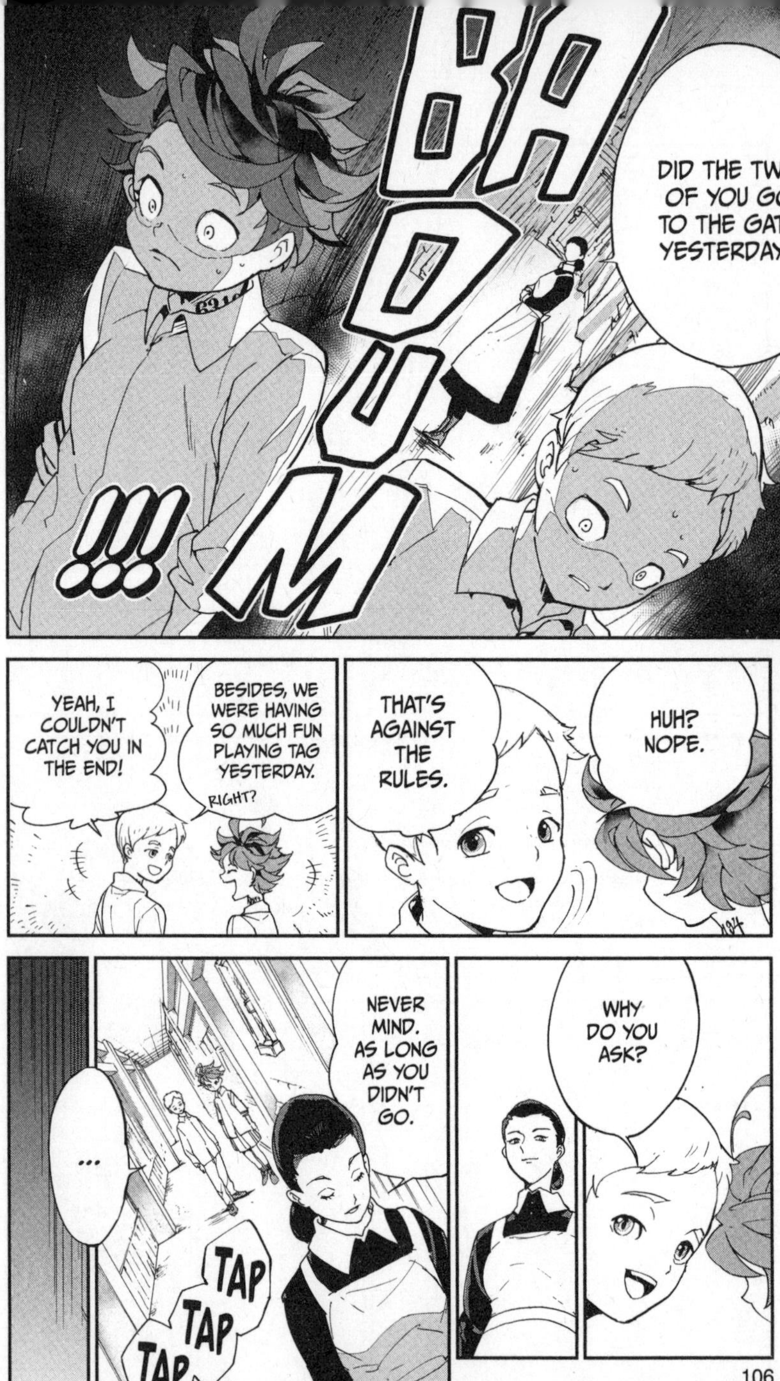
DID THE TWO OF YOU GO TO THE GATE YESTERDAY?
BADUM
!!!
HUH? NOPE.
THAT'S AGAINST THE RULES.
BESIDES, WE WERE HAVING SO MUCH FUN PLAYING TAG YESTERDAY.
RIGHT?
YEAH, I COULDN'T CATCH YOU IN THE END!
WHY DO YOU ASK?
NEVER MIND. AS LONG AS YOU DIDN'T GO.
TAP
TAP
TAP
...

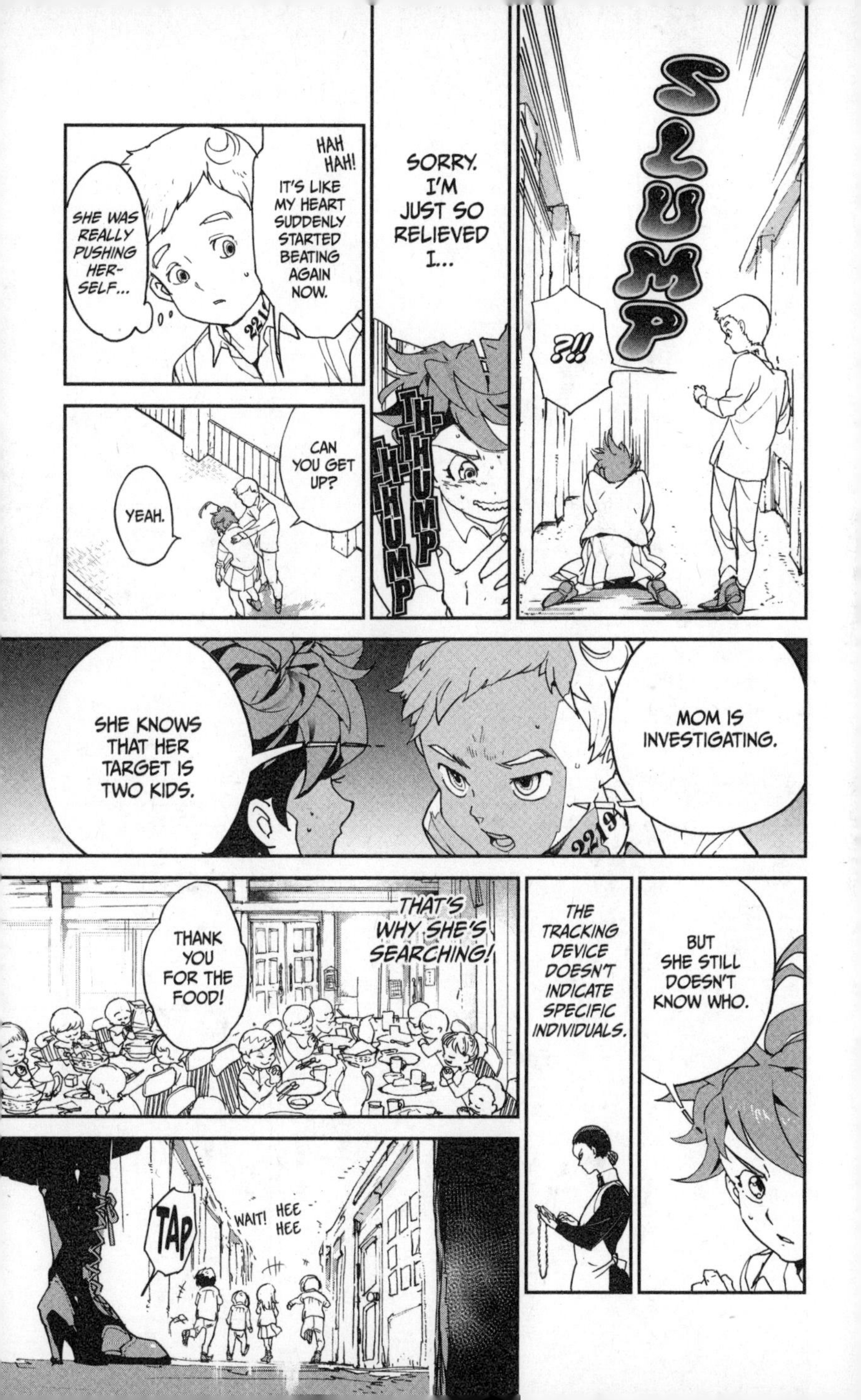
SLUMP
?!!
SORRY. I'M JUST SO RELIEVED I...
TH-THUMP
TH-THUMP
HAH HAH!
IT'S LIKE MY HEART SUDDENLY STARTED BEATING AGAIN NOW.
SHE WAS REALLY PUSHING HER-SELF...
CAN YOU GET UP?
YEAH.
MOM IS INVESTIGATING.
SHE KNOWS THAT HER TARGET IS TWO KIDS.
BUT SHE STILL DOESN'T KNOW WHO.
THE TRACKING DEVICE DOESN'T INDICATE SPECIFIC INDIVIDUALS.
THAT'S WHY SHE'S SEARCHING!
THANK YOU FOR THE FOOD!
WAIT! HEE HEE
TAP

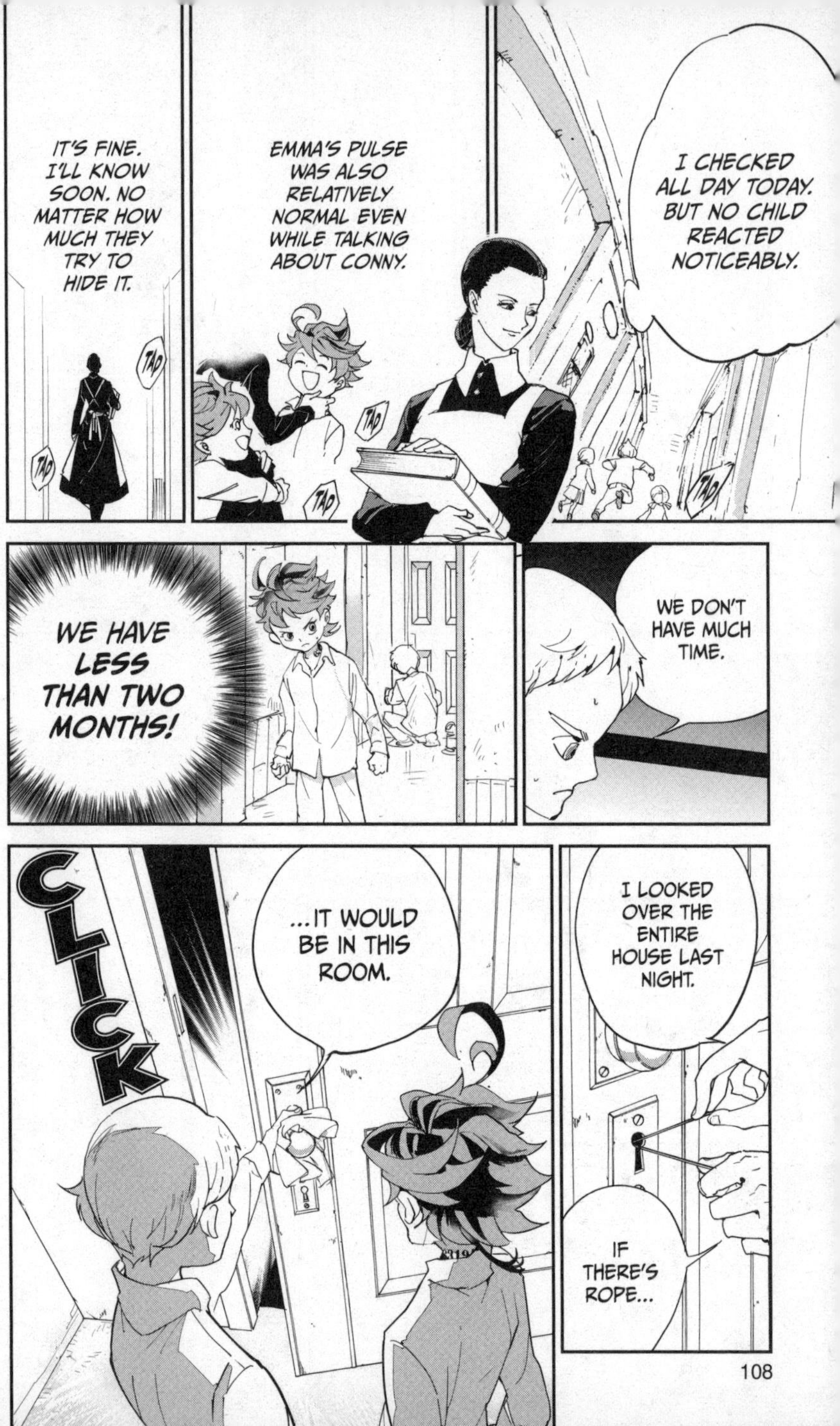
I CHECKED ALL DAY TODAY. BUT NO CHILD REACTED NOTICEABLY.
TAD
EMMA'S PULSE WAS ALSO RELATIVELY NORMAL EVEN WHILE TALKING ABOUT CONNY.
TAD
TAD
IT'S FINE. I'LL KNOW SOON. NO MATTER HOW MUCH THEY TRY TO HIDE IT.
TAD
TAD
WE DON'T HAVE MUCH TIME.
WE HAVE LESS THAN TWO MONTHS!
I LOOKED OVER THE ENTIRE HOUSE LAST NIGHT.
IF THERE'S ROPE...
...IT WOULD BE IN THIS ROOM.
CLICK

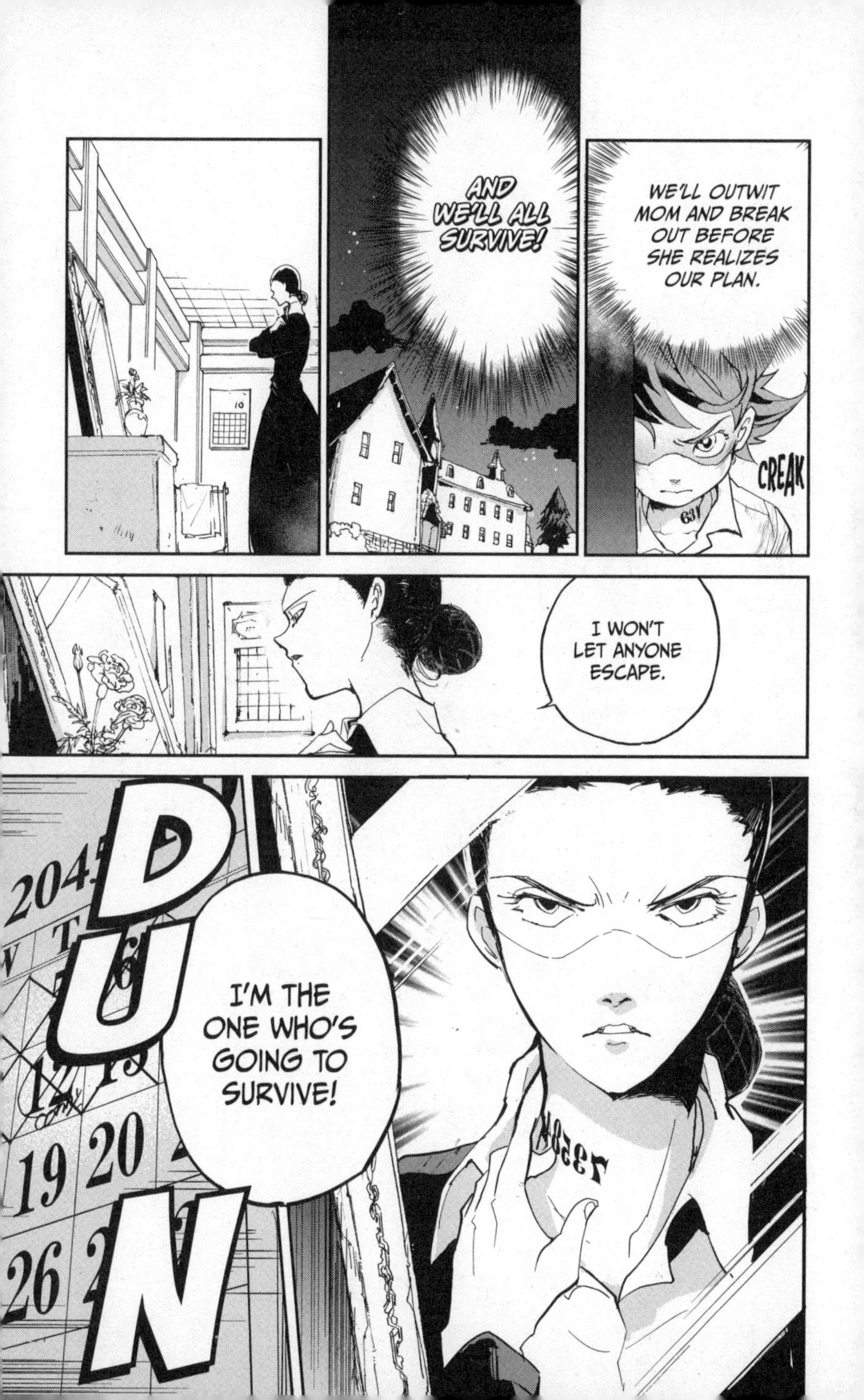
WE'LL OUTWIT MOM AND BREAK OUT BEFORE SHE REALIZES OUR PLAN.
CREAK
AND WE'LL ALL SURVIVE!
I WON'T LET ANYONE ESCAPE.
I'M THE ONE WHO'S GOING TO SURVIVE!
DUN

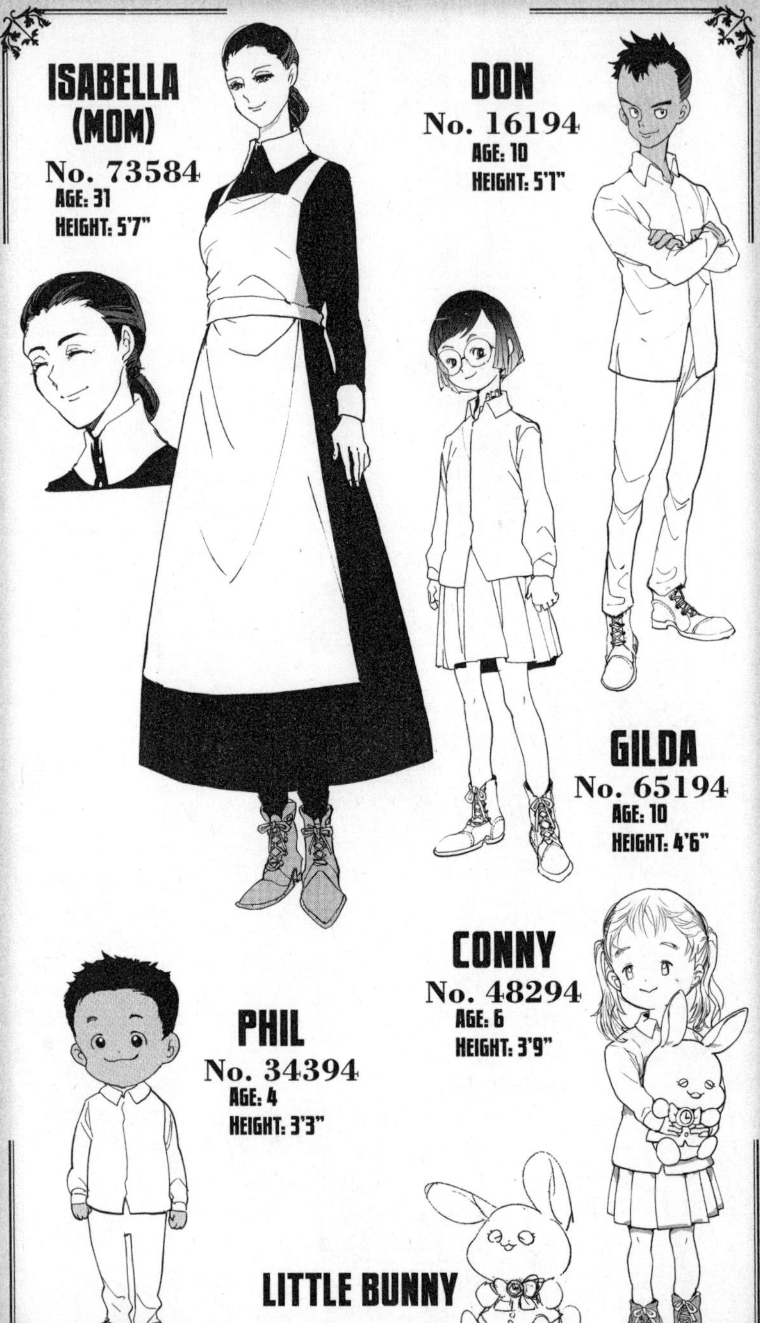
ISABELLA (MOM)
No. 73584
AGE: 31
HEIGHT: 5'7"
DON
No. 16194
AGE: 10
HEIGHT: 5'1"
GILDA
No. 65194
AGE: 10
HEIGHT: 4'6"
CONNY
No. 48294
AGE: 6
HEIGHT: 3'9"
PHIL
No. 34394
AGE: 4
HEIGHT: 3'3"
LITTLE BUNNY

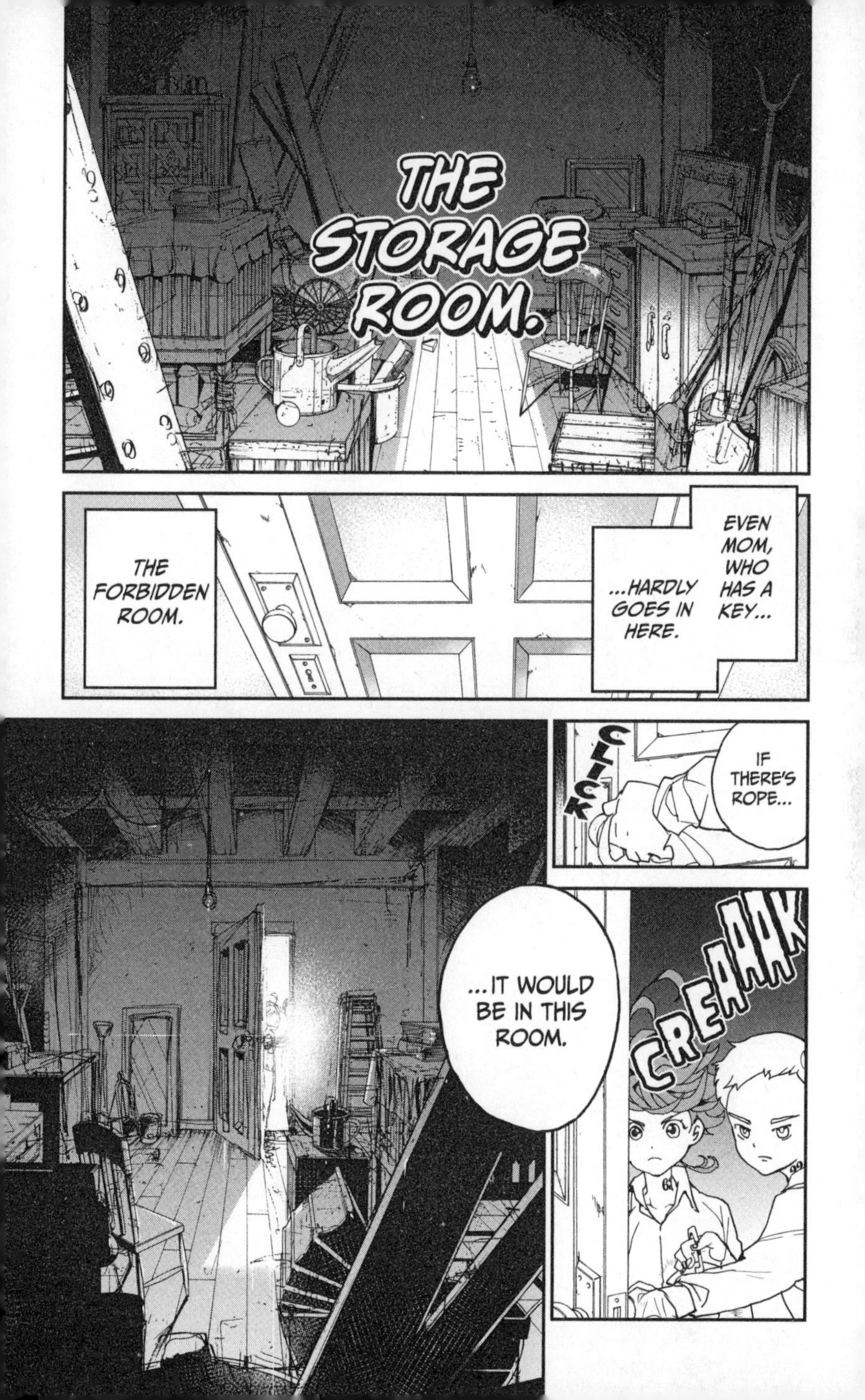
THE STORAGE ROOM.
EVEN MOM, WHO HAS A KEY...
...HARDLY GOES IN HERE.
THE FORBIDDEN ROOM.
CLICK
IF THERE'S ROPE...
CREAAAK
...IT WOULD BE IN THIS ROOM.

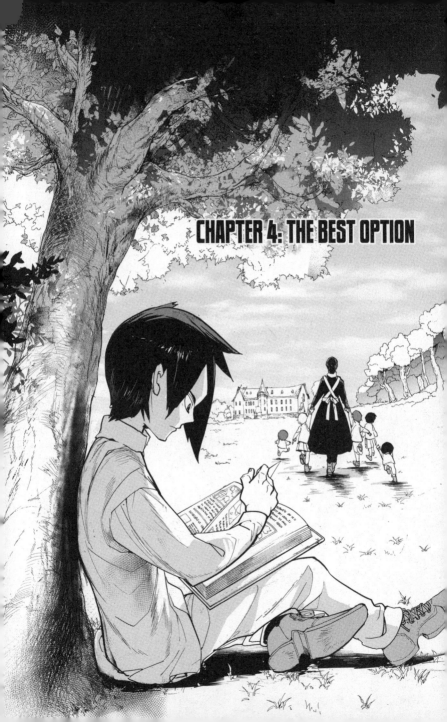

CHAPTER 4: THE BEST OPTION

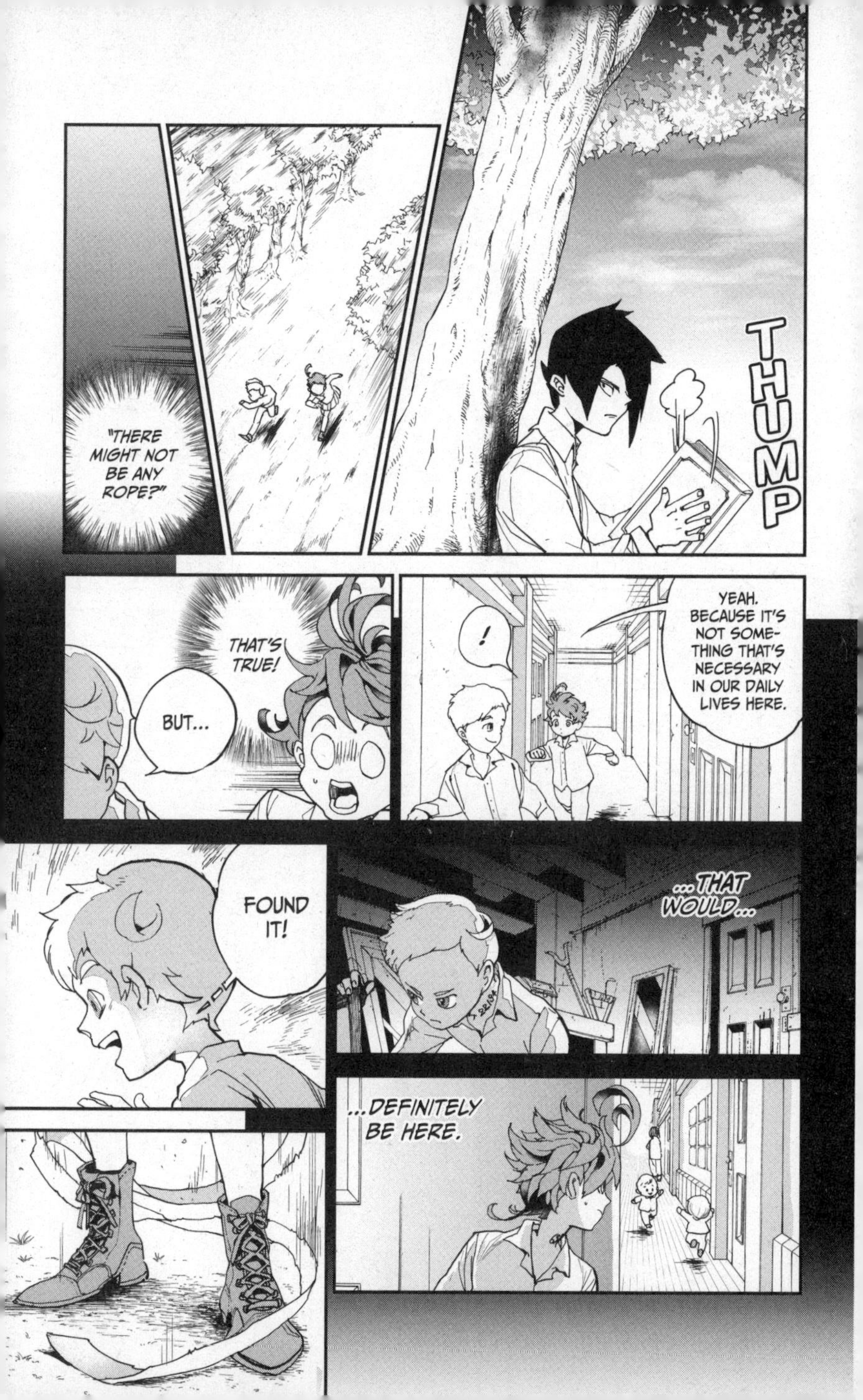
THUMP
"THERE MIGHT NOT BE ANY ROPE?"
YEAH. BECAUSE IT'S NOT SOME-THING THAT'S NECESSARY IN OUR DAILY LIVES HERE.
!
THAT'S TRUE!
BUT...
...THAT WOULD...
...DEFINITELY BE HERE.
FOUND IT!

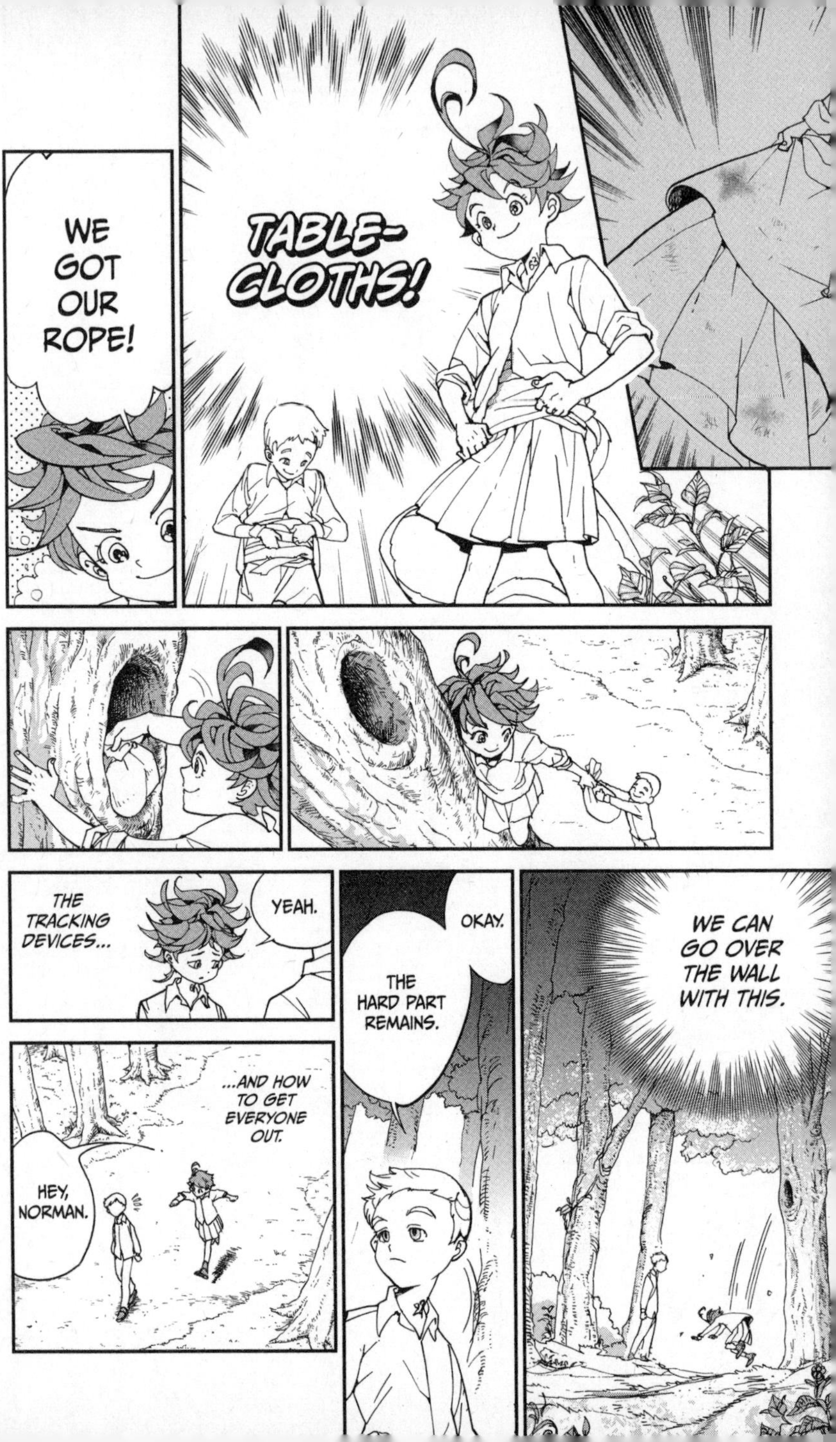
TABLE-CLOTHS!
WE GOT OUR ROPE!
WE CAN GO OVER THE WALL WITH THIS.
OKAY.
THE HARD PART REMAINS.
YEAH.
THE TRACKING DEVICES...
...AND HOW TO GET EVERYONE OUT.
HEY, NORMAN.

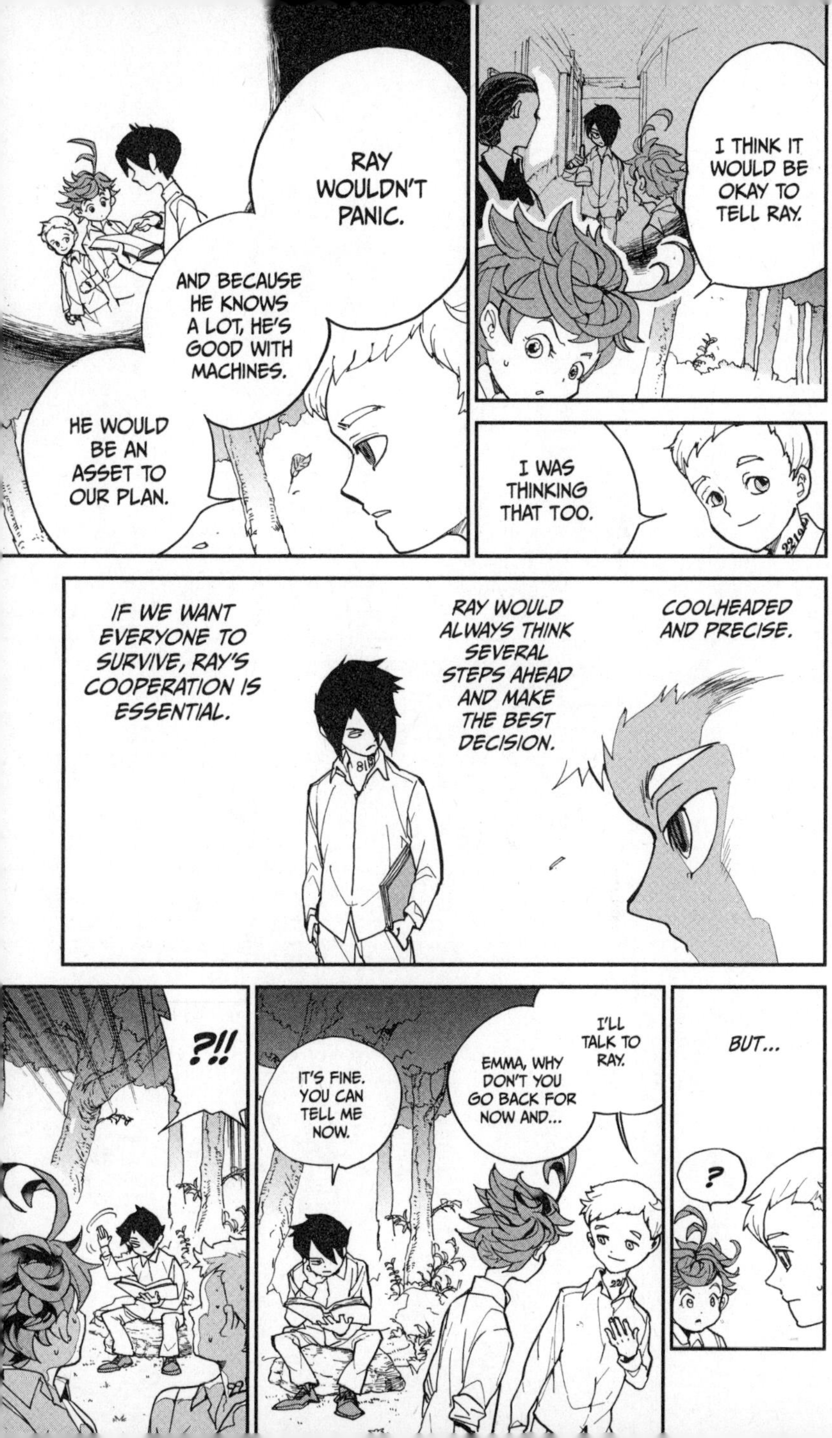
I THINK IT WOULD BE OKAY TO TELL RAY.
I WAS THINKING THAT TOO.
RAY WOULDN'T PANIC.
AND BECAUSE HE KNOWS A LOT, HE'S GOOD WITH MACHINES.
HE WOULD BE AN ASSET TO OUR PLAN.
COOLHEADED AND PRECISE.
RAY WOULD ALWAYS THINK SEVERAL STEPS AHEAD AND MAKE THE BEST DECISION.
IF WE WANT EVERYONE TO SURVIVE, RAY'S COOPERATION IS ESSENTIAL.
BUT...
?
I'LL TALK TO RAY.
EMMA, WHY DON'T YOU GO BACK FOR NOW AND...
IT'S FINE. YOU CAN TELL ME NOW.
?!!

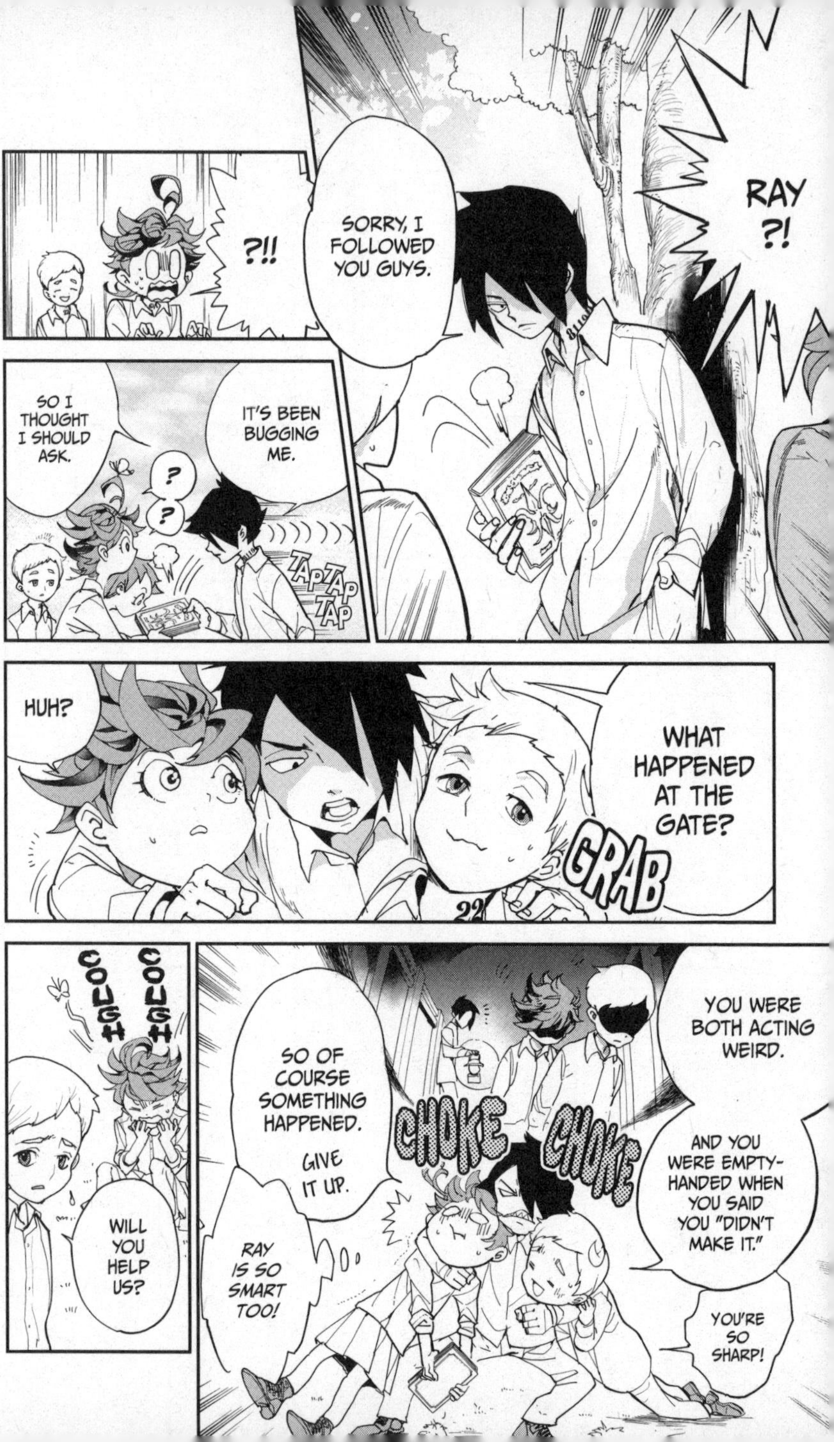
RAY ?!
SORRY, I FOLLOWED YOU GUYS.
?!!
IT'S BEEN BUGGING ME.
SO I THOUGHT I SHOULD ASK.
?
?
TAP TAP TAP
WHAT HAPPENED AT THE GATE?
GRAB
HUH?
YOU WERE BOTH ACTING WEIRD.
AND YOU WERE EMPTY-HANDED WHEN YOU SAID YOU "DIDN'T MAKE IT."
SO OF COURSE SOMETHING HAPPENED.
GIVE IT UP.
CHOKE
CHOKE
YOU'RE SO SHARP!
RAY IS SO SMART TOO!
COUGH
COUGH
WILL YOU HELP US?

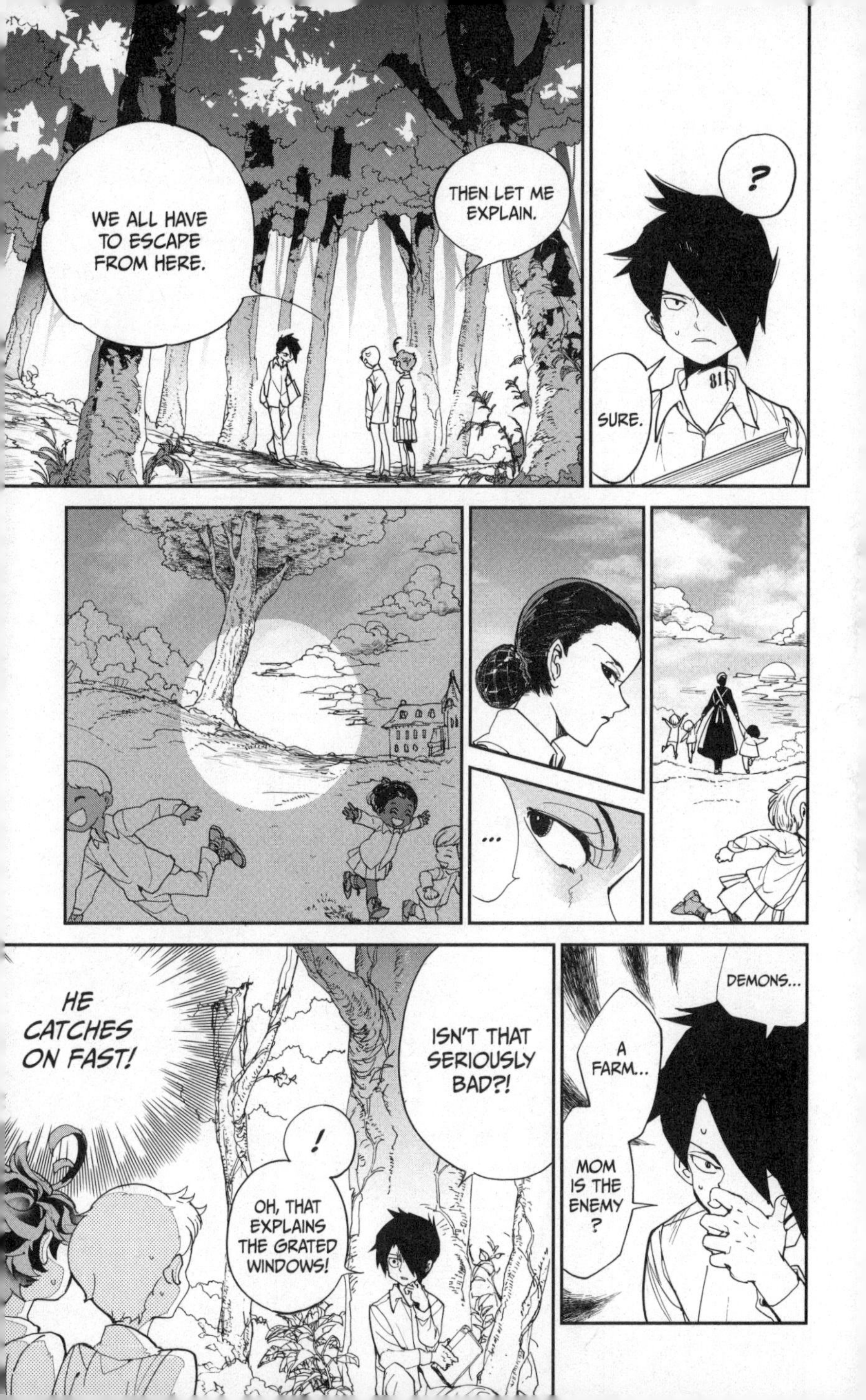
?
SURE.
THEN LET ME EXPLAIN.
WE ALL HAVE TO ESCAPE FROM HERE.
...
DEMONS...
A FARM...
MOM IS THE ENEMY?
ISN'T THAT SERIOUSLY BAD?!
!
OH, THAT EXPLAINS THE GRATED WINDOWS!
HE CATCHES ON FAST!

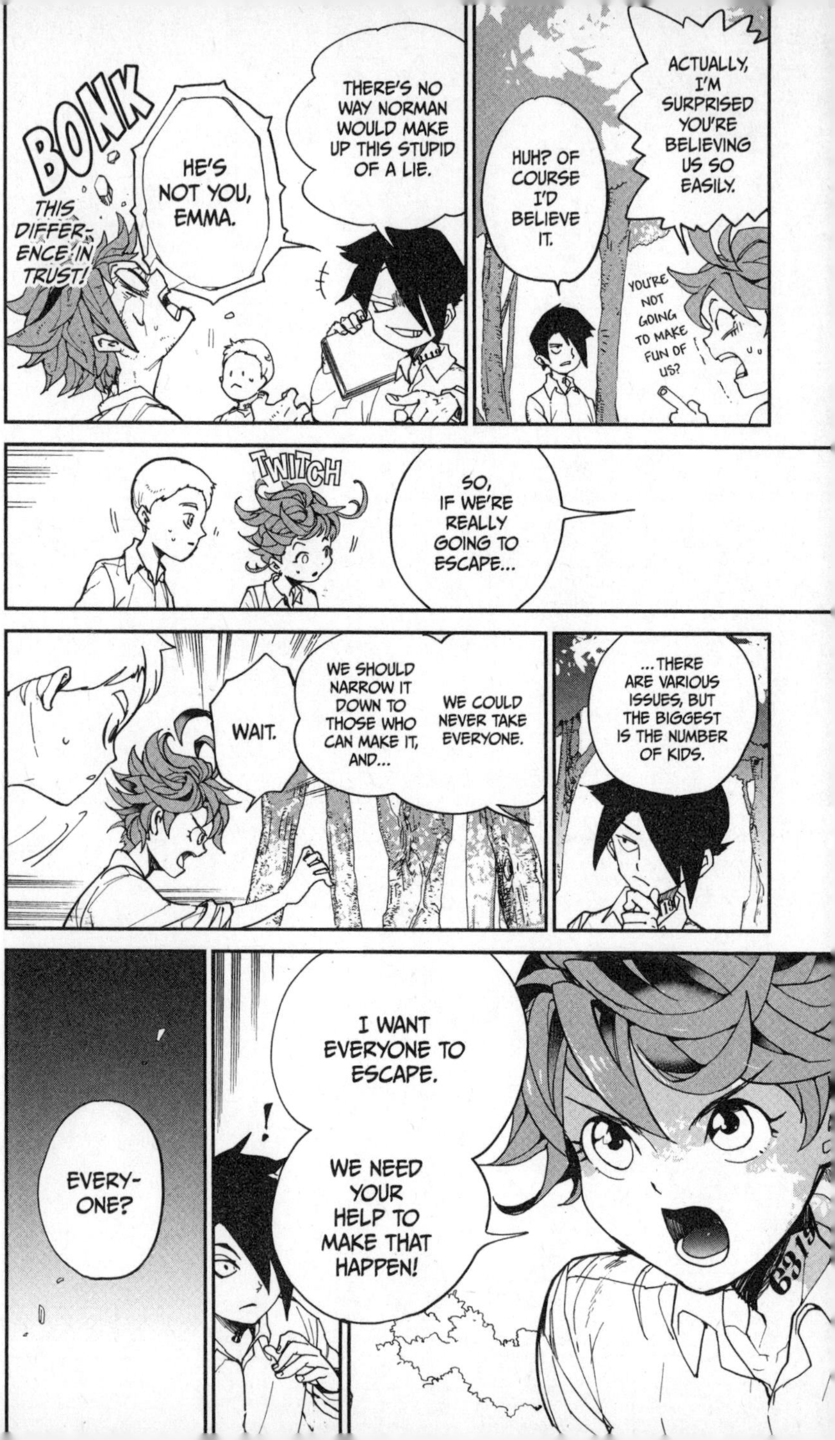
ACTUALLY, I'M SURPRISED YOU'RE BELIEVING US SO EASILY.
YOU'RE NOT GOING TO MAKE FUN OF US?
HUH? OF COURSE I'D BELIEVE IT.
THERE'S NO WAY NORMAN WOULD MAKE UP THIS STUPID OF A LIE.
BONK
HE'S NOT YOU, EMMA.
THIS DIFFER-ENCE IN TRUST!
SO, IF WE'RE REALLY GOING TO ESCAPE...
TWITCH
...THERE ARE VARIOUS ISSUES, BUT THE BIGGEST IS THE NUMBER OF KIDS.
WE COULD NEVER TAKE EVERYONE.
WE SHOULD NARROW IT DOWN TO THOSE WHO CAN MAKE IT, AND...
WAIT.
I WANT EVERYONE TO ESCAPE.
WE NEED YOUR HELP TO MAKE THAT HAPPEN!
!
EVERY-ONE?

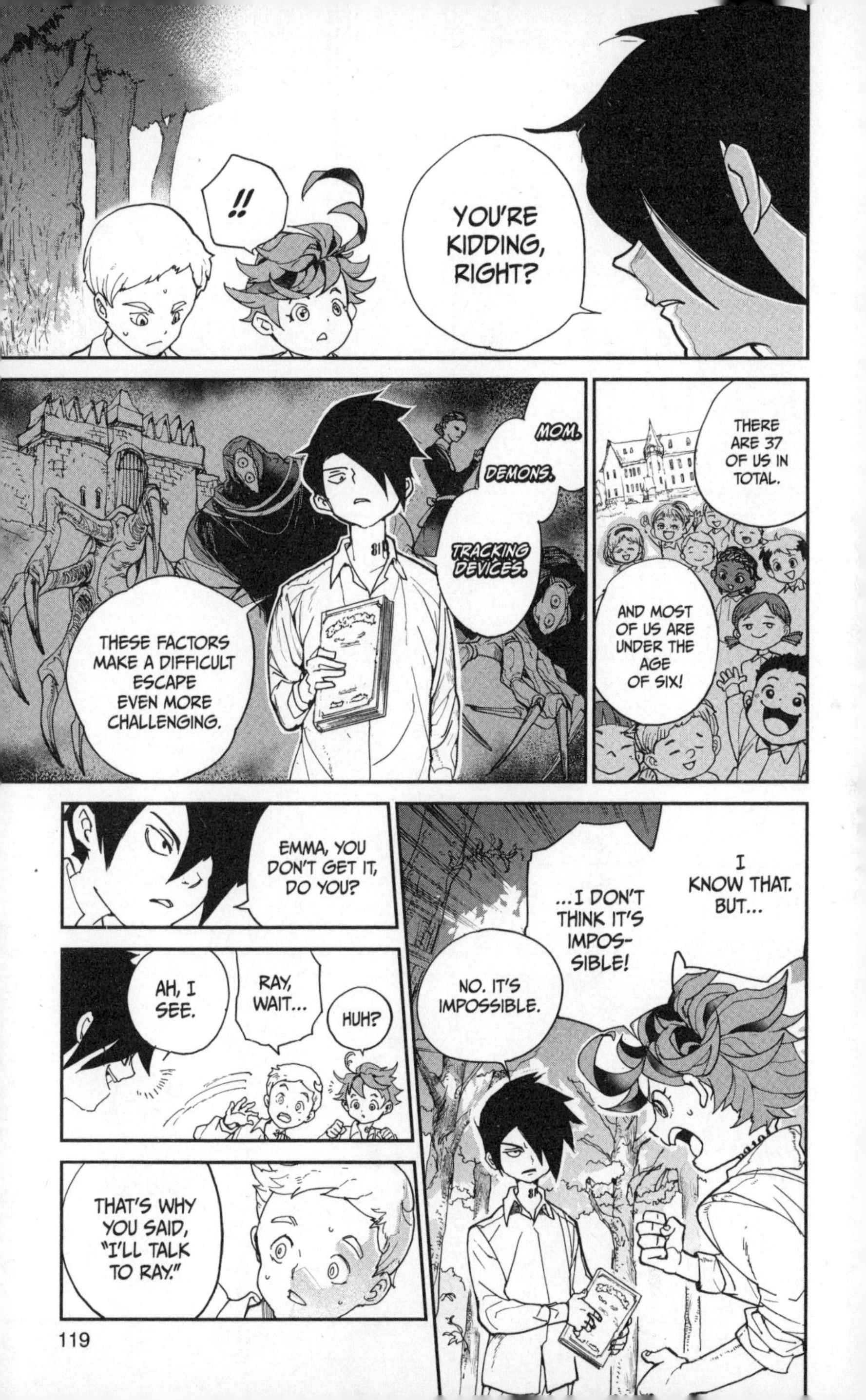
YOU'RE KIDDING, RIGHT?
!!
THERE ARE 37 OF US IN TOTAL.
AND MOST OF US ARE UNDER THE AGE OF SIX!
MOM.
DEMONS.
TRACKING DEVICES.
THESE FACTORS MAKE A DIFFICULT ESCAPE EVEN MORE CHALLENGING.
I KNOW THAT. BUT...
...I DON'T THINK IT'S IMPOS-SIBLE!
NO. IT'S IMPOSSIBLE.
EMMA, YOU DON'T GET IT, DO YOU?
RAY, WAIT...
HUH?
AH, I SEE.
THAT'S WHY YOU SAID, "I'LL TALK TO RAY."

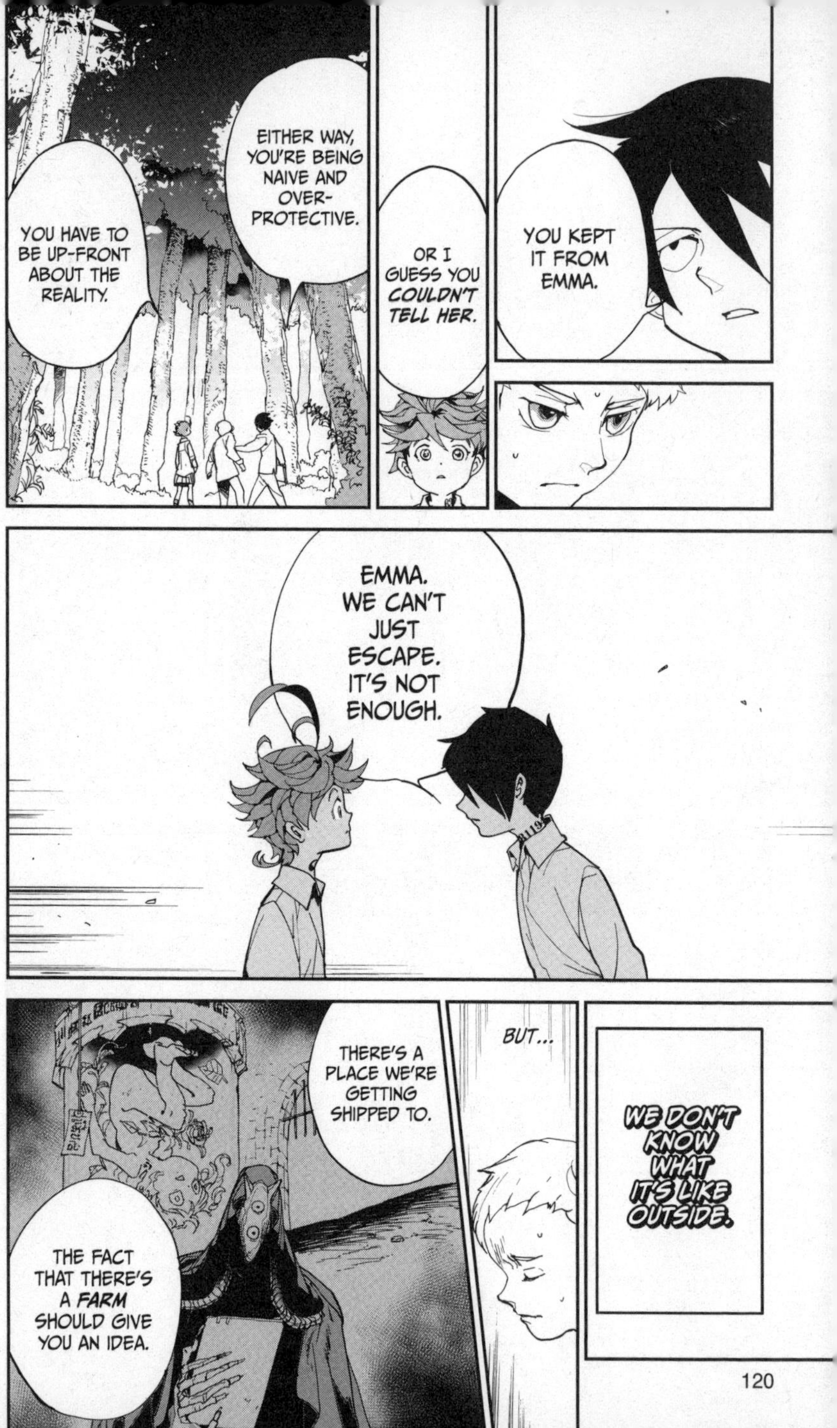
YOU KEPT IT FROM EMMA.
OR I GUESS YOU *COULDN'T TELL HER.*
EITHER WAY, YOU'RE BEING NAIVE AND OVER-PROTECTIVE.
YOU HAVE TO BE UP-FRONT ABOUT THE REALITY.
EMMA. WE CAN'T JUST ESCAPE. IT'S NOT ENOUGH.
WE DON'T KNOW WHAT IT'S LIKE OUTSIDE.
BUT...
THERE'S A PLACE WE'RE GETTING SHIPPED TO.
THE FACT THAT THERE'S A *FARM* SHOULD GIVE YOU AN IDEA.

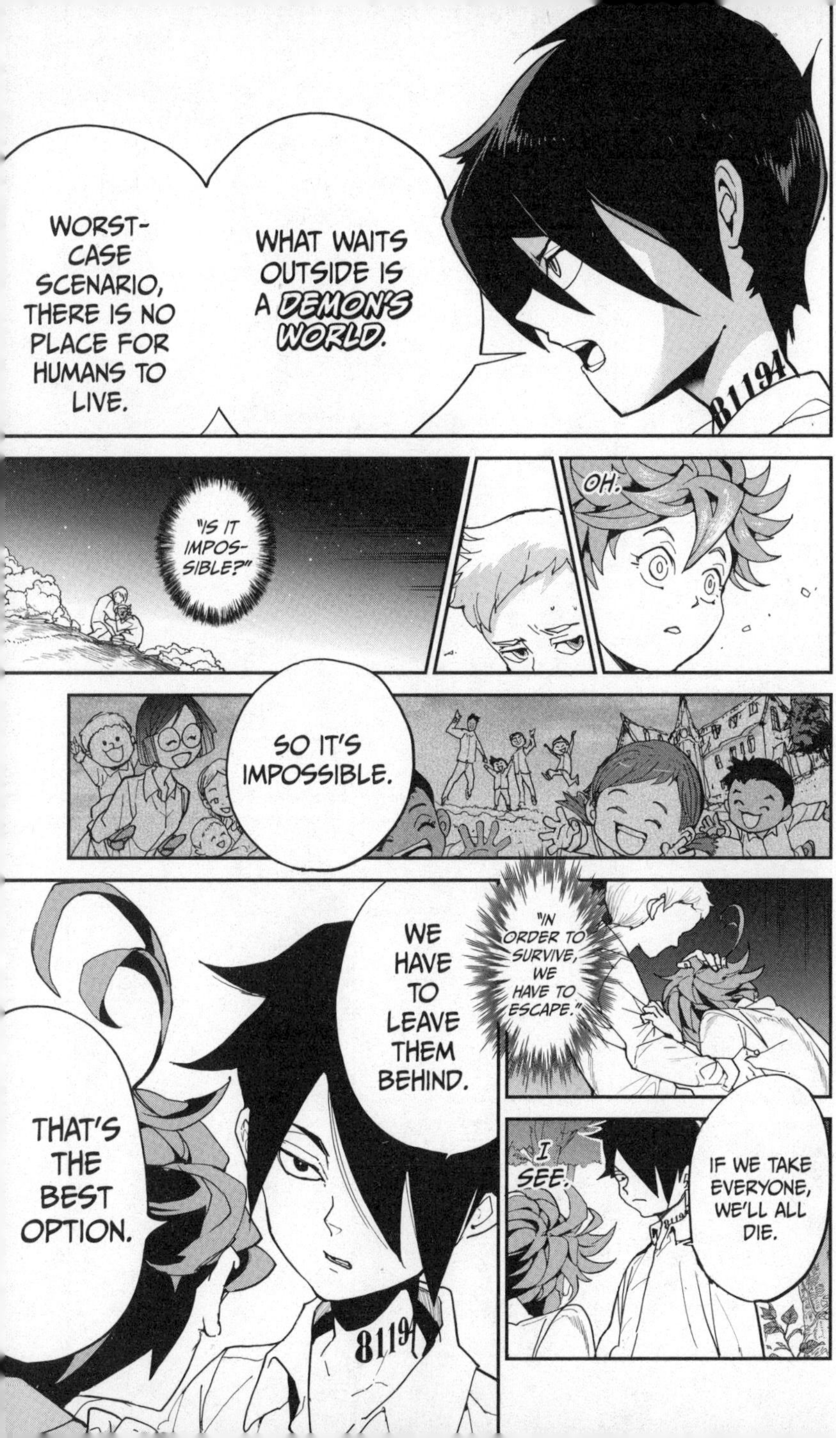
WHAT WAITS OUTSIDE IS A DEMON'S WORLD.
WORST-CASE SCENARIO, THERE IS NO PLACE FOR HUMANS TO LIVE.
OH.
"IS IT IMPOSSIBLE?"
SO IT'S IMPOSSIBLE.
"IN ORDER TO SURVIVE, WE HAVE TO ESCAPE."
IF WE TAKE EVERYONE, WE'LL ALL DIE.
I SEE.
WE HAVE TO LEAVE THEM BEHIND.
THAT'S THE BEST OPTION.

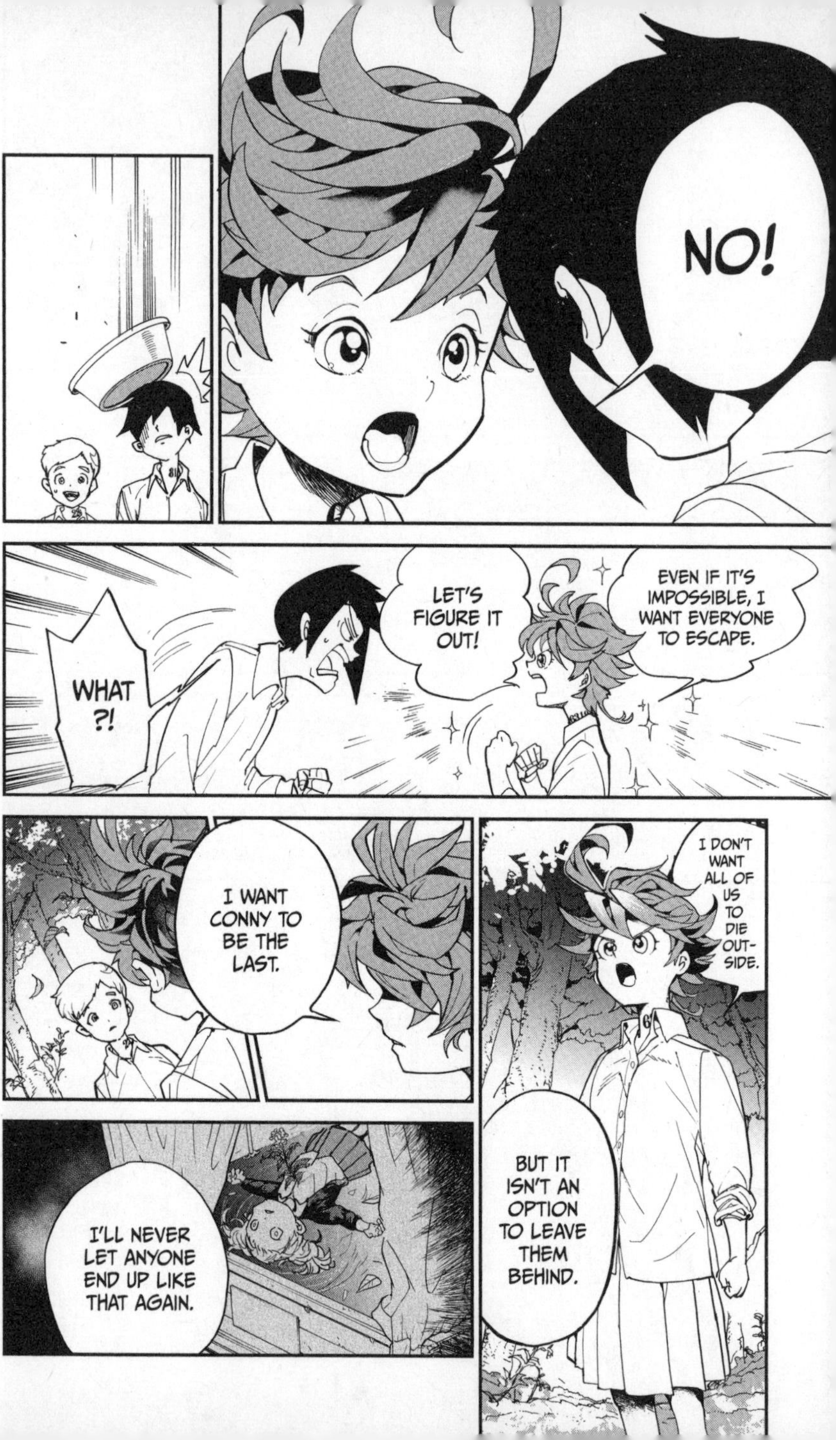
NO!
EVEN IF IT'S IMPOSSIBLE, I WANT EVERYONE TO ESCAPE.
LET'S FIGURE IT OUT!
WHAT ?!
I DON'T WANT ALL OF US TO DIE OUT-SIDE.
BUT IT ISN'T AN OPTION TO LEAVE THEM BEHIND.
I WANT CONNY TO BE THE LAST.
I'LL NEVER LET ANYONE END UP LIKE THAT AGAIN.

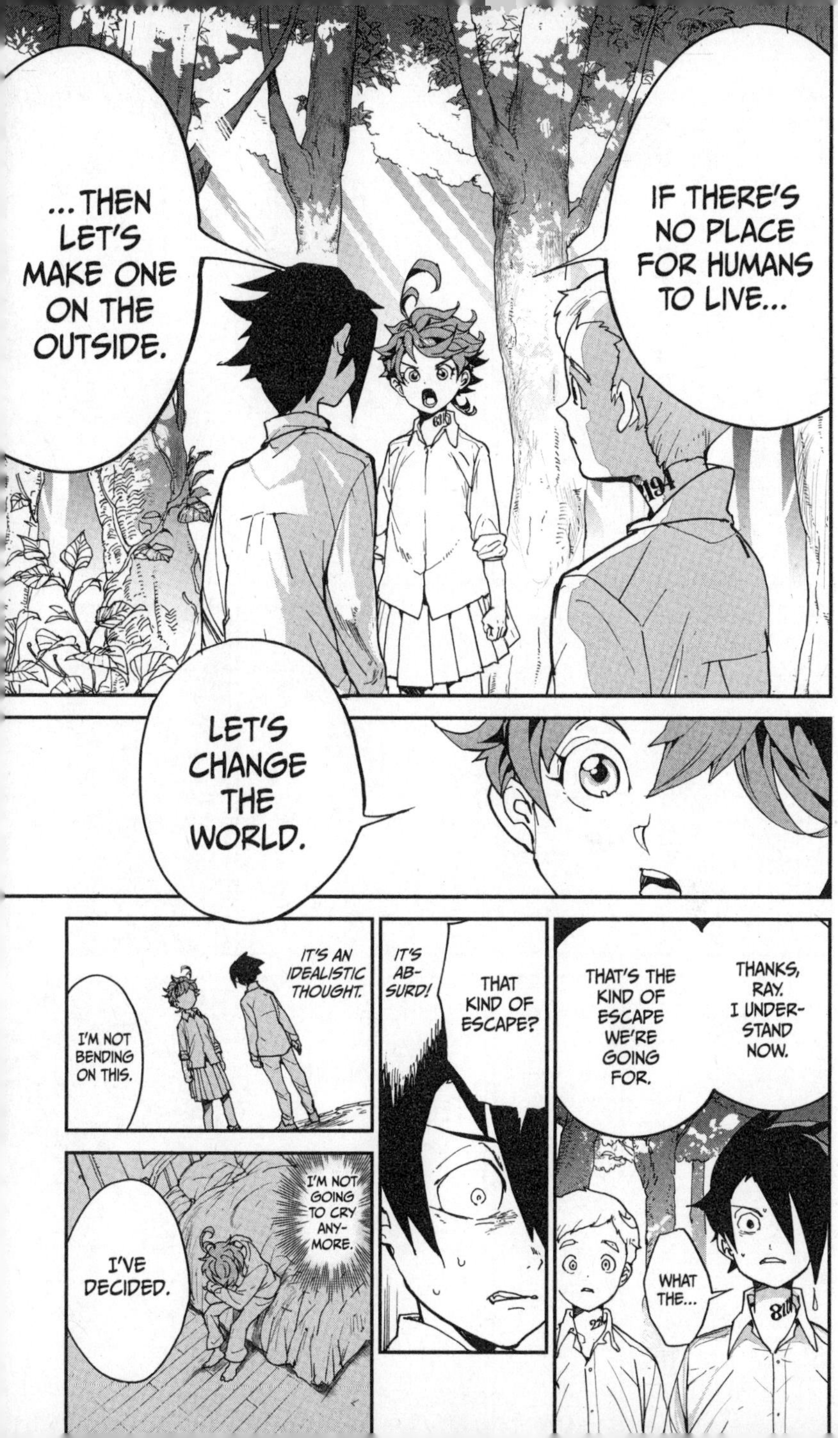
IF THERE'S NO PLACE FOR HUMANS TO LIVE...
...THEN LET'S MAKE ONE ON THE OUTSIDE.
LET'S CHANGE THE WORLD.
THANKS, RAY. I UNDERSTAND NOW.
THAT'S THE KIND OF ESCAPE WE'RE GOING FOR.
WHAT THE...
THAT KIND OF ESCAPE?
IT'S ABSURD!
IT'S AN IDEALISTIC THOUGHT.
I'M NOT BENDING ON THIS.
I'M NOT GOING TO CRY ANYMORE.
I'VE DECIDED.

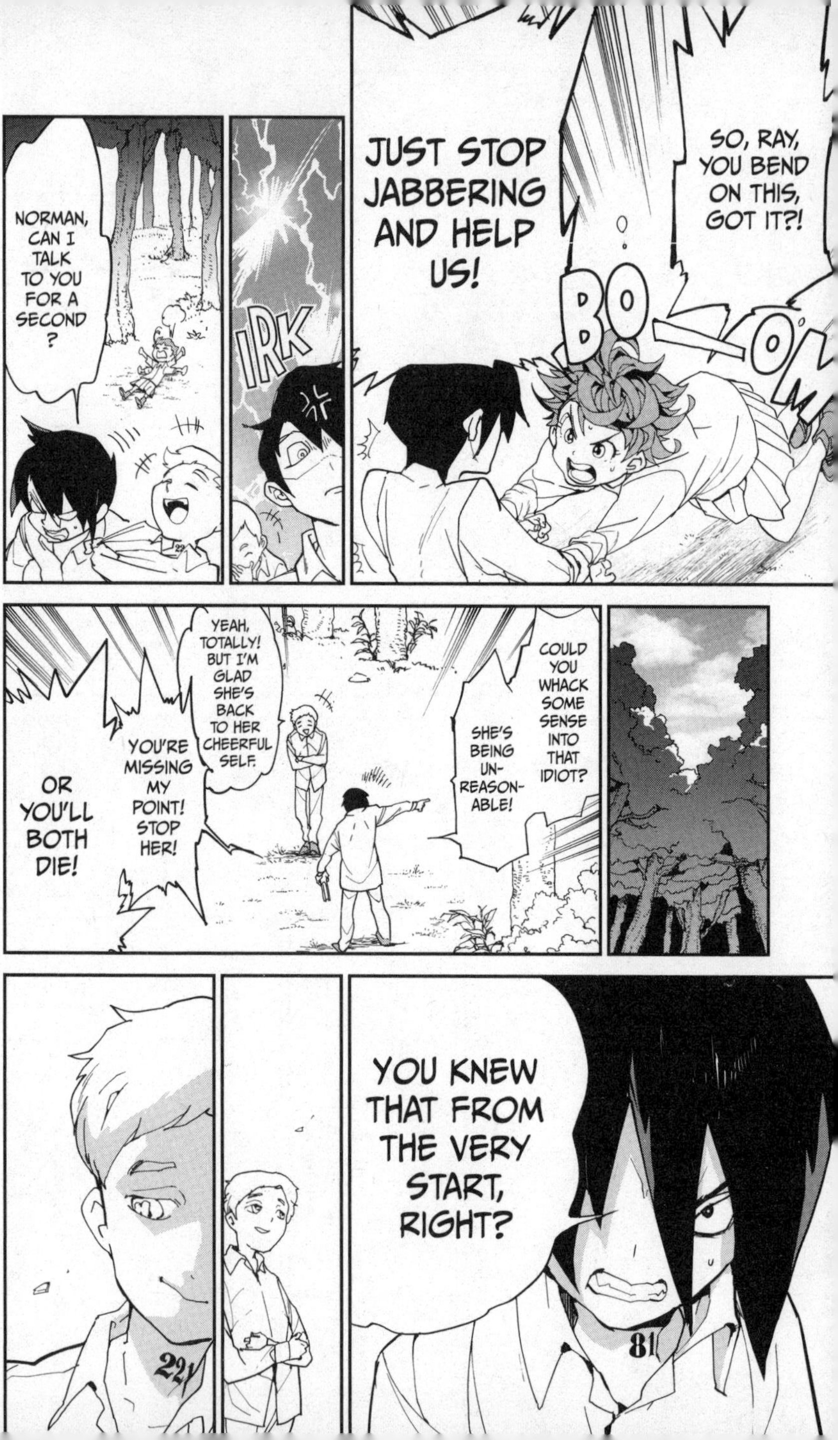
SO, RAY, YOU BEND ON THIS, GOT IT?!
BO-OM
JUST STOP JABBERING AND HELP US!
IRK
NORMAN, CAN I TALK TO YOU FOR A SECOND?
COULD YOU WHACK SOME SENSE INTO THAT IDIOT?
SHE'S BEING UN-REASON-ABLE!
YEAH, TOTALLY! BUT I'M GLAD SHE'S BACK TO HER CHEERFUL SELF.
YOU'RE MISSING MY POINT! STOP HER!
OR YOU'LL BOTH DIE!
YOU KNEW THAT FROM THE VERY START, RIGHT?

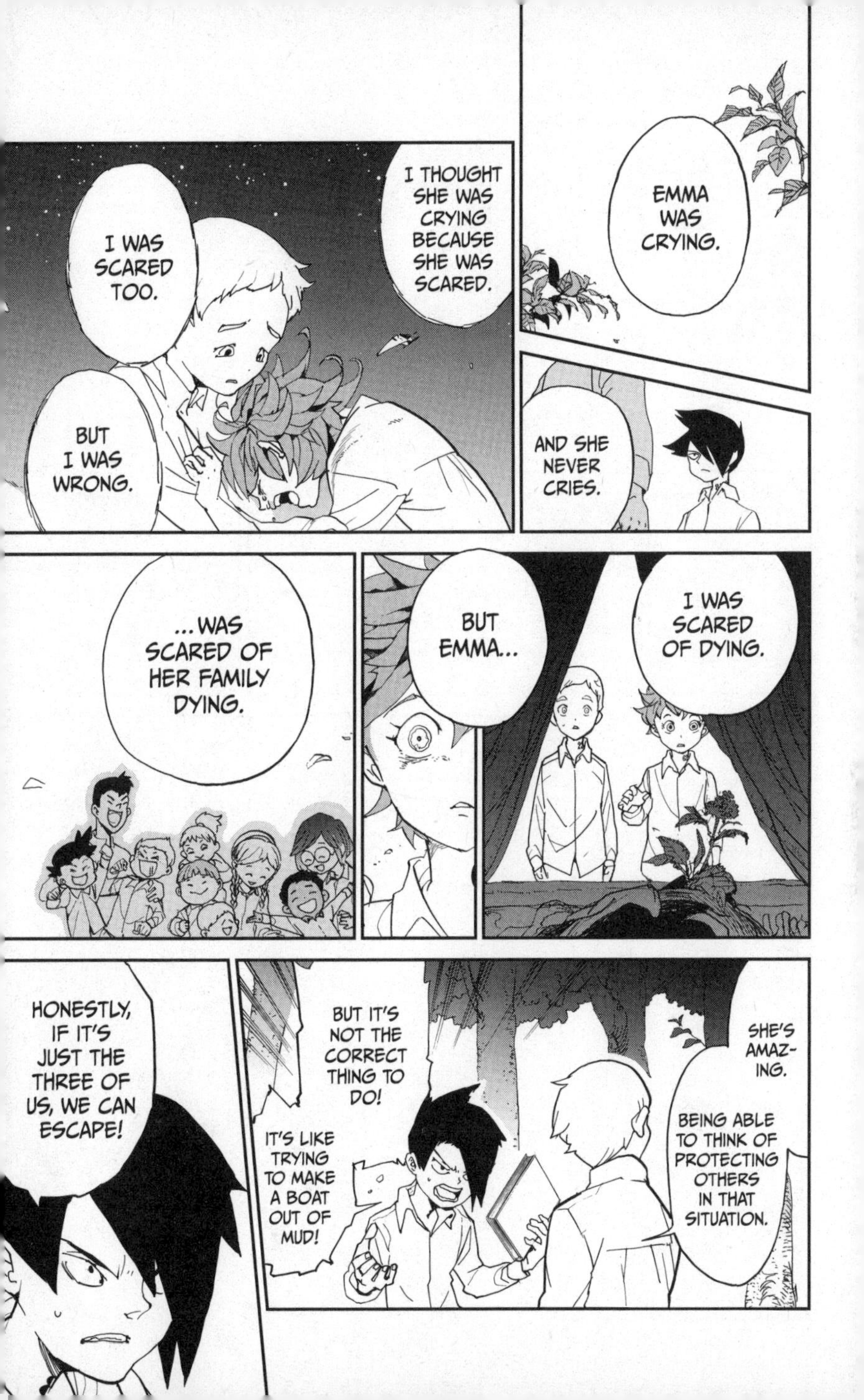
EMMA WAS CRYING.
I THOUGHT SHE WAS CRYING BECAUSE SHE WAS SCARED.
I WAS SCARED TOO.
BUT I WAS WRONG.
AND SHE NEVER CRIES.
I WAS SCARED OF DYING.
BUT EMMA...
...WAS SCARED OF HER FAMILY DYING.
SHE'S AMAZ-ING.
BEING ABLE TO THINK OF PROTECTING OTHERS IN THAT SITUATION.
BUT IT'S NOT THE CORRECT THING TO DO!
IT'S LIKE TRYING TO MAKE A BOAT OUT OF MUD!
HONESTLY, IF IT'S JUST THE THREE OF US, WE CAN ESCAPE!

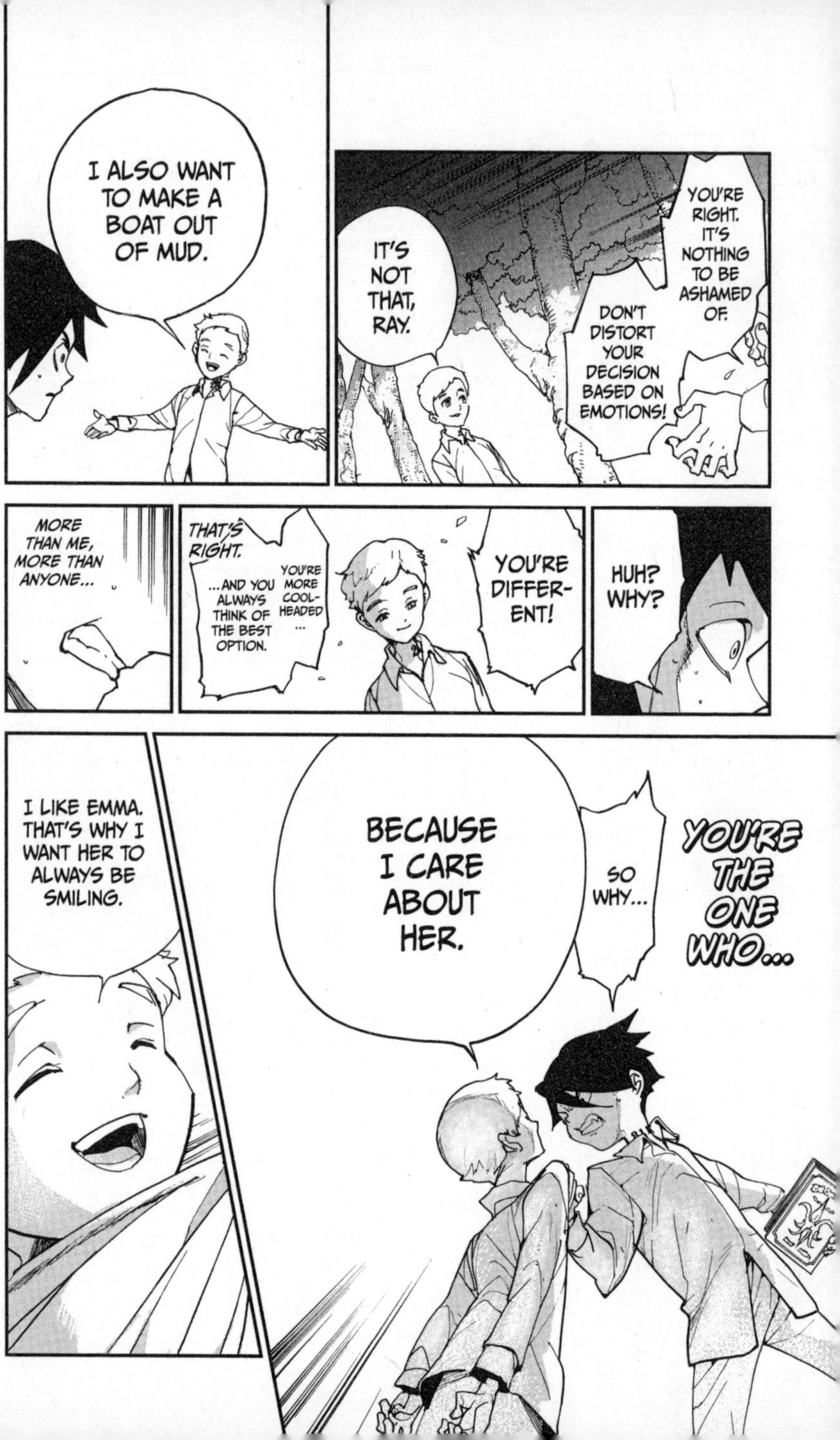
YOU'RE RIGHT. IT'S NOTHING TO BE ASHAMED OF.
DON'T DISTORT YOUR DECISION BASED ON EMOTIONS!
IT'S NOT THAT, RAY.
I ALSO WANT TO MAKE A BOAT OUT OF MUD.
HUH? WHY?
YOU'RE DIFFER-ENT!
THAT'S RIGHT.
YOU'RE MORE COOL-HEADED...
...AND YOU ALWAYS THINK OF THE BEST OPTION.
MORE THAN ME, MORE THAN ANYONE...
YOU'RE THE ONE WHO...
SO WHY...
BECAUSE I CARE ABOUT HER.
I LIKE EMMA. THAT'S WHY I WANT HER TO ALWAYS BE SMILING.

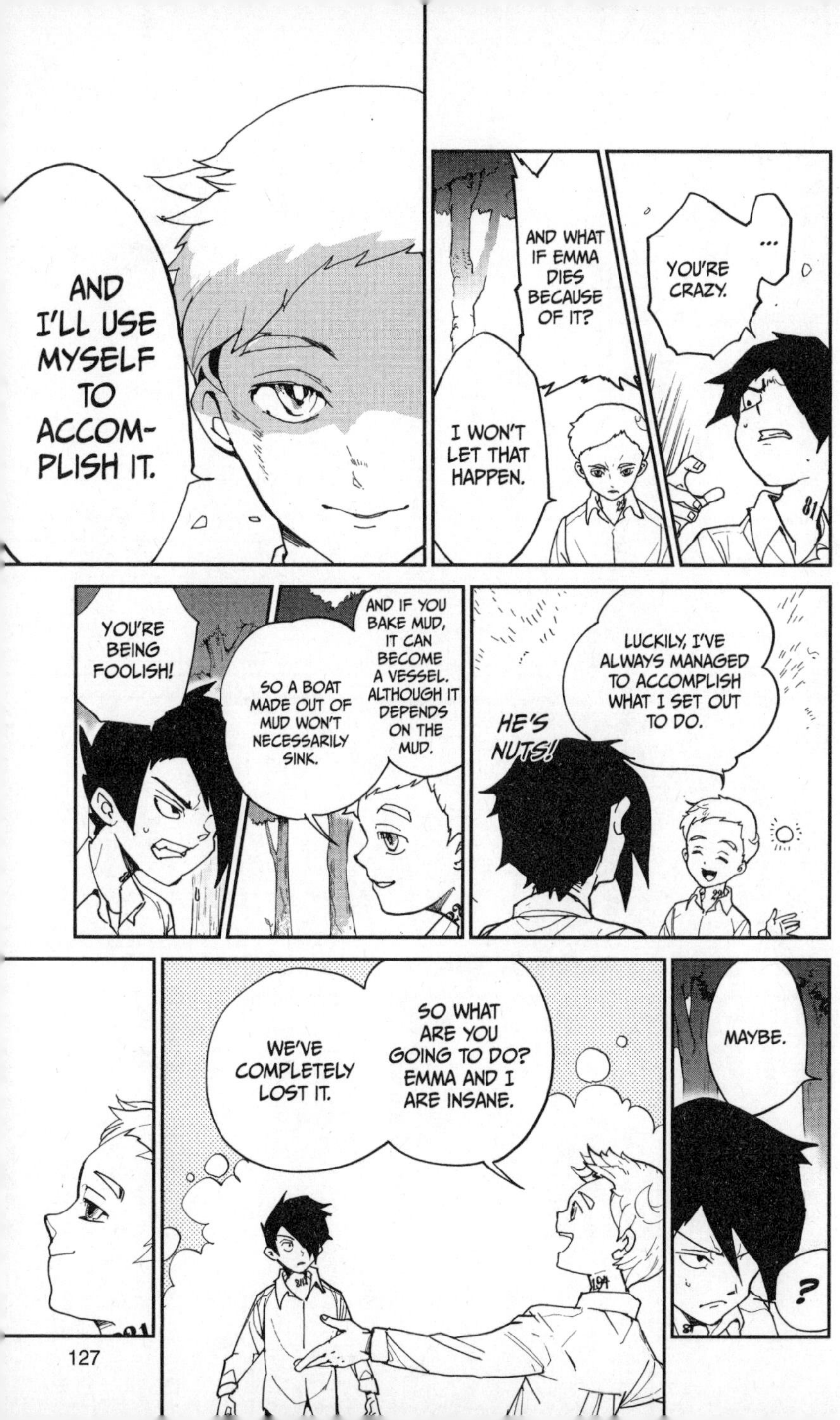
...
YOU'RE CRAZY.
AND WHAT IF EMMA DIES BECAUSE OF IT?
I WON'T LET THAT HAPPEN.
AND I'LL USE MYSELF TO ACCOMPLISH IT.
LUCKILY, I'VE ALWAYS MANAGED TO ACCOMPLISH WHAT I SET OUT TO DO.
HE'S NUTS!
AND IF YOU BAKE MUD, IT CAN BECOME A VESSEL. ALTHOUGH IT DEPENDS ON THE MUD.
SO A BOAT MADE OUT OF MUD WON'T NECESSARILY SINK.
YOU'RE BEING FOOLISH!
MAYBE.
?
SO WHAT ARE YOU GOING TO DO? EMMA AND I ARE INSANE.
WE'VE COMPLETELY LOST IT.

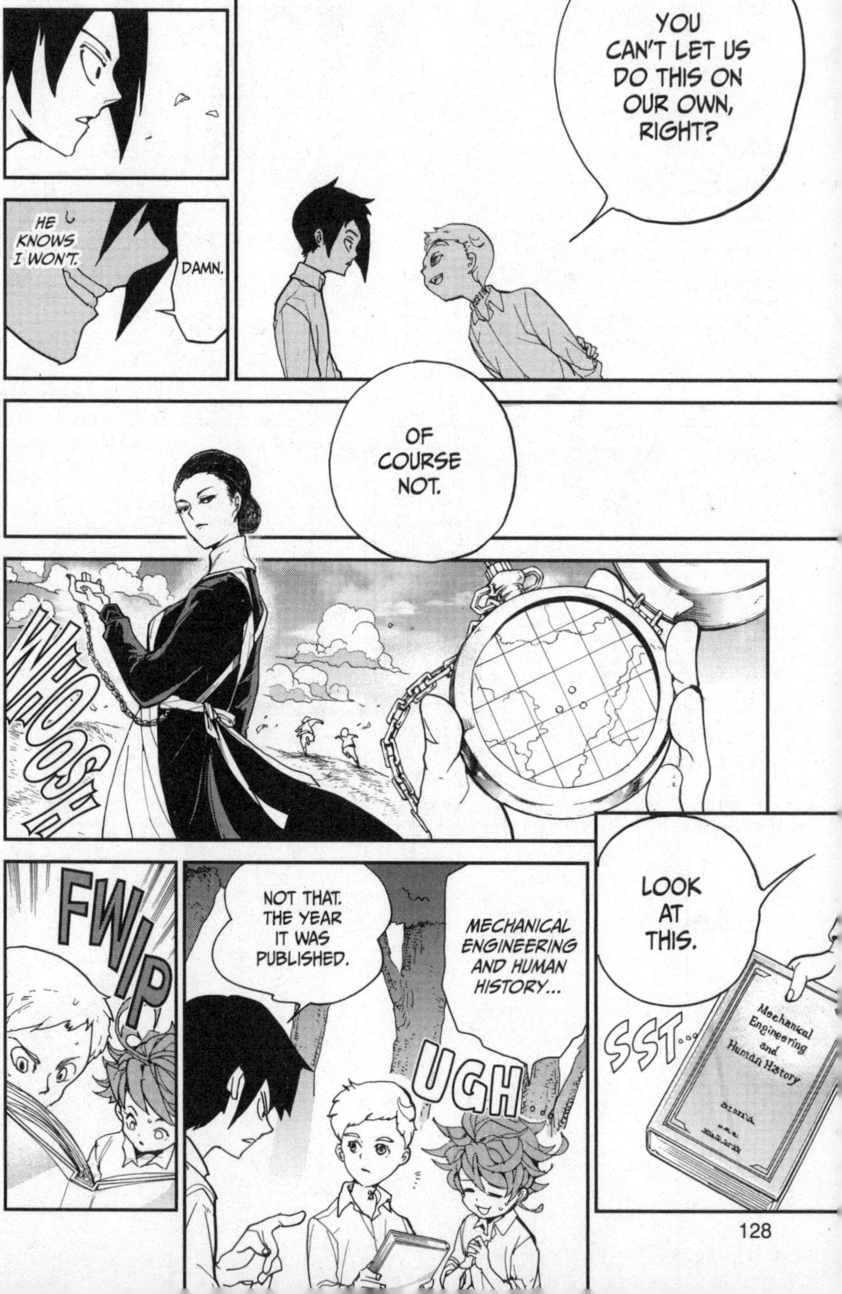
YOU CAN'T LET US DO THIS ON OUR OWN, RIGHT?
DAMN.
HE KNOWS I WON'T.
OF COURSE NOT.
WHOOSH
LOOK AT THIS.
SST...
Mechanical Engineering and Human History
MECHANICAL ENGINEERING AND HUMAN HISTORY...
NOT THAT. THE YEAR IT WAS PUBLISHED.
UGH
FWIP

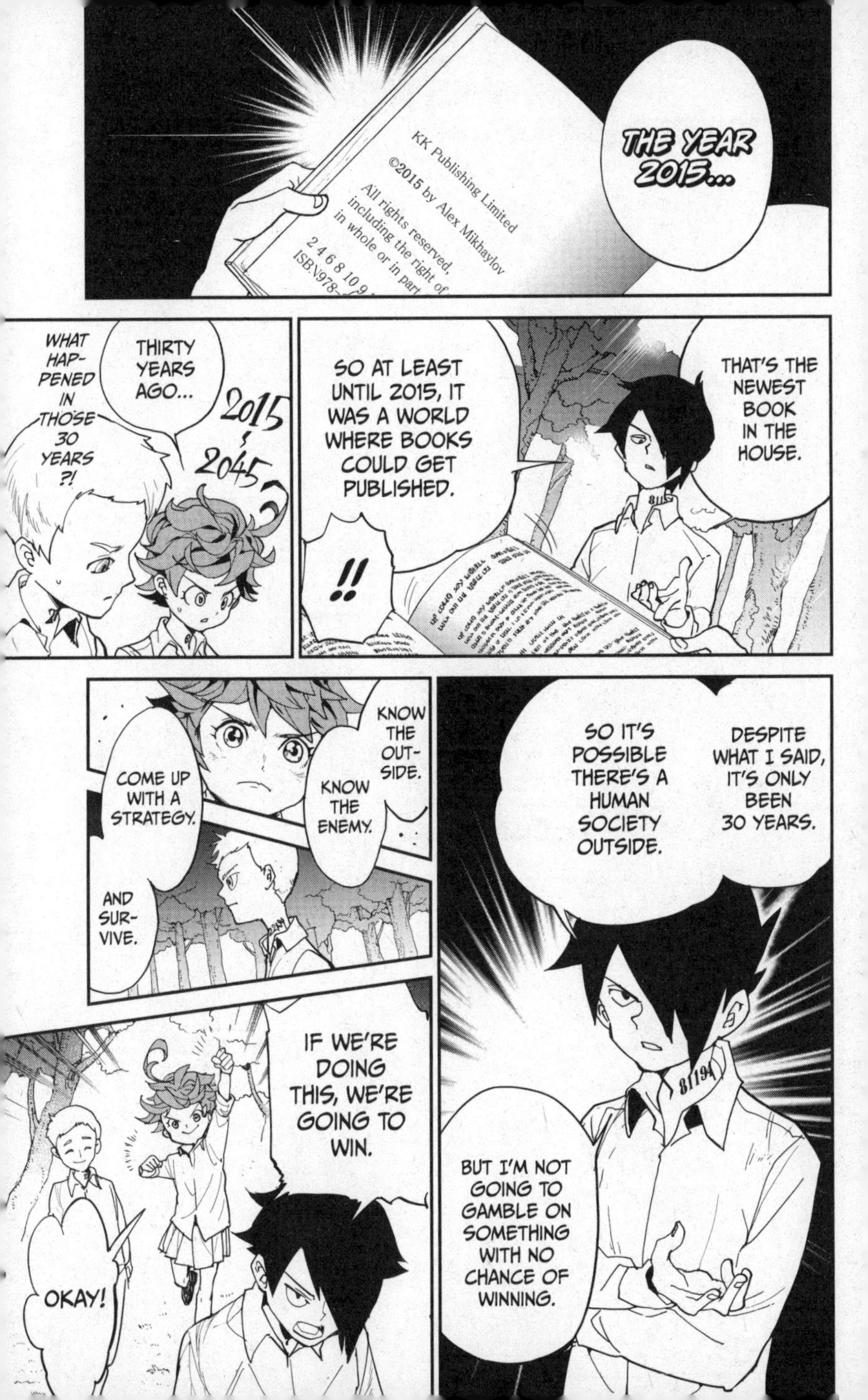
KK Publishing Limited
©2015 by Alex Mikhaylov
All rights reserved, including the right of in whole or in part
2 4 6 8 10 9
ISBN978-
THE YEAR 2015...
THAT'S THE NEWEST BOOK IN THE HOUSE.
SO AT LEAST UNTIL 2015, IT WAS A WORLD WHERE BOOKS COULD GET PUBLISHED.
!!
THIRTY YEARS AGO...
2015 ~ 2045
WHAT HAPPENED IN THOSE 30 YEARS?!
DESPITE WHAT I SAID, IT'S ONLY BEEN 30 YEARS.
SO IT'S POSSIBLE THERE'S A HUMAN SOCIETY OUTSIDE.
BUT I'M NOT GOING TO GAMBLE ON SOMETHING WITH NO CHANCE OF WINNING.
KNOW THE OUTSIDE.
KNOW THE ENEMY.
COME UP WITH A STRATEGY.
AND SURVIVE.
IF WE'RE DOING THIS, WE'RE GOING TO WIN.
OKAY!

INITIAL DESIGNS

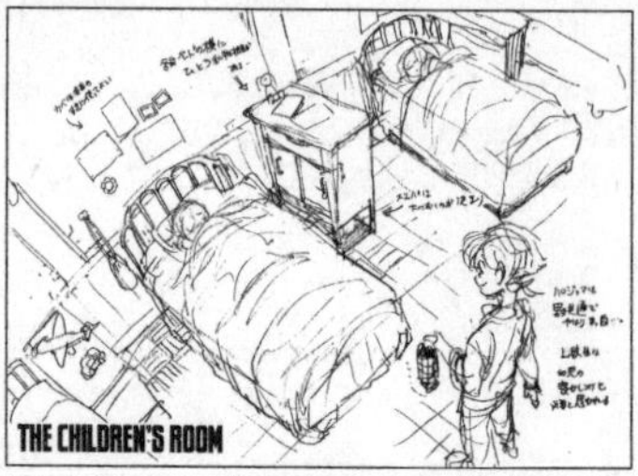
THE CHILDREN'S ROOM

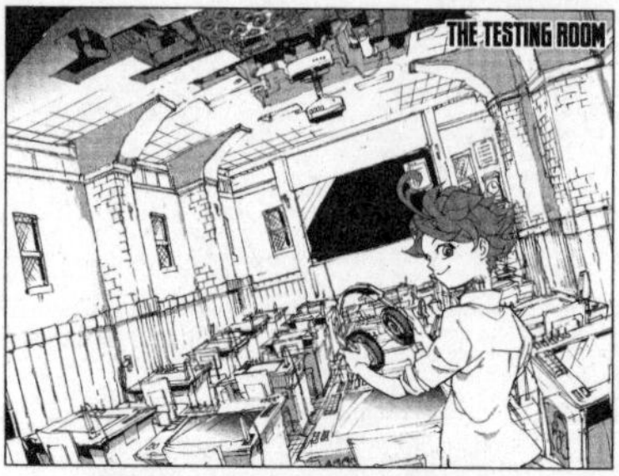
THE TESTING ROOM

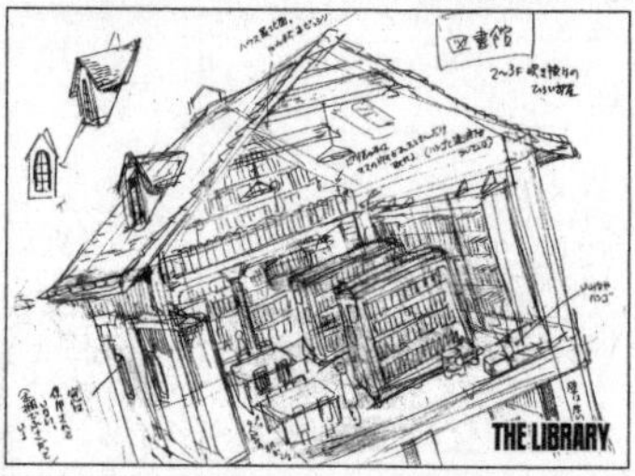
THE LIBRARY

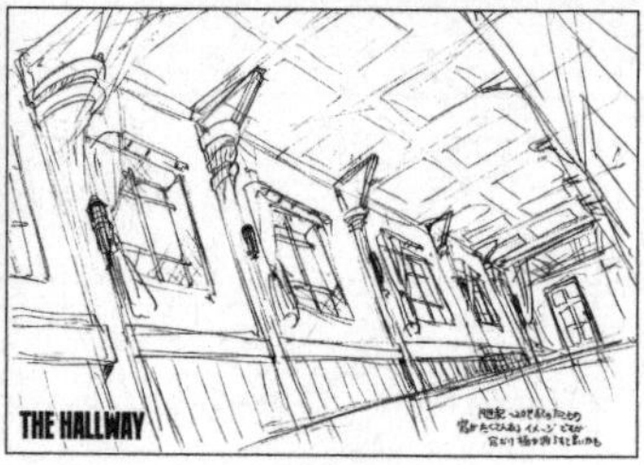
THE HALLWAY

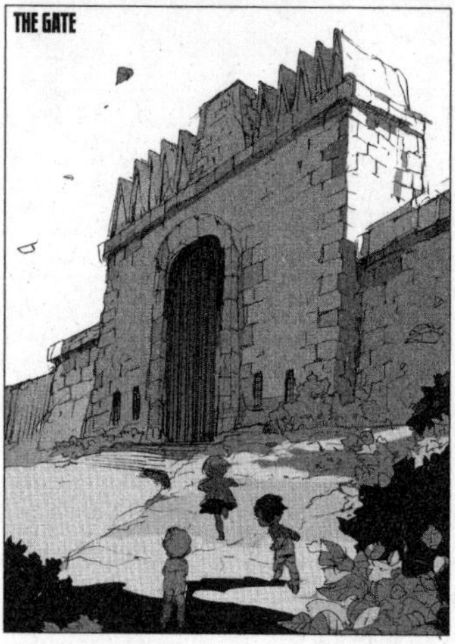
THE GATE

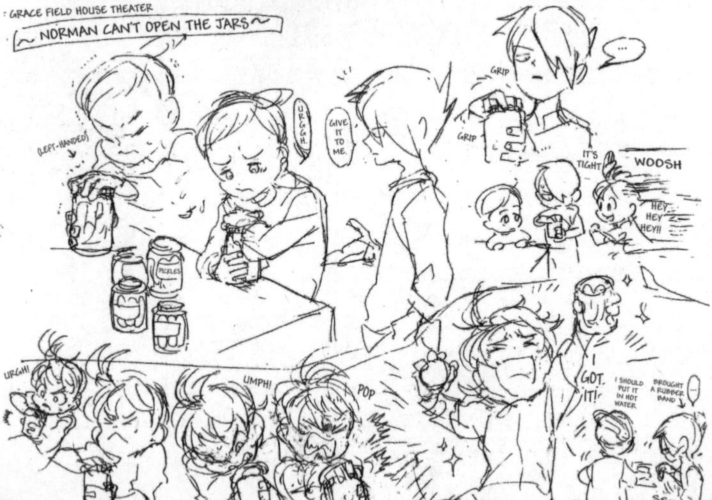
: GRACE FIELD HOUSE THEATER
~ NORMAN CAN'T OPEN THE JARS ~
...
GRIP
GRIP
GIVE IT TO ME.
URGGH.
(LEFT-HANDED)
PICKLES
WOOSH
HEY HEY HEY!!
IT'S TIGHT
...
BROUGHT A RUBBER BAND
I SHOULD PUT IT IN HOT WATER
GOT IT!
POP
UMPH!
URGH!
SST

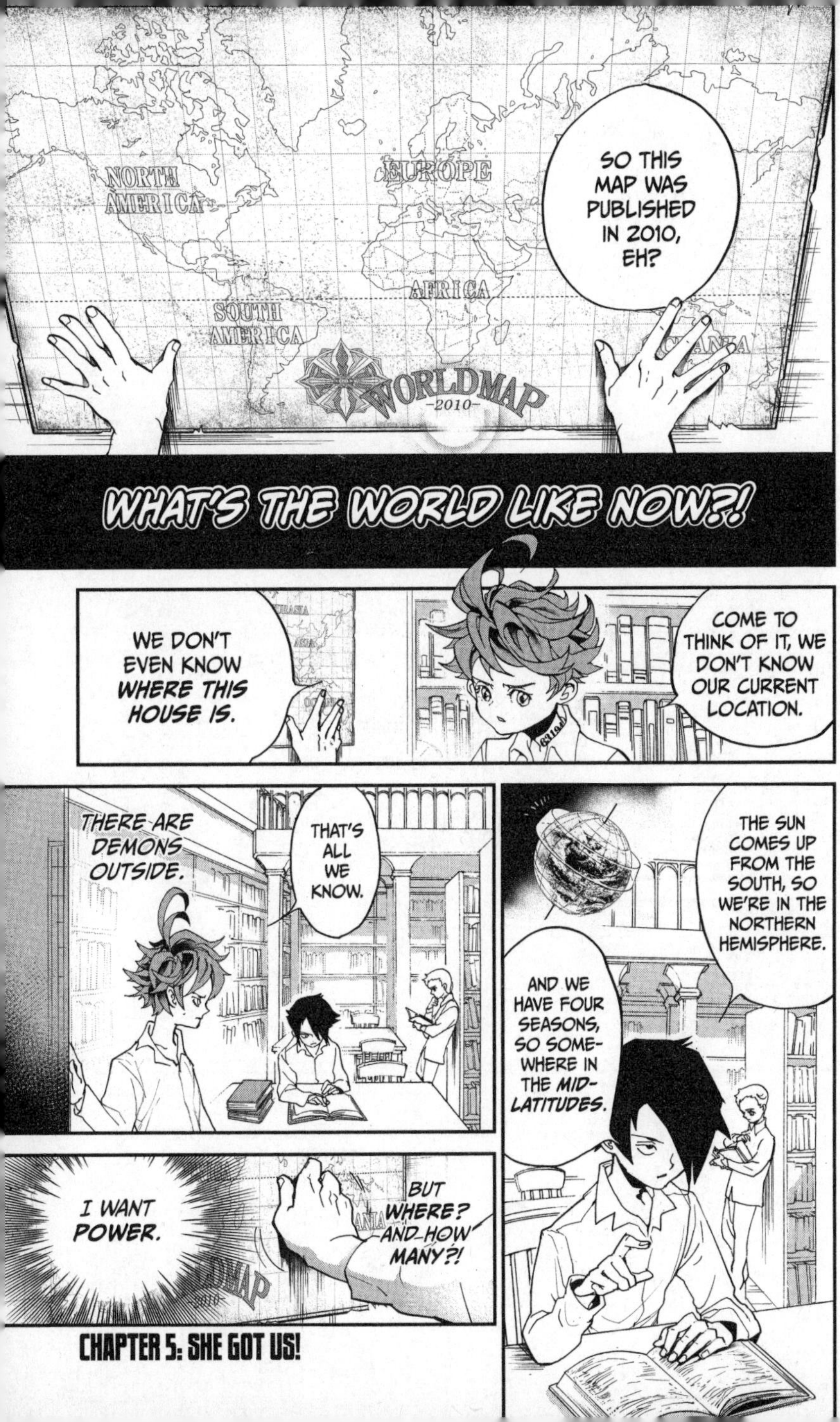
EUROPE
NORTH AMERICA
AFRICA
SOUTH AMERICA
WORLDMAP
-2010-
SO THIS MAP WAS PUBLISHED IN 2010, EH?
WHAT'S THE WORLD LIKE NOW?!
COME TO THINK OF IT, WE DON'T KNOW OUR CURRENT LOCATION.
WE DON'T EVEN KNOW *WHERE THIS HOUSE IS.*
THE SUN COMES UP FROM THE SOUTH, SO WE'RE IN THE NORTHERN HEMISPHERE.
AND WE HAVE FOUR SEASONS, SO SOME-WHERE IN THE *MID-LATITUDES.*
THERE ARE DEMONS OUTSIDE.
THAT'S ALL WE KNOW.
BUT WHERE? AND HOW MANY?!
I WANT POWER.

CHAPTER 5: SHE GOT US!

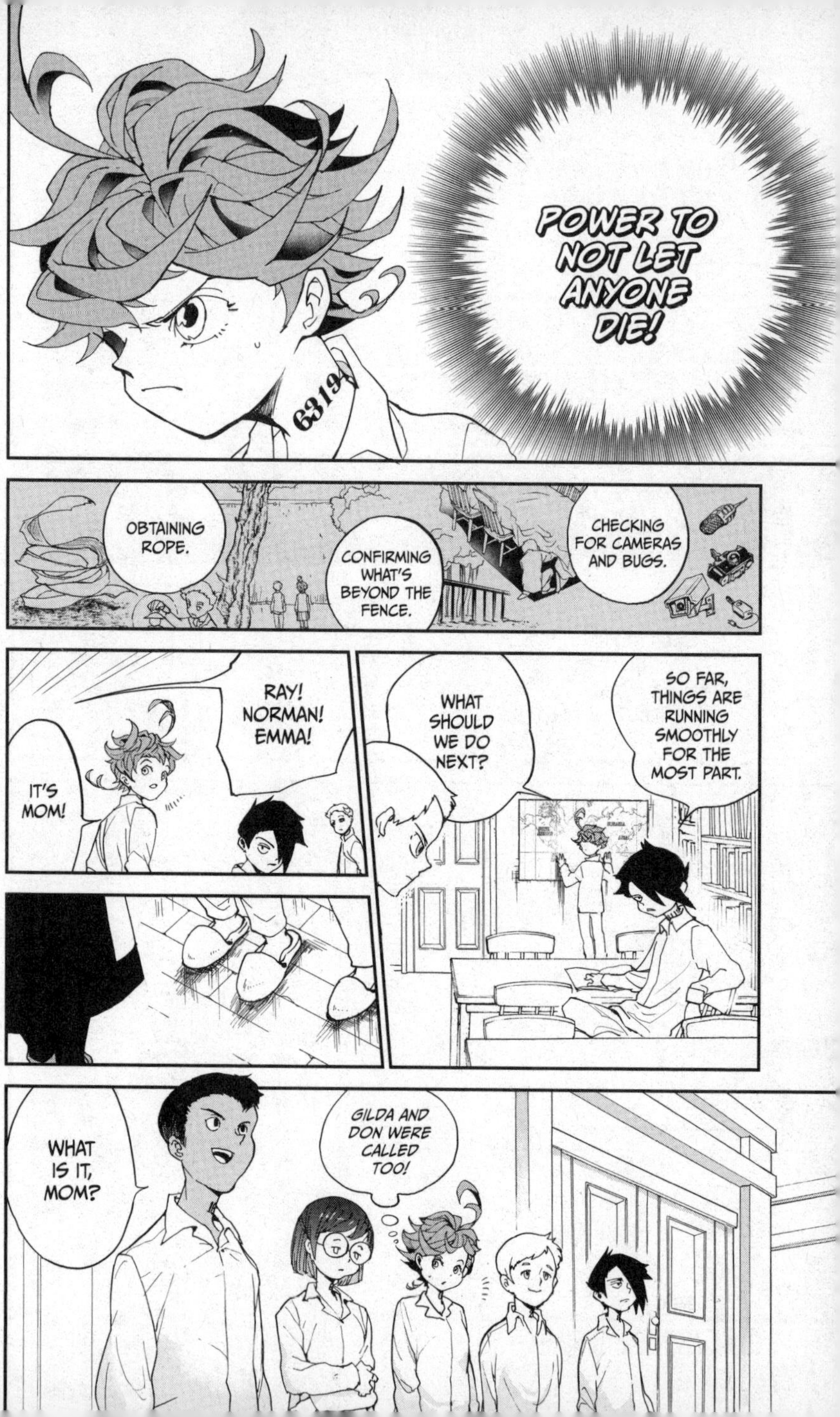
POWER TO NOT LET ANYONE DIE!
CHECKING FOR CAMERAS AND BUGS.
CONFIRMING WHAT'S BEYOND THE FENCE.
OBTAINING ROPE.
SO FAR, THINGS ARE RUNNING SMOOTHLY FOR THE MOST PART.
WHAT SHOULD WE DO NEXT?
RAY! NORMAN! EMMA!
IT'S MOM!
GILDA AND DON WERE CALLED TOO!
WHAT IS IT, MOM?

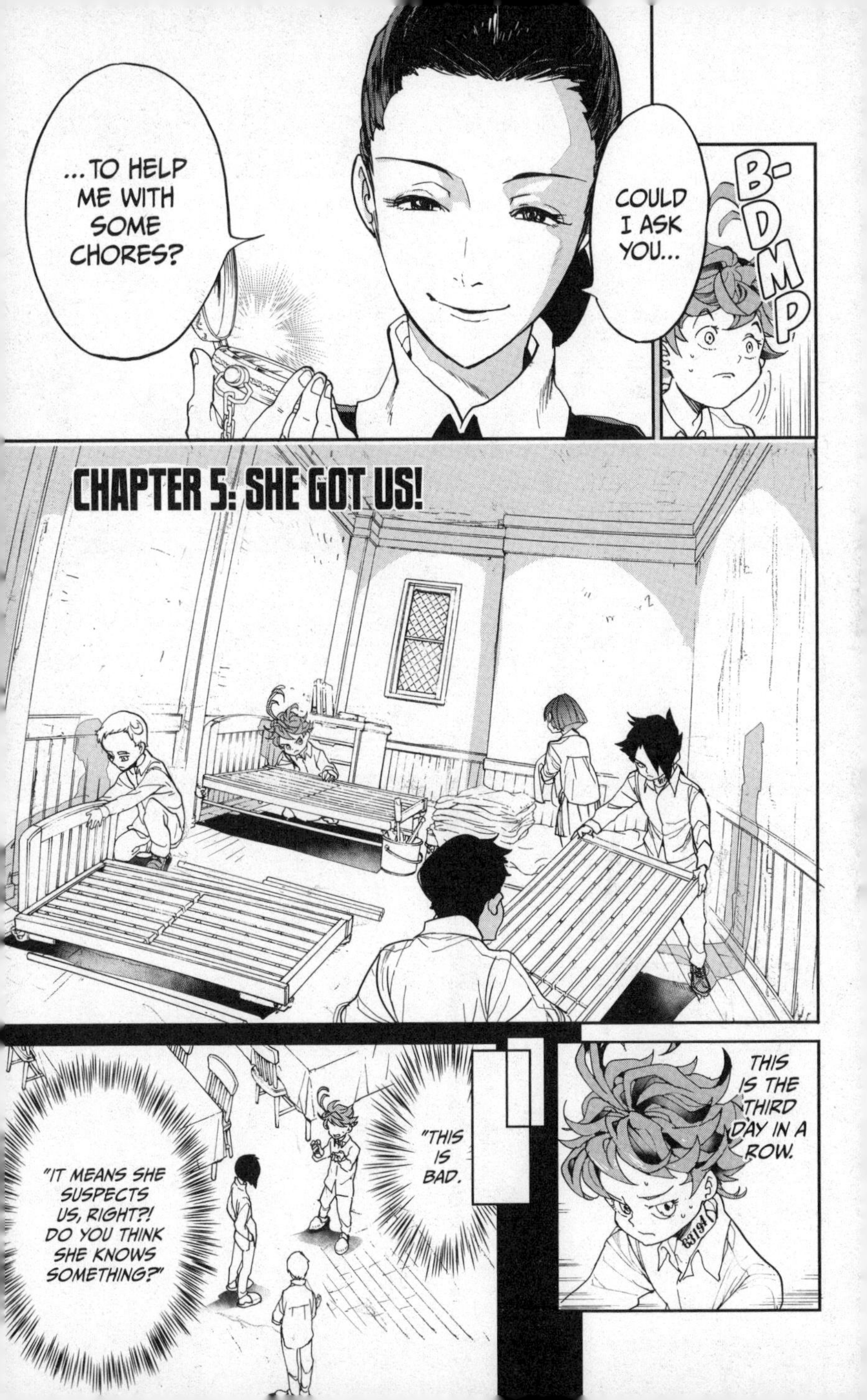
B-DMP
COULD I ASK YOU...
...TO HELP ME WITH SOME CHORES?
CHAPTER 5: SHE GOT US!
THIS IS THE THIRD DAY IN A ROW.
"THIS IS BAD.
"IT MEANS SHE SUSPECTS US, RIGHT?! DO YOU THINK SHE KNOWS SOMETHING?"

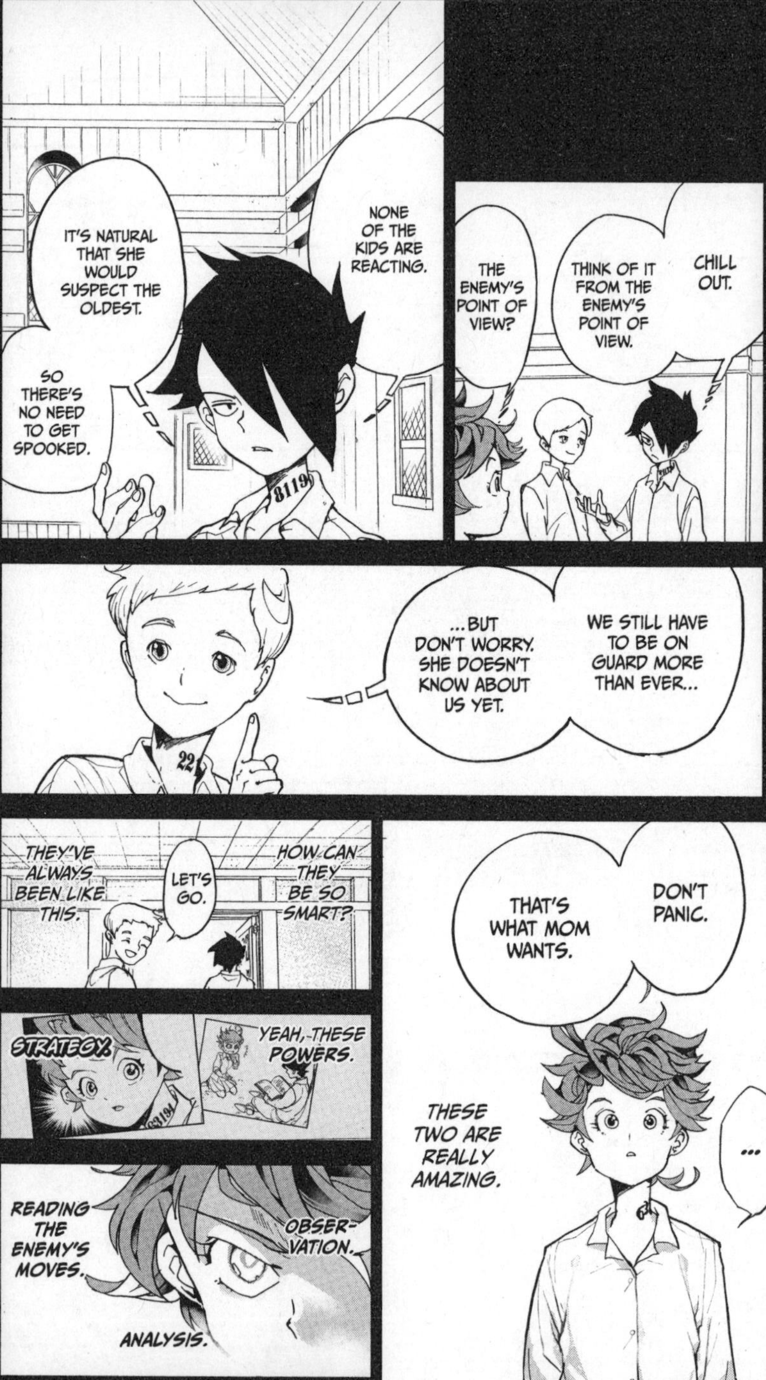
CHILL OUT.
THINK OF IT FROM THE ENEMY'S POINT OF VIEW.
THE ENEMY'S POINT OF VIEW?
NONE OF THE KIDS ARE REACTING.
IT'S NATURAL THAT SHE WOULD SUSPECT THE OLDEST.
SO THERE'S NO NEED TO GET SPOOKED.
WE STILL HAVE TO BE ON GUARD MORE THAN EVER...
...BUT DON'T WORRY. SHE DOESN'T KNOW ABOUT US YET.
DON'T PANIC.
THAT'S WHAT MOM WANTS.
THESE TWO ARE REALLY AMAZING.
...
HOW CAN THEY BE SO SMART?
LET'S GO.
THEY'VE ALWAYS BEEN LIKE THIS.
YEAH, THESE POWERS.
STRATEGY.
OBSERVATION.
READING THE ENEMY'S MOVES.
ANALYSIS.

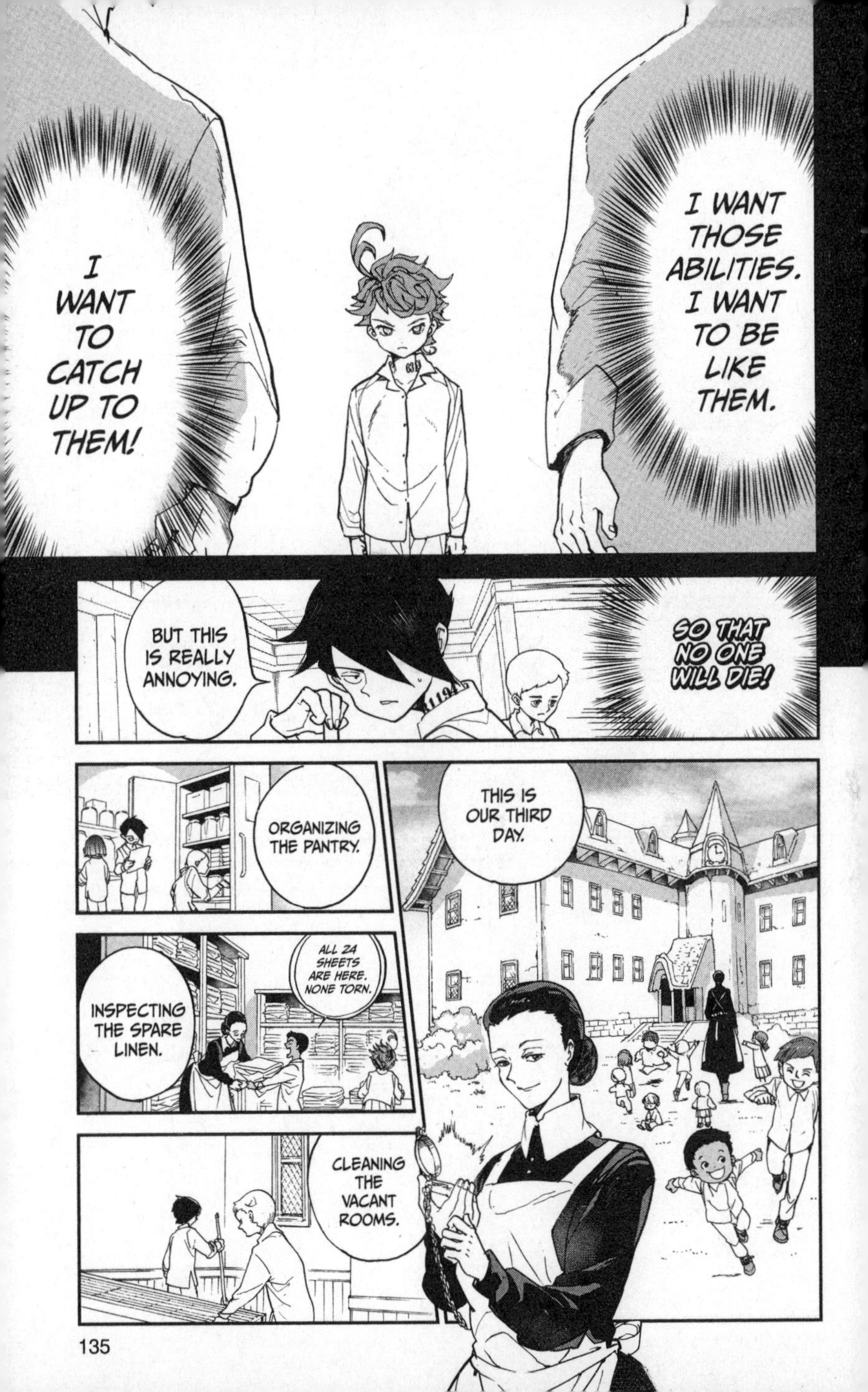
I WANT THOSE ABILITIES. I WANT TO BE LIKE THEM.
I WANT TO CATCH UP TO THEM!
SO THAT NO ONE WILL DIE!
BUT THIS IS REALLY ANNOYING.
THIS IS OUR THIRD DAY.
ORGANIZING THE PANTRY.
ALL 24 SHEETS ARE HERE. NONE TORN.
INSPECTING THE SPARE LINEN.
CLEANING THE VACANT ROOMS.

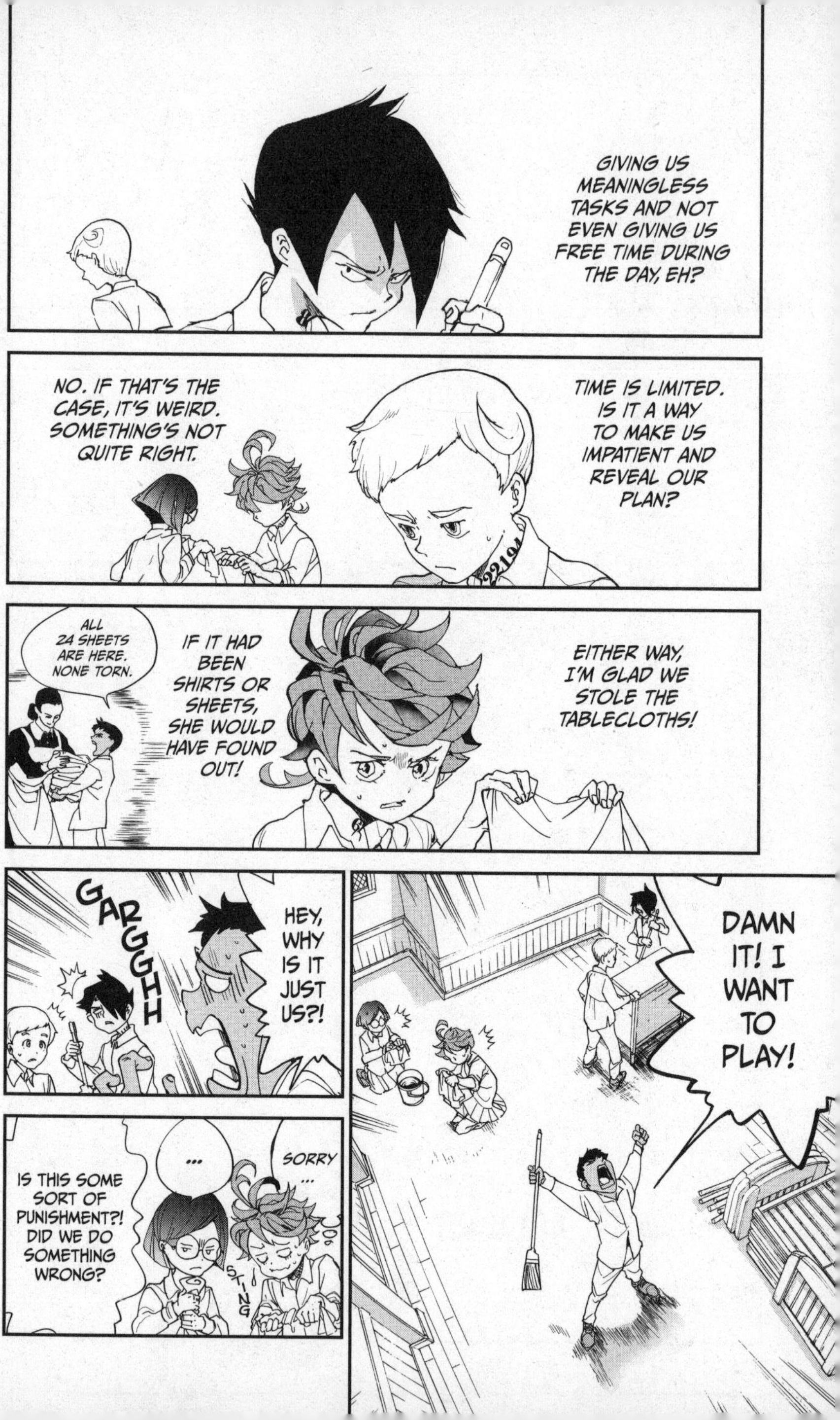
GIVING US MEANINGLESS TASKS AND NOT EVEN GIVING US FREE TIME DURING THE DAY, EH?
TIME IS LIMITED. IS IT A WAY TO MAKE US IMPATIENT AND REVEAL OUR PLAN?
NO. IF THAT'S THE CASE, IT'S WEIRD. SOMETHING'S NOT QUITE RIGHT.
EITHER WAY, I'M GLAD WE STOLE THE TABLECLOTHS!
IF IT HAD BEEN SHIRTS OR SHEETS, SHE WOULD HAVE FOUND OUT!
ALL 24 SHEETS ARE HERE. NONE TORN.
DAMN IT! I WANT TO PLAY!
HEY, WHY IS IT JUST US?!
GARRGGHH
SORRY ...
...
IS THIS SOME SORT OF PUNISHMENT?! DID WE DO SOMETHING WRONG?
STING

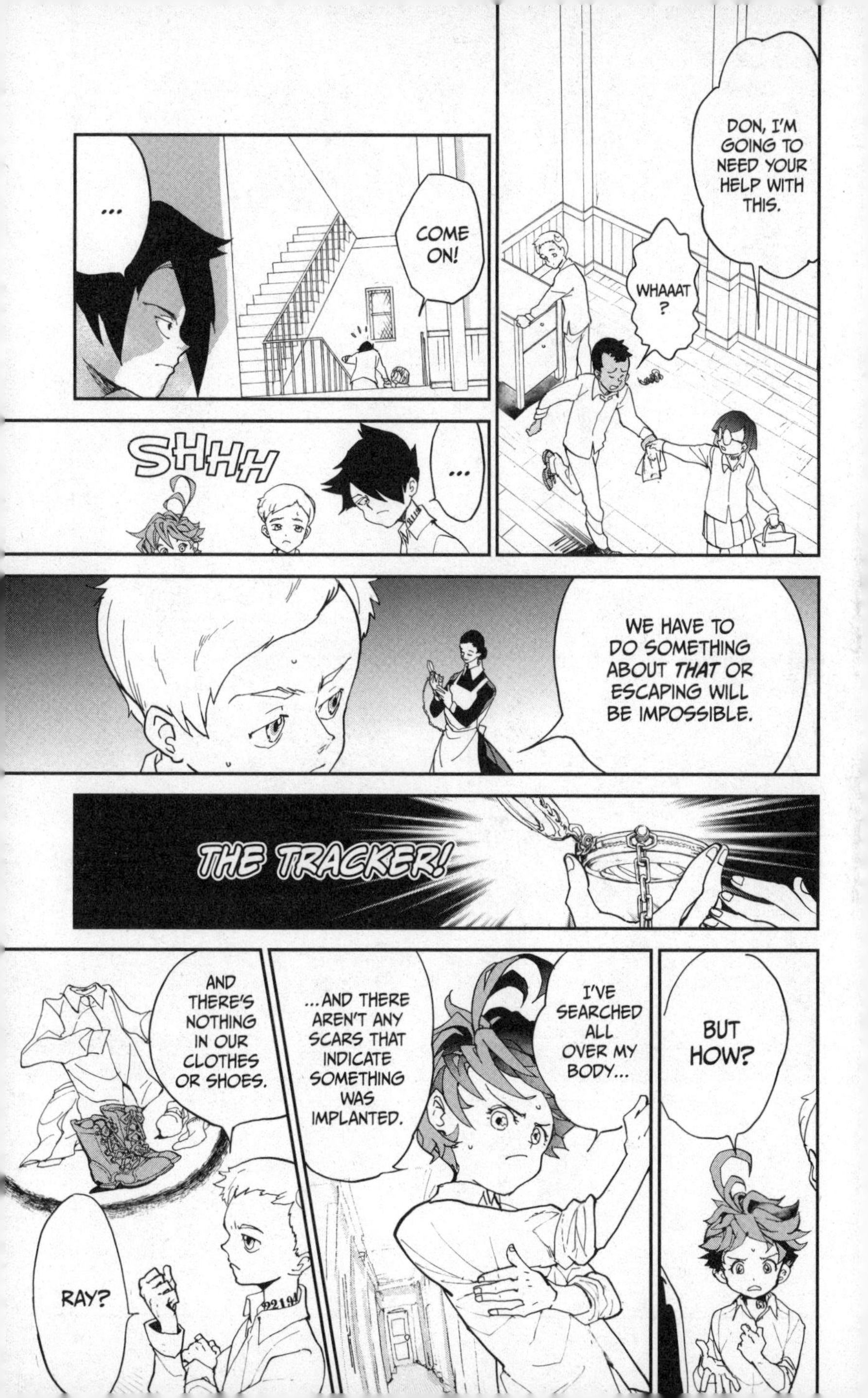
DON, I'M GOING TO NEED YOUR HELP WITH THIS.
WHAAAT?
COME ON!
...
...
SHHH
WE HAVE TO DO SOMETHING ABOUT *THAT* OR ESCAPING WILL BE IMPOSSIBLE.
THE TRACKER!
BUT HOW?
I'VE SEARCHED ALL OVER MY BODY...
...AND THERE AREN'T ANY SCARS THAT INDICATE SOMETHING WAS IMPLANTED.
AND THERE'S NOTHING IN OUR CLOTHES OR SHOES.
RAY?

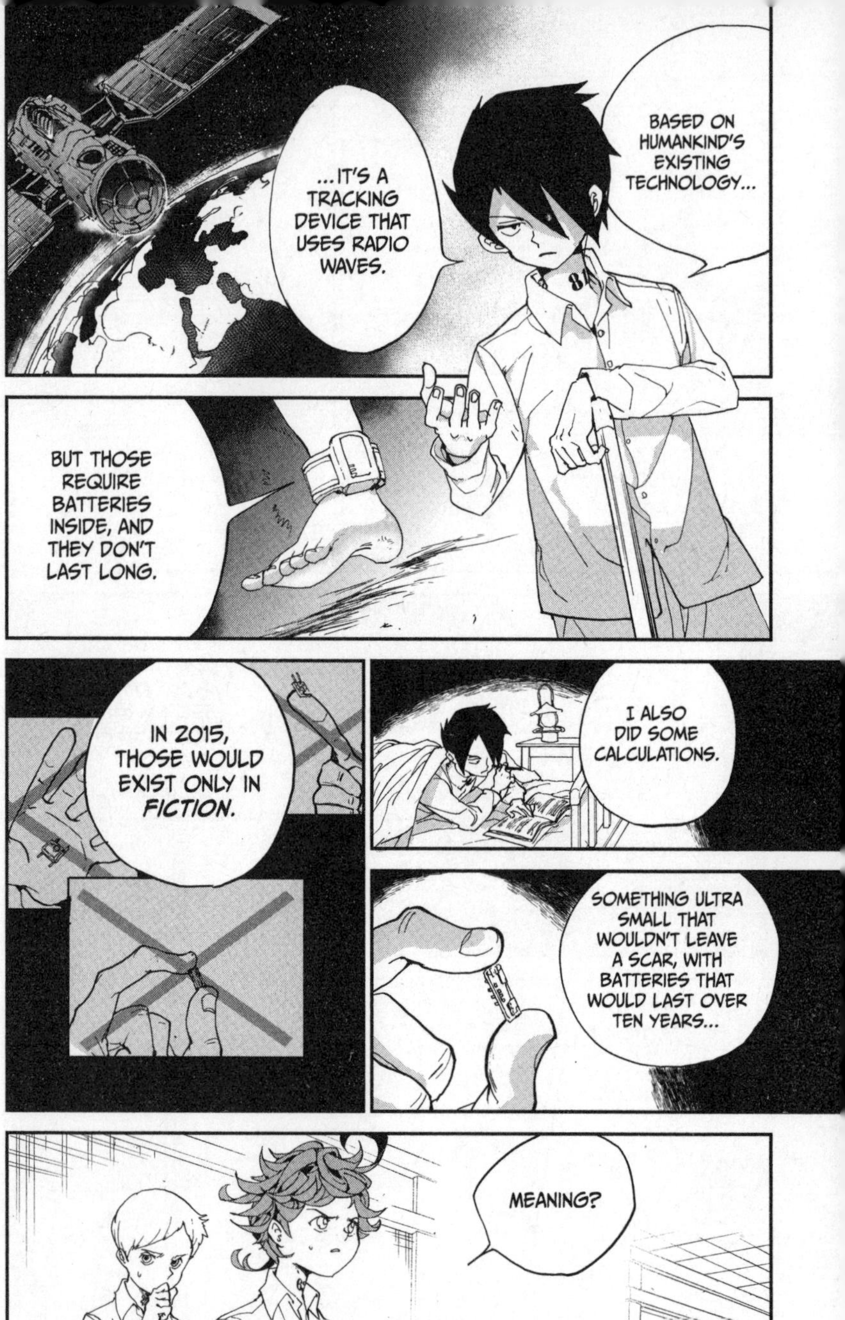
BASED ON HUMANKIND'S EXISTING TECHNOLOGY...
...IT'S A TRACKING DEVICE THAT USES RADIO WAVES.
BUT THOSE REQUIRE BATTERIES INSIDE, AND THEY DON'T LAST LONG.
I ALSO DID SOME CALCULATIONS.
SOMETHING ULTRA SMALL THAT WOULDN'T LEAVE A SCAR, WITH BATTERIES THAT WOULD LAST OVER TEN YEARS...
IN 2015, THOSE WOULD EXIST ONLY IN *FICTION*.
MEANING?

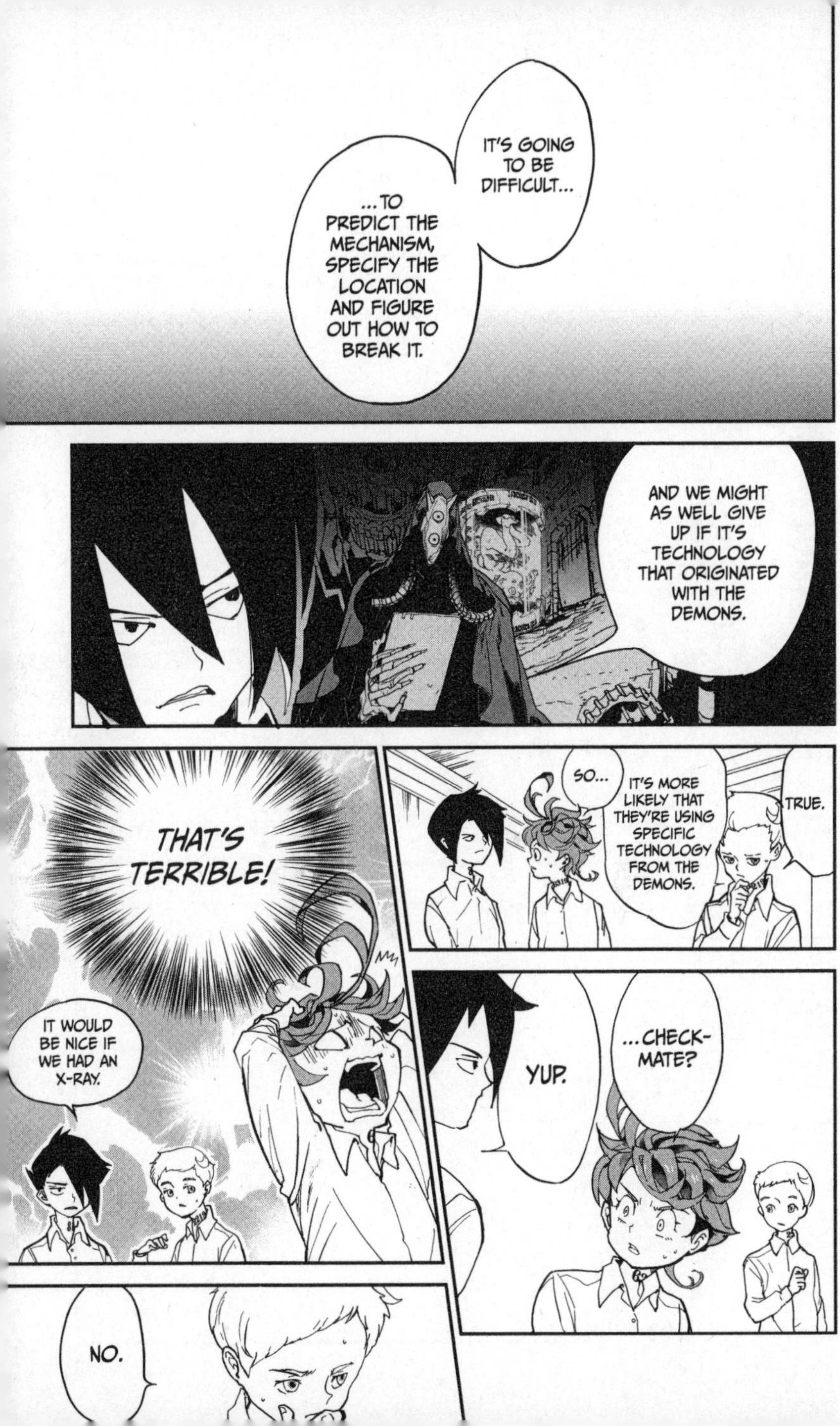
IT'S GOING TO BE DIFFICULT...
...TO PREDICT THE MECHANISM, SPECIFY THE LOCATION AND FIGURE OUT HOW TO BREAK IT.
AND WE MIGHT AS WELL GIVE UP IF IT'S TECHNOLOGY THAT ORIGINATED WITH THE DEMONS.
SO...
IT'S MORE LIKELY THAT THEY'RE USING SPECIFIC TECHNOLOGY FROM THE DEMONS.
TRUE.
...CHECK-MATE?
YUP.
THAT'S TERRIBLE!
IT WOULD BE NICE IF WE HAD AN X-RAY.
NO.

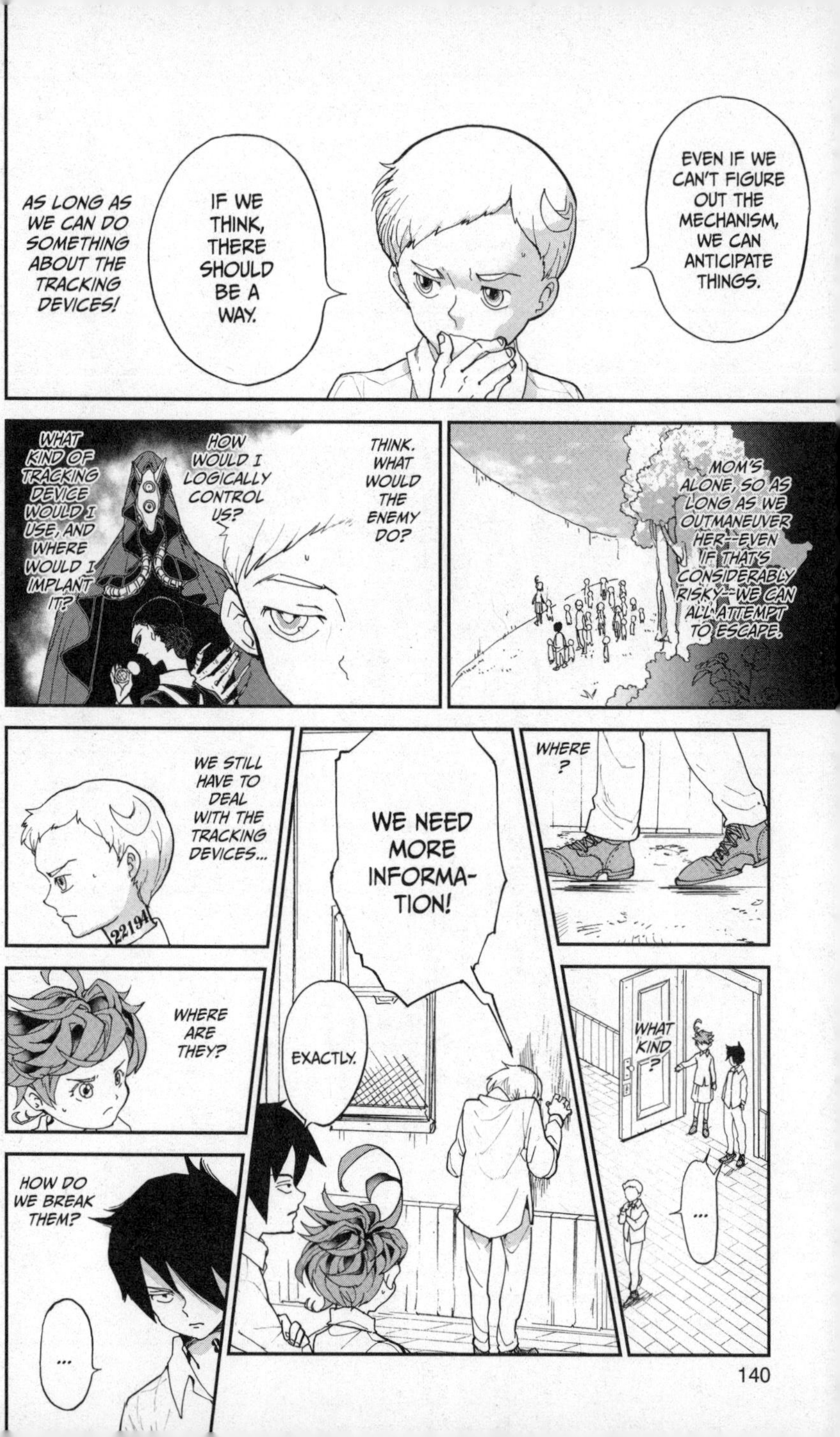
EVEN IF WE CAN'T FIGURE OUT THE MECHANISM, WE CAN ANTICIPATE THINGS.
IF WE THINK, THERE SHOULD BE A WAY.
AS LONG AS WE CAN DO SOMETHING ABOUT THE TRACKING DEVICES!
MOM'S ALONE, SO AS LONG AS WE OUTMANEUVER HER--EVEN IF THAT'S CONSIDERABLY RISKY--WE CAN ALL ATTEMPT TO ESCAPE.
THINK. WHAT WOULD THE ENEMY DO?
HOW WOULD I LOGICALLY CONTROL US?
WHAT KIND OF TRACKING DEVICE WOULD I USE, AND WHERE WOULD I IMPLANT IT?
WHERE?
WHAT KIND?
...
WE NEED MORE INFORMATION!
EXACTLY.
WE STILL HAVE TO DEAL WITH THE TRACKING DEVICES...
22194
WHERE ARE THEY?
HOW DO WE BREAK THEM?
...

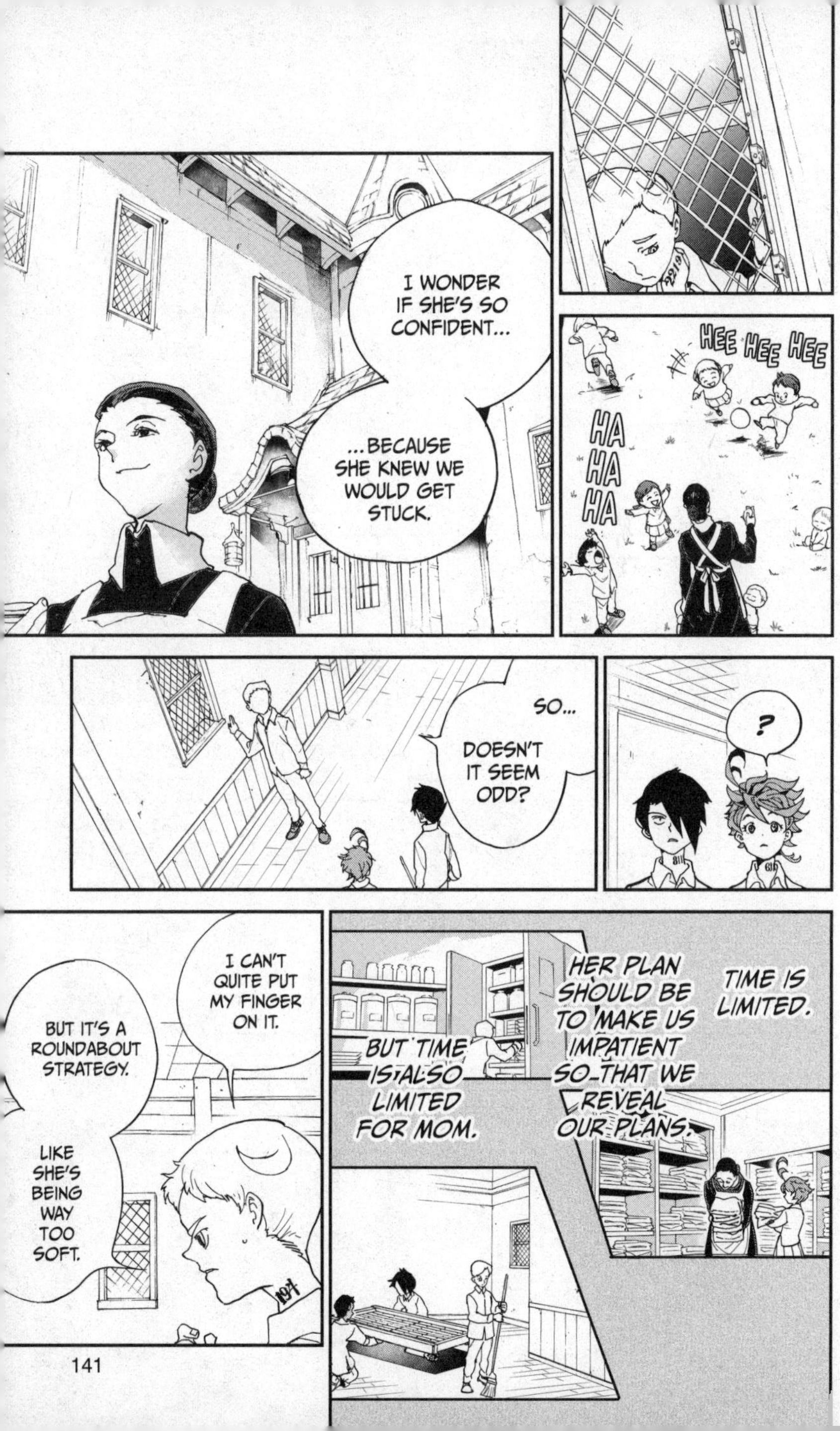
HEE HEE HEE
HA HA HA
I WONDER IF SHE'S SO CONFIDENT...
...BECAUSE SHE KNEW WE WOULD GET STUCK.
?
SO... DOESN'T IT SEEM ODD?
TIME IS LIMITED.
HER PLAN SHOULD BE TO MAKE US IMPATIENT SO THAT WE REVEAL OUR PLANS.
BUT TIME IS ALSO LIMITED FOR MOM.
I CAN'T QUITE PUT MY FINGER ON IT.
BUT IT'S A ROUNDABOUT STRATEGY.
LIKE SHE'S BEING WAY TOO SOFT.

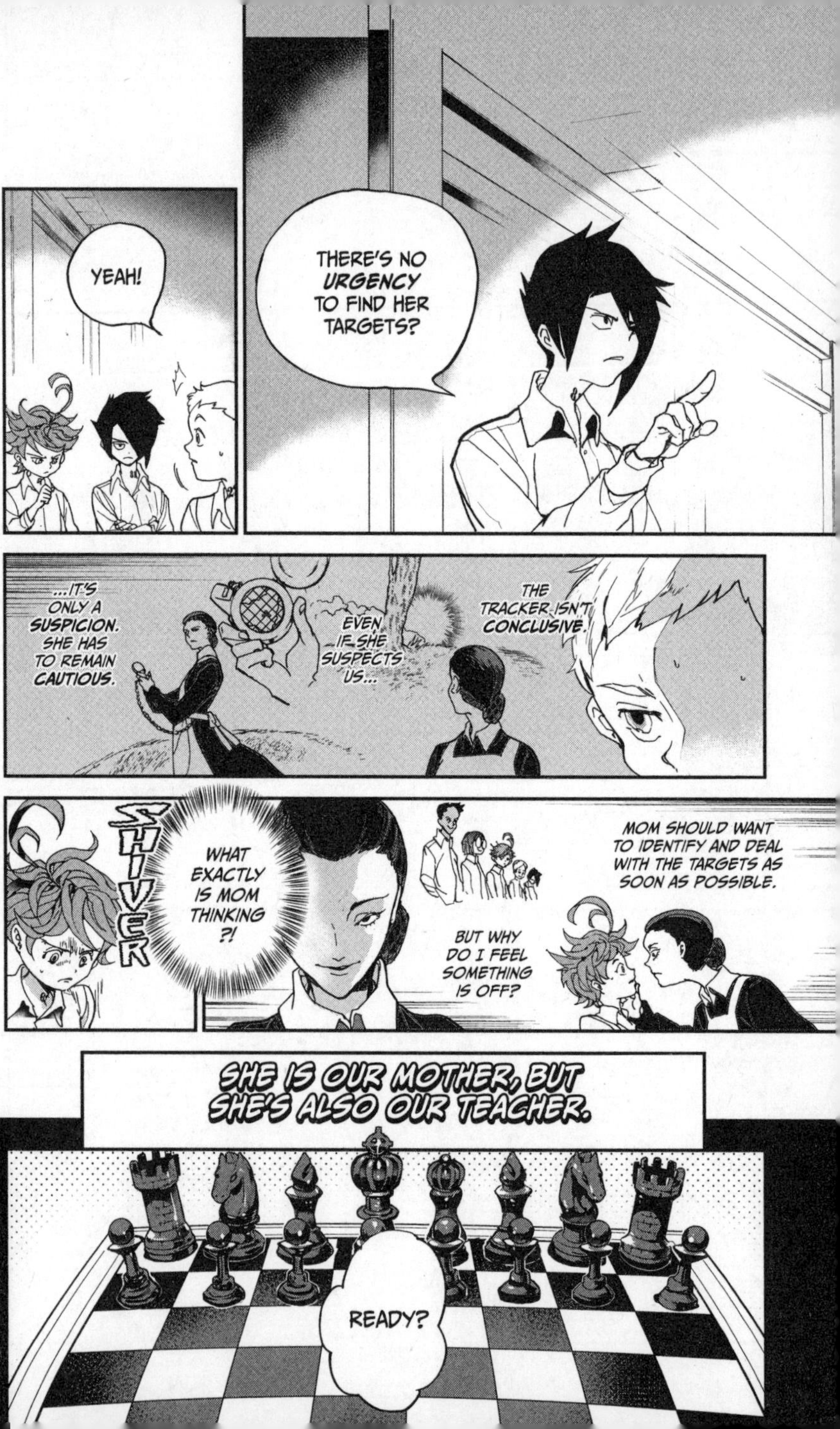
THERE'S NO URGENCY TO FIND HER TARGETS?
YEAH!
THE TRACKER ISN'T CONCLUSIVE.
EVEN IF SHE SUSPECTS US...
...IT'S ONLY A SUSPICION. SHE HAS TO REMAIN CAUTIOUS.
MOM SHOULD WANT TO IDENTIFY AND DEAL WITH THE TARGETS AS SOON AS POSSIBLE.
BUT WHY DO I FEEL SOMETHING IS OFF?
WHAT EXACTLY IS MOM THINKING?!
SHIVER
SHE IS OUR MOTHER, BUT SHE'S ALSO OUR TEACHER.
READY?

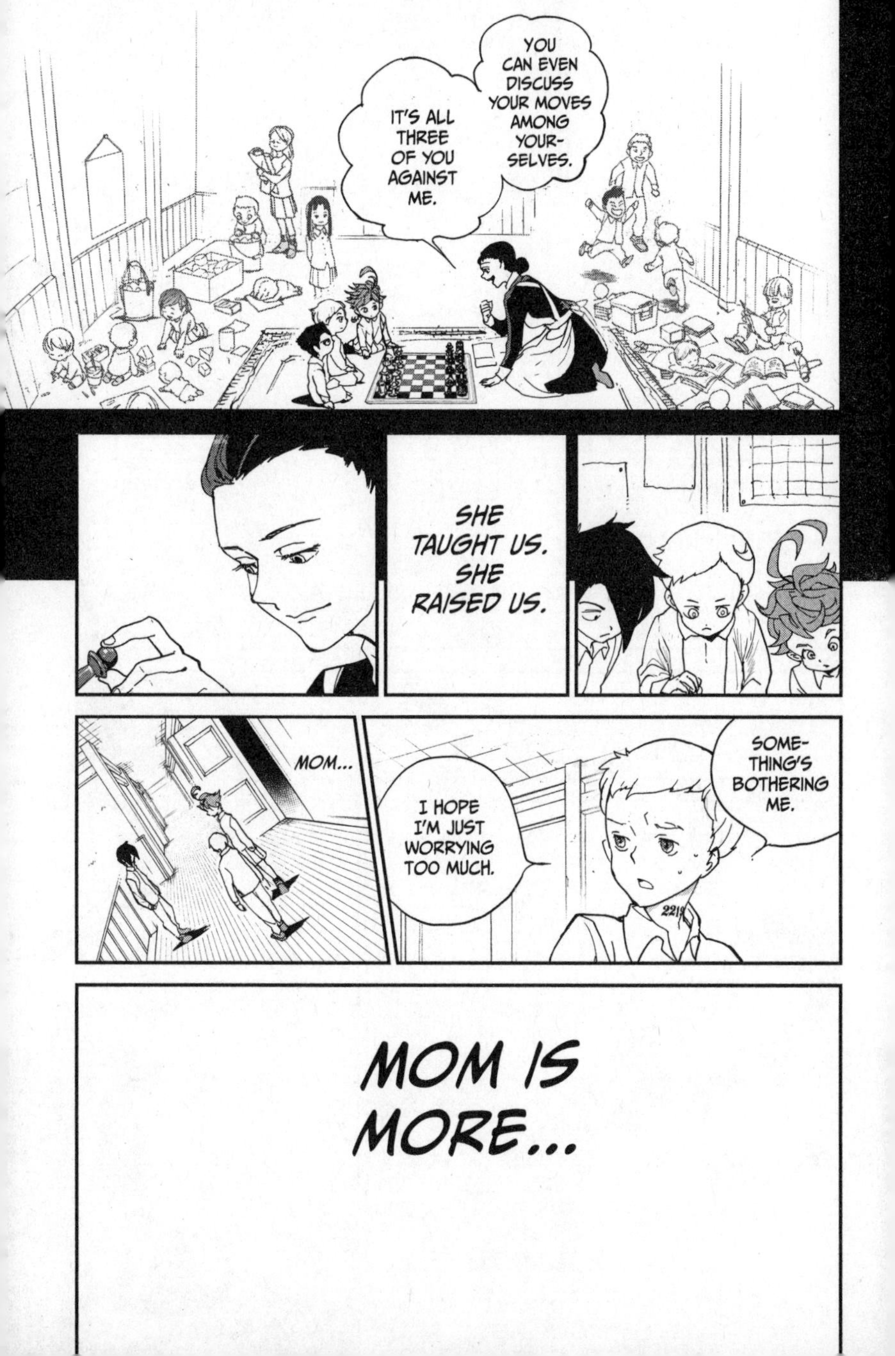
YOU CAN EVEN DISCUSS YOUR MOVES AMONG YOUR-SELVES.
IT'S ALL THREE OF YOU AGAINST ME.
SHE TAUGHT US. SHE RAISED US.
SOME-THING'S BOTHERING ME.
I HOPE I'M JUST WORRYING TOO MUCH.
MOM...
MOM IS MORE...

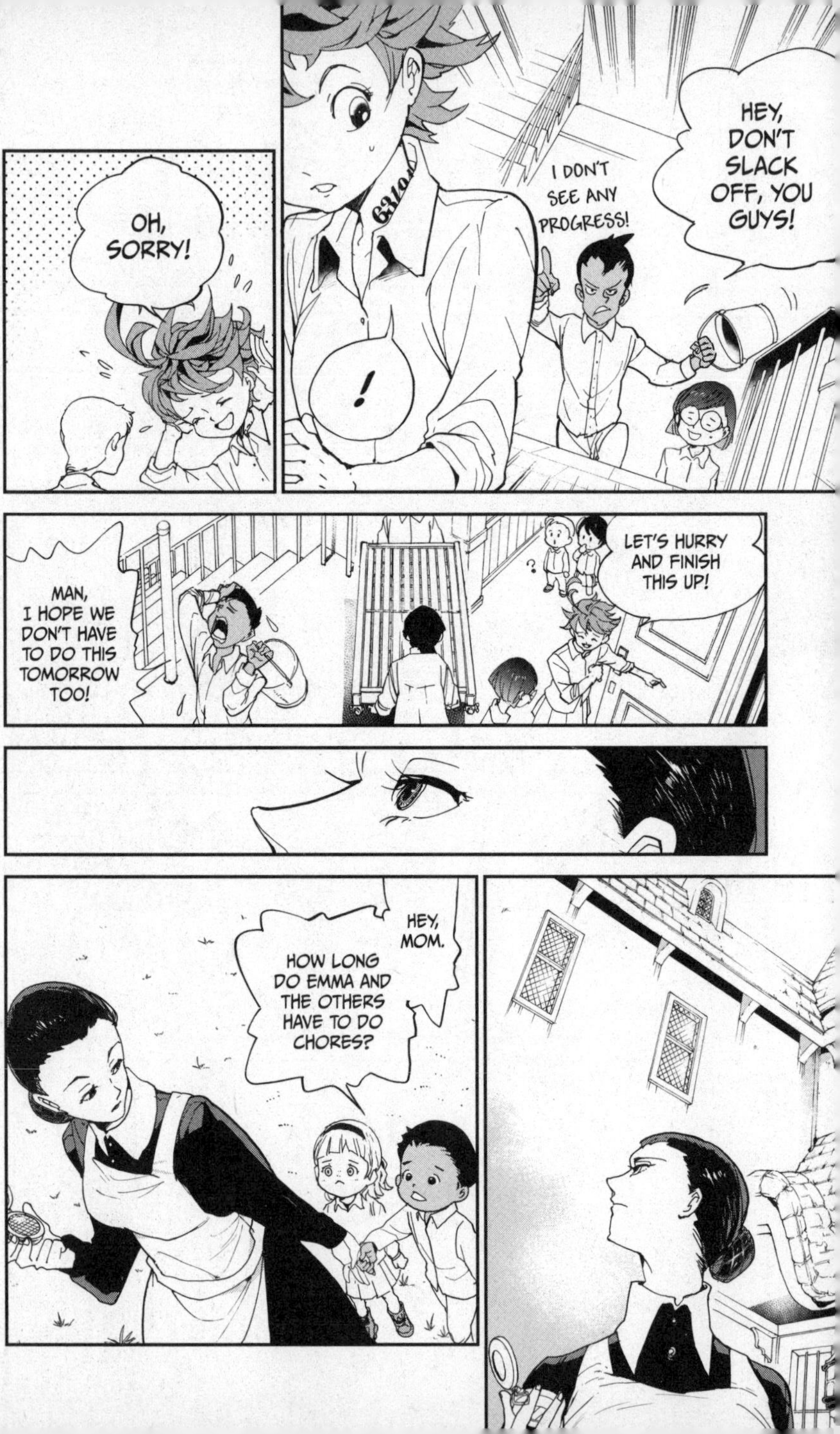
HEY, DON'T SLACK OFF, YOU GUYS!
I DON'T SEE ANY PROGRESS!
!
OH, SORRY!
LET'S HURRY AND FINISH THIS UP!
MAN, I HOPE WE DON'T HAVE TO DO THIS TOMORROW TOO!
HEY, MOM.
HOW LONG DO EMMA AND THE OTHERS HAVE TO DO CHORES?

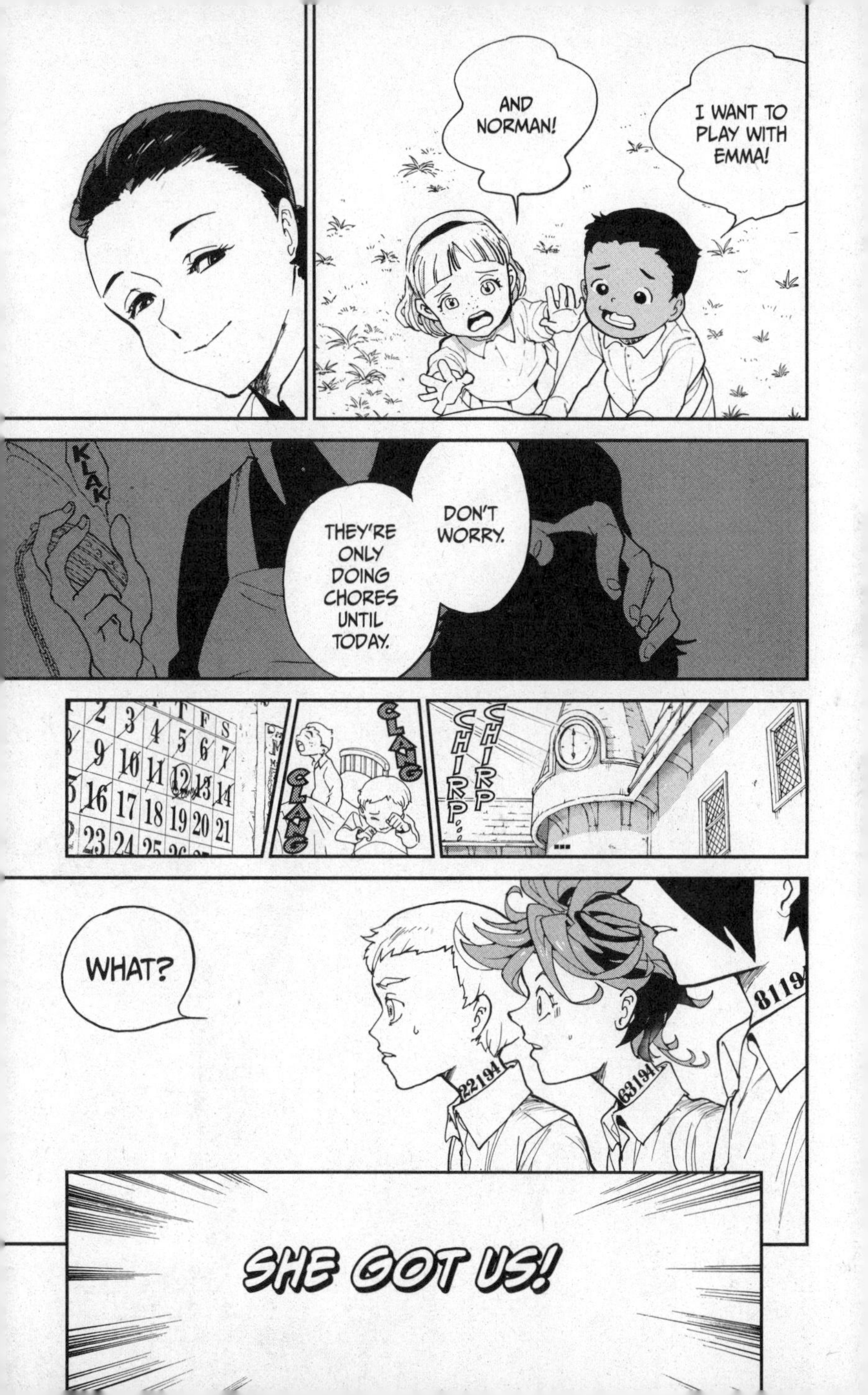
I WANT TO PLAY WITH EMMA!
AND NORMAN!
DON'T WORRY.
THEY'RE ONLY DOING CHORES UNTIL TODAY.
KLAK
CHIRP CHIRP...
CLANG CLANG
WHAT?
22194
63194
SHE GOT US!

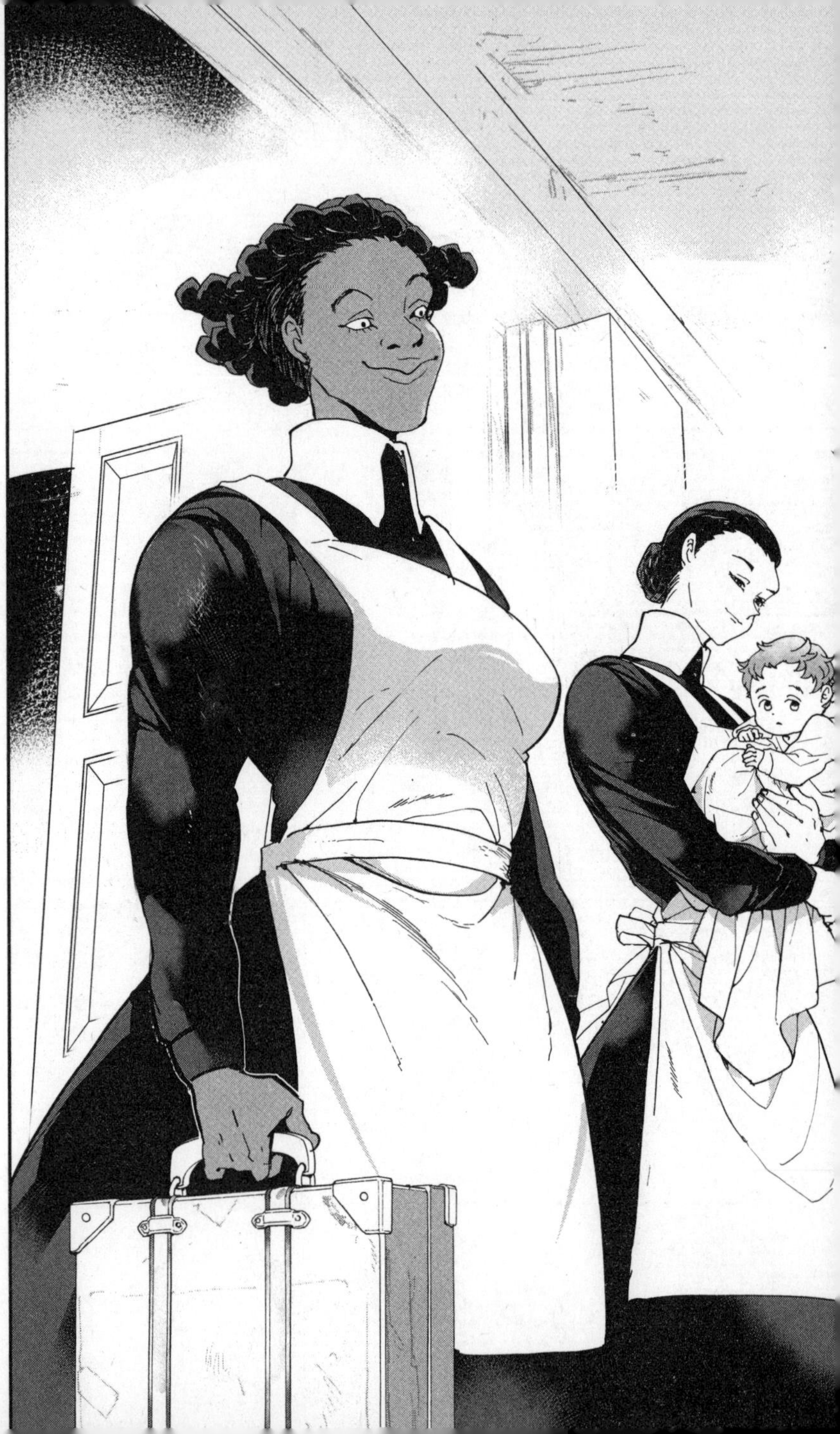

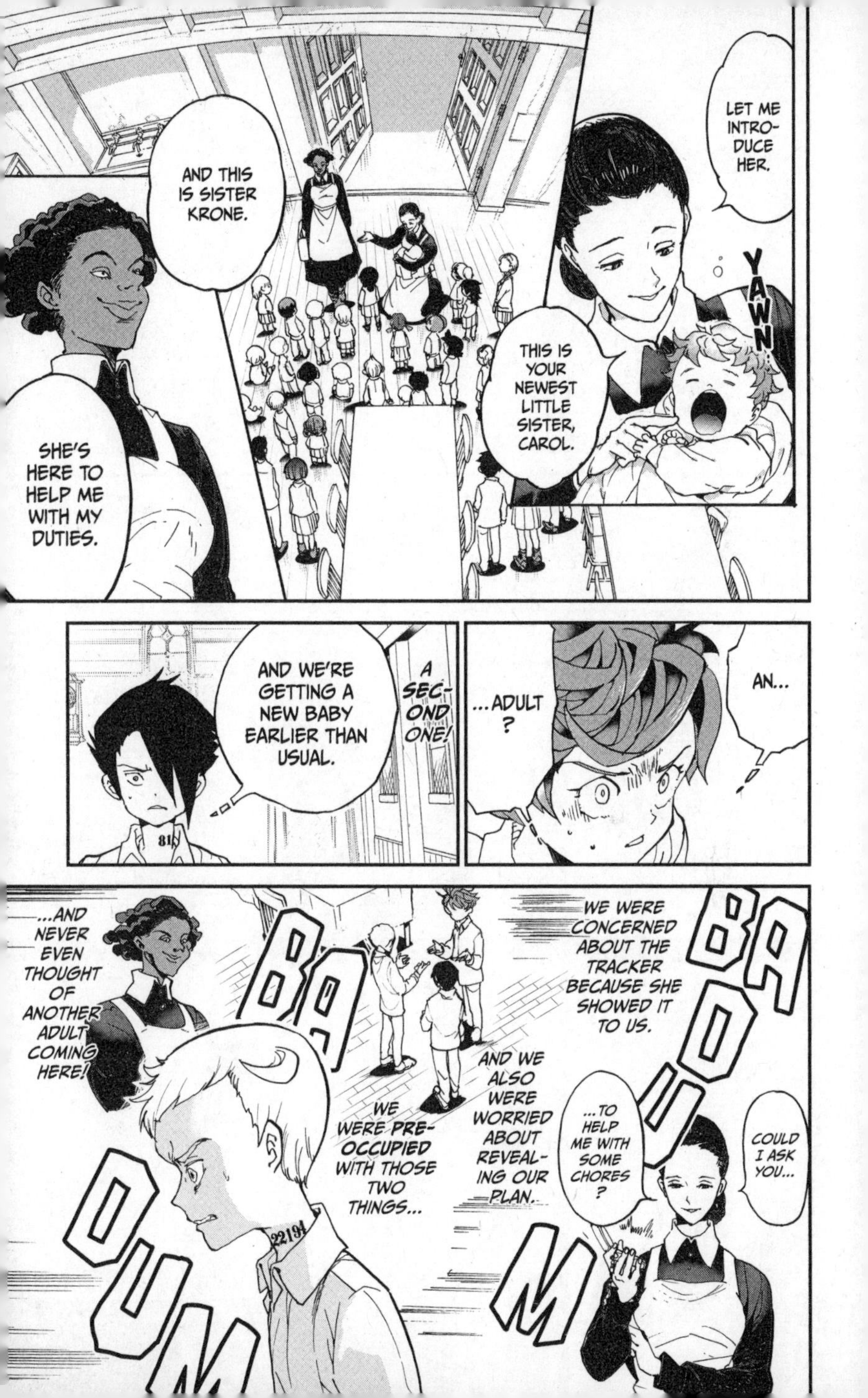
LET ME INTRODUCE HER.
YAWN
THIS IS YOUR NEWEST LITTLE SISTER, CAROL.
AND THIS IS SISTER KRONE.
SHE'S HERE TO HELP ME WITH MY DUTIES.
AN...
...ADULT ?
A SECOND ONE!
AND WE'RE GETTING A NEW BABY EARLIER THAN USUAL.
81
BADUM
COULD I ASK YOU...
...TO HELP ME WITH SOME CHORES ?
WE WERE CONCERNED ABOUT THE TRACKER BECAUSE SHE SHOWED IT TO US.
AND WE ALSO WERE WORRIED ABOUT REVEALING OUR PLAN.
WE WERE PREOCCUPIED WITH THOSE TWO THINGS...
BA
...AND NEVER EVEN THOUGHT OF ANOTHER ADULT COMING HERE!
22194
DUM

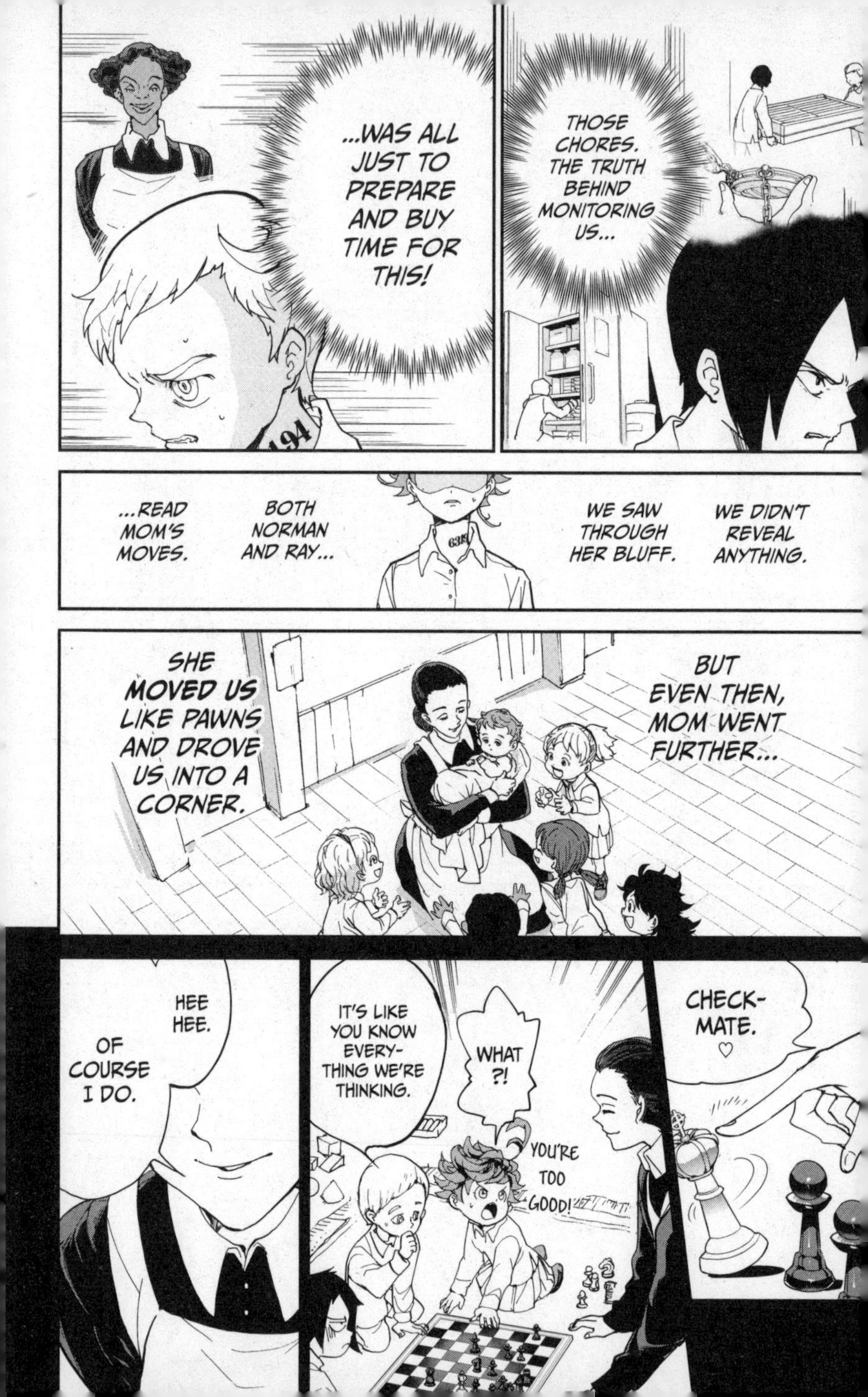
THOSE CHORES. THE TRUTH BEHIND MONITORING US...
...WAS ALL JUST TO PREPARE AND BUY TIME FOR THIS!
WE DIDN'T REVEAL ANYTHING.
WE SAW THROUGH HER BLUFF.
BOTH NORMAN AND RAY...
...READ MOM'S MOVES.
BUT EVEN THEN, MOM WENT FURTHER...
SHE MOVED US LIKE PAWNS AND DROVE US INTO A CORNER.
CHECK-MATE. ♡
WHAT?!
YOU'RE TOO GOOD!
IT'S LIKE YOU KNOW EVERY-THING WE'RE THINKING.
HEE HEE.
OF COURSE I DO.

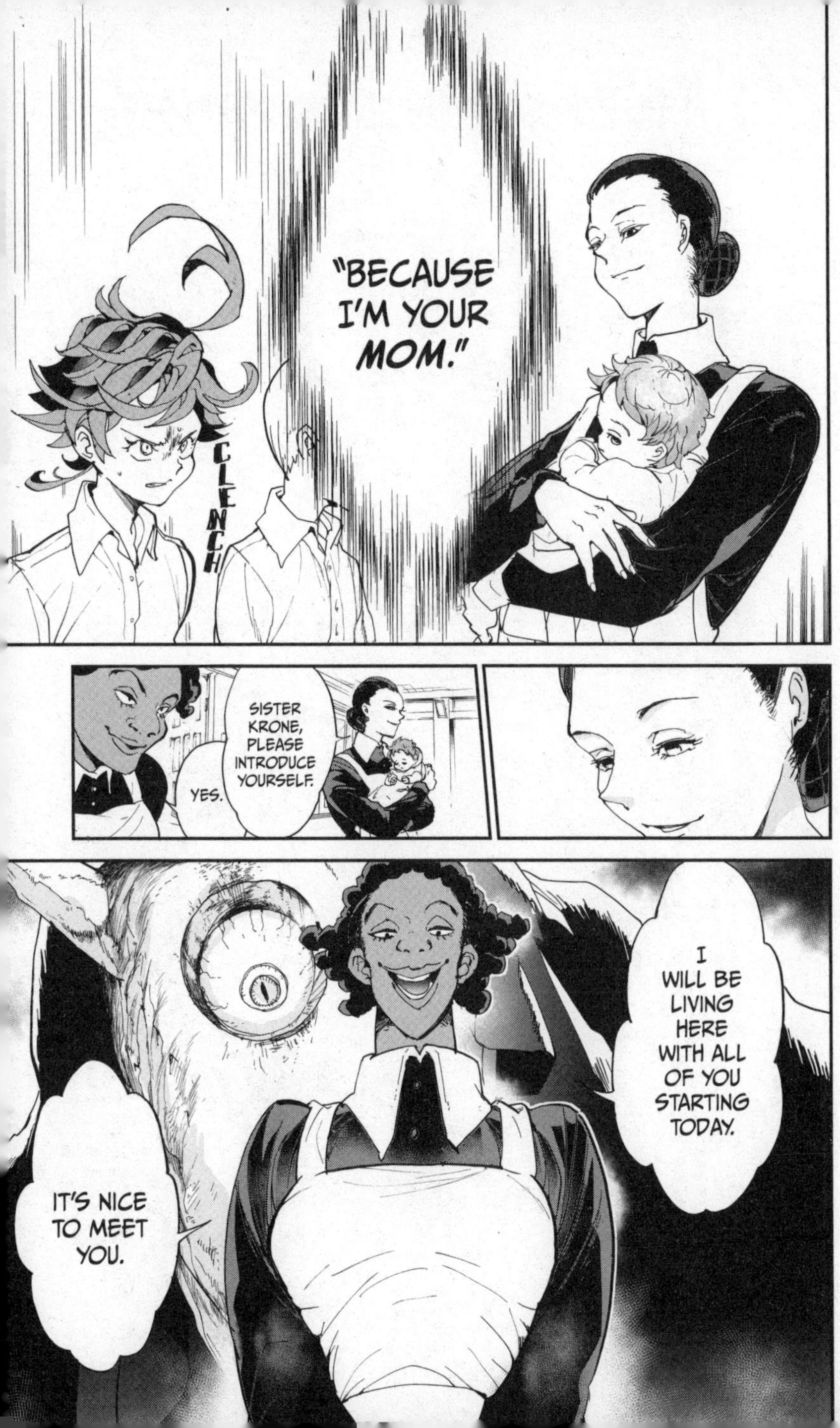
"BECAUSE I'M YOUR MOM."
CLENCH
SISTER KRONE, PLEASE INTRODUCE YOURSELF.
YES.
I WILL BE LIVING HERE WITH ALL OF YOU STARTING TODAY.
IT'S NICE TO MEET YOU.

THE PROMISED NEVERLAND SIDE SCENE 002

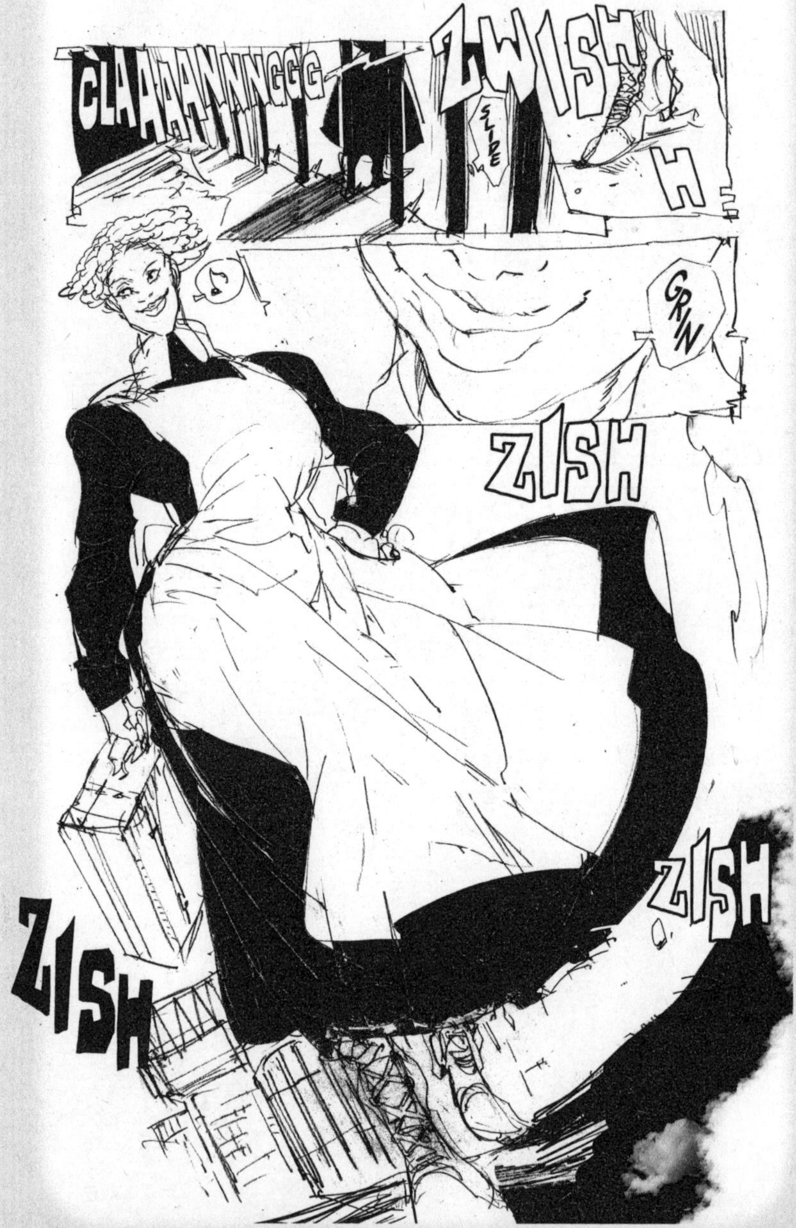
ZWISH
H
SLIDE
CLAAAANNNGGG
GRIN
♪
ZISH
ZISH
ZISH

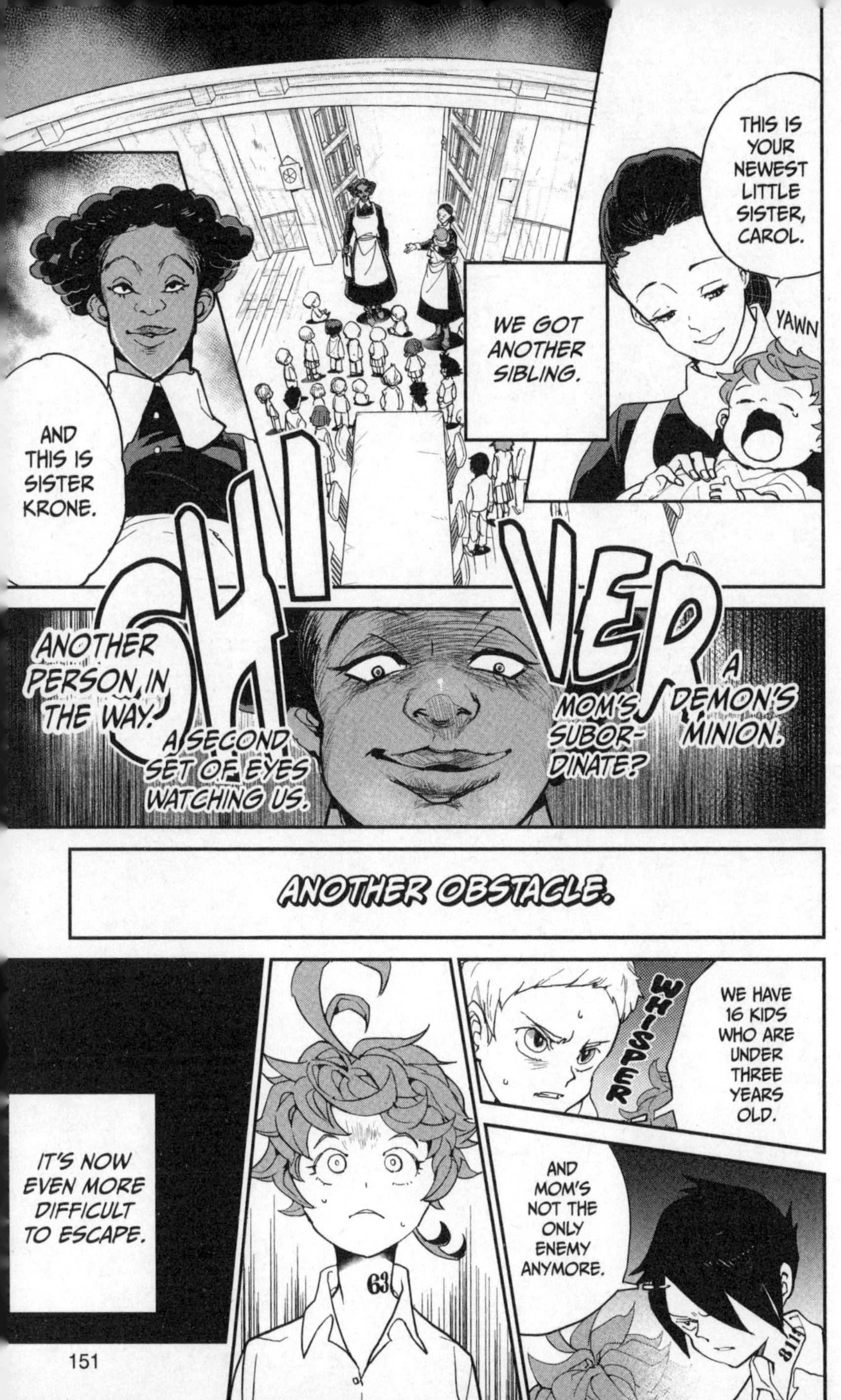
THIS IS YOUR NEWEST LITTLE SISTER, CAROL.
YAWN
WE GOT ANOTHER SIBLING.
AND THIS IS SISTER KRONE.
SHIVER
A DEMON'S MINION.
MOM'S SUBORDINATE?
A SECOND SET OF EYES WATCHING US.
ANOTHER PERSON IN THE WAY.
ANOTHER OBSTACLE.
WHISPER
WE HAVE 16 KIDS WHO ARE UNDER THREE YEARS OLD.
AND MOM'S NOT THE ONLY ENEMY ANYMORE.
63
IT'S NOW EVEN MORE DIFFICULT TO ESCAPE.

CHAPTER 6: CAROL AND KRONE

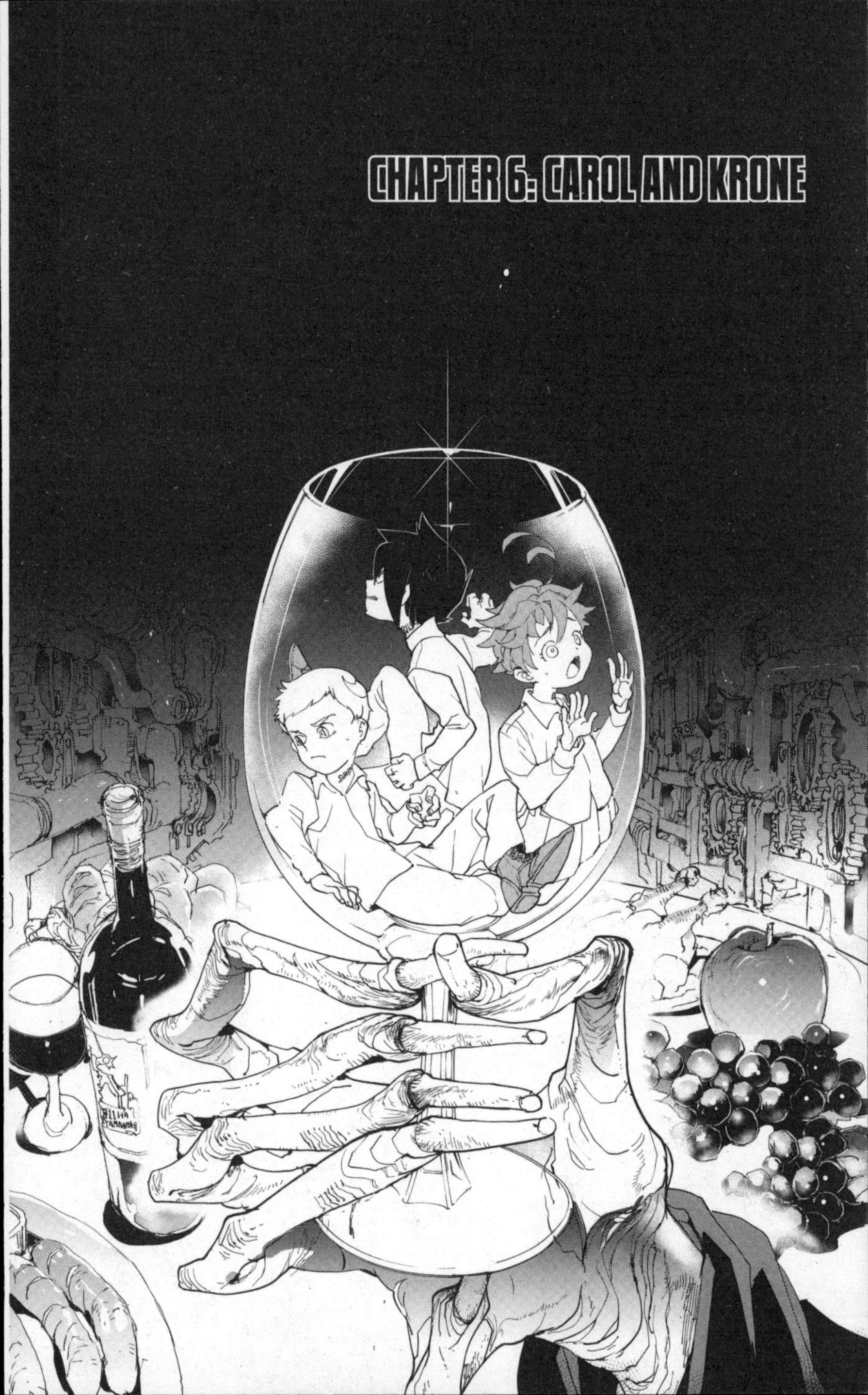

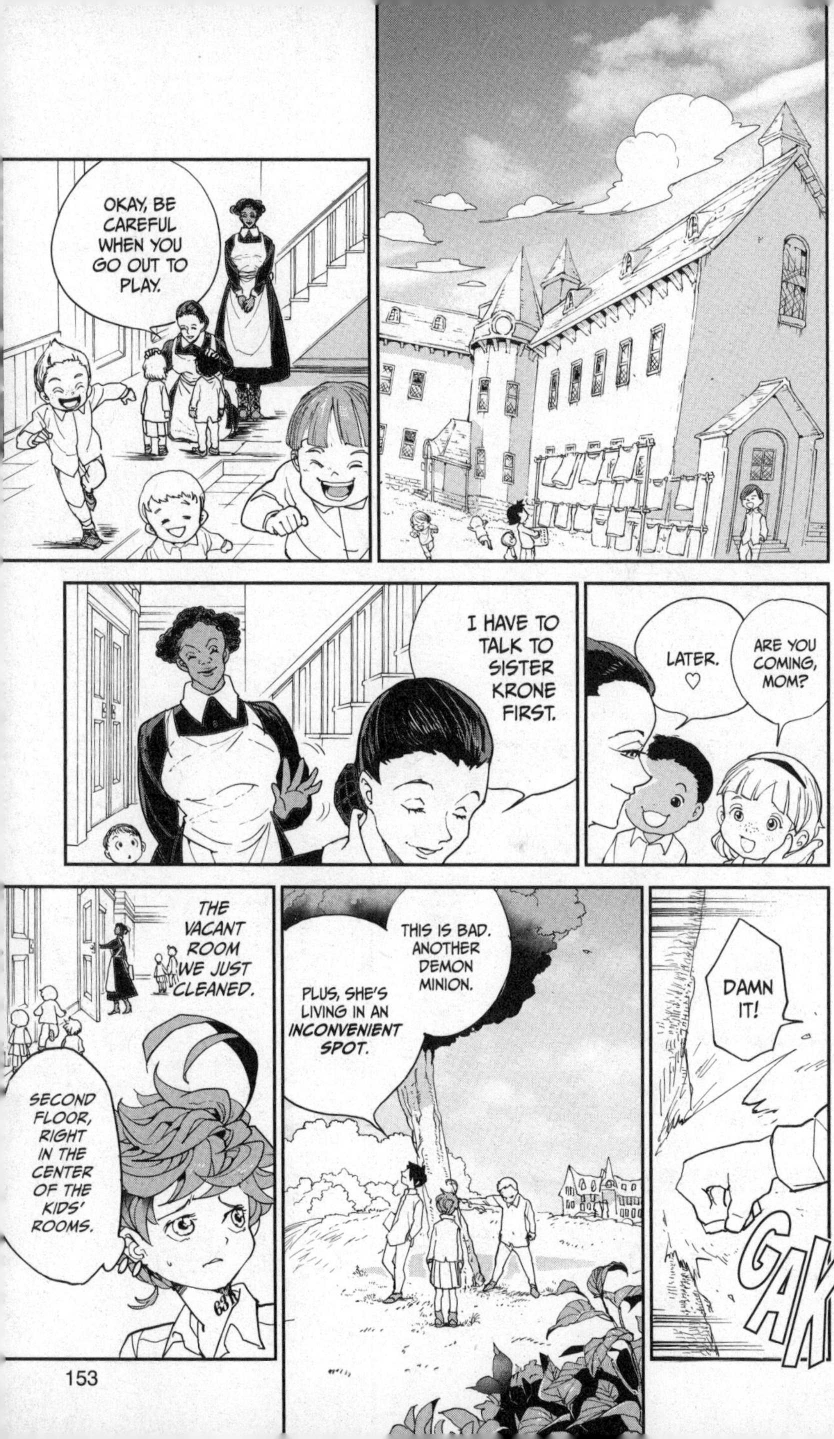
OKAY, BE CAREFUL WHEN YOU GO OUT TO PLAY.
ARE YOU COMING, MOM?
LATER. ♡
I HAVE TO TALK TO SISTER KRONE FIRST.
DAMN IT!
GAK
THIS IS BAD. ANOTHER DEMON MINION.
PLUS, SHE'S LIVING IN AN *INCONVENIENT* SPOT.
THE VACANT ROOM WE JUST CLEANED.
SECOND FLOOR, RIGHT IN THE CENTER OF THE KIDS' ROOMS.

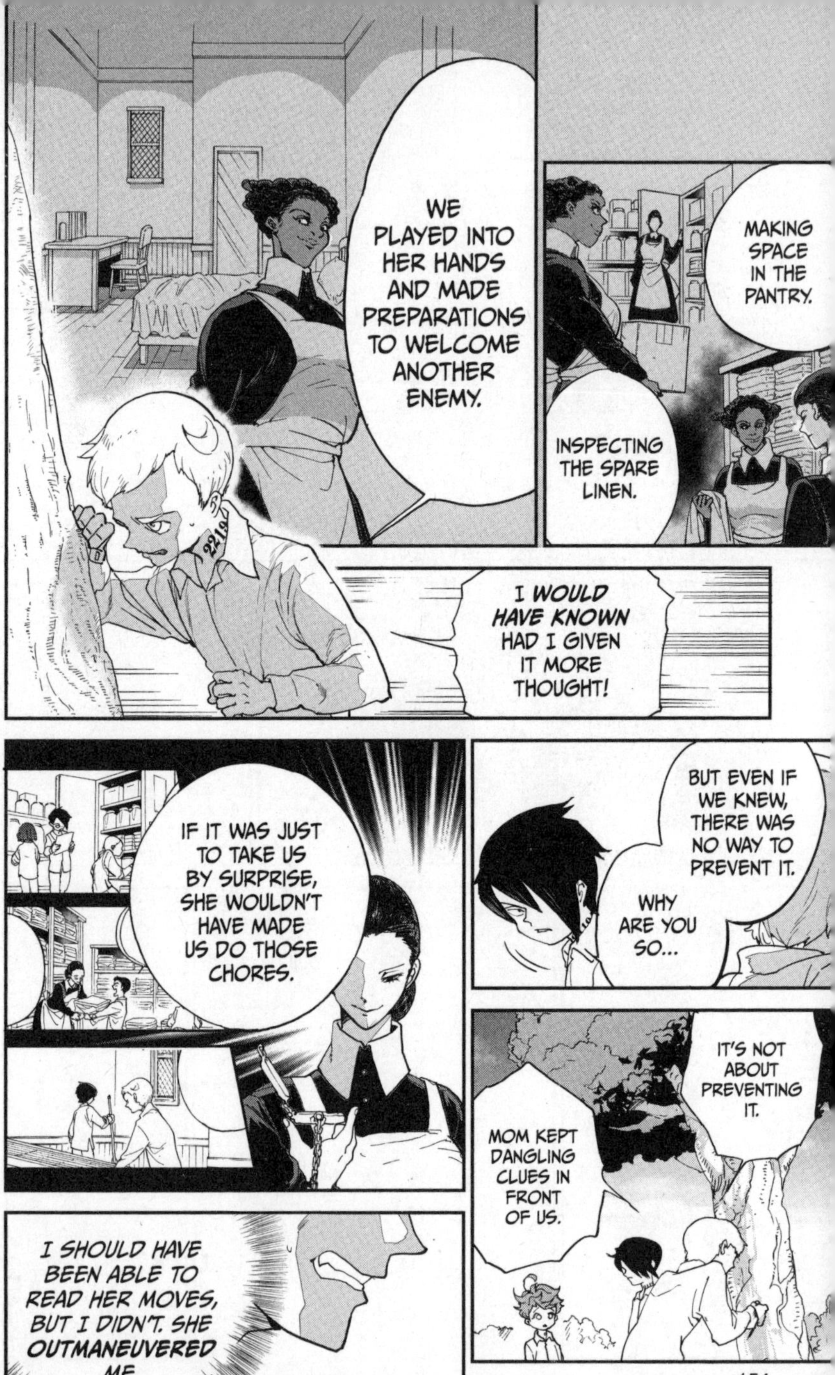
MAKING SPACE IN THE PANTRY.
INSPECTING THE SPARE LINEN.
WE PLAYED INTO HER HANDS AND MADE PREPARATIONS TO WELCOME ANOTHER ENEMY.
I *WOULD HAVE KNOWN* HAD I GIVEN IT MORE THOUGHT!
BUT EVEN IF WE KNEW, THERE WAS NO WAY TO PREVENT IT.
WHY ARE YOU SO...
IT'S NOT ABOUT PREVENTING IT.
MOM KEPT DANGLING CLUES IN FRONT OF US.
IF IT WAS JUST TO TAKE US BY SURPRISE, SHE WOULDN'T HAVE MADE US DO THOSE CHORES.
*I SHOULD HAVE BEEN ABLE TO READ HER MOVES, BUT I DIDN'T. SHE **OUTMANEUVERED** ME.*

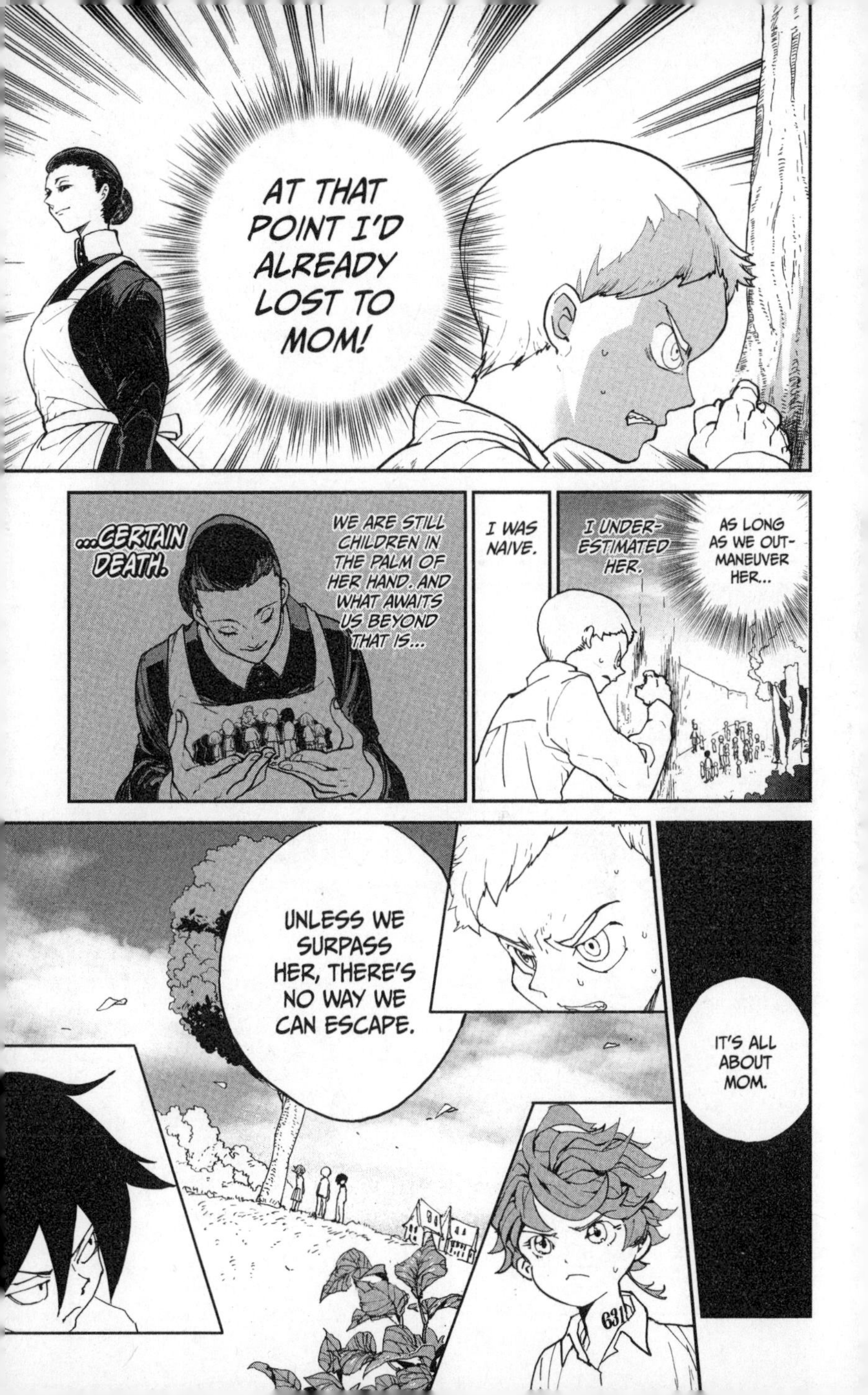
AT THAT POINT I'D ALREADY LOST TO MOM!
AS LONG AS WE OUT-MANEUVER HER...
I UNDER-ESTIMATED HER.
I WAS NAIVE.
WE ARE STILL CHILDREN IN THE PALM OF HER HAND. AND WHAT AWAITS US BEYOND THAT IS...
...CERTAIN DEATH.
IT'S ALL ABOUT MOM.
UNLESS WE SURPASS HER, THERE'S NO WAY WE CAN ESCAPE.
631

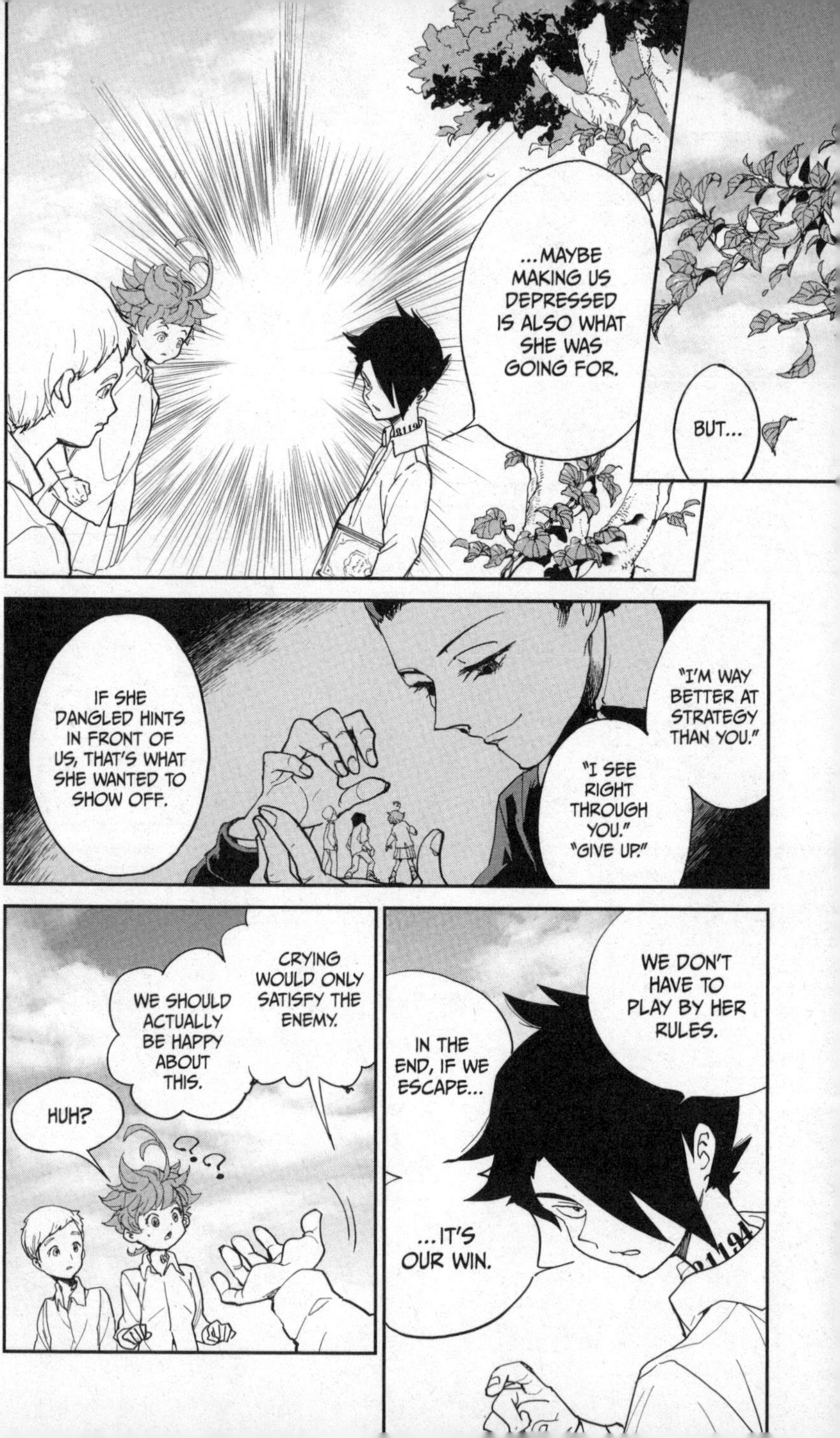
...MAYBE MAKING US DEPRESSED IS ALSO WHAT SHE WAS GOING FOR.
BUT...
"I'M WAY BETTER AT STRATEGY THAN YOU."
"I SEE RIGHT THROUGH YOU." "GIVE UP."
IF SHE DANGLED HINTS IN FRONT OF US, THAT'S WHAT SHE WANTED TO SHOW OFF.
WE DON'T HAVE TO PLAY BY HER RULES.
IN THE END, IF WE ESCAPE...
...IT'S OUR WIN.
CRYING WOULD ONLY SATISFY THE ENEMY.
WE SHOULD ACTUALLY BE HAPPY ABOUT THIS.
HUH?

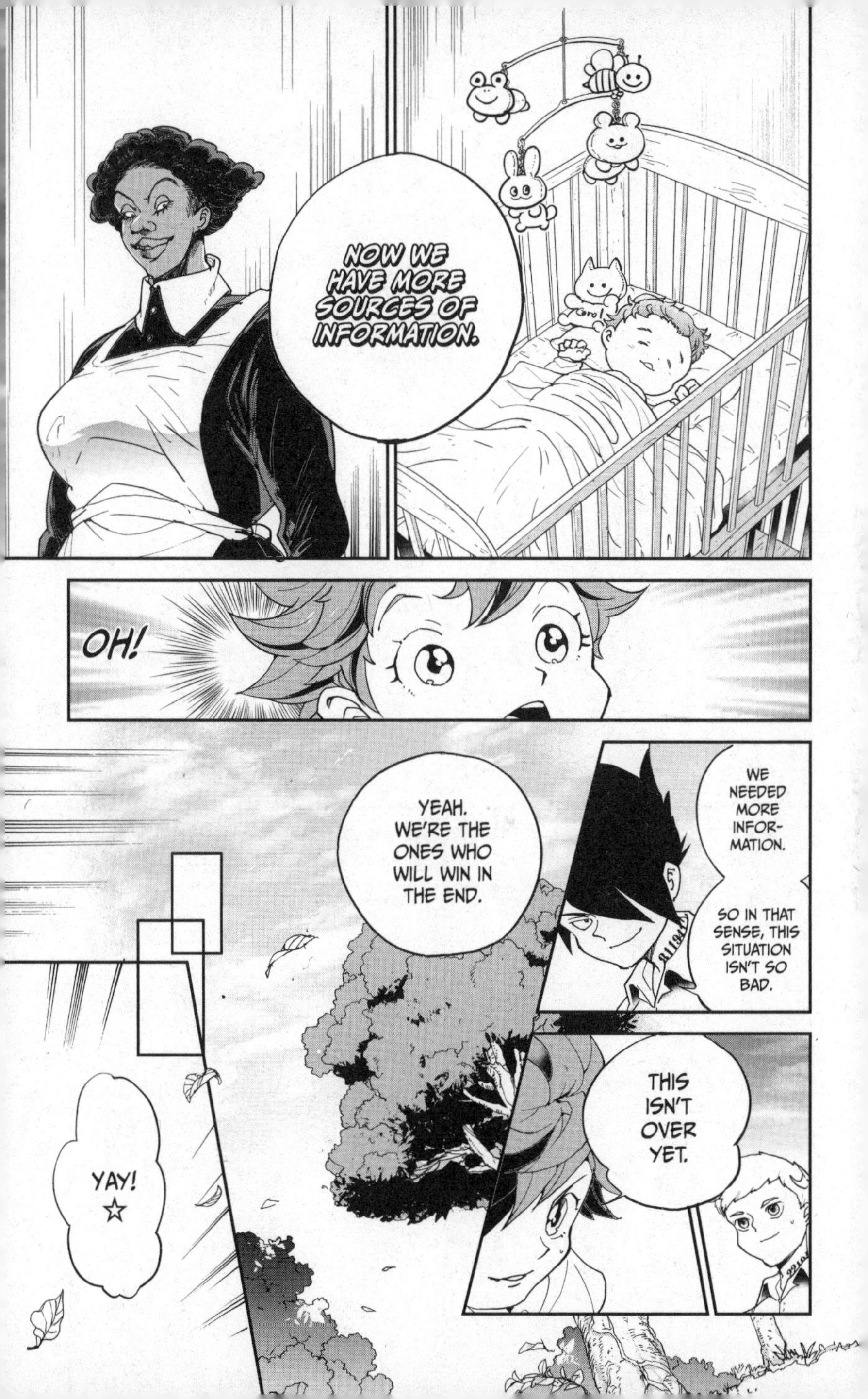
NOW WE HAVE MORE SOURCES OF INFORMATION.
OH!
WE NEEDED MORE INFOR-MATION.
SO IN THAT SENSE, THIS SITUATION ISN'T SO BAD.
THIS ISN'T OVER YET.
YEAH. WE'RE THE ONES WHO WILL WIN IN THE END.
YAY! ☆

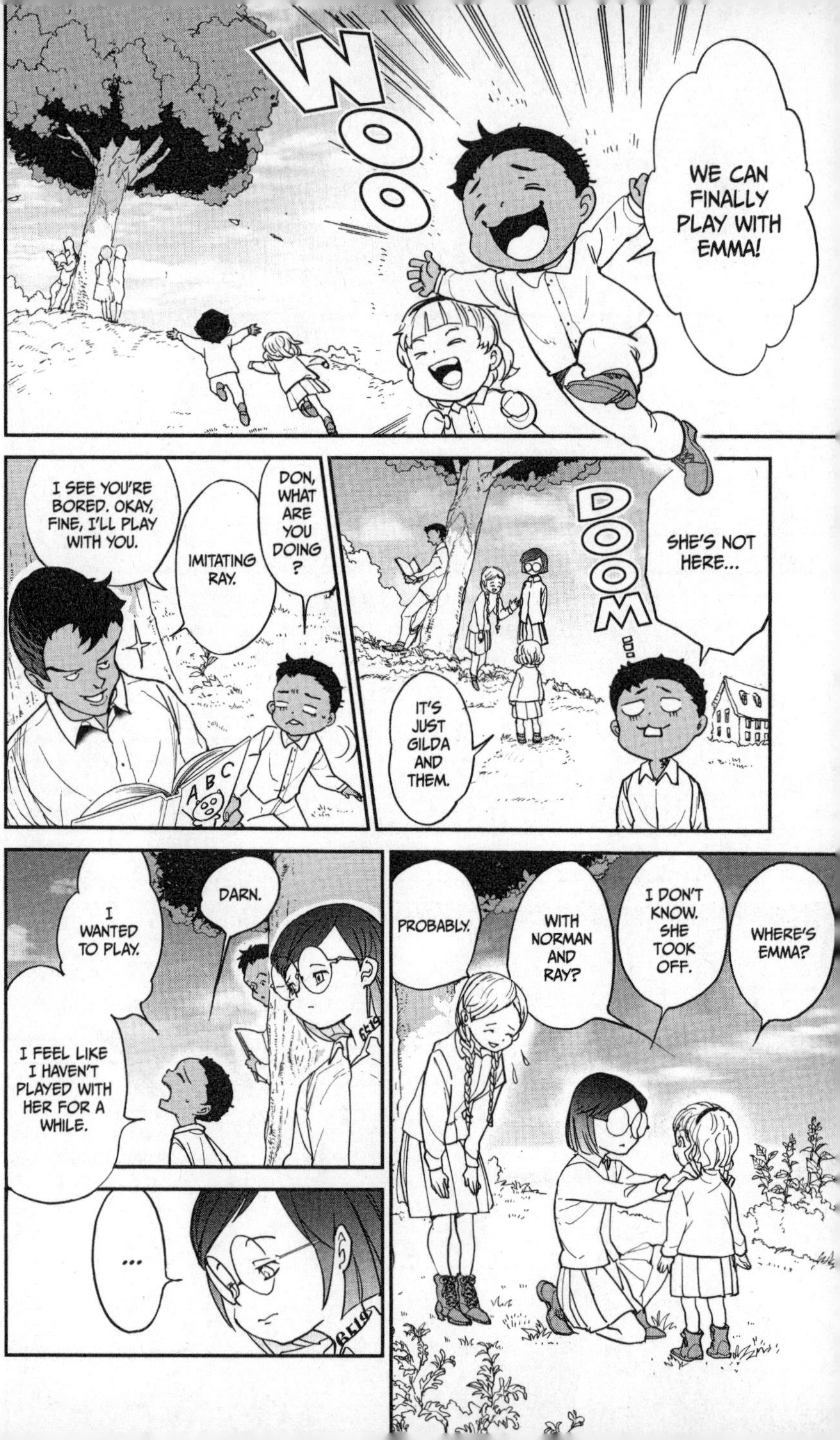
WOOO
WE CAN FINALLY PLAY WITH EMMA!
DOOM
SHE'S NOT HERE...
IT'S JUST GILDA AND THEM.
DON, WHAT ARE YOU DOING?
IMITATING RAY.
I SEE YOU'RE BORED. OKAY, FINE, I'LL PLAY WITH YOU.
WHERE'S EMMA?
I DON'T KNOW. SHE TOOK OFF.
WITH NORMAN AND RAY?
PROBABLY.
DARN.
I WANTED TO PLAY.
I FEEL LIKE I HAVEN'T PLAYED WITH HER FOR A WHILE.
...

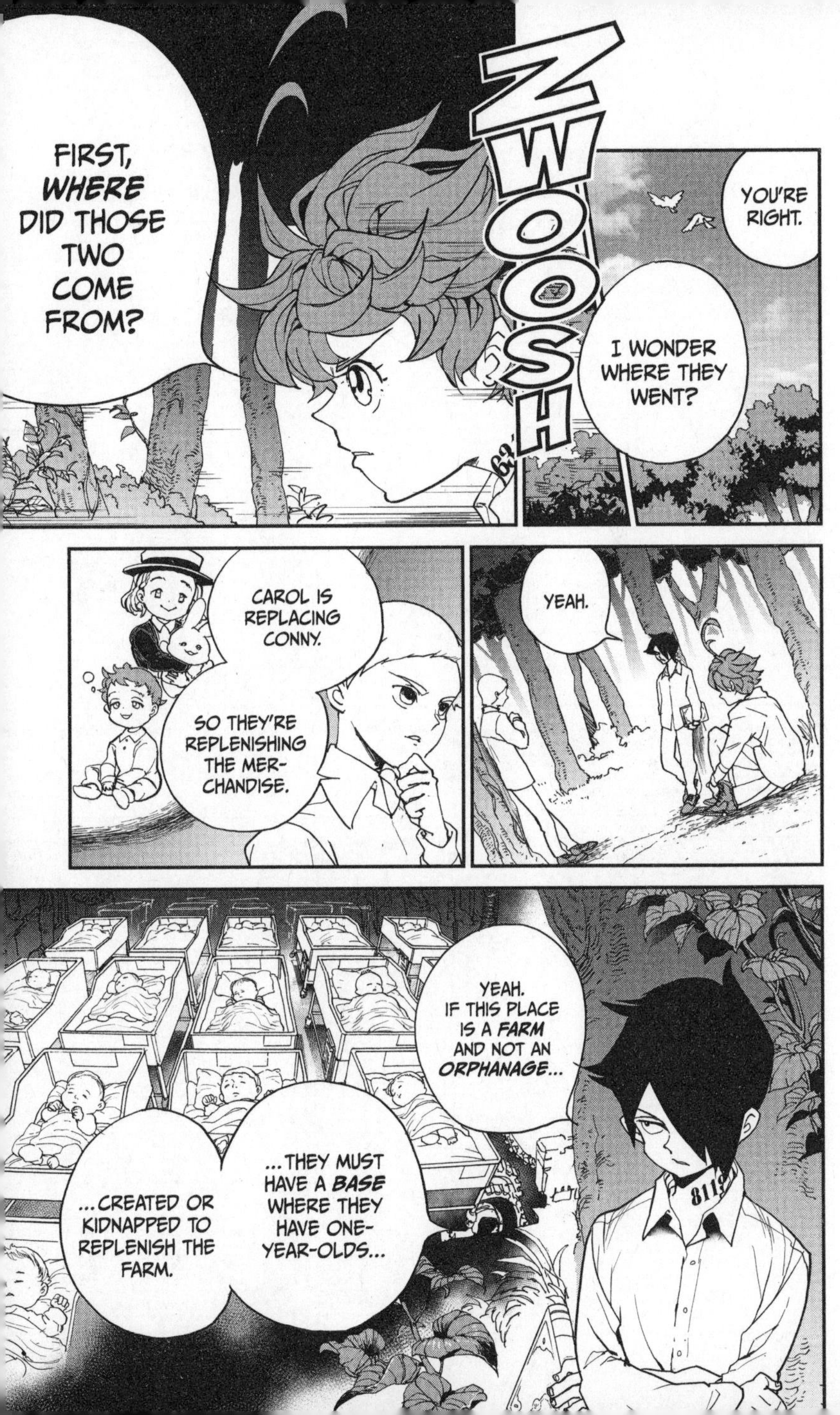
YOU'RE RIGHT.
I WONDER WHERE THEY WENT?
WHOOSH
FIRST, *WHERE* DID THOSE TWO COME FROM?
YEAH.
CAROL IS REPLACING CONNY.
SO THEY'RE REPLENISHING THE MER-CHANDISE.
YEAH. IF THIS PLACE IS A *FARM* AND NOT AN *ORPHANAGE*...
...THEY MUST HAVE A *BASE* WHERE THEY HAVE ONE-YEAR-OLDS...
...CREATED OR KIDNAPPED TO REPLENISH THE FARM.

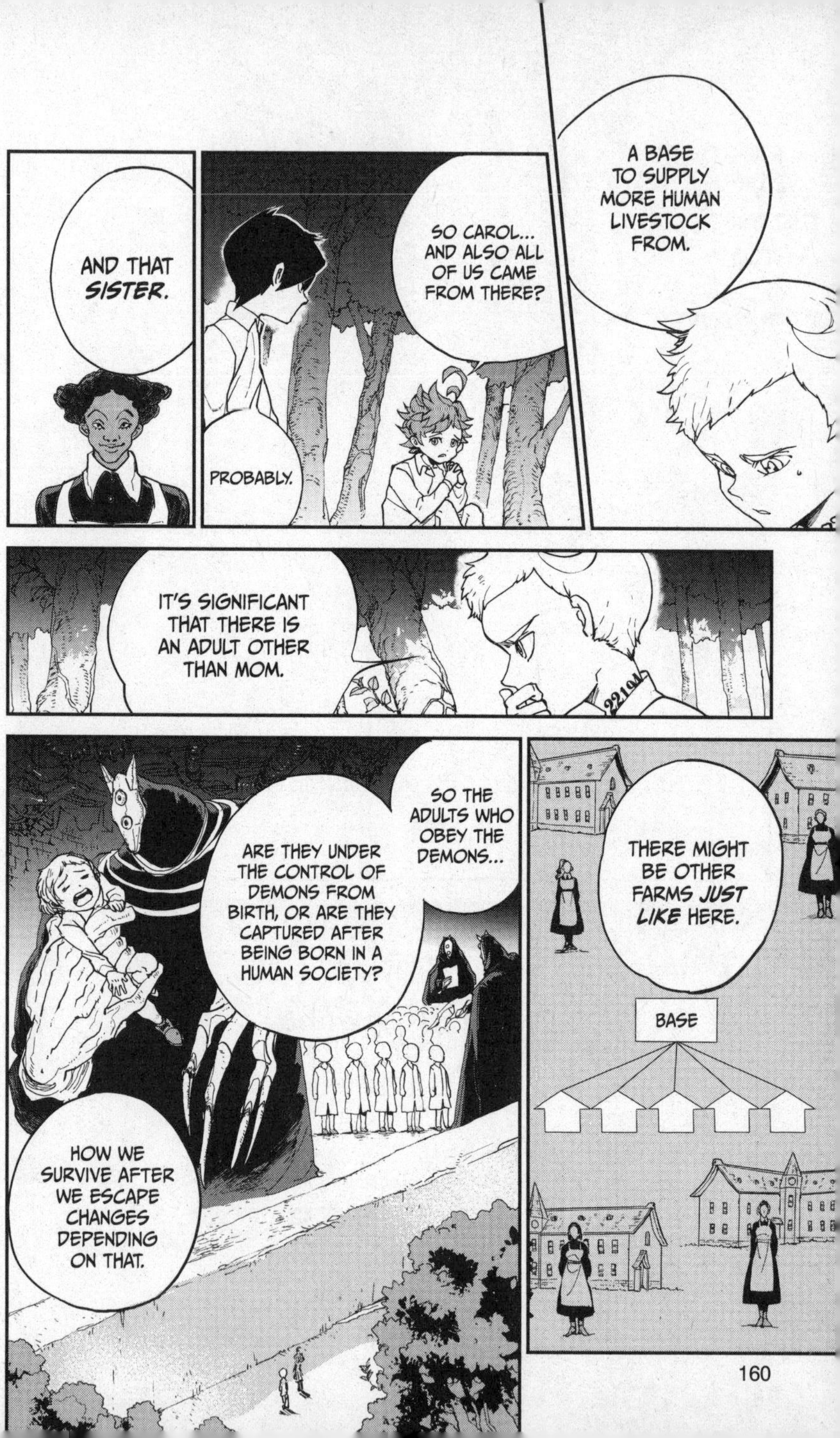
A BASE TO SUPPLY MORE HUMAN LIVESTOCK FROM.
SO CAROL... AND ALSO ALL OF US CAME FROM THERE?
PROBABLY.
AND THAT *SISTER.*
IT'S SIGNIFICANT THAT THERE IS AN ADULT OTHER THAN MOM.
THERE MIGHT BE OTHER FARMS *JUST LIKE* HERE.
BASE
SO THE ADULTS WHO OBEY THE DEMONS...
ARE THEY UNDER THE CONTROL OF DEMONS FROM BIRTH, OR ARE THEY CAPTURED AFTER BEING BORN IN A HUMAN SOCIETY?
HOW WE SURVIVE AFTER WE ESCAPE CHANGES DEPENDING ON THAT.

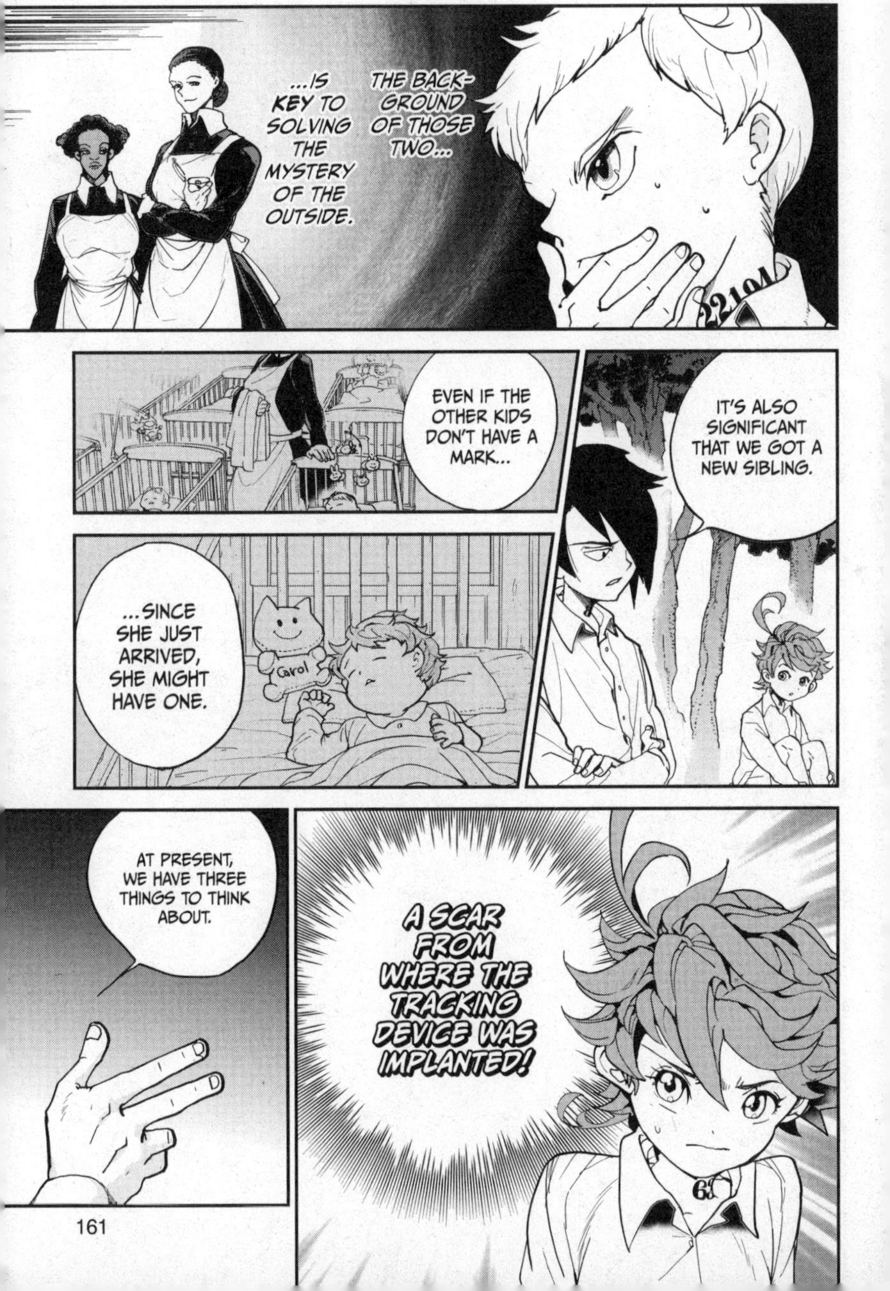
THE BACK-GROUND OF THOSE TWO...
...IS KEY TO SOLVING THE MYSTERY OF THE OUTSIDE.
IT'S ALSO SIGNIFICANT THAT WE GOT A NEW SIBLING.
EVEN IF THE OTHER KIDS DON'T HAVE A MARK...
...SINCE SHE JUST ARRIVED, SHE MIGHT HAVE ONE.
Carol
A SCAR FROM WHERE THE TRACKING DEVICE WAS IMPLANTED!
AT PRESENT, WE HAVE THREE THINGS TO THINK ABOUT.

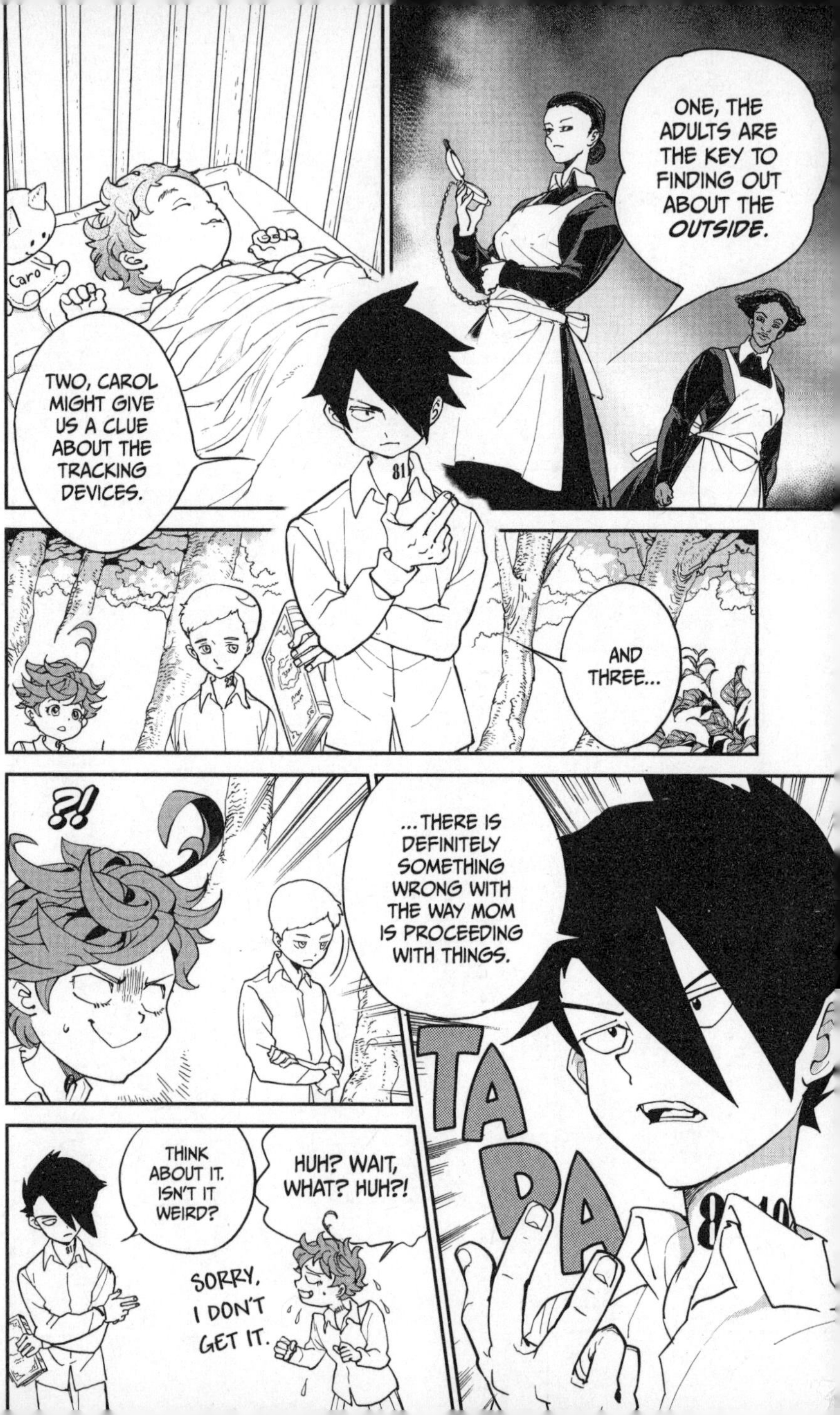
ONE, THE ADULTS ARE THE KEY TO FINDING OUT ABOUT THE *OUTSIDE*.
Caro
TWO, CAROL MIGHT GIVE US A CLUE ABOUT THE TRACKING DEVICES.
AND THREE...
...THERE IS DEFINITELY SOMETHING WRONG WITH THE WAY MOM IS PROCEEDING WITH THINGS.
TA DA
?!
HUH? WAIT, WHAT? HUH?!
THINK ABOUT IT. ISN'T IT WEIRD?
SORRY, I DON'T GET IT.

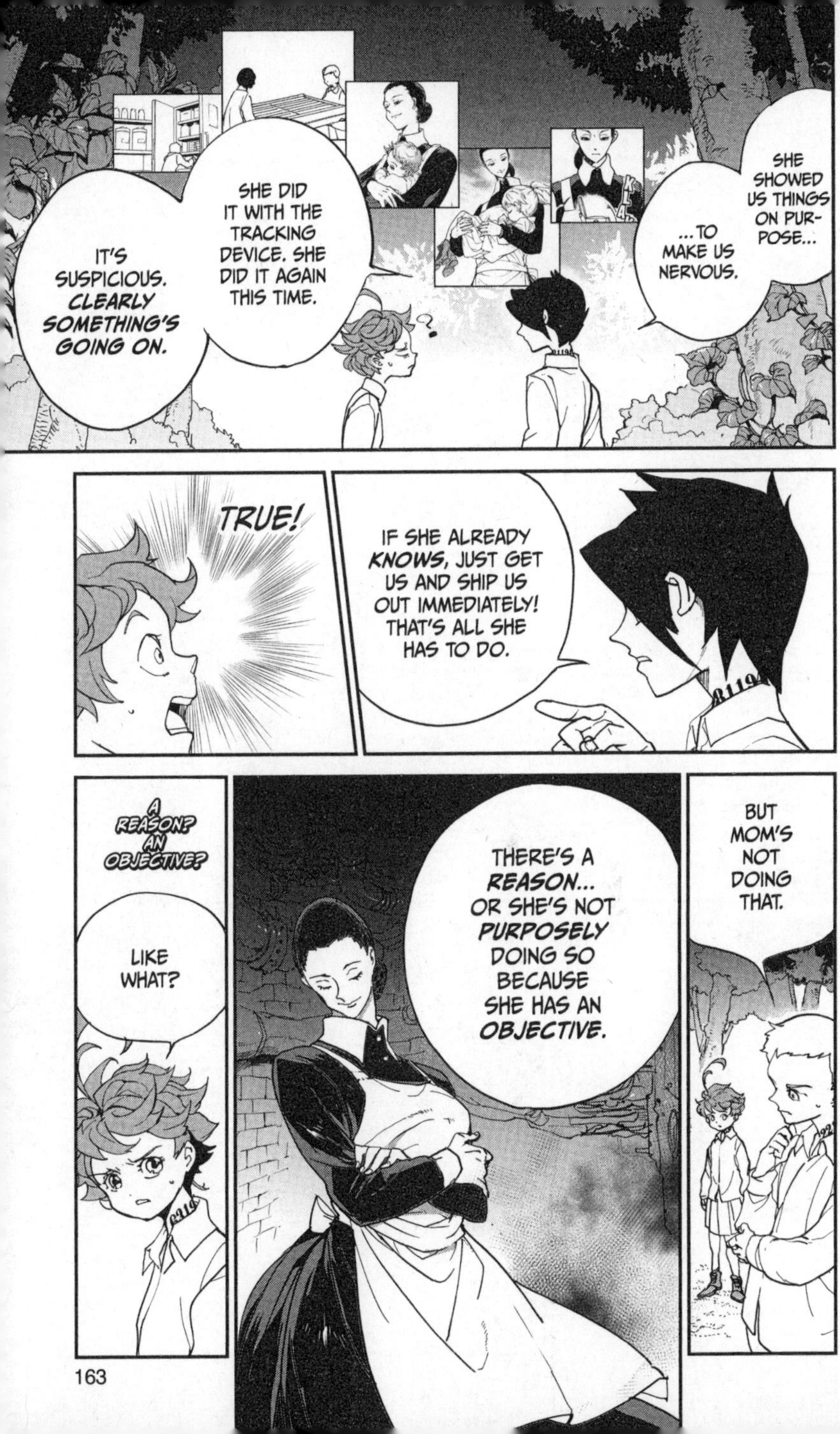
SHE SHOWED US THINGS ON PURPOSE...
...TO MAKE US NERVOUS.
SHE DID IT WITH THE TRACKING DEVICE. SHE DID IT AGAIN THIS TIME.
IT'S SUSPICIOUS. CLEARLY SOMETHING'S GOING ON.
IF SHE ALREADY KNOWS, JUST GET US AND SHIP US OUT IMMEDIATELY! THAT'S ALL SHE HAS TO DO.
TRUE!
BUT MOM'S NOT DOING THAT.
THERE'S A REASON... OR SHE'S NOT PURPOSELY DOING SO BECAUSE SHE HAS AN OBJECTIVE.
A REASON? AN OBJECTIVE?
LIKE WHAT?

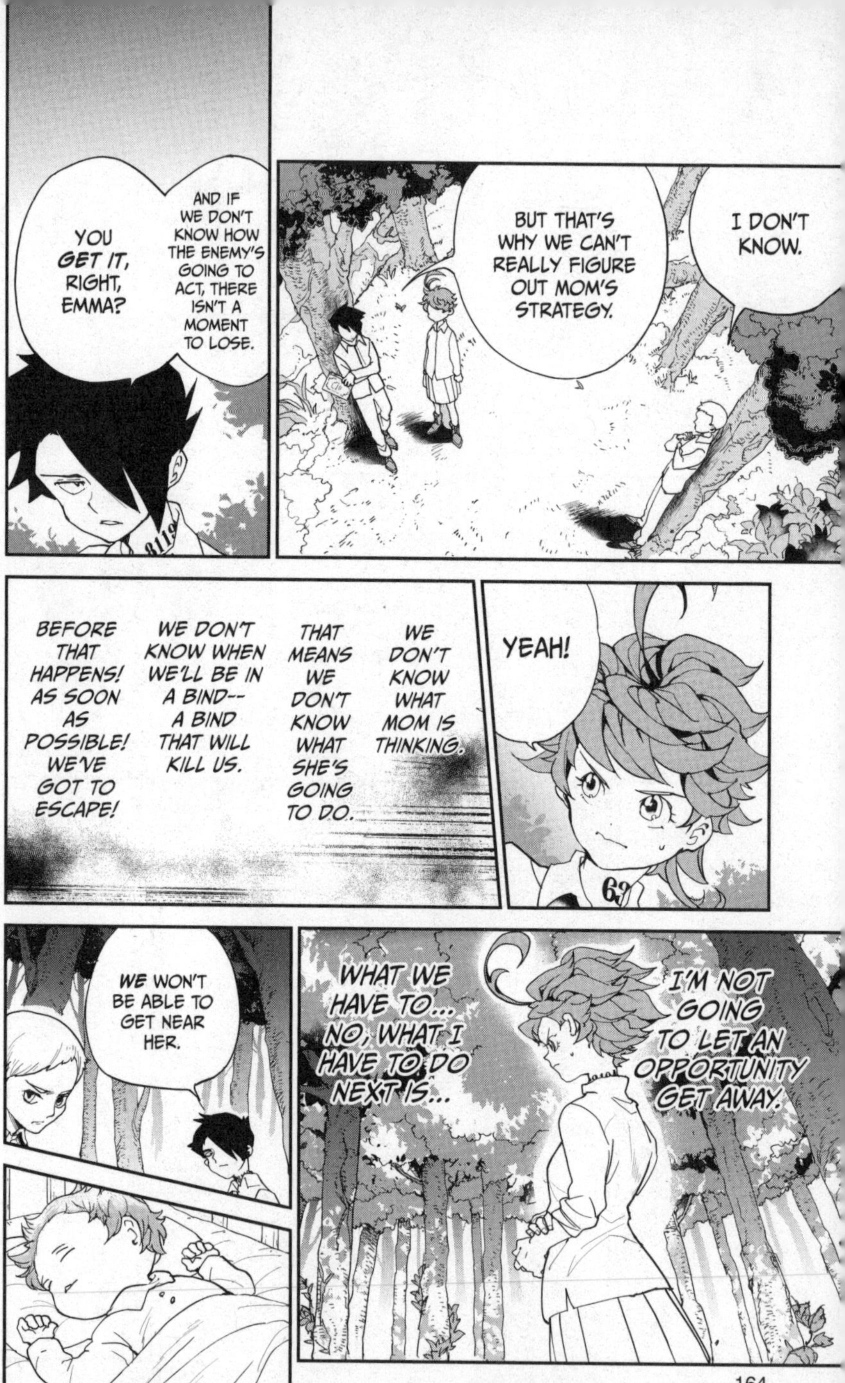
I DON'T KNOW.
BUT THAT'S WHY WE CAN'T REALLY FIGURE OUT MOM'S STRATEGY.
AND IF WE DON'T KNOW HOW THE ENEMY'S GOING TO ACT, THERE ISN'T A MOMENT TO LOSE.
YOU GET IT, RIGHT, EMMA?
YEAH!
WE DON'T KNOW WHAT MOM IS THINKING.
THAT MEANS WE DON'T KNOW WHAT SHE'S GOING TO DO.
WE DON'T KNOW WHEN WE'LL BE IN A BIND-- A BIND THAT WILL KILL US.
BEFORE THAT HAPPENS! AS SOON AS POSSIBLE! WE'VE GOT TO ESCAPE!
I'M NOT GOING TO LET AN OPPORTUNITY GET AWAY.
WHAT WE HAVE TO... NO, WHAT I HAVE TO DO NEXT IS...
WE WON'T BE ABLE TO GET NEAR HER.

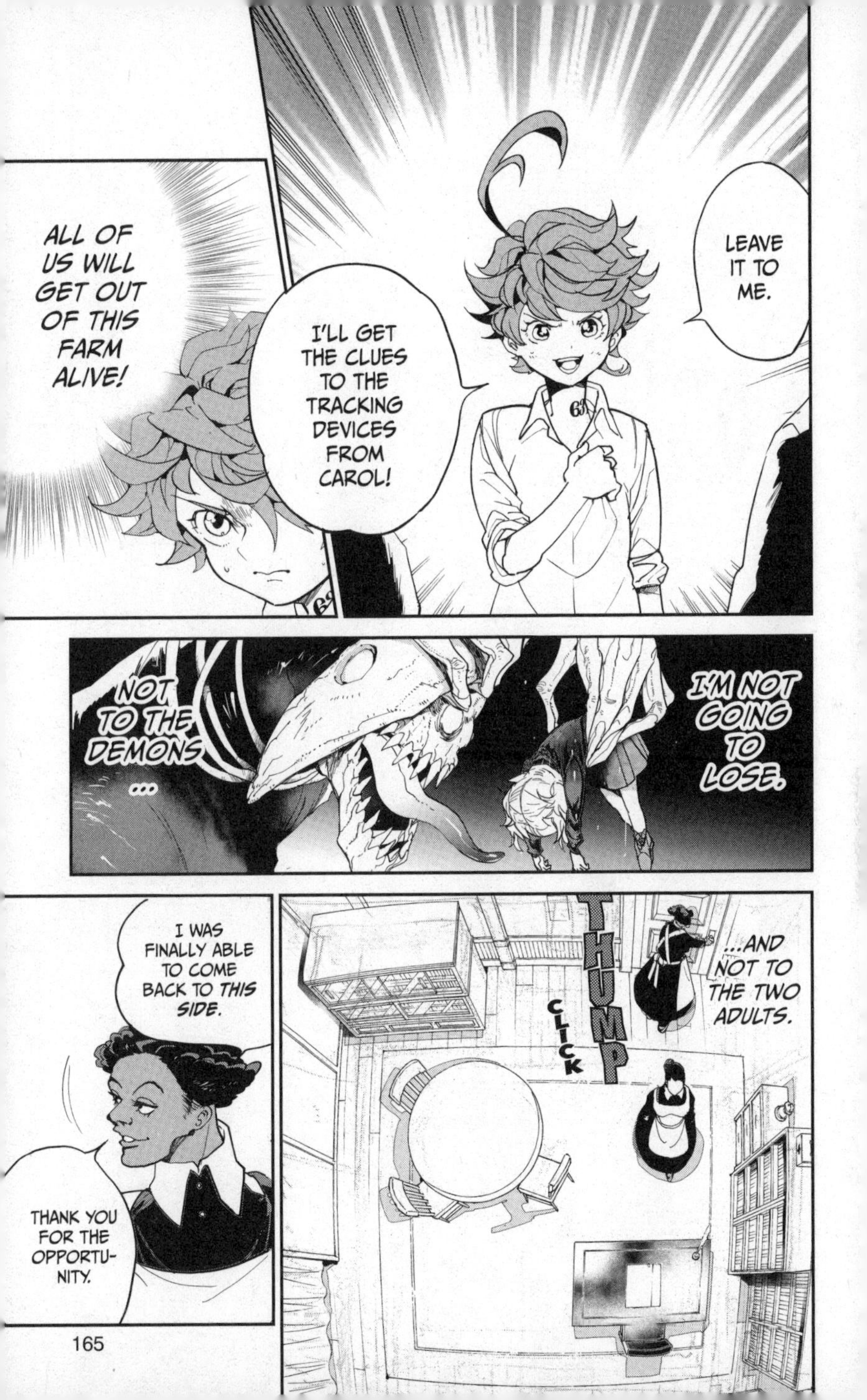
LEAVE IT TO ME.
I'LL GET THE CLUES TO THE TRACKING DEVICES FROM CAROL!
ALL OF US WILL GET OUT OF THIS FARM ALIVE!
I'M NOT GOING TO LOSE.
NOT TO THE DEMONS ...
...AND NOT TO THE TWO ADULTS.
THUMP
CLICK
I WAS FINALLY ABLE TO COME BACK TO THIS SIDE.
THANK YOU FOR THE OPPORTUNITY.

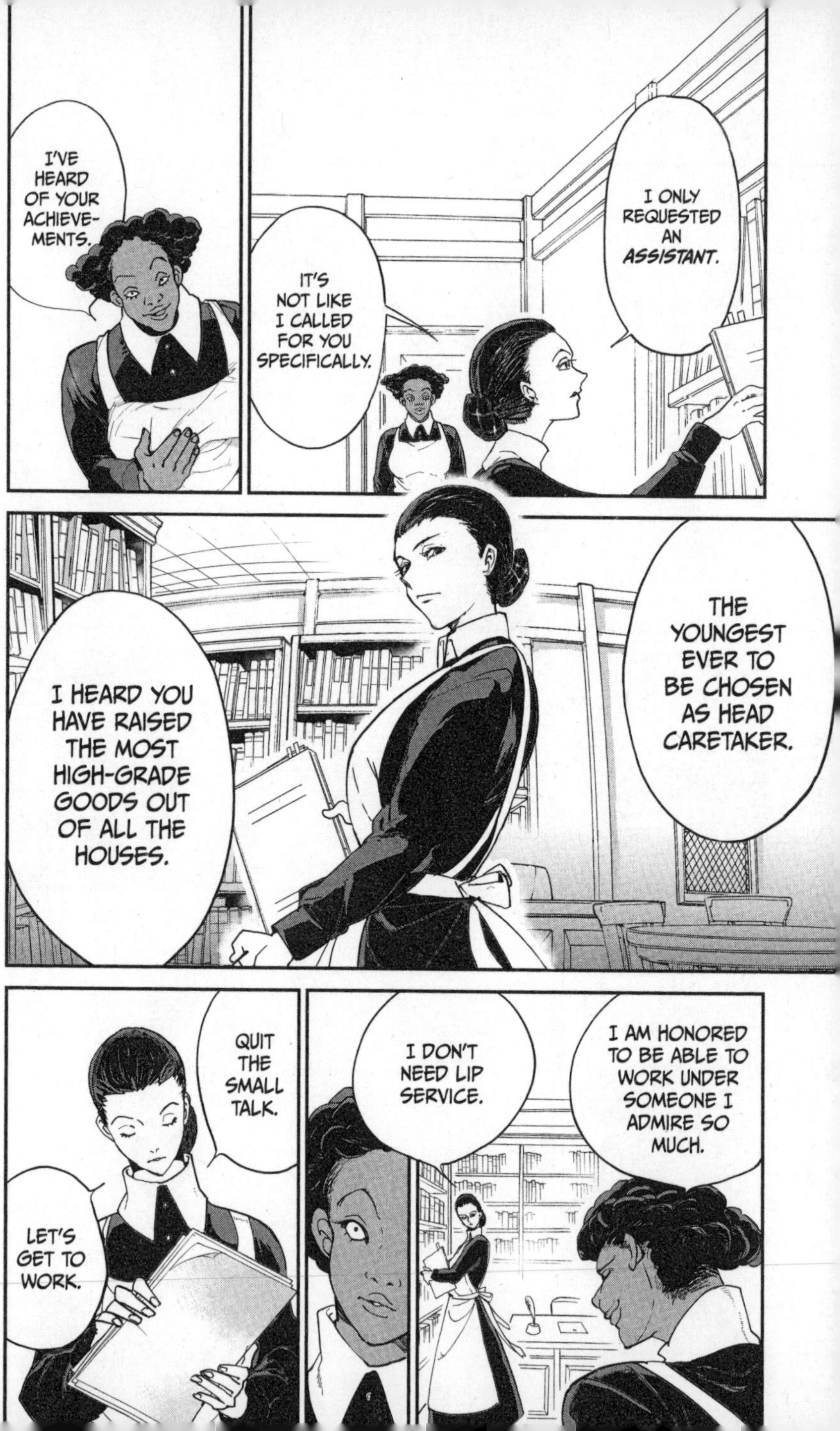
I ONLY REQUESTED AN ASSISTANT.
IT'S NOT LIKE I CALLED FOR YOU SPECIFICALLY.
I'VE HEARD OF YOUR ACHIEVEMENTS.
THE YOUNGEST EVER TO BE CHOSEN AS HEAD CARETAKER.
I HEARD YOU HAVE RAISED THE MOST HIGH-GRADE GOODS OUT OF ALL THE HOUSES.
I AM HONORED TO BE ABLE TO WORK UNDER SOMEONE I ADMIRE SO MUCH.
I DON'T NEED LIP SERVICE.
QUIT THE SMALL TALK.
LET'S GET TO WORK.

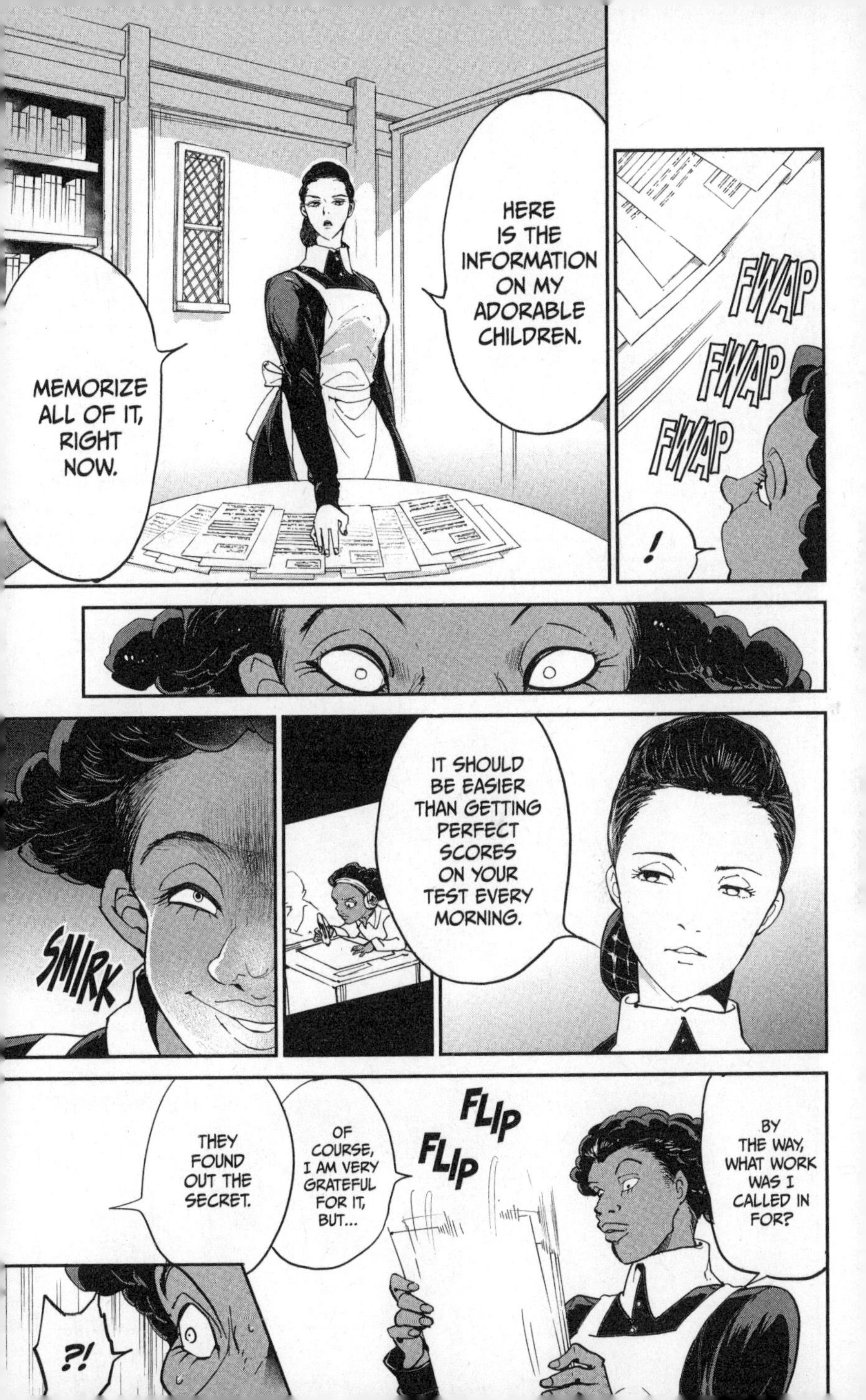
FWAP
FWAP
FWAP
!
HERE IS THE INFORMATION ON MY ADORABLE CHILDREN.
MEMORIZE ALL OF IT, RIGHT NOW.
IT SHOULD BE EASIER THAN GETTING PERFECT SCORES ON YOUR TEST EVERY MORNING.
SMIRK
BY THE WAY, WHAT WORK WAS I CALLED IN FOR?
FLIP
FLIP
OF COURSE, I AM VERY GRATEFUL FOR IT, BUT...
THEY FOUND OUT THE SECRET.
?!

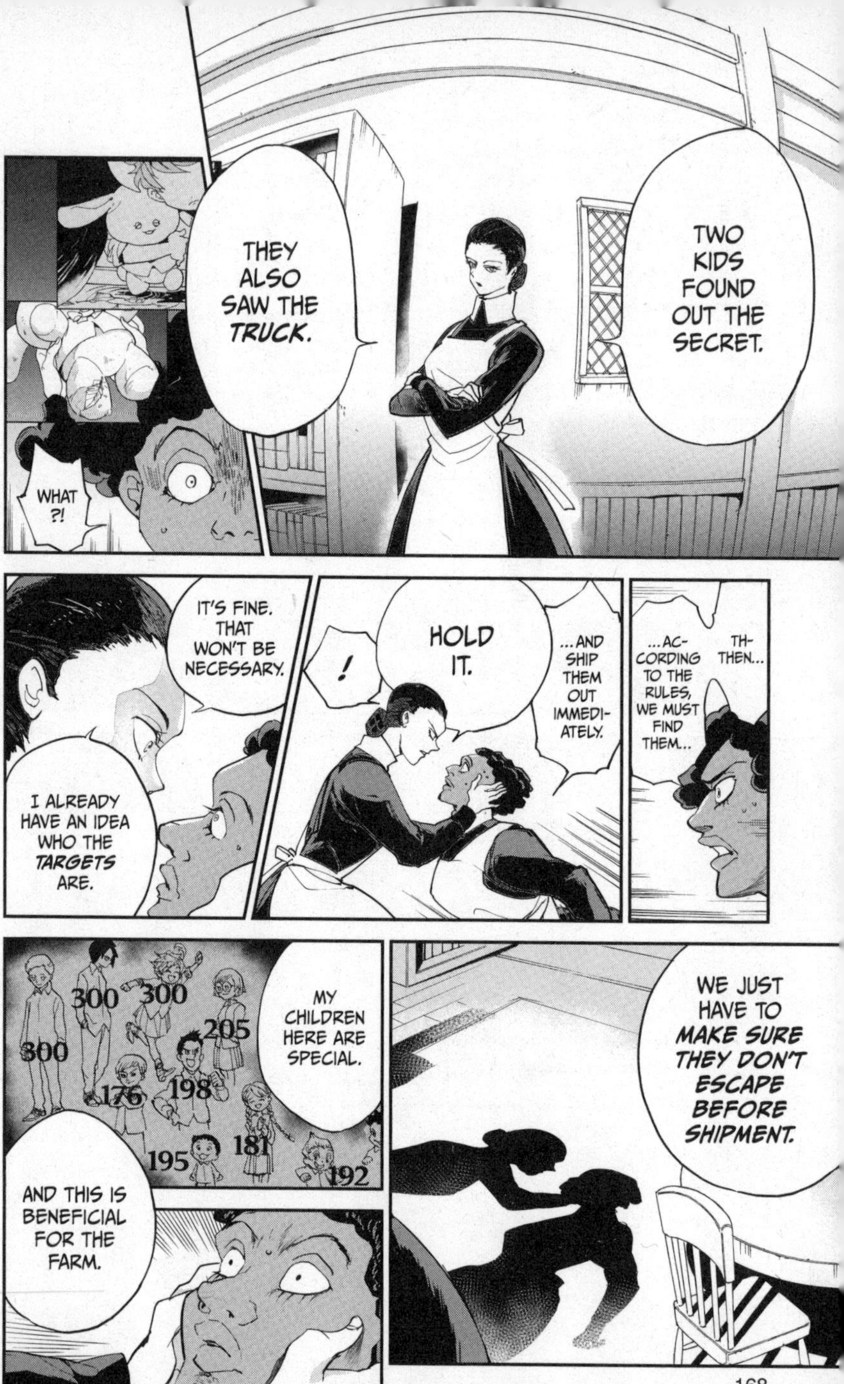
TWO KIDS FOUND OUT THE SECRET.
THEY ALSO SAW THE *TRUCK.*
WHAT?!
TH-THEN...
...ACCORDING TO THE RULES, WE MUST FIND THEM...
...AND SHIP THEM OUT IMMEDIATELY.
HOLD IT.
!
IT'S FINE. THAT WON'T BE NECESSARY.
I ALREADY HAVE AN IDEA WHO THE *TARGETS* ARE.
WE JUST HAVE TO *MAKE SURE THEY DON'T ESCAPE BEFORE SHIPMENT.*
MY CHILDREN HERE ARE SPECIAL.
300
300
300
205
198
176
195
181
192
AND THIS IS BENEFICIAL FOR THE FARM.

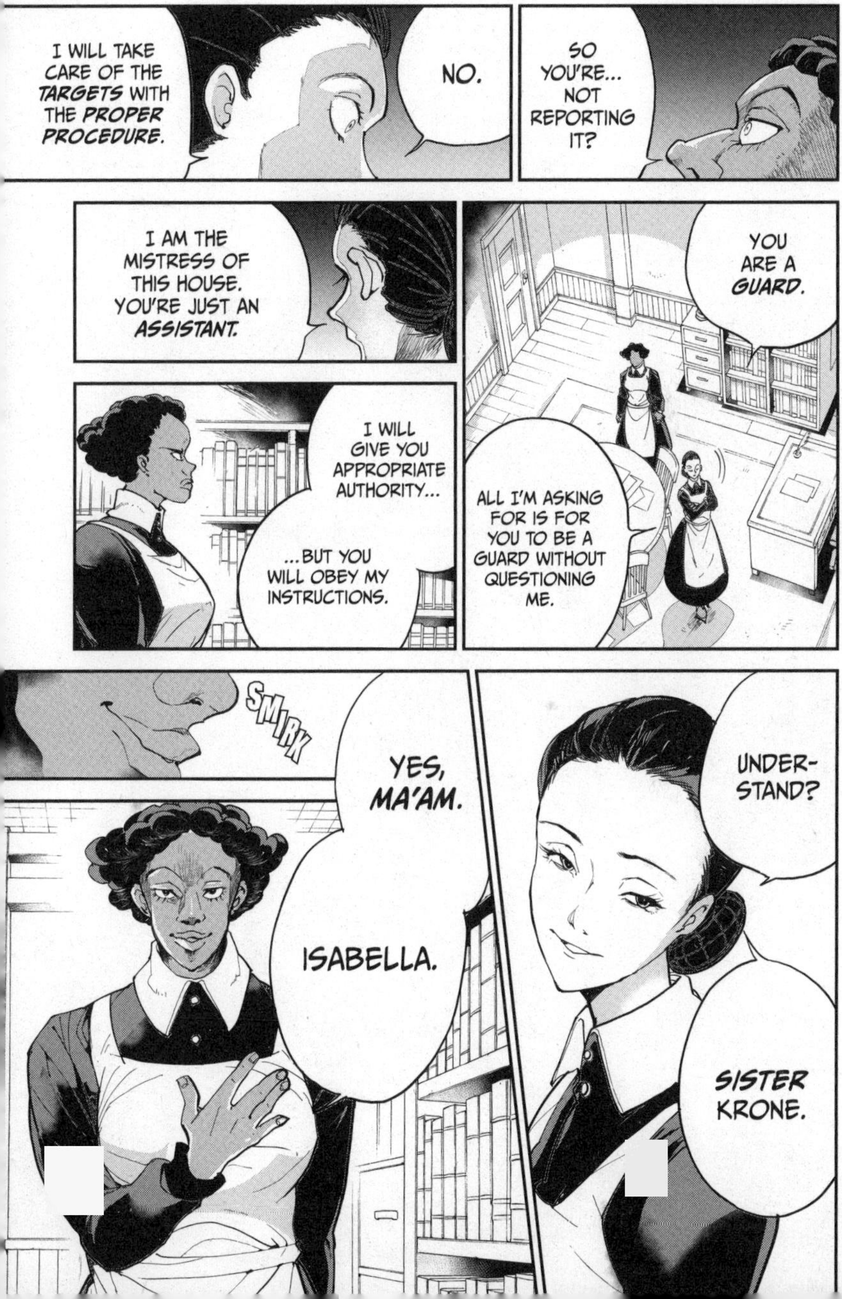

SO YOU'RE... NOT REPORTING IT?
NO.
I WILL TAKE CARE OF THE TARGETS WITH THE PROPER PROCEDURE.
YOU ARE A GUARD.
ALL I'M ASKING FOR IS FOR YOU TO BE A GUARD WITHOUT QUESTIONING ME.
I AM THE MISTRESS OF THIS HOUSE. YOU'RE JUST AN ASSISTANT.
I WILL GIVE YOU APPROPRIATE AUTHORITY...
...BUT YOU WILL OBEY MY INSTRUCTIONS.
UNDER-STAND?
SISTER KRONE.
SMIRK
YES, MA'AM.
ISABELLA.

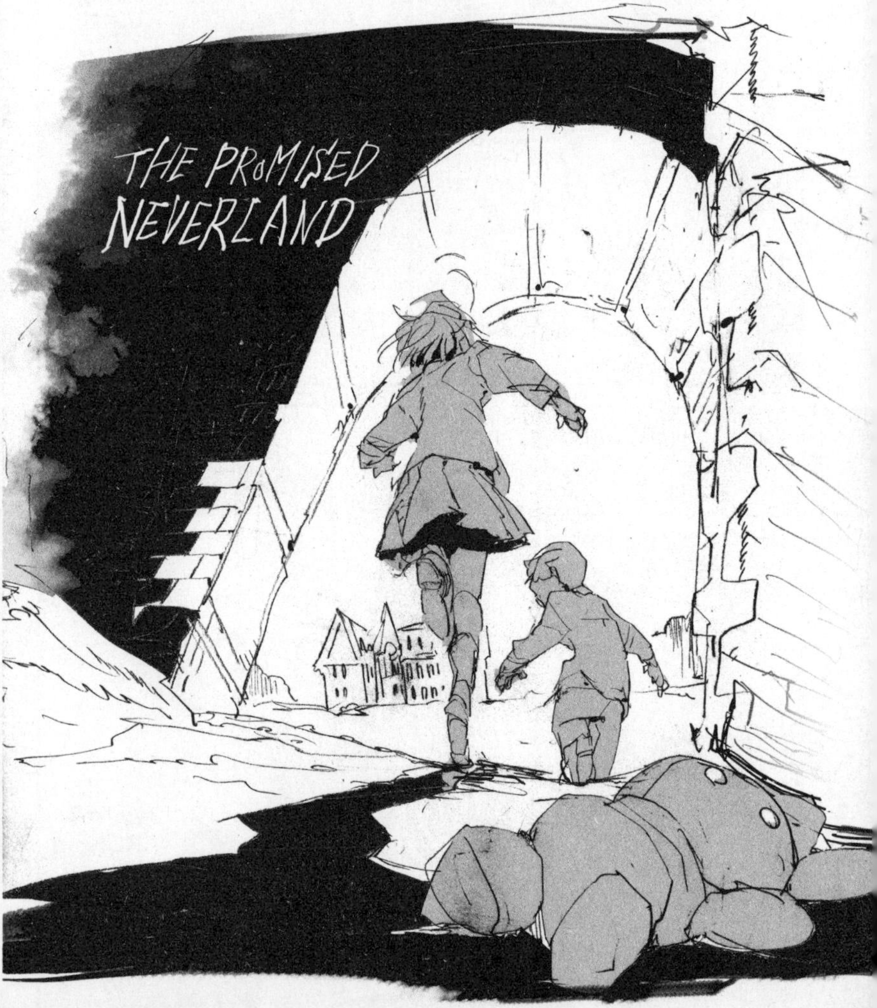
THE PROMISED NEVERLAND

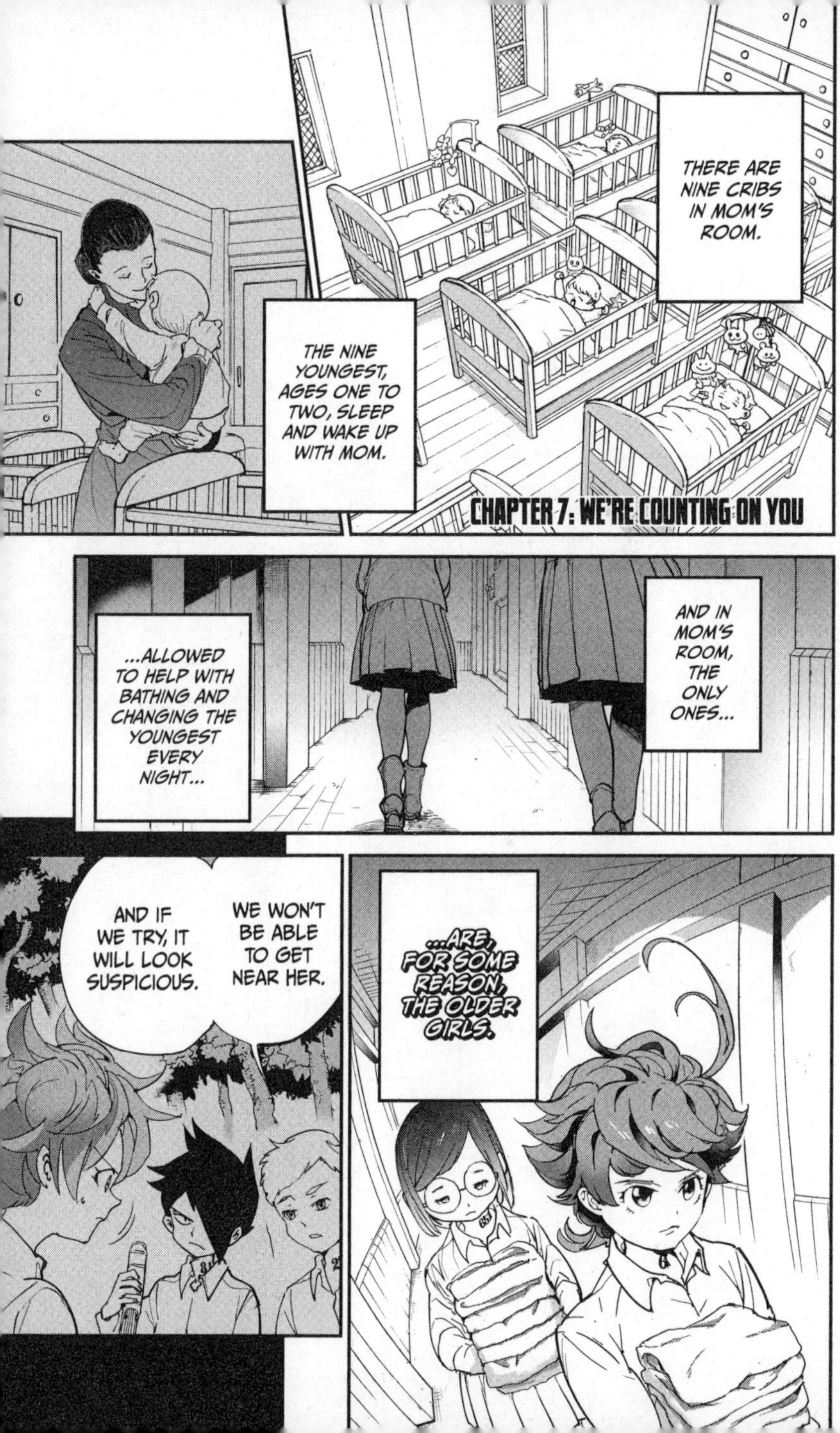
THERE ARE NINE CRIBS IN MOM'S ROOM.
THE NINE YOUNGEST, AGES ONE TO TWO, SLEEP AND WAKE UP WITH MOM.
CHAPTER 7: WE'RE COUNTING ON YOU
AND IN MOM'S ROOM, THE ONLY ONES...
...ALLOWED TO HELP WITH BATHING AND CHANGING THE YOUNGEST EVERY NIGHT...
...ARE, FOR SOME REASON, THE OLDER GIRLS.
WE WON'T BE ABLE TO GET NEAR HER.
AND IF WE TRY, IT WILL LOOK SUSPICIOUS.

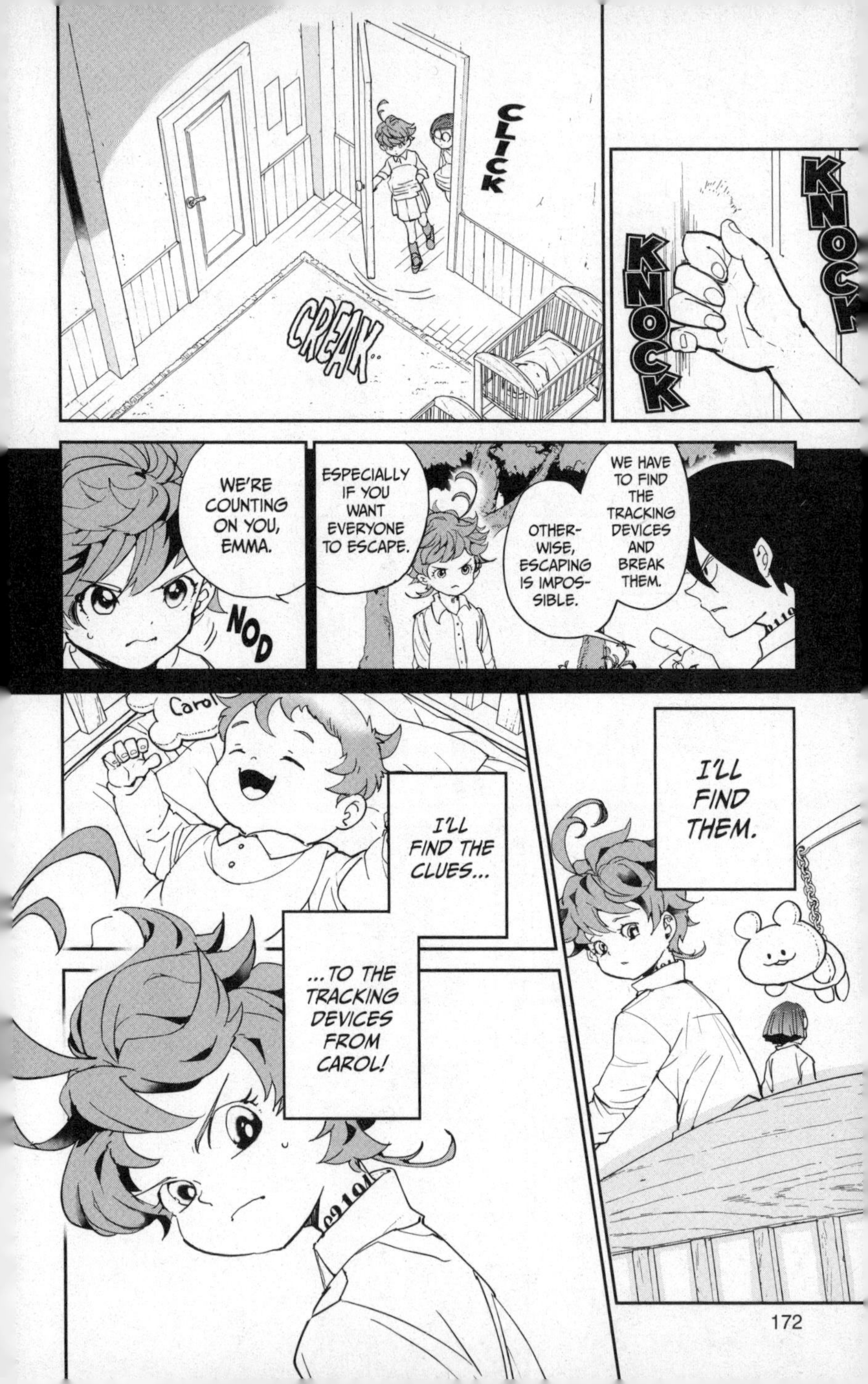
KNOCK
KNOCK
CLICK
CREAK..
WE HAVE TO FIND THE TRACKING DEVICES AND BREAK THEM.
OTHERWISE, ESCAPING IS IMPOSSIBLE.
ESPECIALLY IF YOU WANT EVERYONE TO ESCAPE.
WE'RE COUNTING ON YOU, EMMA.
NOD
I'LL FIND THEM.
Carol
I'LL FIND THE CLUES...
...TO THE TRACKING DEVICES FROM CAROL!

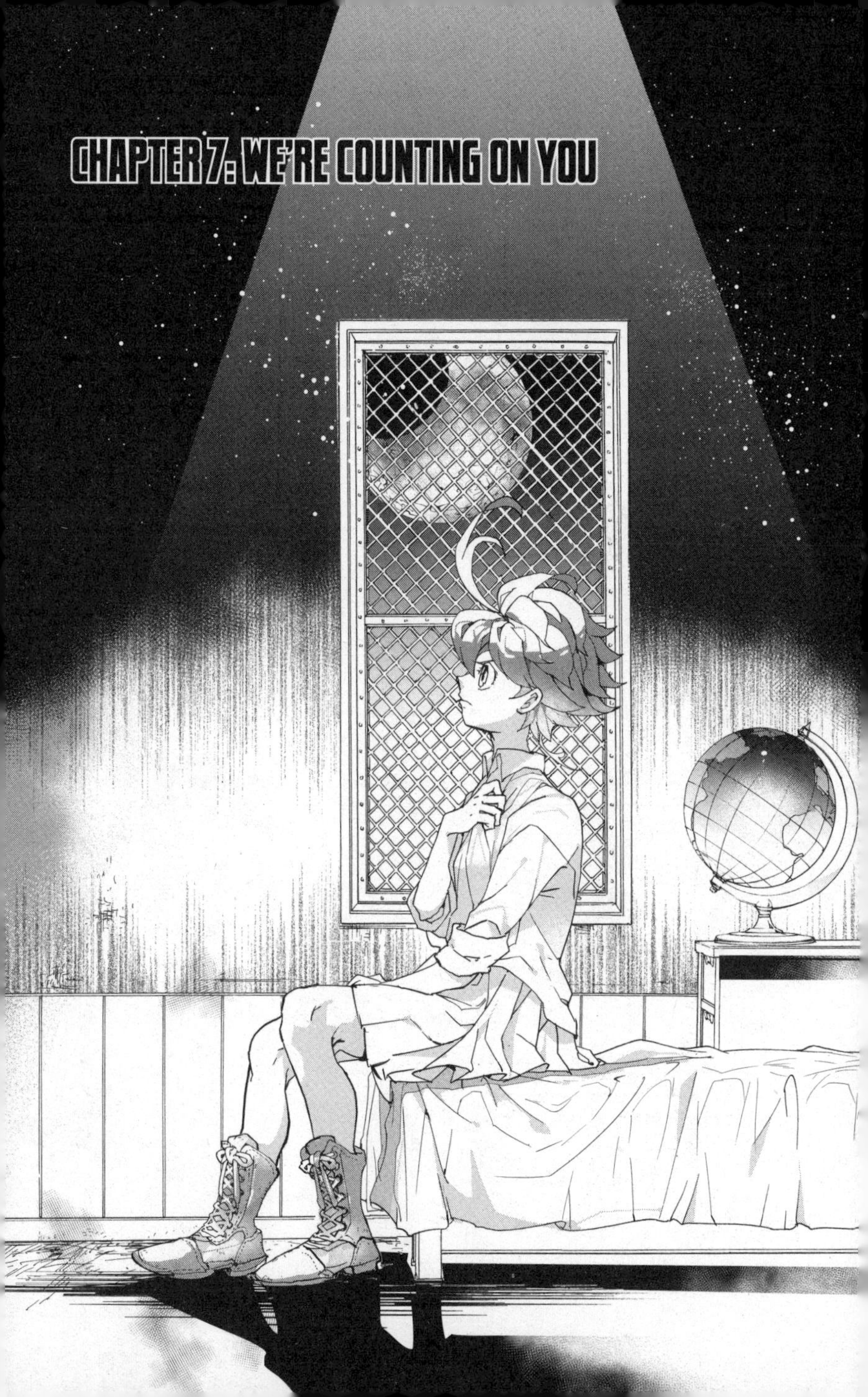
CHAPTER 7: WE'RE COUNTING ON YOU

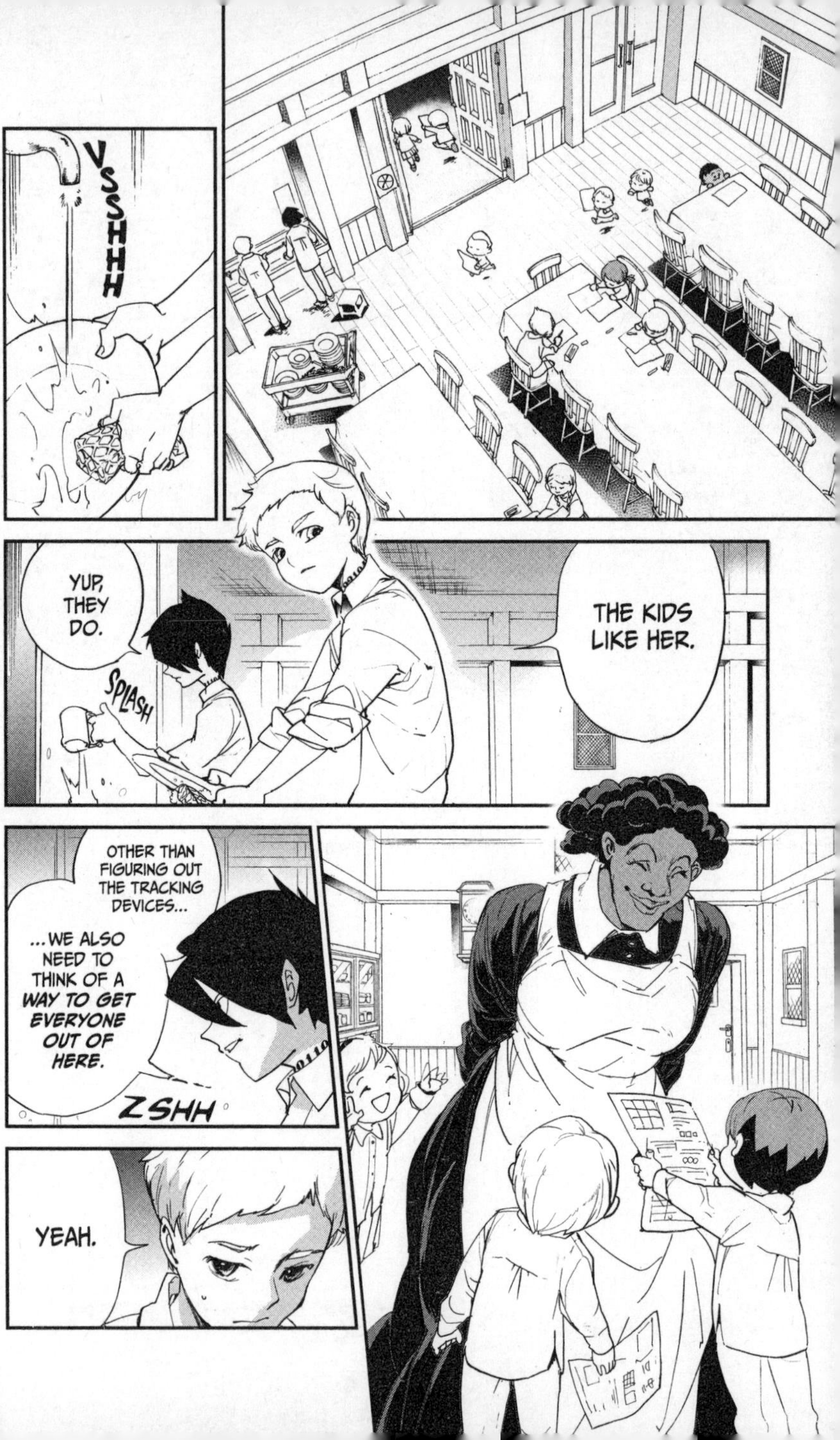
VSSHHH
THE KIDS LIKE HER.
YUP, THEY DO.
SPLASH
OTHER THAN FIGURING OUT THE TRACKING DEVICES...
...WE ALSO NEED TO THINK OF A WAY TO GET EVERYONE OUT OF HERE.
ZSHH
YEAH.

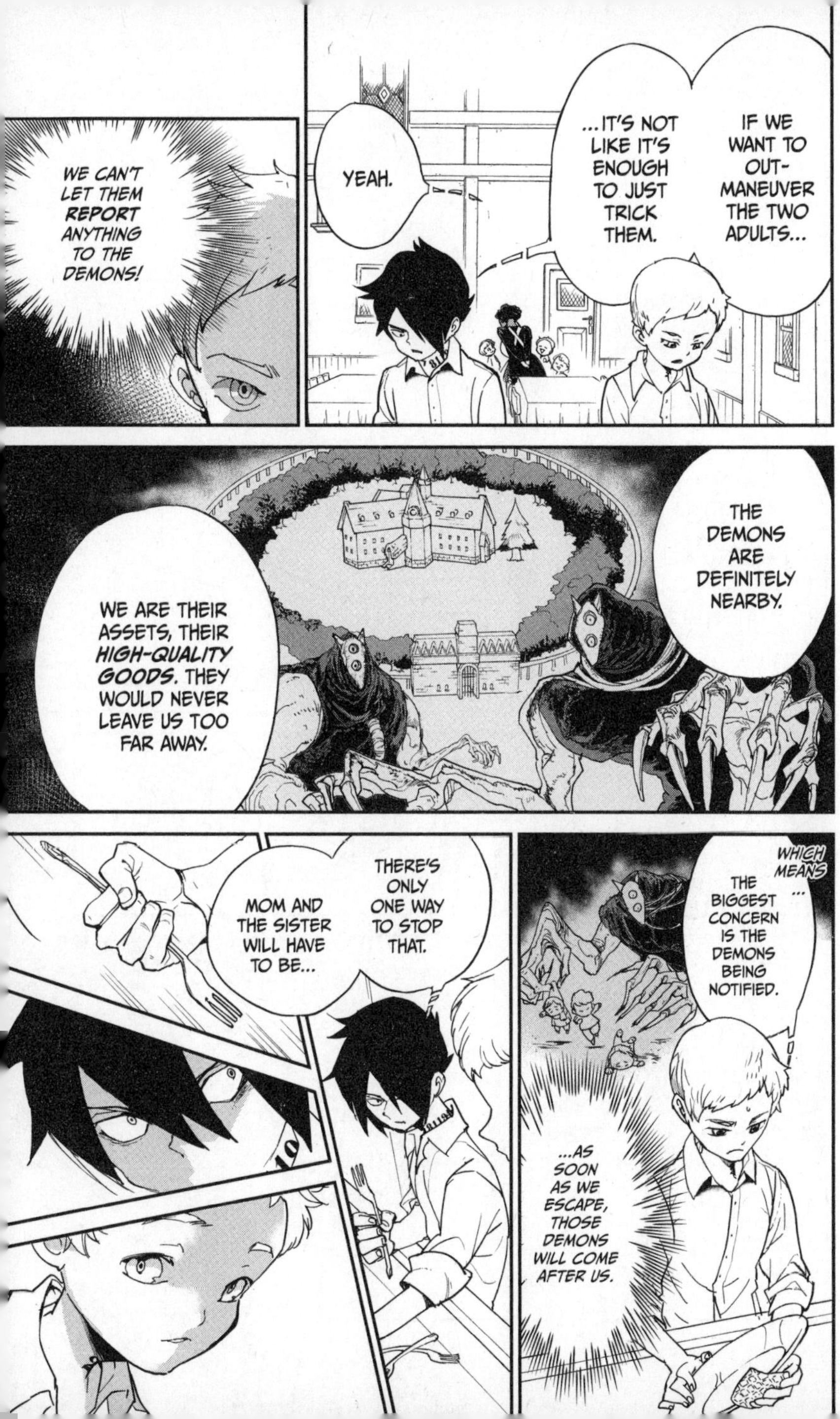
IF WE WANT TO OUT-MANEUVER THE TWO ADULTS...
...IT'S NOT LIKE IT'S ENOUGH TO JUST TRICK THEM.
YEAH.
WE CAN'T LET THEM REPORT ANYTHING TO THE DEMONS!
THE DEMONS ARE DEFINITELY NEARBY.
WE ARE THEIR ASSETS, THEIR *HIGH-QUALITY GOODS*. THEY WOULD NEVER LEAVE US TOO FAR AWAY.
WHICH MEANS...
THE BIGGEST CONCERN IS THE DEMONS BEING NOTIFIED.
...AS SOON AS WE ESCAPE, THOSE DEMONS WILL COME AFTER US.
THERE'S ONLY ONE WAY TO STOP THAT.
MOM AND THE SISTER WILL HAVE TO BE...

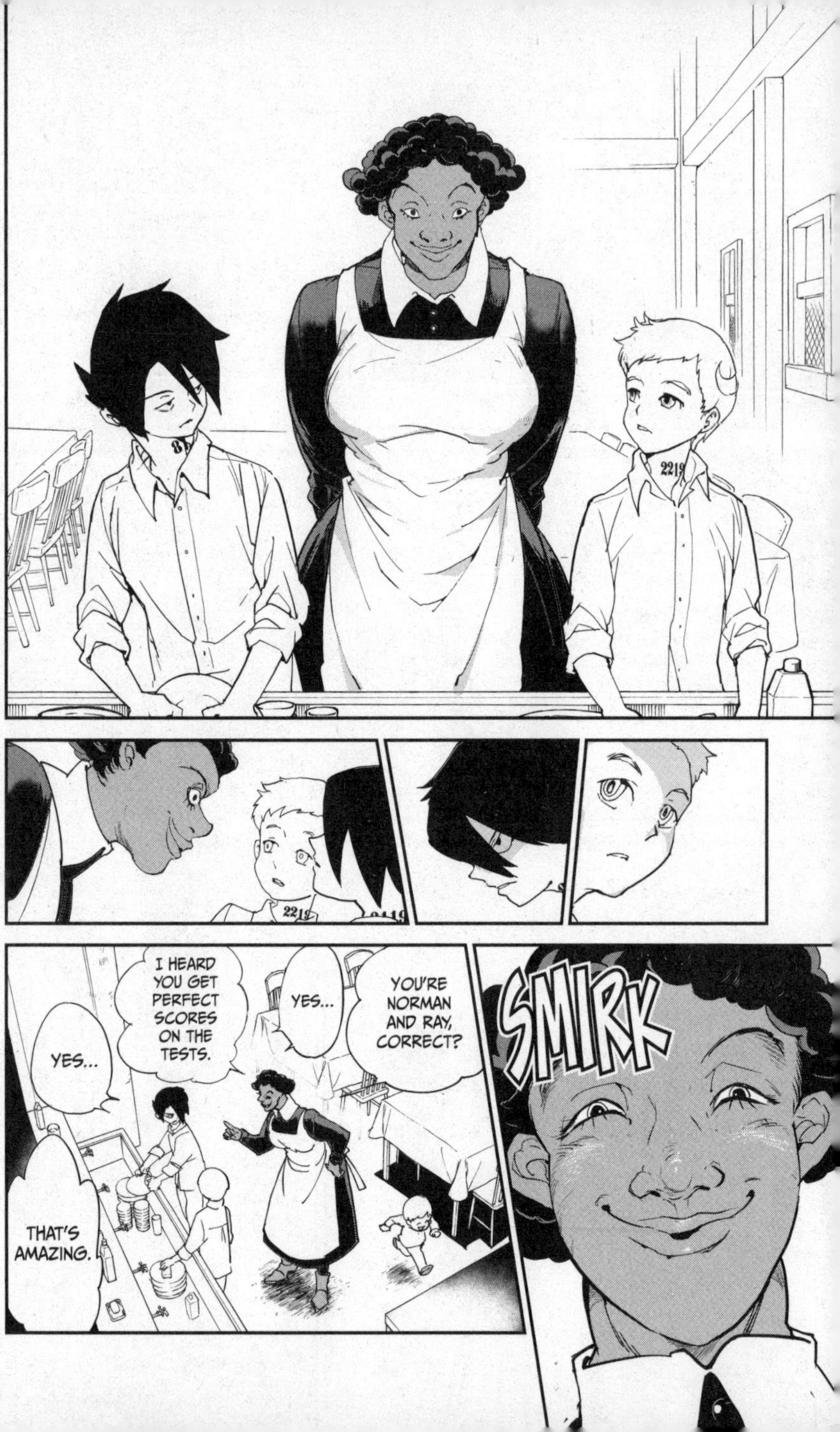
SMIRK
YOU'RE NORMAN AND RAY, CORRECT?
YES...
I HEARD YOU GET PERFECT SCORES ON THE TESTS.
YES...
THAT'S AMAZING.

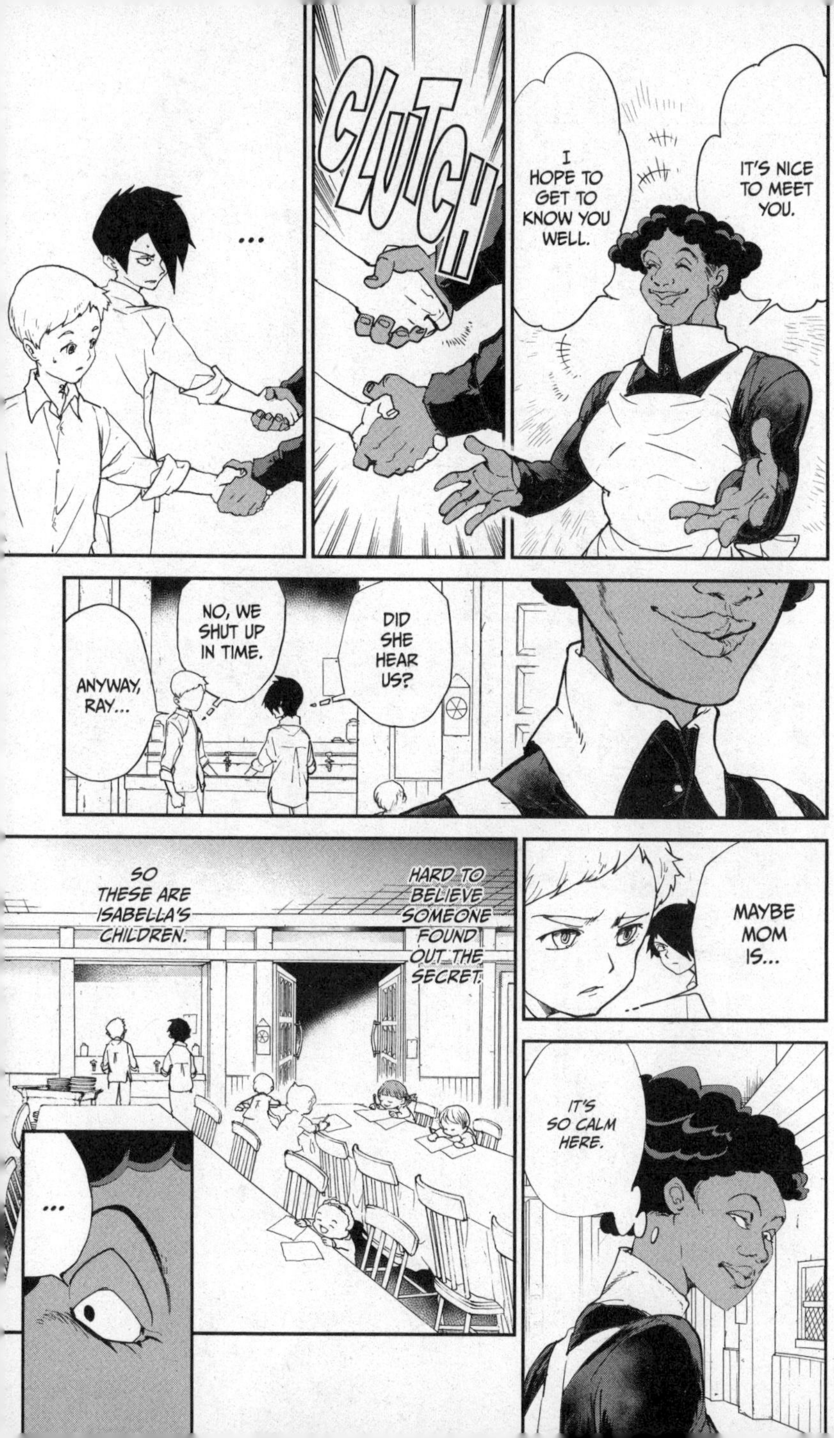
IT'S NICE TO MEET YOU.
I HOPE TO GET TO KNOW YOU WELL.
CLUTCH
...
DID SHE HEAR US?
NO, WE SHUT UP IN TIME.
ANYWAY, RAY...
MAYBE MOM IS...
IT'S SO CALM HERE.
HARD TO BELIEVE SOMEONE FOUND OUT THE SECRET.
SO THESE ARE ISABELLA'S CHILDREN.
...

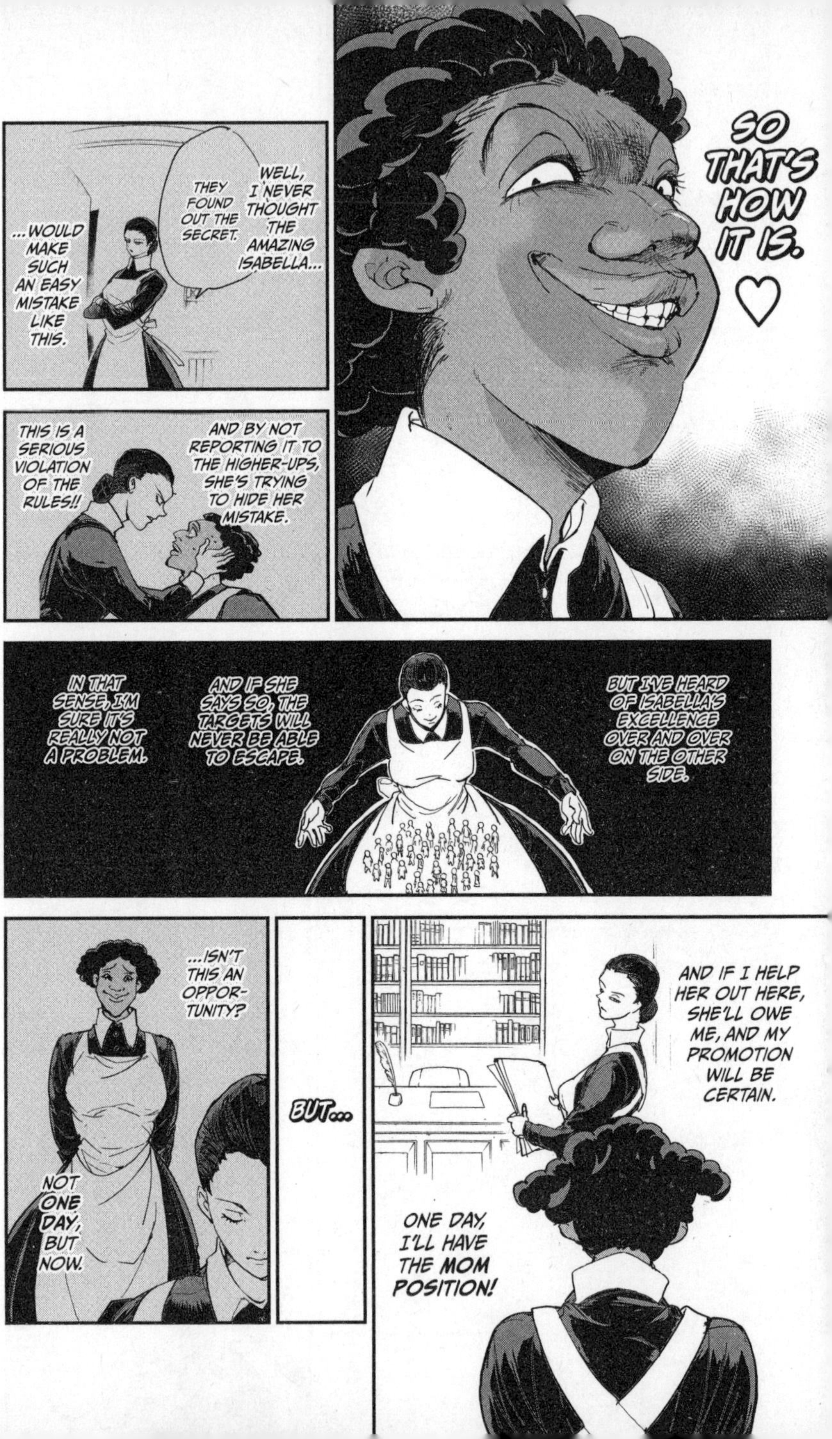
SO THAT'S HOW IT IS. ♥
WELL, I NEVER THOUGHT THE AMAZING ISABELLA...
THEY FOUND OUT THE SECRET.
...WOULD MAKE SUCH AN EASY MISTAKE LIKE THIS.
AND BY NOT REPORTING IT TO THE HIGHER-UPS, SHE'S TRYING TO HIDE HER MISTAKE.
THIS IS A SERIOUS VIOLATION OF THE RULES!!
BUT I'VE HEARD OF ISABELLA'S EXCELLENCE OVER AND OVER ON THE OTHER SIDE.
AND IF SHE SAYS SO, THE TARGETS WILL NEVER BE ABLE TO ESCAPE.
IN THAT SENSE, I'M SURE IT'S REALLY NOT A PROBLEM.
AND IF I HELP HER OUT HERE, SHE'LL OWE ME, AND MY PROMOTION WILL BE CERTAIN.
ONE DAY, I'LL HAVE THE MOM POSITION!
BUT...
...ISN'T THIS AN OPPORTUNITY?
NOT ONE DAY, BUT NOW.

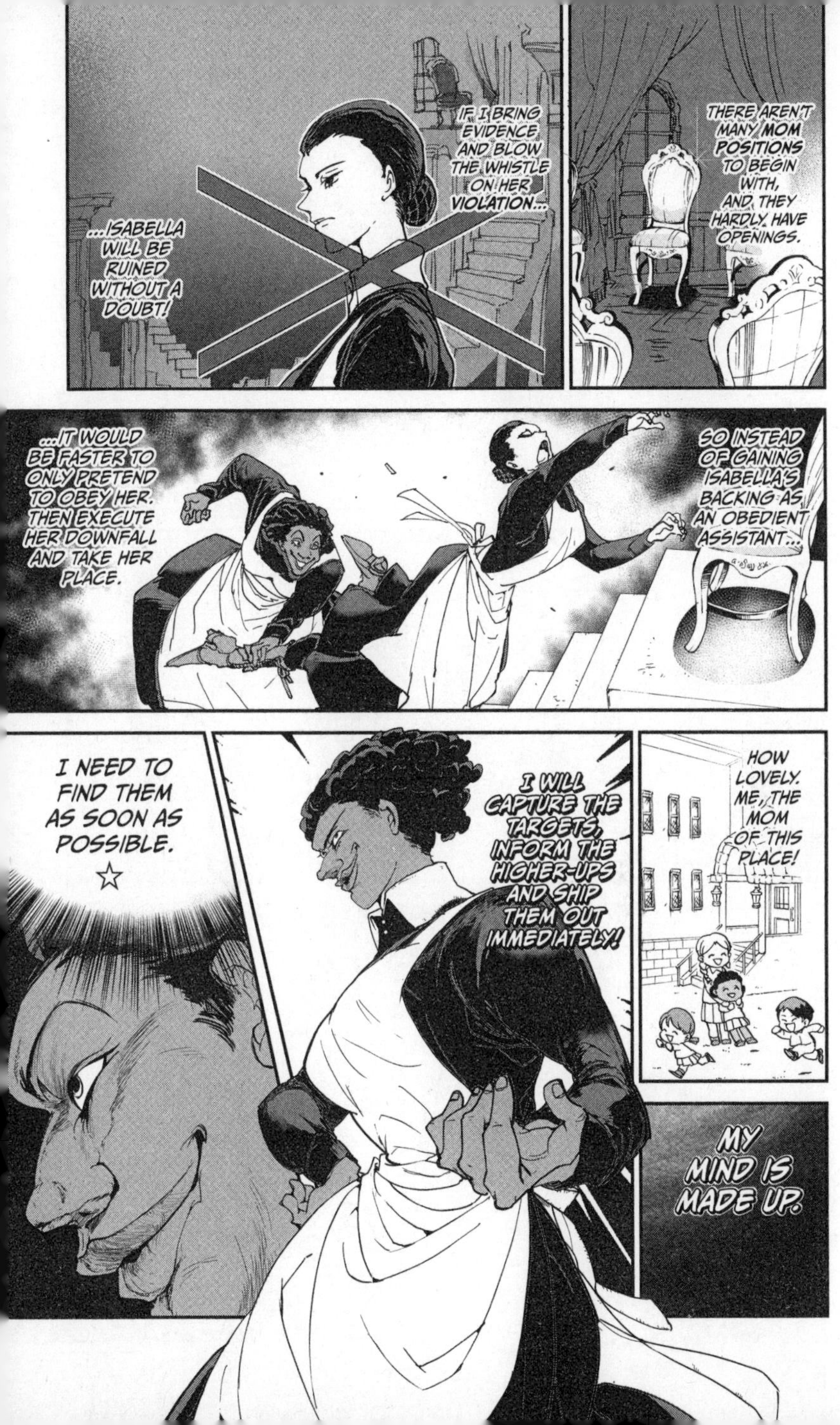
THERE AREN'T MANY MOM POSITIONS TO BEGIN WITH, AND THEY HARDLY HAVE OPENINGS.
IF I BRING EVIDENCE AND BLOW THE WHISTLE ON HER VIOLATION...
...ISABELLA WILL BE RUINED WITHOUT A DOUBT!
SO INSTEAD OF GAINING ISABELLA'S BACKING AS AN OBEDIENT ASSISTANT...
...IT WOULD BE FASTER TO ONLY PRETEND TO OBEY HER. THEN EXECUTE HER DOWNFALL AND TAKE HER PLACE.
HOW LOVELY. ME, THE MOM OF THIS PLACE!
MY MIND IS MADE UP.
I WILL CAPTURE THE TARGETS, INFORM THE HIGHER-UPS AND SHIP THEM OUT IMMEDIATELY!
I NEED TO FIND THEM AS SOON AS POSSIBLE. ☆

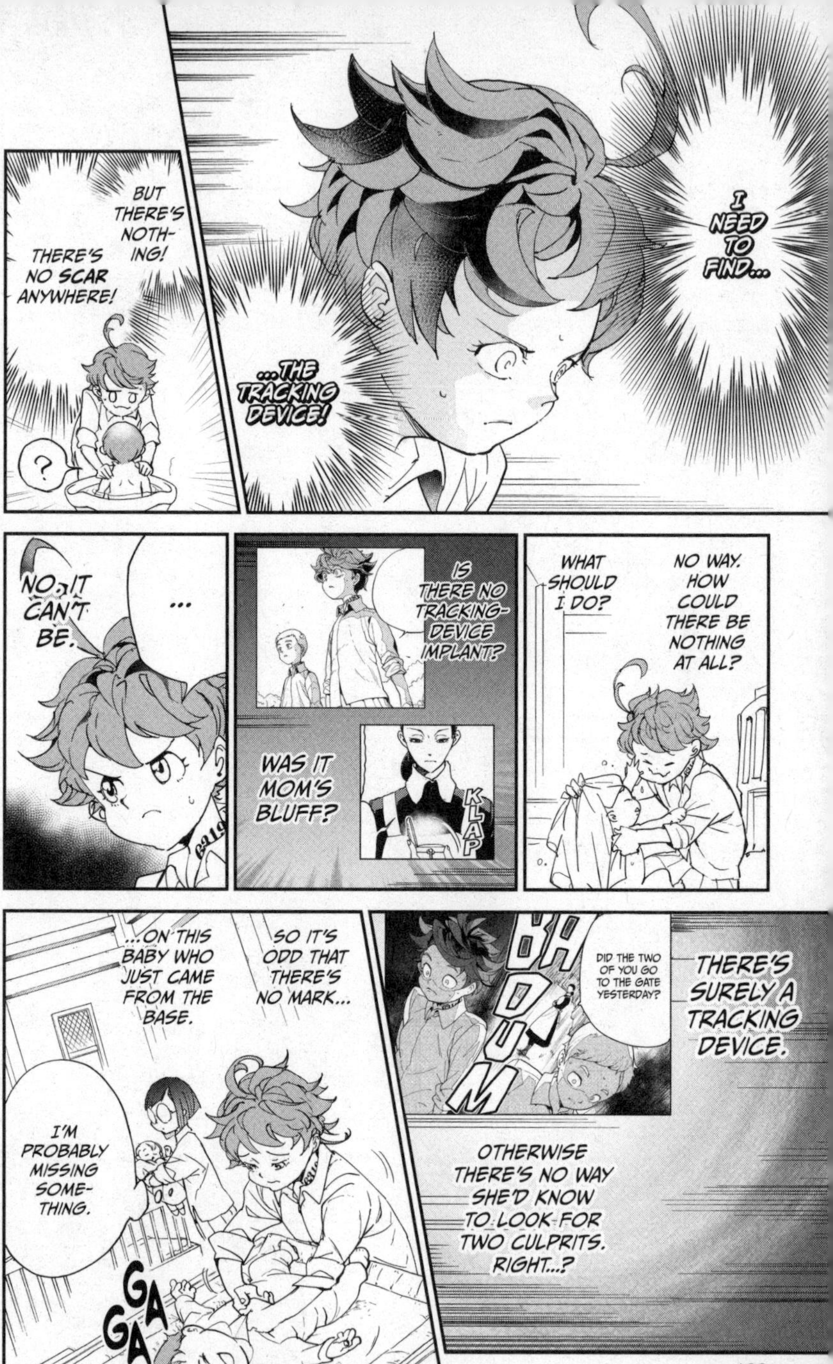
I NEED TO FIND...
...THE TRACKING DEVICE!
BUT THERE'S NOTHING!
THERE'S NO SCAR ANYWHERE!
?
NO WAY. HOW COULD THERE BE NOTHING AT ALL?
WHAT SHOULD I DO?
IS THERE NO TRACKING-DEVICE IMPLANT?
WAS IT MOM'S BLUFF?
KLAP
...
NO, IT CAN'T BE.
THERE'S SURELY A TRACKING DEVICE.
DID THE TWO OF YOU GO TO THE GATE YESTERDAY?
BADUM
OTHERWISE THERE'S NO WAY SHE'D KNOW TO LOOK FOR TWO CULPRITS. RIGHT...?
SO IT'S ODD THAT THERE'S NO MARK...
...ON THIS BABY WHO JUST CAME FROM THE BASE.
I'M PROBABLY MISSING SOMETHING.
GAGA

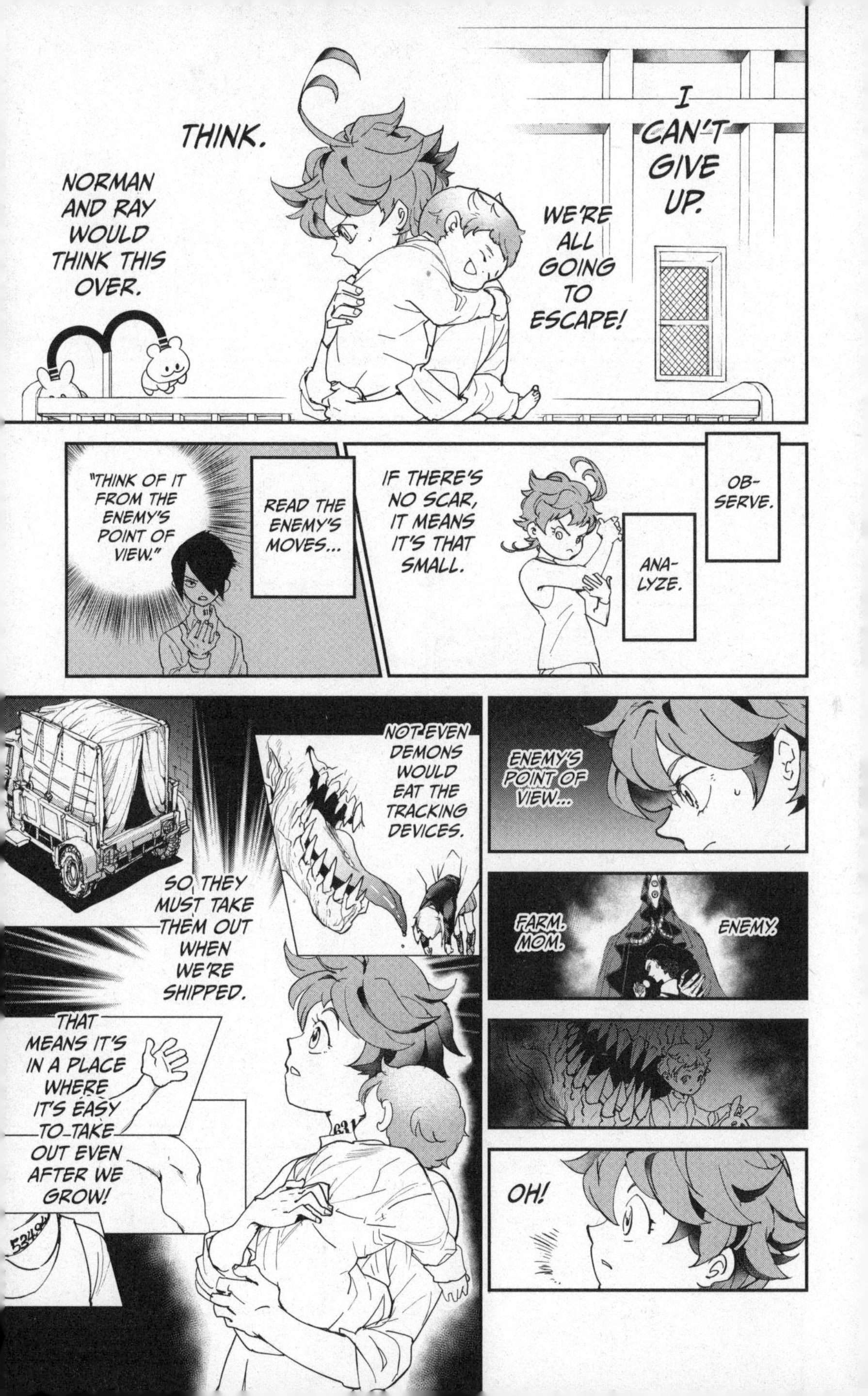
I CAN'T GIVE UP.
WE'RE ALL GOING TO ESCAPE!
THINK.
NORMAN AND RAY WOULD THINK THIS OVER.
OB-SERVE.
ANA-LYZE.
IF THERE'S NO SCAR, IT MEANS IT'S THAT SMALL.
READ THE ENEMY'S MOVES...
"THINK OF IT FROM THE ENEMY'S POINT OF VIEW."
ENEMY'S POINT OF VIEW...
ENEMY.
FARM. MOM.
OH!
NOT EVEN DEMONS WOULD EAT THE TRACKING DEVICES.
SO THEY MUST TAKE THEM OUT WHEN WE'RE SHIPPED.
THAT MEANS IT'S IN A PLACE WHERE IT'S EASY TO TAKE OUT EVEN AFTER WE GROW!

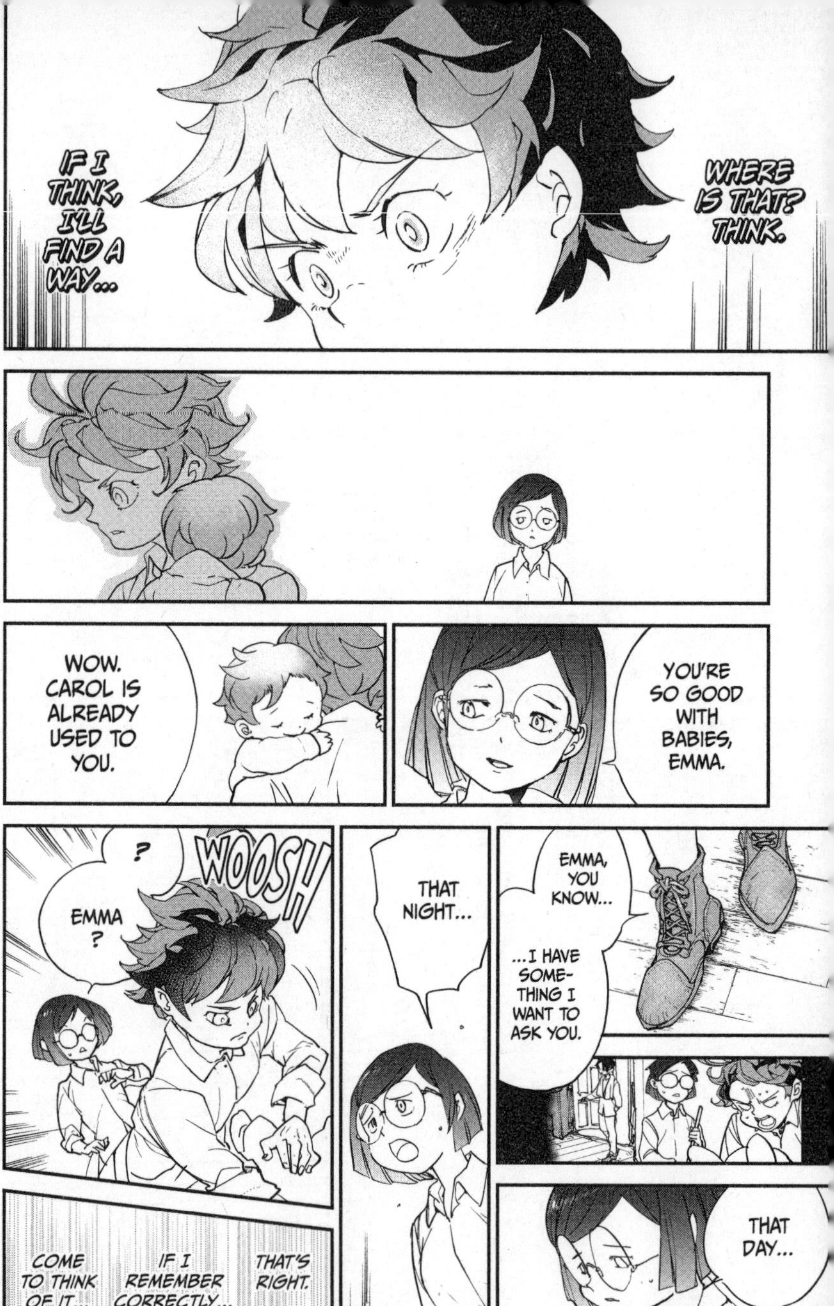
WHERE IS THAT? THINK.
IF I THINK, I'LL FIND A WAY...
YOU'RE SO GOOD WITH BABIES, EMMA.
WOW. CAROL IS ALREADY USED TO YOU.
EMMA, YOU KNOW...
...I HAVE SOME-THING I WANT TO ASK YOU.
THAT DAY...
THAT NIGHT...
WOOSH
?
EMMA ?
THAT'S RIGHT.
IF I REMEMBER CORRECTLY...
COME TO THINK OF IT...

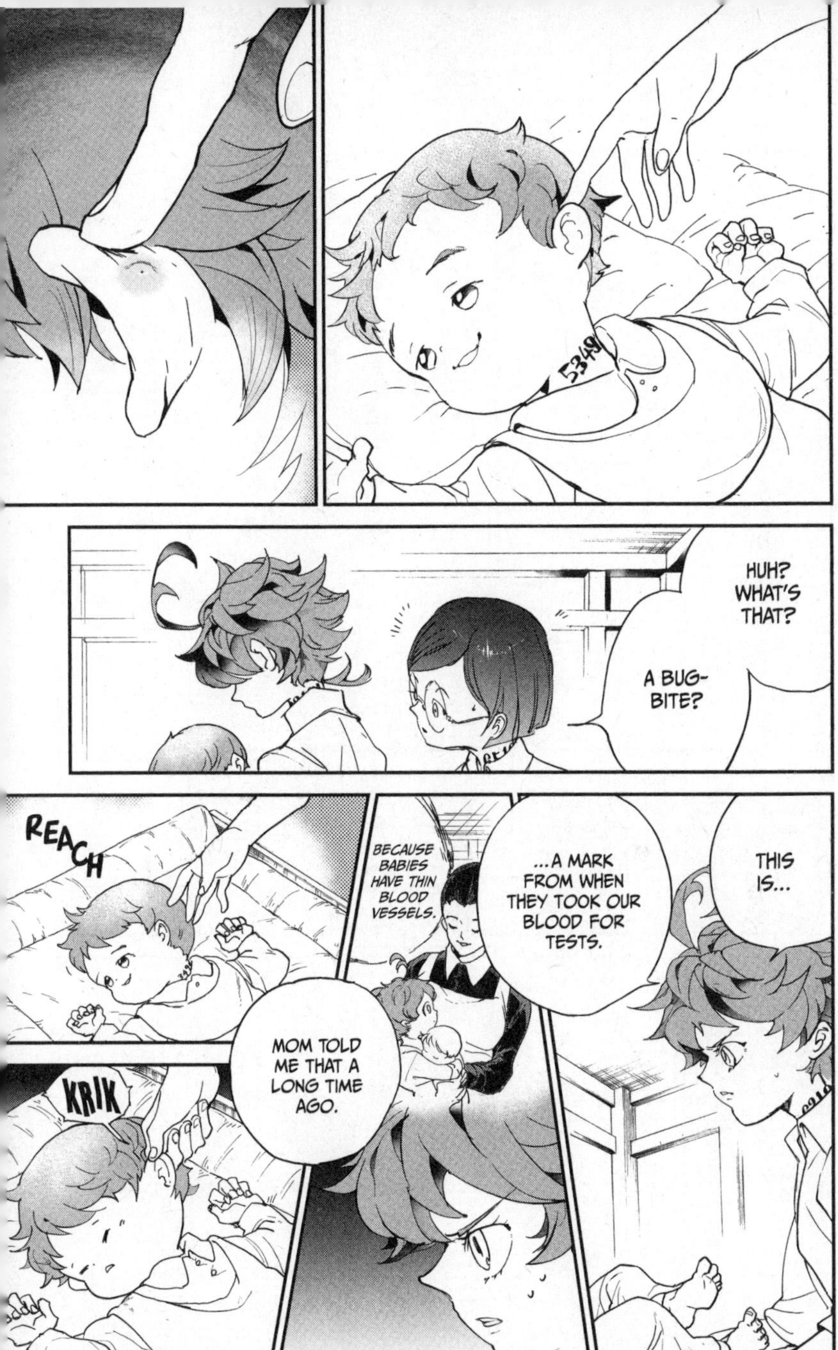
HUH? WHAT'S THAT?
A BUG-BITE?
THIS IS...
...A MARK FROM WHEN THEY TOOK OUR BLOOD FOR TESTS.
BECAUSE BABIES HAVE THIN BLOOD VESSELS.
MOM TOLD ME THAT A LONG TIME AGO.
REACH
KRIK

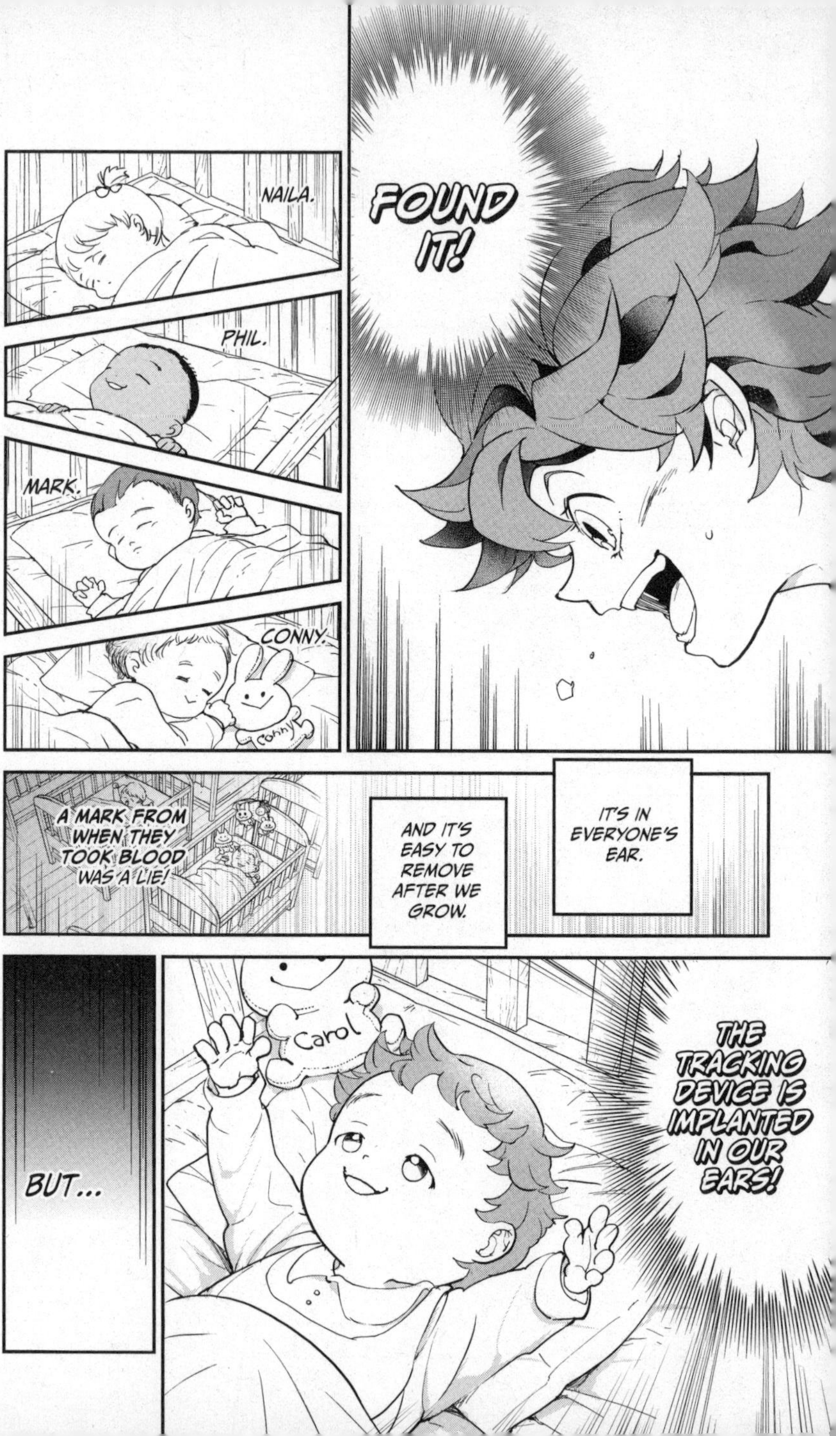
FOUND IT!
NAILA.
PHIL.
MARK.
CONNY.
Conny
IT'S IN EVERYONE'S EAR.
AND IT'S EASY TO REMOVE AFTER WE GROW.
A MARK FROM WHEN THEY TOOK BLOOD WAS A LIE!
THE TRACKING DEVICE IS IMPLANTED IN OUR EARS!
Carol
BUT...

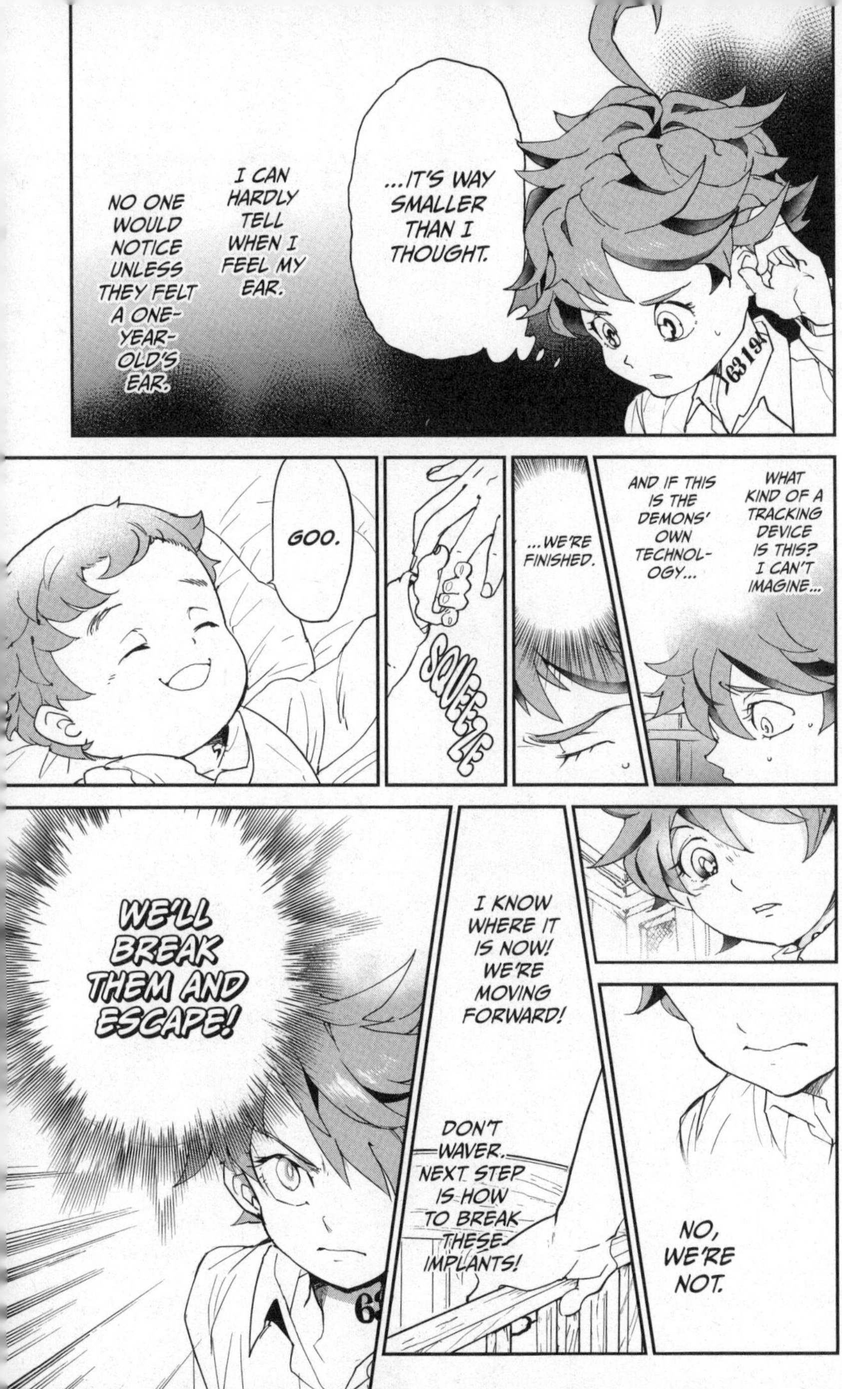
...IT'S WAY SMALLER THAN I THOUGHT.
I CAN HARDLY TELL WHEN I FEEL MY EAR.
NO ONE WOULD NOTICE UNLESS THEY FELT A ONE-YEAR-OLD'S EAR.
WHAT KIND OF A TRACKING DEVICE IS THIS? I CAN'T IMAGINE...
AND IF THIS IS THE DEMONS' OWN TECHNOLOGY...
...WE'RE FINISHED.
SQUEEEZE
GOO.
NO, WE'RE NOT.
I KNOW WHERE IT IS NOW! WE'RE MOVING FORWARD!
DON'T WAVER. NEXT STEP IS HOW TO BREAK THESE IMPLANTS!
WE'LL BREAK THEM AND ESCAPE!

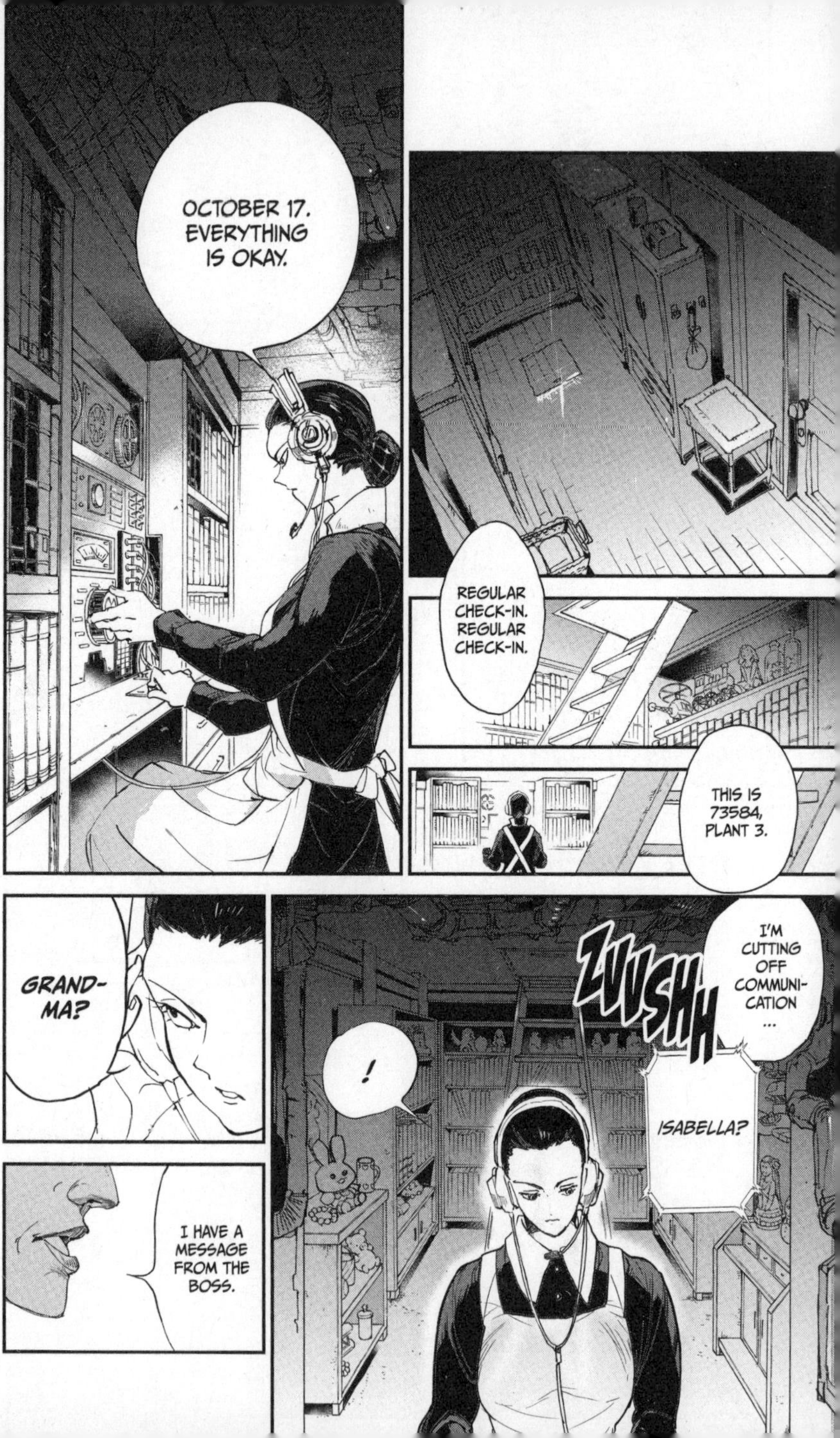
REGULAR CHECK-IN. REGULAR CHECK-IN.
THIS IS 73584, PLANT 3.
OCTOBER 17. EVERYTHING IS OKAY.
I'M CUTTING OFF COMMUNICATION...
ZUUSHH
ISABELLA?
!
GRAND-MA?
I HAVE A MESSAGE FROM THE BOSS.

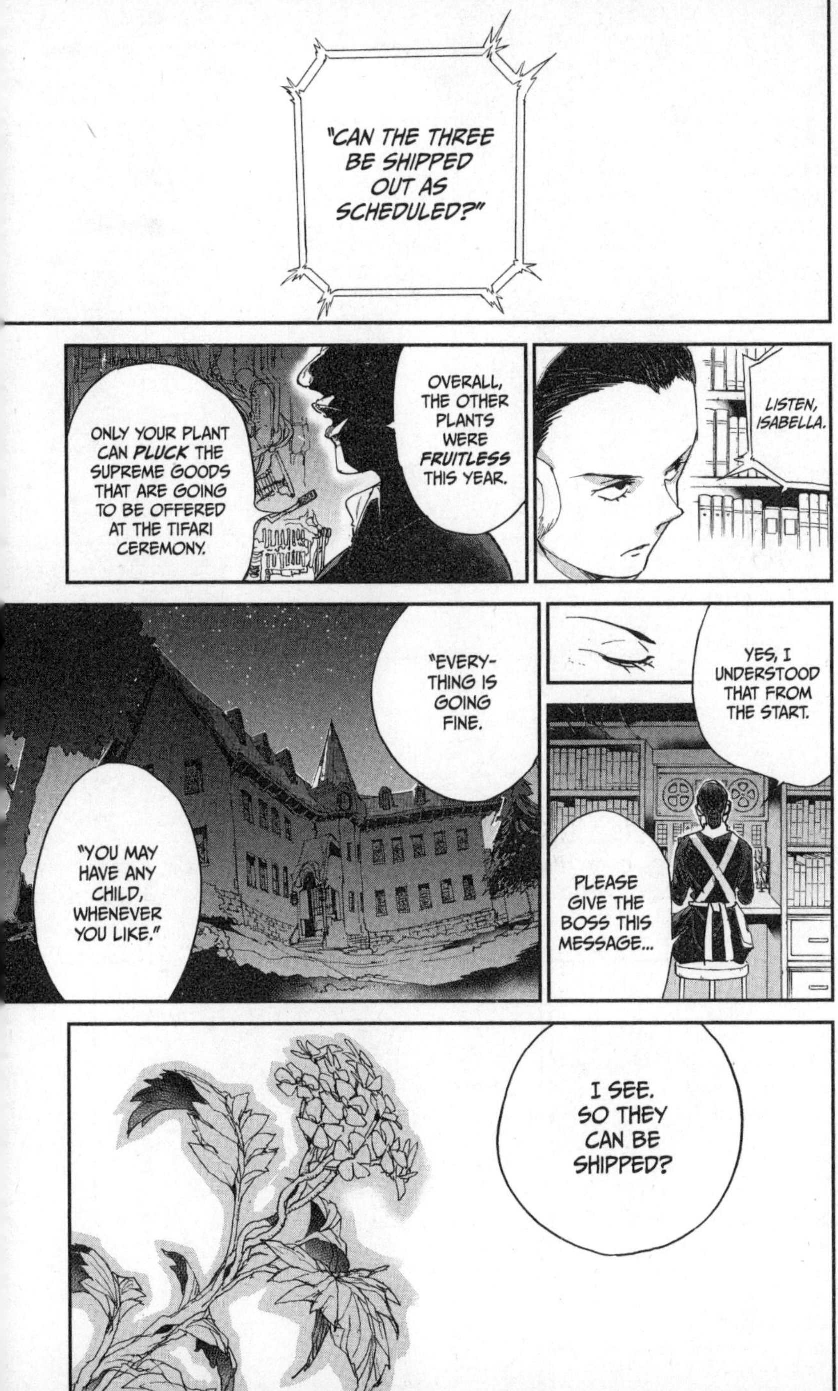
"CAN THE THREE BE SHIPPED OUT AS SCHEDULED?"
LISTEN, ISABELLA.
OVERALL, THE OTHER PLANTS WERE *FRUITLESS* THIS YEAR.
ONLY YOUR PLANT CAN *PLUCK* THE SUPREME GOODS THAT ARE GOING TO BE OFFERED AT THE TIFARI CEREMONY.
YES, I UNDERSTOOD THAT FROM THE START.
PLEASE GIVE THE BOSS THIS MESSAGE...
"EVERYTHING IS GOING FINE.
"YOU MAY HAVE ANY CHILD, WHENEVER YOU LIKE."
I SEE. SO THEY CAN BE SHIPPED?

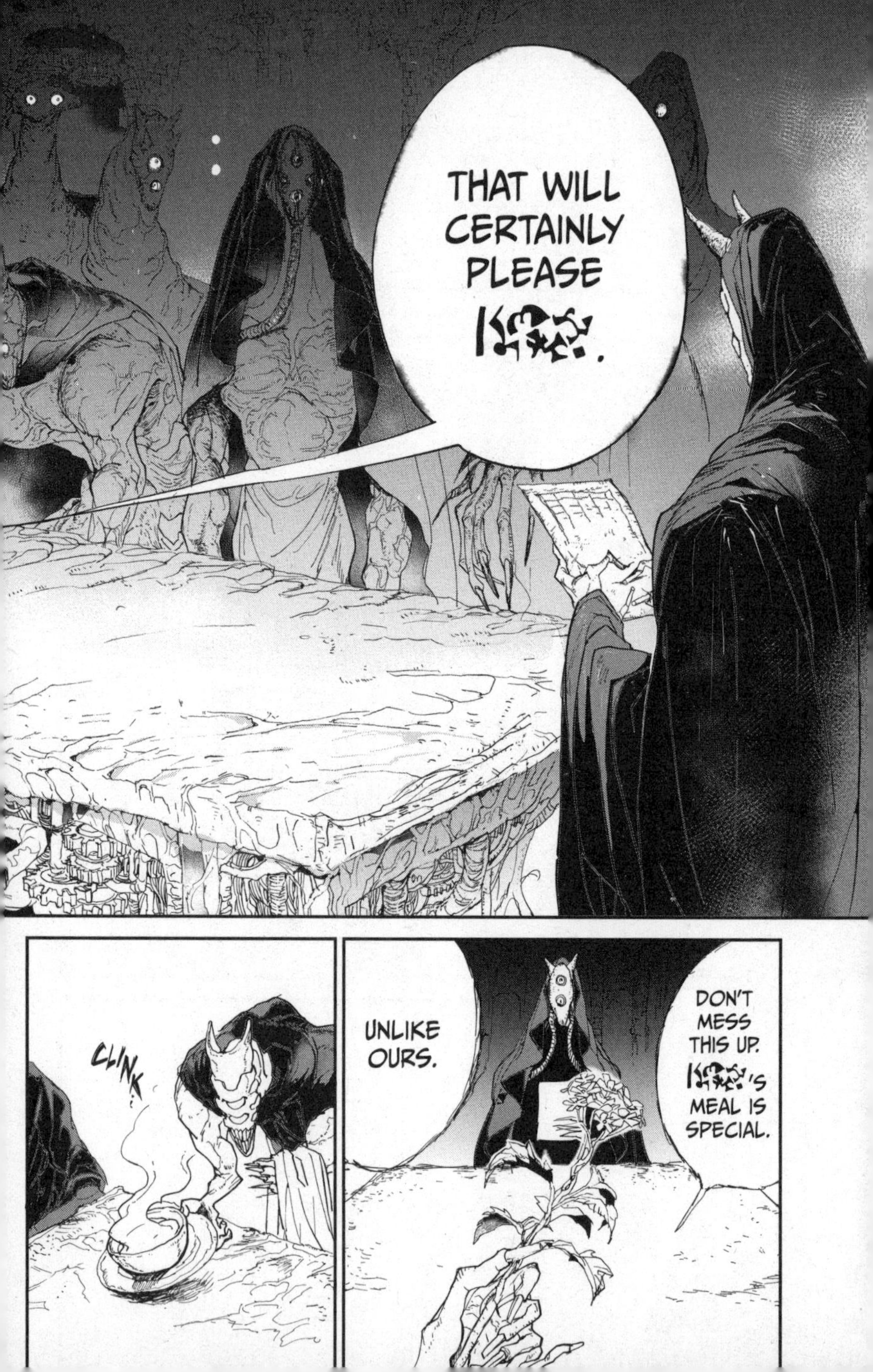
THAT WILL CERTAINLY PLEASE .
DON'T MESS THIS UP. 'S MEAL IS SPECIAL.
UNLIKE OURS.
CLINK

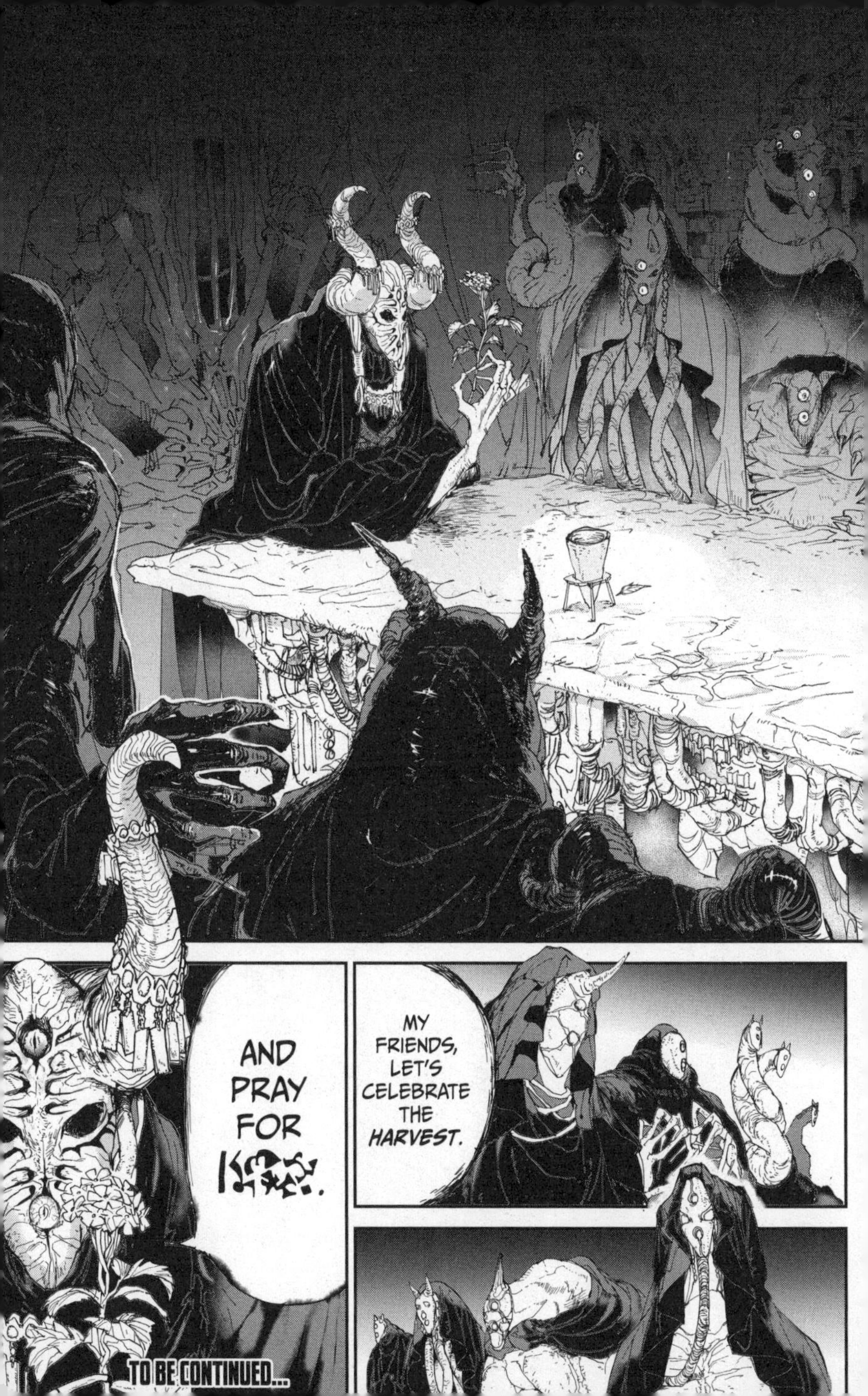
MY FRIENDS, LET'S CELEBRATE THE *HARVEST*.
AND PRAY FOR
TO BE CONTINUED...

YOU'RE READING THE **WRONG WAY!**

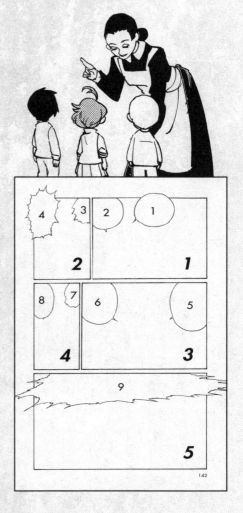

The Promised Neverland reads from right to left, starting in the upper-right corner. Japanese is read from right to left, meaning that action, sound effects and word-balloon order are completely reversed from English order.